A HISTORY OF THE CHURCH IN THE MIDDLE AGES

A History of the Church in the Middle Ages traces the story of the Christian church in Western Europe over the thousand years or so that comprise the medieval age. While this period witnessed the continuities of belief, ritual and even institutions, it also experienced remarkable changes when old forms were renewed or replaced and when new forms were created. Saint Francis of Assisi, the gentle *poverello* of Umbria, the martyr Thomas Becket, the ill-fated lovers Abelard and Heloise, the visionary Hildegard of Bingen, all testify to the diversity and richness of the medieval church.

In this fascinating survey, Donald Logan introduces the reader to the Christian church, from the conversion of the Celtic and Germanic peoples up to the discovery of the New World. He reveals how the church unified the people of Western Europe as they worshipped with the same ceremonies and used Latin as the language of civilized communication. From the remote, rural parish church, where simple peasants came to pray, to the magnificent urban cathedral, where choirs chanted the psalms, *A History of the Church in the Middle Ages* explores the role of the church as a central element in determining a thousand years of history.

F. Donald Logan is Professor Emeritus of History at Emmanuel College, Boston. His previous publications include *The Vikings in History* (second edition, 1991 and translated into four languages) and *Runaway Religious in Medieval England* (1996).

D0209220

A HISTORY OF THE CHURCH IN THE MIDDLE AGES

F. Donald Logan

Routledge
Taylor & Francis Group

LONDON AND NEW YORK

First published 2002
by Routledge
2 Park Square, Milton Park, Abingdon, Oxford OX14 4RN

Simultaneously published in the USA and Canada
by Routledge
270 Madison Ave, New York, NY10016

Reprinted 2003, 2004, 2005, 2006 (twice), 2007, 2008

Routledge is an imprint of the Taylor & Francis Group, an informa business

Typeset in Goudy by
Keystroke, Jacaranda Lodge, Wolverhampton
Printed in the United States of America

British Library Cataloguing in Publication Data
A catalogue record for this book is available from the British Library

Library of Congress Cataloging in Publication Data
has been applied for

ISBN 10: 0–415–13288–6 (hbk)
ISBN 10: 0–415–13289–4 (pbk)

ISBN 13: 978–0–415–13288–6 (hbk)
ISBN 13: 978–0–415–13289–3 (pbk)

For my sister, Mary Eleanor Logan,
and my brother, Joseph Logan

CONTENTS

LIST OF PLATES

MAPS

FIGURES

PREFACE

This book is an introduction. It is meant to be more than a brief survey and less – considerably less – than an encyclopedic work. The emphasis here is largely chronological and the presentation mostly in the form of a narrative. It is based on the premise that the study of history must begin with chronology. I hope that it will not end there and that readers of this book will wish to pursue aspects of the subject to another level: the selected readings sections appended to each chapter can provide a starting point.

As a young scholar, I felt – and would tell anyone who would listen – that no serious research scholar should write a book like this: there are just too many areas of history crying out for scholarly investigation. Yet, without in any way abandoning a firm belief in the fundamental importance of original research, I have softened the tone and have even changed my mind. It is my hope that a straightforward narrative which presupposes no detailed knowledge of either the Middle Ages or the Christian religion will encourage the reader to share the author's enthusiasm for the subject and will stimulate an interest in the general study of history.

A book of this kind, which covers a thousand years or so, requires difficult choices about what to include and, conversely, what to exclude. I realize that no two historians would make exactly the same choices. I am all too conscious that, in the nature of things, there is bound to be something arbitrary about inclusions and exclusions, but I take some solace in knowing that readers can turn to such books as Steven Fanning's work on mystics and Jonathan Riley-Smith's studies on the Crusades to fill in the *lacunae* left where these difficult choices have been made.

Over the past few years I have taken advantage of friends by going on and on, almost shamelessly, about topics that appear in these pages. I thank them for their patience and tolerance. It is a pleasure to record my debt and gratitude to scholars who have generously read parts of the text and made helpful suggestions: Katherine Cushing, Keith Egan, Robin Fleming, Linda Grant, Michael Robson, Sarah Stever and Daniel Williman. The readers for the press in their thoughtful comments and suggestions have helped to improve the text enormously. To no one am I more indebted than to Michael Clanchy, who read the entire text, chapter by chapter, as it came from my printer. His comments and encouragement have been of inestimable value to me in preparing this book, and I cannot thank him adequately. I greatly appreciate the suggestions made by all of these scholars and have departed from them rarely and then, I fear, at my own peril.

Writing a book such as this reminds one of the great wealth of scholarly work that has been done and is being done in the field of medieval history. The substance of this book owes its existence to untold hundreds of scholars working in this field in the past and in the present. It is an exceptionally rich vein one is privileged to mine.

F. Donald Logan
21 September 2001
Brookline, Massachusetts

INTRODUCTION

The Christian church was a defining element in medieval society. There were others, of course, but the Middle Ages without the church would not be the historic Middle Ages. It was the one international ingredient which bound together disparate peoples in a shared faith and ritual and by a common learned language. Variations there indeed were, but the same Creed was recited at the same kinds of liturgical ceremonies from Iceland to Sicily and in tens of thousands of villages throughout Western Europe. The general councils of the church drew members to Lyons, Rome, Vienne, Constance and elsewhere in the only truly international assemblies of the Middle Ages. Theologians and canon lawyers not only spoke the same Latin language, but they discussed the same issues. The existence of local customs and traditions added to the flavour of the religious culture of the times and also served to emphasize the overarching transcendence of the medieval church.

The underlying assumptions about the nature and purpose of life were common currency. A triune God exists and is involved in human affairs. Christ is God and man, who came to earth to redeem the human race. Life on earth is a pilgrimage to another life, where the obvious injustices of this life will be redressed in eternal bliss or eternal punishment. Even Christians who diverted from traditional Christianity – and who were labelled heretics – generally shared the same basic world-view. Scepticism and disbelief, on the evidence, were extremely rare but not totally absent. Yet it was the religious assumptions of society generally, whether questioned or unquestioned, that helped to define the age.

If the medieval church can be said to have a body and a soul, then the external institution pertains to the body and the inner spiritual life of Christian people pertains to the soul. A history of the church cannot limit itself to the institution nor, on the other hand, should it omit the institution or treat it almost incidentally. History records how an institution, which was believed to have been divinely founded, was ruled by human beings, who were not divine, sometimes far from being even spiritual. This institution grew and, as it grew, required organization and rules. From the time that we might want to use the word medieval, perhaps from the sixth century, we can see a network of bishops with one, at Rome, claiming authority over the others. That institution then, following the mandate to 'teach all nations', sent missionaries to Celtic and Germanic peoples. And as these new peoples began to establish political control, the church as an institution made the decision to interact with these new leaders, at times even asserting authority over them. This external church constructed places of worship and places of education, giving the world great churches and universities. The leaders of this institution helped to organize military campaigns to reconquer once Christian lands in the East from the hands of the Muslims. Yet, even as an institution, the church was more than the papacy, more than its central government, which gained greater and greater control over the course of time. It was about new religious orders and persons like Benedict and Bernard and Francis of Assisi, and the countless numbers of men and women who followed them. Since records tend to be kept by and for great men, institutional history can understandably become the story of the great men – seldom women – popes and abbots rather than of parish priests and simple monks and nuns, or ordinary laymen and laywomen. It was a church whose fortunes can be charted, particularly at its higher reaches.

Yet a church without an essential spirituality is a body without a soul, form without substance, a hollow and empty contrivance. Nevertheless, the inner life of the church leaves less obvious, less certain traces than the institution. How deep was an individual's commitment or what part prayer or contemplation played in one's life or, indeed, how religious a person actually was it is difficult, nearly impossible to say. It is not given to the historian, mercifully, to be able to look into the souls of others, past or present, yet the historian must try, however diffidently, to examine the inner life of the church and try to get some sense of what religion really meant to Christian people. Inferences can be made from existing evidence such as acts of devotion and works of piety, where these can be seen, but one remains ever aware of the inherent difficulty in doing so.

The history of the church in a period extending over a thousand years, with its continuities and changes, demands a healthy amount of caution and constraint. Generalizations must respect the variations and modalities of a long period of human history and of its different peoples and places. The expression 'medieval church' might be seen to imply a greater sameness than the historical record would permit. The 'church in the Middle Ages' allows us to regard the church in a historical period, during which the church experienced profound changes. In this view, generalizations should not be made lightly and, when made, spoken only in the subjunctive mood. *Caveat lector.*

1

THE PRE-MEDIEVAL CHURCH

The central figure of the medieval church died almost half a millennium before the date usually given for the beginning of the Middle Ages. Enigmatic as it may sound, Christ was born Before Christ. When in the sixth century Dionysius Exiguus used the birth of Christ to date the beginning of the Christian era, he mistakenly believed that Christ was born in the Roman year 754 *ab urbe condita* ('from the founding of the city'), and that year is called the first year of the Christian era: AD 1. In fact, King Herod, during whose reign Christ was born, died in the Roman year 750, and the date given by modern scholars for Christ's birth generally falls between 8 and 4 BC. The date of Christ's death – and, indeed, his age at the time of his death – are not known for certain, but he was probably executed in the year AD 30.

To some of his fellow Jews Jesus of Nazareth was the long-awaited Messiah, the fulfilment of the prophecies, the saviour of his people, the expected of the nations. They believed he was born of a virgin, whose cult was to become a significant feature of medieval religious life. They heard him preach not a new law but the fulfilment of the Jewish law, summarized in the Sermon on the Mount (Matthew, chs 5–6) in a doctrine of universal love: not an eye for an eye and a tooth for a tooth (*lex talionis*), but 'turn the other cheek', 'love your enemies and pray for your persecutors'. When asked how to pray, he told them to say, 'Our Father, who art in heaven' and gave the world the central prayer of the Christian faith. The political problems that he posed for the rabbinical leaders and for the Roman authorities led to his execution by crucifixion on a hill outside Jerusalem between two thieves. His followers were strongly motivated by the conviction that he had actually risen from the dead three days after his death. Many said that they saw him during the next forty days and that then on the fortieth day that they saw him ascend bodily into heaven. Huddled together in fear and confusion ten days later, his followers were said to have been inspired by the Holy Spirit under the appearance of tongues of fire.

They believed that the human race had fallen by reason of the sins of Adam and Eve, the consequences of which affected all peoples. To redeem mankind from this sin God sent his Son to earth in the form of a human being, whose death on the cross was a redemptive sacrifice for the whole human race. Christ, the God–man, was redeemer, saviour, reconciler; it was through belief in him that salvation – a heavenly life in the next world – was to come. This was the message his followers were to preach.

The apostolic church

The band of twelve, the place of Judas the suicide now taken by Matthias, plus several score disciples and a loyal band of holy women – a scant hundred or so in total – formed the core group from which the Christian church was to grow. They had been given no master plan, no blueprint, for an institution, merely the mandate to preach the good news (*gospel*) to all peoples, baptizing them in the name of the Father, Son and Holy Spirit (Matthew 28, 19; Mark 16, 15; Acts 1, 8). The pages of the Acts of the Apostles tell in detail the story of the infant church or, more accurately, the story of the growth of this small band of Jewish followers of Christ to a movement. The author of Acts (probably the evangelist Luke) with unconcealed pleasure quotes the learned rabbi Gamaliel: 'If this idea of theirs or its execution is of human origin, it will collapse; but if it is from God, you will never be able to put them down' (5, 38–9). This band of early Christians were all Jews and viewed themselves as part of the Jewish religious tradition: we would say that they formed a sect of Judaism. They soon made a decision of monumental historical significance.

The question they asked themselves was: Should gentile converts be compelled to undergo circumcision (the Jewish rite of initiation) and become subject to the dietary and other obligations of Judaism? At what has been anachronistically called the 'Council' of Jerusalem (AD 49 or 50) this issue was discussed, and the assembled group of Christian leaders endorsed the opinion of Peter: gentiles need not first become religious Jews. This decision opened the way to the conversion of non-Jews, its significance impossible to exaggerate. Tradition has traced apostles to far-flung parts of the world. Christians of south India trace their Christianity back to the apostle Thomas, who they believe is buried near Madras. John was believed to have been at the city of Ephesus in Asia Minor (Efes in modern Turkey). Matthew may have been active in Ethiopia. Pilgrims still climb mountain passes to the legendary burial place of the apostle James at Compostela in northern Spain. On the historical side of tradition and legend we see the figure of the 'apostle of the gentiles', Paul, the persecutor who was struck down on the road to Damascus and rose as the missionary *par excellence*. He has been well served by Luke, who, in great detail in Acts, describes the missionary journeys of Paul through the Mediterranean world. Etched in the consciousness of peoples for centuries to come was Luke's picture of this learned Jew, Paul, in the *agora* at Athens, where Socrates had spoken four centuries earlier, and also the picture of him talking to men of wisdom on the Areopagus hill below the Acropolis.

> Men of Athens, I see that in everything that concerns religion you
> are uncommonly scrupulous. For as I was going around looking at

the objects of your worship I noticed among other things an altar bearing the inscription 'To an Unknown God'. What you worship but do not know – that is what I proclaim.

(Acts 17, 22–3)

Paul, when later arrested, claimed his rights as a Roman citizen – he was from Tarsus – appealed to Caesar and arrived in Rome in chains.

Already at Rome there was a Christian community. Emperor Claudius *c.*AD 51 expelled Jews from the city because of trouble concerning a certain 'Crestos'. It requires little historical imagination to see in this matter some discord within the Jewish community at Rome concerning the believers in Christ. When Paul arrived there (*c.*AD 60), Roman Christians, to whom he had already sent an epistle, welcomed him. The Roman historian Tacitus relates that in the year 64 Christians constituted a vast multitude (*ingens multitudo*), and, even if we allow here for exaggeration, it seems clear that by then they formed a definable group distinct from the Jewish community at Rome. That the apostle Peter was at Rome is undeniable and that he died during the persecution of Nero (64–67) seems more than likely. Excavations under St Peter's Basilica have unearthed a shrine built in the second century on a slope of the Vatican, which may very well mark the spot of Peter's burial. Also, it was from Rome that a tradition holds that Paul wrote to a follower the words,

Already my life is being poured out on the altar, and the hour for my departure is upon me: I have run the great race, I have finished the course, I have kept faith.

(2 Timothy 4, 6–7)

It is generally believed that, like Peter, Paul too perished in the Neronian persecution, and there is a fairly early tradition that his body lies beneath the church of St Paul's-Without-the-Walls. What is historically certain is that Peter and Paul both died at Rome and a fairly early tradition links them as 'founders' of the Roman church, the Christian Romulus and Remus, as it were.

The spread of Christianity

How to explain the rapid growth of Christianity from the small band of Jews in Jerusalem to the dominant religion of the Roman Empire, which it was to become? Some may perceive in all this the workings of a divine providence, but the historian as historian lacks that kind of vision and, by definition, can and should only see the workings of human agents and natural forces. Over two centuries ago Edward Gibbon, writing probably with a considerable measure of irony, asked, 'What were the secondary causes of the rapid growth of Christianity?' (*Decline and Fall*, chapter 15) Modern historians eschew 'causes' and discuss 'factors': what factors contributed to the growth of Christianity?

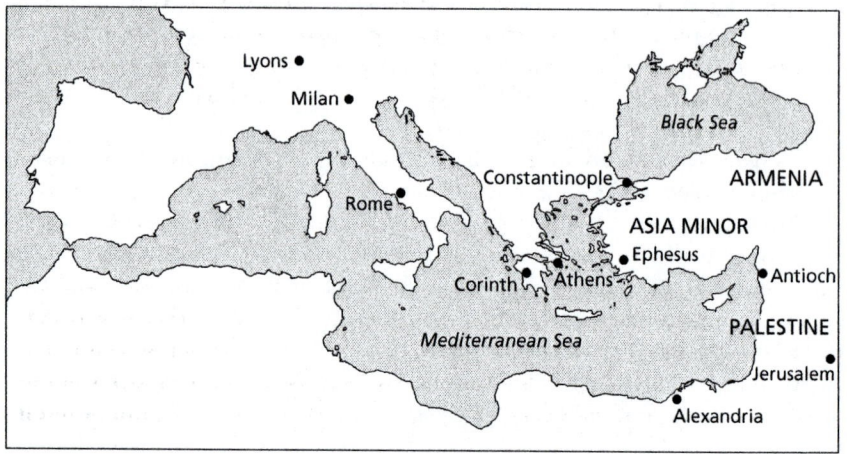

Map 1 Mediterranean region with early Christian sites.

Two will be singled out here: the existence of the Roman Empire and a spiritual vacuum in the Roman world.

It would be difficult to exaggerate the significance of the where and when of the birth of the Christian religion: Jesus was born in the Roman Empire, albeit at a remote edge of that empire. The Romans under Pompey had conquered Palestine in 63 BC, and at once this tiny land with an ancient people became part of a mighty empire which was to stretch from Scotland in the north to the Sahara in the south and from Spain in the west to Syria in the east. Jesus was born while Herod, a part-Jew, ruled as local king and Roman surrogate. When asked about tribute in a trick question, Jesus replied to 'render to Caesar the things that are Caesar's . . .' He was executed while Pontius Pilate was the Roman procurator of Judea. A large diaspora of Jews lived outside Palestine in other parts of the Roman Empire: perhaps four million – four times the Jewish population of Palestine – in such cities as Alexandria, Ephesus, Antioch, Corinth and even Rome. Paul himself was from Tarsus, capital of Cilicia, in the south-eastern part of modern Turkey. He had a Greek name, Paul, and was a Roman citizen. No frontiers need be crossed within the Roman world. Roman engineers had constructed thousands of miles of roads, which, like modern railways, linked the remotest parts. And the Mediterranean Sea, as its name implies ('the water in the midst of the land'), was an inland lake with Roman lands along all its shores. No wonder the Romans called it *mare nostrum* ('our sea'). For two hundred years a population of perhaps as many as seventy million people at a given time lived in a peace (*Pax Romana*) of a length seldom known in human history before or since. Although wars were fought at trouble spots along its long exterior borders and two rebellions were savagely put down in Judea and two brief civil wars occurred over the emperorship, the period was essentially one of a general, prolonged peace and extensive, if not universal, prosperity. Two languages – Greek and Latin – were linguistic equipment enough to allow one to travel with ease across the over two-thousand-mile east–west axis. Problems were to arise – and these will be visited shortly – but it is difficult to imagine more favourable circumstances for the spread of Christianity.

Favourable in another way was what we might call a spiritual void, a yearning for personal fulfilment of the inner person, a need largely unsatisfied by the formal state religion of Rome. Whatever appeal the cults of the ancient gods might have once had, by the first century they had become formalized festivities, like in our times the trooping of the colours by the monarch or Fourth-of-July parades and fireworks. They were largely civic and even patriotic events, which hardly brought meaning to the deeper parts of the human soul, where reside questions of the ultimate meaning of life. Some Romans found answers in the teachings of their Stoic philosophers, like Seneca, who saw virtue, not material success, as the path of wisdom leading to human happiness. Attractive in many ways, Stoicism appealed by and large to a small elite. Of wider appeal were the religions which entered the West from the more remote eastern parts of the Roman world and even beyond. Usually said to have been brought back by returning Roman legionaries, cults such as those to Mithras and Isis touched a responsive chord. For many the search for meaning went beyond the coolly rational teachings of the philosophers, and for them these mystery religions could have an appealing affective element. Men who pledged themselves to Mithras, the Persian sun god, were formally initiated, ate meals together, committed themselves to such manly virtues as loyalty and courage and held secret meetings in caves or cave-like places, and a happy life after death was promised to its votaries. Hundreds of shrines of Mithras, frequently showing a suffering Mithras, have been found throughout the Roman world: one of the most well known lies far beneath the church of San Clemente in Rome. Was Christianity but another Eastern mystery religion, similar in some ways to the cult of Mithras? Despite obvious points of external similarity, Christianity differed in essential ways from these other religions from the East. It alone was monotheistic. At its centre was not a mythological person but an actual historical person. A religion based on a rigid moral code, Christianity stood apart from the mystery cults, yet it tapped some of the same human yearnings. What was perceived as a high moral code – in Tertullian's familiar phrase 'See the Christians: how they love one another' – provided a powerful attraction to souls in search of a religion which affected their whole lives.

With these favourable factors contributing, Christian communities were to be found by the end of the first century in every city of the empire, no longer submerged within the Jewish community. About the year 112 Pliny the Younger, once consul in Rome, wrote from Asia Minor that Christianity was reaching even into the villages. By the end of that century Christianity had reached remotest Britain. Numbers are difficult to come at in all this, but, by the conversion of Constantine in 312, perhaps as many as six or seven million Christians lived within the empire and an untold but no doubt smaller number beyond its borders. By any measure a remarkable achievement, perhaps unsurpassed in conversion history.

The persecutions: a historical problem

Few subjects in this process have exercised the talents of historians more than the significance of the persecution of the Christians by the Roman state. The facts are not really in dispute; it is their interpretation which divides their students. In 64 the emperor Nero singled out the nascent Christian community at Rome as a scapegoat for the burning of Rome. It was a local persecution, restricted to the city itself, and it lasted perhaps three years. What Nero did was to create a precedent that permitted the persecution of Christians as Christians. Clearer reasons for their persecution were in time to be enunciated: they were atheists in not worshipping the gods and traitors in not honouring the emperor as a god. For the next two hundred years after Nero's scapegoating, Christians were persecuted sporadically but only in specific locations – now at Alexandria, now at Smyrna, now at Rome, etc. – and never for a prolonged period in any of these. Even the seemingly benign Marcus Aurelius, whose *Meditations* continue to inspire thoughtful readers, in 177 sanctioned persecution, including the brutal executions of forty-eight Christians at Lyons: some strangled and beheaded, others given, while still living, to the wild beasts in the amphitheatre. A period of prolonged peace lasted from 211 to 250. Matters changed in 250 when Emperor Decius ordered all Christians to deny their Christian belief and to worship the Roman gods; those who refused paid with their lives. Continued by his successor, this total persecution finally ended in 260. The forty years that followed saw a de facto toleration, even to the extent of Christians becoming provincial governors. The mightiest persecution was the last: Diocletian moved against the Christians in 303 and in the following year decreed death to all Christians throughout the empire. Before this general persecution ended in 311, more Christians were slaughtered than in all previous persecutions combined.

Some may see the Roman persecutions of the Christians as a main theme in the first three centuries of the Christian era, others see them at most as a minor theme. What is clear is that the picture of Christians in an 'underground' church, worshipping by stealth in the catacombs, being ruthlessly sought out by a uniformly hostile state and fed to lions is a picture hardly borne out by the facts. Sporadic and affecting only a very small number of Christians, the persecutions probably were not major negative forces in the process of the growth of the Christian religion. Yet throughout this period from the time of Nero to the conversion of Constantine (312) the Christian religion was not only officially proscribed but, perhaps more importantly, was the object of suspicion, hideous rumours and popular outbursts of ill-treatment. Not totally secure in the Roman state, the early Christians did not know when or where persecution or rioting might erupt against them. Also – and its weight defies measurement – the heroic and peaceful way in which many Christians received the 'martyr's crown' attracted the admiration of pagans. Tertullian's well-known epigram that the blood of martyrs acted as a seed for the growth of the Christian religion (*semen est sanguis Christianorum*) reflects the view that persecution merely strengthened Christianity. Still, it is fair to say that an overemphasis of the popular opposition and official persecutions probably distorts the historical realities.

Constantine, controversy and conversion

At the time of Constantine's conversion (312) and the Edict of Milan (313) the Christians composed perhaps one-tenth or so of the population of the empire with a somewhat larger concentration in the East than in the West. While Constantine's motives can be debated, the effect of his policy transformed the religious culture of the Roman world and was clearly a defining moment in the history of the church. Free now from persecution – a tolerated church (*ecclesia tolerabilis*) – the Christian religion prospered as it never had before. By century's end the majority of the people professed Christianity, which in 392, in effect, became the official religion of the Roman state.

From apostolic times the movement had some organization: the unit was the local church (*ecclesia*). The local community at Corinth was known as the church of Corinth, and so it was with the other local Christian communities. At each church some person presided; he was called by different names but has become known as 'bishop'. He and his community welcomed new members in an initiation rite (baptism with water and affirmation of the Christian name). They worshipped together in private homes at a Eucharist ('thanks-giving') that memorialized the Last Supper of Christ with his apostles. By the time of Constantine the 'bishops' of the great churches at Antioch, Alexandria and Rome exercised authority beyond their local churches. Constantine's establishment of a 'new Rome' on the Bosporus at the small port of Byzantium, to which he gave his own name, meant that Constantinople would take its place with these three and would play a prominent part in church affairs.

The emergence of Christianity into the full light of day provided the opportunity and, indeed, the necessity for Christians to reflect on the nature of their religion. The New Testament provided inspirational reading but not an organized body of Christian theology. Differences soon emerged and focused on the central issue of the Christian religion: the nature of Christ. The gospels declared that he was the Messiah, the fulfilment of the prophecies, the redeemer of mankind, the expectation of the nations. But what was he? Was he merely a good and great man whose message of hope and love and the pre-eminence of the spirit touched the hearts of men and women? Or was he more? Did Jesus of Nazareth partake of the deity in some way? If so, how? Was the 'Son of God' really God? And if so, how could this be if there is only one God? Simply put, the two related issues which were to trouble Christianity in its long history were the divinity of Christ and the nature of the Godhead. The issues are obviously intertwined and go to the very heart of Christian belief.

In a moment of great theatre Emperor Constantine, in 325, took the place of pre-eminence at a council of bishops at Nicaea to resolve the dispute about the nature of Christ. A holy priest of Alexandria, Arius, had been teaching that there was a time when Christ was not, that God the Father created his son out of nothing (*ex nihilo*) and endowed his creature with extraordinary, divine-like powers. This was not Christ the God, but Christ the creature. Before the matter was officially resolved by this council at Nicaea and later councils at Constantinople (381) and Chalcedon (451), much of Christendom was riven into two camps over the issue of the divinity of Christ. In the fourth century, the debate centred on which Greek word accurately described the relationship of Christ to God the Father: was he of the same substance as the Father ὁμοούσιον (*homo-ousion*) or merely of like substance to the Father ὁμοιούσιον (*homoi-ousion*)? Only the frivolous would scorn this as a debate over the Greek letter ι (*iota*): it was, in fact, a debate over whether Christ is God or only god-like. The creed developed by these councils, generally called the Nicene Creed and still used in the rites of Christian churches, asserts that Christ is God (i.e., ὁμοούσιος, of the same substance as the Father). The Arians were defeated, but their teaching was to live on among many German tribes who were converted to Christianity in its Arian form. Subsequent debate centred on how Christ could be both the immutable God and the clearly mutable human? How could the Son of God become incarnate in time and place? What is the nature of this incarnate God ('the Word made flesh')? Are there two persons, one divine and one human? The councils, while leaving room for theological speculation, taught that Christ was one person who is fully God and fully human. This union of the divine and human (the hypostatic union) theologians were later to explain by distinguishing between person and nature: they are metaphysically different and, hence, the person Christ could have two natures, one divine and one human.

A clearly related issue was apparent to all: if Jesus is God and is distinct from God the Father, why are there not two gods? how could Christianity escape from polytheism? And the matter was further involved by the belief that the Holy Spirit also is God and also is distinct from the Father and the Son. Monotheism was obviously at stake in this trinitarian debate. The Christian orthodoxy that emerged held to a Trinity: one God and three divine persons. It was later to be summed up in the Athanasian Creed:

> Ita deus pater, deus filius, deus spiritus sanctus,
> Et tamen non tres dii, sed unus est deus.

> (Thus, God the Father, God the Son, God the Holy Spirit,
> Yet not three gods but one God.)

Here, again, later theologians were to apply to this 'mystery' the same metaphysical distinction between person and nature: God can have one nature (divine) and three persons (Father, Son and Holy Spirit).

The fourth and fifth centuries witnessed more – much more – than doctrinal disputes. The very councils just mentioned attest to the fact that there was a sense of the church, the wider community of Christian believers which was more than a collection of local churches: the whole being not only more but different from the sum of its parts. This sense of the Christian – authors by this time used the word 'Catholic' – church can also be seen in the body of Christian literature, from East and West, which was written not merely for the local church but for the whole body of Christian believers. If examples are only given here from the Latin West, it is because these became part of the medieval library. Augustine (354–430) was the greatest mind of his age and devoted much of his talents to writing theological works (e.g., *De trinitate, On the Trinity*), which became the subject of commentaries throughout the Middle Ages. His *Confessions* describes for the ages the story of the anguish of a soul in search of rest. In the *City of God* he presented a theological view of human history which still finds an audience. If Augustine was anguished, his contemporary Jerome (d. 420) was irascible. An often-repeated anecdote has a modern pope shaking his fist at a statue of St Jerome in the Vatican garden and saying 'How did you become a saint?' Yet, despite his irascibility, Jerome was to give the Middle Ages its greatest book, the translation of the Greek Bible into Latin, known historically as the Latin Vulgate. And completing the trinity of these Latin 'Fathers of the Church' is the urbane Ambrose (d. 397), Roman official who became bishop of Milan and humbled the emperor Theodosius the Great. His prose reflected the *sonoritas* of the prose of Cicero, whose *De officiis* (*On Duties*) Ambrose used as a model to write about Christian ethics. These great Fathers of the Latin church – to be joined later by Gregory the Great – were impelled by a sense of the church which transcended the merely local and provincial and which was the community of all believers.

One of the most remarkable events in world history has to be the conversion of the Roman Empire to Christianity, a process largely of the fourth century. Students of Roman history are used to a division of their subject into the Roman Republic and the Roman Empire. To these a third should be added, the Christian Roman Empire, which was clearly a part of ancient history. From a small minority in 312 Christians came to form the majority by at least the 380s. Christian churches were built in the basilica style. In Rome, St Paul's-Without-the-Walls, built about 380 and rebuilt after a fire in 1823 to the original design, remains perhaps the best example of its type. By the end of the fourth century there were several thousand monks living in the deserts outside Alexandria in Egypt. Even in distant Britain, Christianity had become firmly established. It had already, in the third century, had its first martyr, Alban, slain at Verulamium. And after Christian emancipation three bishops from Britain attended the church council held at Arles in 314 and bishops from Britain are known to have attended the council at Rimini in 359. Also, the remains of a Christian church at Silchester, a large cemetery at Dorchester and a hoard of Christian plate at Water Newton (Northamptonshire) attest to a large Christian community in Roman Britain. At the other end of the Roman world, a Christian community was being established in the lands below the Caucasus in Armenia, where Tiridates (d. 314), client king to the Roman emperor, was converted and his people soon followed. These examples could be multiplied. While the actual process of Christianization challenges precise definition and measurement, it is clear that, within decades after its toleration by Constantine, rather than centuries, Christianity had a predominant place in the religious life of the Roman world.

Further reading

The starting place, of course, is the New Testament. The four gospels and the Acts of the Apostles describe the life of Christ and the life of the early Christian community, while the epistles of early Christian leaders provide insight into the issues that concerned them and their flocks.

Of contemporary histories the most accessible is *The History of the Church: From Christ to Constantine*, published as a Penguin Classic (Harmondsworth, Mddsx, 1960, and frequently reprinted) by Eusebius (*c*.260–*c*.340), who suffered imprisonment, became a bishop and was a friend of Emperor Constantine. It sheds much light on the experiences of the early Christians. A survey of this period is W.H.C. Frend, *The Early Church from the Beginning to 461* (3rd edn; London, 1991). For the early post-apostolic period one may consult W.A. Meeks, *The First Urban Christians: The Social World of the Apostle Paul* (New Haven and London, 1983), which adopts the approach of social history.

On persecutions one may begin with W.H.C. Frend, *Martyrdom and Persecution in the Early Church* (Oxford, 1965). A lively debate on the question can be found in the journal *Past and Present*, vols 26 (1963) and 27 (1964). Also, one should see P.S. Davies, 'The Origin and Purpose of the Persecution of AD 303', *Journal of Theological Studies* 40 (1989), 66–94.

Ramsey MacMullen makes interesting observations about the spread of Christianity in *Christianizing the Roman Empire (A.D. 100–400)* (New Haven and London, 1984). J.N.D. Kelly provides a description of the theological developments in *Early Christian Doctrine* (5th edn; London, 1977) as does Jaroslav Pelikan in *The Emergence of the Catholic Tradition, 100–600* (vol. 1 of *The Christian Tradition: A History of the Development of Doctrine*, Chicago and London, 1971). For a more specialized work see R.P.C. Hanson, *The Search for the Christian Doctrine of God: The Arian Controversy, 318–381* (Edinburgh, 1988).

2

THE BEGINNING OF THE MIDDLE AGES

The Middle Ages did not begin in the year 500, although that date is often used in a shorthand way, a usage to which only the pedantic will take exception. Yet the world and Western Europe, in particular, were little changed between 499 and 501. It makes more historical sense to see a period of time during which the ancient world was ending and the medieval world beginning. This age of transition, in which old and new were intermixed, lasted for several centuries, and the historical reality that emerged was essentially different from that which preceded, as different as the world of Charlemagne was from the world of Theodosius I. Even to put dates to this age of transition is hazardous, but dates placing these two historical figures at either end would fit the historical realities, very roughly from 400 to 750. At the end of the fourth century the historical focus was on the Mediterranean Sea and the lands of the Roman Empire along its entire littoral. Its southern boundary was the Sahara desert and its northern boundary along the lines of the Rhine and Danube Rivers from the North Sea to the Black Sea. In the eighth century that political and cultural world no longer existed. The Roman Empire that existed by that time was but a fragment: the eastern part of the old empire north of the Mediterranean Sea. The western part of the old empire north of the Mediterranean Sea – Iberia excepted – was under the political control of Germanic peoples. And the southern, eastern and even the western shores of the sea were controlled by a new and powerful force, Islam, whose world stretched from the Pyrenees to the Punjab. In the next chapter we shall briefly view the East, the attempts of Justinian to sew together that which was irreparable, and also the extraordinary emergence of Islam. But our main focus must be on Western Europe, for the Middle Ages were a phenomenon of Western Europe, although, to be sure, there were relations with neighbours, Byzantium and the Eastern church to the east and Islam to the south and south-west. The geographical boundaries of medieval Europe had the Mediterranean as its southern boundary and, in time, extended beyond the Arctic Circle to the north. Its western boundary was the great sea and its eastern boundary the easternmost lands of the Germans, yet both of these boundaries were to expand. Any cultural map of medieval Europe from the tenth and eleventh centuries onwards would have to include Iceland and southern Greenland, and the eastern line moved further eastward – a medieval *Drang nach Osten* – as Slavic peoples adopted Latin Christianity.

The peoples in these lands were not the same at the beginning and end of this transition. The Romans and the Romanized populated the Roman Empire, whereas medieval Europe had a decidedly Germanic element. Some scholars define the Middle Ages as the fusion of three elements: Roman, Germanic and Christian. An absolutely crucial phenomenon was the entrance and settlement of Germanic tribes within the old empire in the West. The empire after 487 – and some would say even earlier – had little effective power in the West. When the barbarian migration ended, political unity in the West was no more and a plurality of successor states had come into being under Germanic kings, and, when larger political ambitions were voiced, they were in the Germanic tones of Frankish kings. If the Roman world can be described as having an east–west axis, then the medieval world can be said to have a north–south axis that linked the Mediterranean peninsulas with lands to the north, even, in time, with the Scandinavian lands to the far north. These were changes not of a day but of centuries.

The Germans

A word about terminology. Anthropologists see the complex elements in these peoples whom we call German and warn of the danger in calling these people 'German', whereas 'German-speaking' better respects their differences and their own social structures, where ethnic purity should not be assumed. Where the word 'German' is used here, let it be understood in this latter sense.

It would be easy to see the migration of Germanic peoples into the Roman Empire as the end result of events which took place in central Asia in the late first century AD. It might be said that, if the Chinese had not inflicted a devastating defeat on tribal peoples called the Hiung-nu (Huns), the Middle Ages would never have occurred. This domino theory of history sees a series of events leading from this defeat of the Huns to the dismemberment of the Roman Empire. The Huns, fierce warriors on horseback, licking their wounds, headed westward and eventually (and, indeed, abruptly) appeared in south-eastern Europe in the fourth century. To escape their fury the people who were in their way – various groups calling themselves Goths – moved westward, eventually into the empire as did other similarly pressed Germanic peoples. The integrity of the empire was lost, and new structures replaced the old. So the domino theory goes.

There is, no doubt, some truth in this scenario, and those events can be so described, but history as it unfolds is very rarely a sequence of simple causes: monocausality reduces the study of history to meaningless simplicities. Other factors occurred at every stage in these developments, and there were always pressures – economic, social and military – which could force peoples to move on. And there were inevitable minglings of peoples, which makes ethnic identities

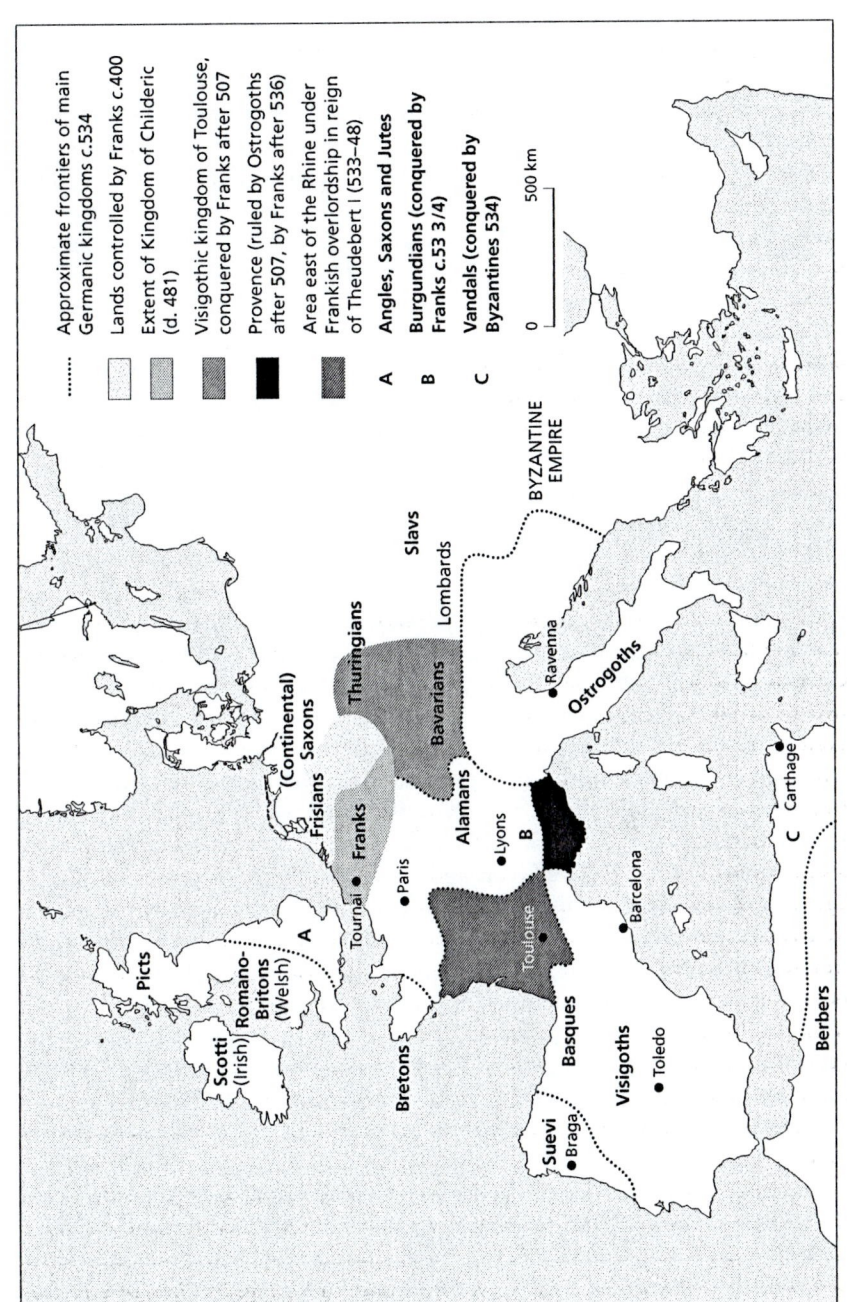

Map 2 Germanic settlement pattern, c.534.

among migrating tribes difficult to verify. Although a sequence of migrations can be plotted on the map, the historian must allow for unmappable complexities and multiple causes.

The Germanic peoples who in the 370s lay in the path of the Hunnic horde had over several centuries migrated south from homelands near the Baltic Sea. Although these peoples had not been clearly differentiated there, the migrations produced more clearly defined groupings, called 'tribes' in our historiography. The Goths – a reminder of remote origins remains in the name of the island of Gotland in the Baltic Sea – should not be seen on the eve of the Hunnic invasions as existing in a clear-cut division of two groups, Ostrogoths and Visigoths. These terms are anachronistic. They were not used in contemporary sources, where the peoples are commonly called simply Goths. Two groups are indeed known to us, but it would be rash indeed to think that there were not other Gothic peoples. The groupings that appear are (i) the Tervingi, who lived west of the Dneister River in Moldavia and perhaps in part of Wallachia, and (ii) the Greuthungi, who were in the steppeland north of the Black Sea and east of the Dneister. The Goths were a people who, no doubt with significant indigenous populations, lived in the lands between the Danube and the Don Rivers. It was these people, the Goths, whom the Huns met as they invaded the rich lands of the modern Ukraine in 376. More particularly, it was elements of these people living in the eastern parts of these Gothic lands who were stunned by the fierce – ferocious and beast-like, say hardly impartial sources – horde of the Huns. In desperation, refuge was sought within the confines of the empire, and in that year most, but not all, of the Tervingi and some of the Greuthungi, who had fled west, were allowed to enter the empire. Perhaps it was because the emperor Valens was distracted by troubles on the Persian frontier that he agreed that these Goths could cross the Danube and settle in northern Thrace. He further agreed to provision them in return for their military service when required. (The descendants of these Goths who crossed the Danube into Thrace in 376 would soon be called Visigoths, and we may now conveniently call them by that name.) Almost immediate discontent – not enough food soon enough – turned into violence. This caught Valens's attention, but Roman miscalculation continued and the imperial army was defeated at Adrianople by these Visigoths (378), the emperor falling with his soldiers. While modern historians dispute the significance of this battle, its contemporary historian Ammianus Marcellinus had no doubt and prophetically called it 'this irreparable disaster, whose consequences will long weigh upon the destinies of the empire'. Thereafter, Germans were to be a constant feature within the Roman Empire, and, whatever the arguments of some modern historians, the world was never the same after Adrianople.

The Roman Empire towards the end of the fourth century, before the Gothic incursions across the Danube and their military successes, was little different in size and shape from the empire of two hundred years earlier. The external boundaries were virtually the same. The northern boundary, the great stretch of the Rivers Rhine and Danube with a system of fortifications (*limes*) stretching between them near their headwaters, was always the most difficult frontier to maintain. It was extended at one point to include the province of Dacia, from which Romania traces itself. The major changes concerned internal divisions, chiefly the work of Diocletian (284–305): the one empire had two emperors, one in the West at Rome and the other in the East at Constantinople, each with a Caesar assisting. These internal administrative divisions notwithstanding, the empire was intact in 376. Yet by the early sixth century it was a different world. From 476 there was no emperor in the West, and the eastern emperor had only nominal authority west of the Adriatic. In the West itself Germanic kings ruled where once ruled Augustus, Hadrian, Marcus Aurelius, Septimius Severus and Constantine. The Vandals, their name now, perhaps unfairly, having a pejorative meaning, had crossed the upper Rhine, pillaged their way through Gaul and Iberia before settling in North Africa. Behind them, as it were, came the Visigoths, who, several decades after Adrianople, marched into Italy, briefly 'sacked' Rome (410) and, for want of food, moved into south-western Gaul before being pushed by the Franks into what became their historical home, Visigothic Spain. The Ostrogoths – i.e., the Grethungi and others – followed later still, and the emperor adeptly sent them westward, where by 500 they ruled Italy, their leader there called *patricius* and never *imperator*. Of a different sort were those Germans living east of the Rhine, particularly the Franks, who were to become major players in medieval history. The Franks crossed the Rhine and, in various groupings, settled in northern parts of Roman Gaul. By 500 they had a single ruler, Clovis, whose land stretched from what is south-western Germany across Gaul to the Atlantic waters of the Bay of Biscay. Other Germanic peoples were taking control of once Roman lands, as, for example, the Burgundians in the Rhone valley. Britain had been abandoned by the Roman legions (*c.*410), and its native Celtic people (the Britons) were left with little defence against invading Anglo-Saxons.

This much different situation of the early sixth century should not tempt us to conclude that Roman culture was stamped out in a West now ruled by Germanic kings: it was not. That Theodoric, the Ostrogothic king of Italy, never attempted to use the title of emperor is telling. Earlier, according to the historian Orosius, the Visigothic king Ataulf, who had married Placidia, sister of the emperor,

> decided to seek for himself the glory of restoring the fame of Rome
> in all its fullness and of adding to it by the power of the Goths, for
> he wanted to be remembered by posterity as the restorer of the
> Roman Empire, since he could not alter it.

Latin, its classical purity now well in decline, was still the dominant tongue, and the languages spoken today in these places, with only minor exceptions, are Romance languages, offsprings of Latin (Italian in Italy, French in France, Spanish and Portuguese in Iberia). No one would argue that the parts of *Romania* ruled by German kings experienced a golden age, but a period of cultural decline might well have occurred even without the coming of the Germans. Probably never large in number – estimates yield conflicting results – the Germans were never more than a minority in Italy, Iberia and southern Gaul.

The coming of the Germans posed serious issues for the Catholic church. When these peoples entered the empire, none of them was Catholic: they were either Arian or pagan. Crucial in the first stage of their conversion to Christianity was the mission of Ulfilas (c.311–83). He was part Greek and part Goth, and on his Greek side he was Christian. His grandparents had been taken away from their native Cappadocia and abducted by the Goths to their lands to the north. It was the bilingual, Christian Ulfilas who was the pivotal figure in the early Christianization of the Germans. In 341, while at Constantinople with an embassy of Goths, he was made a bishop with a mission to convert his fellow Goths. To say he was a Christian is to tell only part of the story: he, in fact, was an Arian Christian and an Arian bishop and an Arian missionary to his fellow Goths. Their conversion to Arian Christianity contained the seeds of future problems. Besides his missionary successes, Ulfilas accomplished two remarkable feats: he created the written Gothic language by inventing its alphabet and then he translated the Greek Bible into Gothic. When the Visigoths entered the empire in 376, they were led by Fritigern, a convert, and they had Ulfilas in their company. That their holy book was in the German language and their religious services were also in the same language – not as surprising as it may seem, since the West had services in the vernacular, i.e., Latin – served to facilitate the conversion of their brother Germans to Arian Christianity, as they, in turn, entered the empire. Thus, the Ostrogoths in Italy practised what the native Christians considered a heretical form of Christianity. And so it was in North Africa that the Arian Vandals harshly persecuted Catholics. The Visigoths, while in southern Gaul and later in Spain, were long faithful to the religion of Ulfilas.

Two societies, then, were to be found in the West in the fifth century, one Germanic and Arian and the other Roman and Catholic. That there were hostile relations between these two societies is clear enough. Arian Visigoths sacked Rome in 410 and sent a chill through the empire, yet, in truth, they stayed only a short while before moving on in their quest for food. After their settlement in Spain, the Visigoths continued to profess Arianism for over a hundred years. Also, it is true that St Augustine died at Hippo in North Africa while the Vandals besieged his city and that the Vandals decimated the higher ranks of old Roman, Catholic society in their new land. Yet all was not hostility, and remarkable men and achievements give an irenic tint to the picture. Theodoric, the Ostrogothic king of Italy (493–526), while at Ravenna, built the finely decorated church of S. Apollinare Nuovo. In general, he tolerated Catholic Christianity. During the period of Ostrogothic rule in Italy, eminent Catholic writers wrote works which were to resonate through the centuries.

Boethius (c.480–524), representing the full flower of Christian Rome, the scion of a senatorial family, was appointed *magister officiorum* by Theodoric in 522. His imprisonment in the following year on charges of conspiring with the

Byzantine emperor against the king (which he strongly denied) gave the world the classic *Consolations of Philosophy*, which would later be found in virtually every medieval library. It was among the first books translated into vernacular languages – by King Alfred into Old English, by Chaucer into Middle English and by Queen Elizabeth I into modern English. At its end, Philosophy tells Boethius, 'It is not in vain that you place your hope in God, nor are your prayers to him in vain. . . . Your life is known by the judge who knows all.' In the event, Boethius was brutally executed at Pavia as a traitor. In danger of being lost to sight because of the brilliance and dramatic circumstances of the *Consolations* is the scheme that Boethius started, but never finished, of translating the works of the Greek philosophers Aristotle and Plato into Latin. He lived long enough to do the logical works of Aristotle, but his execution deprived the West of Greek thought at that time, a loss which was not made good until the twelfth century. It is not entirely idle to speculate how vastly different the intellectual life of the Middle Ages would have been if Boethius had lived to complete his work. Sir Richard Southern has called him 'the schoolmaster of medieval Europe'.

Theodoric in need of Latinists to compose official documents took on another member of the senatorial class, Cassiodorus (490–*c*.583). His *Variae* is a collection of documents which he composed for the Ostrogothic king; they reveal a skilled rhetorician. Royal employment was but a prelude to his founding the monastery of Vivarium in Calabria, where he was to write the influential *Institutiones* (*c*.562). A description of the curriculum for his monks, the *Institutiones* exercised a profound influence on the history of the West. By dividing his treatise into two parts, the first concerning biblical study and the second concerning secular study of the seven liberal arts, Cassiodorus allowed, probably not by design, the separation of religious studies from secular studies. Knowledge of the liberal arts could have a place on its own, separate from religious knowledge. The full title of this work underlines this distinction: *Institutiones divinarum et saecularium litterarum* (*Institutions of divine and secular learning*). Only three of the surviving manuscripts of the *Institutiones* have both parts, the rest have either part one or part two, thus emphasizing this bifurcation. To a very large extent the position of the liberal arts in the medieval schools and, indeed, the modern universities owes much to this sixth-century Christian Roman intellectual.

More difficult to assess is the historical importance of the contemporary of Boethius and Cassiodorus, the monk Benedict of Nursia (*c*.480–*c*.550). Although St Benedict is frequently hailed as the 'Patriarch of Western Monasticism', it is highly doubtful that such a title can be justified by historical evidence. Why such a sobriquet in the first place? Traditional historiography described this holy man in a version which was long received. He came, it is said, to Rome from near Spoleto as a young student, but, appalled by the excesses of the city, he went off to live as a hermit at Subiaco in the Sabine hills near Rome. Later he founded the best known of Christian monasteries at Monte Cassino on a hill above the town of Cassianum near Naples, a monastery unnecessarily destroyed by allied forces in 1944. His posthumous fame rests solely on the Rule of St Benedict, which, in time, was to become the blueprint for the monastic order in the Middle Ages and beyond. The rule describes the life of cenobitical monks – they ate together a common meal (*coena*) – under the kindly authority of an abbot. It was a life of dedication, yet a life of moderation, avoiding extremes of laxity and severity. The Rule strikes the modern reader as sensible, discreet, practical and, in a word, livable. We read, 'And so we establish a school for God's service (*dominici scola servitii*), in which we hope we are founding an institution where there is nothing harsh or burdensome (*nihil asperum, nihil grave*).' He outlined a stable community with a life lived in prayer (*opus dei*, the work of God) and work. The abbot should mitigate the rule for the aged and infirm. This rule with its lofty idealism and pragmatic flexibility recommended itself to the ages. It is on this subsequent success of the Rule of St Benedict that hinges the historical place of Benedict of Nursia. What we know about his life is largely, almost singly, derived from his biography written by Pope Gregory the Great about 593, over four decades after Benedict's death. A work of hagiography, Gregory's life attributes miracles to Benedict – he made water flow from rocks – and gives the essential lines of his life, summarized above. About the Rule, Gregory merely commended it for its discretion and clarity, but he showed no indication that he was familiar with it. The sixth-century abbot Benedict would be but a minor footnote to the history of that period were it not for his Rule. Yet St Benedict did not write the Rule of St Benedict as it now stands. Very large sections of this rule were taken substantially from the older Rule of the Master and other sections contain striking parallels and echoes of the Rule of the Master. The most famous parts of the Rule of St Benedict (e.g., the prologue, the chapters on obedience, on silence, on the steps of humility) are not the work of St Benedict. Hugh Lawrence writes that 'all the essentials of St Benedict's Rule are to be found in the works of his unknown predecessor'. Of course, it must be granted to St Benedict that he organized what became known as his rule and added some notable contributions of his own to the work of the Master and that this Rule became the model for monasticism in the Middle Ages. Benedict's historical place belongs somewhere between patriarch of Western monasticism and a minor Italian abbot.

Conversion of the Franks

It was as pagans, not Arian Christians, that the Franks entered the Roman Empire in the fifth century. Theirs was not an immigration *en masse* into Roman lands. They expanded from lands north and east of the Rhine: the Salian Franks from the lands near saline sea (the North Sea) north of the upper Rhine and the Ripuarian Franks from the lands east of the banks (*ripa*) of the middle Rhine. The former entered into the Roman province of Belgica Secunda, establishing themselves at Tournai, where among their early chieftains was Merovech, whose name was given to the dynasty (i.e., Merovingian). The Ripuarians crossed the Rhine in the area now called the Rhineland and Luxembourg, taking such cities as Cologne, Trier and Metz. The two branches of Franks became united under the Merovingian king Clovis. Few moments in European history were truly so momentous in their consequences as the conversion of the Frankish king Clovis to Catholic Christianity (*c*.500), about the sincerity of which contemporary sources leave little doubt. It is unfortunate that much of what we know of Clovis comes from the description given by Gregory of Tours in his *Histories of the Franks*, a hostile secondary source written more than six decades after the death of Clovis. There we see a cruel, treacherous, cunning perpetrator of ruses and assassinations, the very stereotype of the worst kind of barbarian. Primary sources, the only truly reliable evidence for him, show another Clovis: the embodiment of the synthesis of Roman, Germanic and Christian attributes, who, in a remarkable way, did much to shape the emerging medieval world. By moving south, first, to the lands between the Seine and the Loire and, later, by defeating the Arian Visigoths (507), thus incorporating much of southern Gaul, Clovis gave the general contours to what was known as *Francia* and now France, which, because of Clovis's conversion (*c*.500), can claim to be 'the eldest daughter of the church'. His contemporary Geneviève constructed a substantial church at the burial site of St Denis near Paris, and, at her grave on the hill that still bears her name (Mont Ste Geneviève) on the left bank of the Seine, Clovis built a church, where in 511 his body was buried: the person whose conversion insured the eventual conversion of other Germanic peoples to Catholic orthodoxy.

Roman Gaul was long a Catholic province, and, thus, to the Romans, the Frankish converts were fellow believers rather than hostile heretics. There had long been bishops in Christian Gaul; they and their flocks could view the Franks as liberators from the Arian Visigoths. Notable among these bishops was Caesarius of Arles (d. 542), a dedicated pastor of souls, some of whose sermons still survive. In the year in which Clovis was to die, he called the Gallo-Roman bishops to a council at Orléans. The Franks did not overturn nor did they attempt to overturn the existing ecclesiastical organization: each bishop ruled over a diocese (*parochia*), which corresponded to the Roman city (*civitas*). By 575 the son of a senatorial family, Gregory, became bishop of Tours, within whose jurisdiction came the bishoprics of Le Mans, Rennes, Angers, Nantes and four others. For the years 575 to 591 Gregory's *History of the Franks* – curious that a Gallo-Roman so titled his book – is a contemporary account of Francia and, especially, of the church in Francia. The conversion of the Franks was attained only in a limited sense by the ceremony of baptism: what in fact occurred, in Rosamond McKitterick's words, was 'a very gradual process by which the very complexion and context of Frankish society, its religion, ethics, law and social institutions, became completely transformed'.

Catholic Spain

The Arian Visigoths, now pushed south of the Pyrenees by the Franks, established themselves in Spain as a minority in a Hispano-Roman, Catholic population.

Before the sixth century was out, there was accomplished what the sword of Clovis had not accomplished, the conversion of the Visigoths. Their great king Leovigild (568–86), faced with the conversion of his son Hermenegild (579), launched a persecution of Catholics. His successor, Recared I (586–601), was converted shortly after his succession, and he then summoned bishops, Catholic and Arian, to a meeting at his capital at Toledo. There at the Third Council of Toledo (589) Catholicism became the official religion of the Visigothic state. Although some Arians refused conversion, the Visigoths, in general, quickly adopted the Catholic faith. An aspect of Visigothic rule that was perhaps not a precedent strictly speaking was the treatment of the Jews, which reminds one of a later chapter in Spanish history. King Sisebut (612–20) gave the Jews the choice between baptism and banishment. Those who remained – the banished fled to Gaul – constituted a majority of the Jews, and they became the first in a long line of crypto-Jews. The scholarly archbishop of Seville, Isidore, opposed this order and, with other bishops, succeeded in having it overturned at the Fourth Council of Toledo (633). The effect was only temporary: subsequent councils of Toledo (notably the Sixth in 638 and the Eighth in 653) renewed anti-Jewish canons. Before the light of Visigothic Spain was extinguished by Islam (711–19), it had been dimmed for some time. The only recent light of any brilliance was Isidore of Seville (d. 636), who knew, frequently through intermediaries, many of the great works of the ancient and early Christian worlds. With his greatest work, *Etymologies*, Isidore joined Cicero, Augustine, Jerome, Boethius and Cassiodorus as one of the most popular authors of the Middle Ages. Extant today in over a thousand manuscripts, *Etymologies* contained much more than the etymological derivations of words: it was a virtual encyclopedia of what was known at that time. Its twenty books treat such subjects as medicine, law, the liberal arts, God and his angels and saints, the earth and universe as well as pastimes, food, drink and furniture. It has been called 'the basic book of the entire Middle Ages'. Bede, in far-off Northumbria a century later, borrowed heavily from Isidore for his *De natura rerum* (*On the Nature of Things*). Yet Isidore was more than a compiler of extant knowledge; his use of sources, particularly with regard to moral behaviour, reveals a practical emphasis. This bishop of Seville has enjoyed a long life in his writings, a life that in Europe lasted till the Reformation and in Spain in some ways into modern times.

Conversion of the Irish

Events at the uttermost extremity of Europe were to have enormous influences on medieval history. The Romans had conquered Celtic peoples in much of Britain – fortifications across the Forth–Clyde isthmus marked the northern frontier – but never attempted to extend their sway over the island they called *Hibernia*. Despite the boast of the Roman general Agricola that he could take Ireland with 'one legion and some auxiliaries', the land which the Romans on a clear day could see to the west remained outside the Roman world. The Celtic

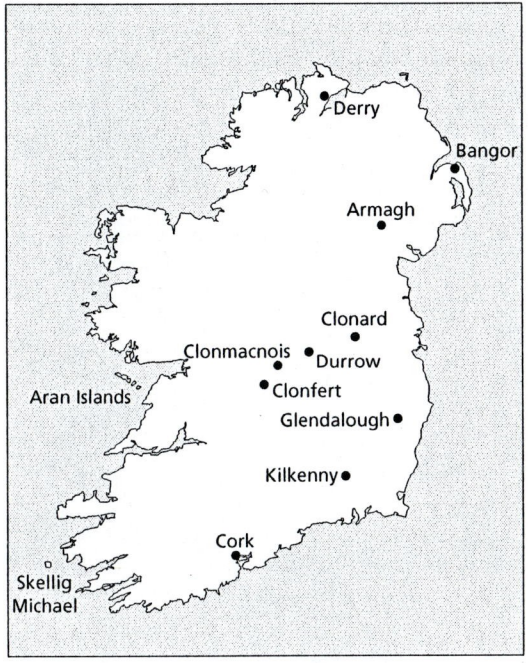

Map 3 Early Christian Ireland.

people living there, the *Scoti*, who later expanded from the north-east of Ireland across the narrow waters to the land that still bears their name, played a remarkable part in the development of the Christian church. About the time that Christianity arrived in Ireland only one thing is certain: it was before the coming of St Patrick. History and myth are not easy to separate in this story. From his own writings we learn that the Christian Patrick was from Britain, the son of a Roman official, that at age sixteen he was carried off into slavery in Ireland, where he remained for six years, that he escaped and that, back in Britain, he heard in a dream the voices of the Irish calling him back. He confesses further that he baptized thousands, ordained countless priests, received the sons and daughters of kings as monks and virgins. Patrick came to Ireland probably as late as about 461 and remained thirty years or so – the precise dates present some problems and once led to a two-Patrick theory. Although other Christian missionaries preceded him, to Patrick should be attributed the principal role in the conversion of the Irish: in one place he described himself as 'bishop to the Irish'. Yet he came not as a missionary but as a pastor to the Christians already there; he later preached in the places of the heathen, no doubt in the west which he knew from his captivity. It makes sense for us to think of the Patrician church as having little formal organization. Patrick made the friendship of local kings, and he also created bishops.

1 Church and round tower, Clonmacnois, Co. Offaly. Reproduced by permission of the Courtauld Institute of Art.

Within a hundred years of Patrick's mission dozens of monasteries were scattered in every part of the island. Near the year 500 there was a bishop-abbot at Armagh and a woman, only centuries later said to be Brigid, had founded a community of holy women at Kildare, which only much later became a double community of men and women under an abbess. Perhaps more important was Darerca, who, early in the sixth century, established a community for women. About all this we would like to know much more, but, alas, reliable sources fail us. To mention only some founders of other monasteries known to have existed at a slightly later date: St Enda on the Aran Islands, St Kieran at Clonmacnois, overlooking the River Shannon on its east bank, St Finian at Clonard, St Brendan at Clonfert, St Kevin at Glendalough ('the valley of the two lakes'), St Finbar on the island at Cork, St Columba at Durrow west of Dublin and also at Derry in the north. In no more dramatic place did Irish monks seek God in solitude than near the top of the seven-hundred-foot rock soaring out of the Atlantic eight miles from the Kerry coast: Skellig Michael with its bee-hive cells and oratories. Yet the view that Patrick imposed an ecclesiastical organization based on bishops which was soon replaced by one based on abbots can no longer be held. The post-Patrician Irish church had a more complicated structure. There were, indeed, great monasteries and their daughters, which together formed federations, but there were also churches allied to great families as well as 'free' churches. Bishops, probably following the lines of the *tuaths* (local tribal groupings), exercised a pastoral role over their churches and clergy. There was no masterplan for organizing the Irish church: what happened was determined by local conditions, and that different structures existed should not surprise us.

The Irish monasticism of this period had three marked characteristics. First, the monks lived stark lives, exposed to the whims of nature and intensified by physical penances. Saints are reputed to have spent nights standing in ice-cold water, while reciting the psalms. Denying the body food, imposing hardships on the body by long vigils and by harsh pilgrimages would have produced an immediate and unmistakable impact as, indeed, would the *vigilia crucis* (standing in prayer with arms extended cross-like for long periods), repeated genuflections, self-flagellations and prolonged total fasts.

Second, the emphasis on penance. Pentitentials, manuals for confessors, existed in Ireland in the sixth century and were to be introduced to the Continent by Celtic and English missionaries. Their appearance coincided with the practice of individuals confessing their sins to a priest followed by absolution and the imposition of a penance. Pentitentials gave lists of appropriate penances for specific sins. For example in one Irish book of the late seventh century we read,

> The penance for murders is seven years on bread and water.
>
> The penance for a mother who kills her own child is twelve years on bread and water.
>
> The penance for eating horse meat is four years on bread and water.

The practice of commuting penalties to prayers relieved some of their severity, but, later, the Franks were to object to the commuting of penalties to the payment of fines. For centuries such penitential books provided the clergy – or at least many of them – with practical instruction in the care of souls.

In this context of penances should be seen the peculiarly Irish practice of the Pilgrimage for Christ (*peregrinatio pro Christo*), by which monks would leave the security of their monastery to live in voluntary exile in strange places among strange peoples or in places where there were no people at all. It was this act of penance that brought not only monks like Columba to Iona and Columbanus to the Continent but also unnamed Irish monks to uninhabited places like the Faroe Islands, 190 miles north of the Shetland islands, and even to Iceland, far out in the North Atlantic, and, further still, according to legend, to lands to the west.

These *peregrini* were not missionaries in the ordinary sense, yet it would be incorrect not to call those who travelled east to the European mainland missionary monks. In Professor Riché's words, they were 'missionaries in spite of themselves'. Columbanus took it as his duty 'to visit the peoples and preach the Gospel to them'. So did his disciples. The mind boggles at the extent of the Irish monastic journeys to the East. Columba's monastery on the island of Iona in the Inner Hebrides off the west coast of Scotland served as a centre for the conversion of the Picts. It was at that thriving monastery that some time later the Book of Kells, the finest example of insular manuscript illumination, was probably produced. If we can date Columba's foundation at Iona to 563, as we perhaps should, then it was only a scant three score years before Iona answered the invitation of Oswald, king of Northumbria, to send monks into his kingdom. In 635 Aidan and the usual twelve monks left Iona and founded Lindisfarne, again on an island, off the north-east coast of England.

The extent of the travels of Columbanus is fairly well known to us. In 590 or 591 this monk of Bangor in Ulster went with twelve companions on their pilgrimage. Before his death in 615 Columbanus had travelled into what we today call France, Belgium, Germany, Switzerland, Austria and Italy, meeting with kings and bishops and opening influential monasteries at Luxeuil, Corbie and Bobbio. These, in turn, spawned countless daughter monasteries. How many others were there who, while not so colourful and prominent as Columbanus, carried Irish monastic ways deep into the European mainland we may never know. We know that Fergil was at Salzburg and Kilian at Würzburg and others at Regensburg and Vienna in the German lands. Still others were at Lucca and Fiesole in Italy, and perhaps St Cataldo, who died in Taranto in Apulia on his way to the Holy Land, was an Irish monk named Cathal.

This extraordinary spread of Irish monasticism on the Continent brought with it the Rule of St Columbanus. This Irish rule reflected Irish asceticism and emphasized severity, particularly physical severity. The Irish rule stated as its guiding principle, 'The chief part of the monk's rule is mortification.' Violations of the rule were to be punished harshly:

He who fails to say grace at table or to answer 'Amen' will be punished with six blows. Also, he who speaks while eating, not because of the needs of another brother, will be punished with six blows.

If through negligence, forgetfulness or carelessness a monk spills an unusual amount of liquids or solids, he will be given the long pardon in church by prostrating himself without moving any limb while the other monks sing twelve psalms at the twelfth hour.

A monk who coughs while chanting the beginning of a psalm will be punished with six blows. Also, he who bites the cup of salvation with his teeth, six blows. He who receives the blessed bread with unclean hands, twelve blows. If a monk comes late to prayers, fifty lashes. If he comes noisily, fifty lashes . . . If he makes a noise during prayers, fifty lashes.

This physical severity did not recommend itself to monks on the Continent. Mixed monasteries, which combined the Columban and Benedictine rules, appeared in the sixth century, and, in the end, it was the more moderate and flexible Rule of St Benedict that prevailed and became the predominant form of monasticism in medieval Europe.

Thirdly, the place of learning in the Irish monastery is universally acknowledged. The judgement of Bernhard Bischoff stands: 'Ireland just a century after its conversion to Christianity became one of the dynamic forces shaping the future civilization of Europe.' The extent to which Irish monasteries used original texts of classical and early Christian writers may not have been great – intermediaries were used, perhaps even to a large extent – but the significance of the Irish contribution to learning lies elsewhere, in two interrelated ways. In the first place, by the sixth century there was developed in Ireland a way – a pedagogy – by which a foreign language, Latin, could be learned from books. The holy books – the Bible and the ceremonials – were all in Latin. It was not only the liturgical but also the theological language of the church to which they were converted. Hence, it was required for ministers of this religion to learn this utterly foreign language, and they learned Latin much as modern students learn it: through the study of grammar and word lists. Although Patrick, calling himself 'a most uncultivated man', had apologized for his Latin, Columbanus had no need to apologize: he had a style vital, verbose and vigorous, a style developed from the book-learning of Latin. This form of pedagogy created by the Irish was later brought to the court of Charlemagne by the English monk Alcuin and became a major influence on the subsequent learning of the universal language of the Middle Ages. And Irish monks contributed to Western civilization in another way: they not only studied manuscripts, they copied them. Their biblical and grammatical commentaries went with them to the Continent. The libraries at Bobbio, St Gall and, later, Salzburg, which were to become manuscript centres, owed their being and their considerable influence as transmitters of ancient learning to monks who had come as pilgrims from the westernmost part of the known world.

Before continuing the story of the conversion of Germanic peoples, we must look to the East and see the transformation there that defined the Middle Ages.

Further reading

Alden Rollins has compiled two helpful works of reference: *The Fall of Rome: A Reference Guide* (Jefferson, NC, and London, 1983) and *Rome in the Fourth Century: An Annotated Bibliography with Historical Overview* (Jeffersonn, NC, and London, 1991). For a work which is both learned and accessible see Peter Brown, *The World of Late Antiquity, A.D. 150–750* (London, 1971). Examining the changes within the Christian world from the fourth to the sixth centuries is Robert A. Markus, *The End of Ancient Christianity* (Cambridge, 1990).

For an overview of the Germanic question see Lucien Musset, *The Germanic Invasions: The Making of Europe, A.D. 400–600* (tr. E. and C. James; London, 1975) and J.M. Wallace-Hadrill, *The Barbarian West: The Early Middle Ages, A.D. 400–600* (Oxford, 1985). For the period of the barbarian incursions see E.A. Thompson, *Romans and Barbarians: The Decline of the Western Empire* (Madison, WI, 1982), Thomas S. Burns, *A History of the Ostrogoths* (Bloomington, IN, 1984), Herwig Wolfram, *History of the Goths* (tr. Thomas J. Dunlap; Berkeley, CA, 1988) and two works by Peter Heather, *Goths and Romans, 332–489* (Oxford, 1991) and *The Goths* (Oxford, 1996). For a work that discusses ethnic identity of 'Roman' and 'Gothic' in an increasingly complex society see Patrick Amory, *People and Identity in Ostrogothic Italy, 489–554* (Cambridge, 1997). Of considerable interest is Stephen C. Fanning, 'Lombard Arianism Reconsidered', *Speculum* 56 (1981), 241–58. Boethius's *The Consolation of Philosophy* is available in a Penguin Classics translation by V.E. Watts (Harmondsworth, Mddsx, 1969).

For Visigothic Spain the reader will find useful E.A. Thompson, *The Goths in Spain* (Oxford, 1969), Edward James (ed.), *Visigothic Spain: New Approaches* (Oxford, 1980) and Roger Collins, *Early Medieval Spain: Unity in Diversity, 400–1000* (New York, 1983) as well as his *The Arab Conquest of Spain, 710–797* (Oxford, 1989). Peter Heather (ed.), *The Visigoths From the Migration Period to the Seventh Century: An Ethnographic Perspective* (*Studies in Historical Archaeoethnology*, vol. 4, Woodbridge, Suffolk, 1999) is a remarkable series of essays, including two on the early history of the Goths. For the Franks see J.M. Wallace-Hadrill, *The Long-Haired Kings* (London, 1962), Edward James, *The Origins of France* (London, 1982) and *The Franks* (Oxford, 1988), Patrick J. Geary, *Before France and Germany: The Creation and Transformation of the Merovingian World* (New York, 1988) and Ian Wood, *The Merovingian Kingdoms, 450–751* (London, 1994). For Clovis, of particular use is William M. Daly's important article, 'Clovis: How Barbaric, How Pagan?', *Speculum* 69 (1994), 619–64. Gregory of Tour's *History of the Franks* is available as a Penguin Classic (tr. Lewis Thorpe; Hammondsworth, Mddsx, 1974). For Gregory and others as historians see Walter Goffart, *Narrators of Barbarian History (A.D. 550–800)* (Princeton, 1988).

The best introduction to monasticism is C.H. Lawrence, *Medieval Monasticism* (3rd edn; London, 2000). There are many English translations of the Rule of St Benedict, among which that in booklet form (Liturgical Press: Collegeville, MN, 1982 and frequently reprinted) may be the most accessible. The *locus classicus* in English on the relation of Benedict's rule to the Rule of the Master is David Knowles, 'The Regula Magistri and the Rule of St Benedict', *Great Historical Enterprises: Problems in Monastic History* (London, 1963), pp. 139–95. A challenge to the views presented in this chapter has been made by Marilyn Dunn, 'Mastering Benedict: Monastic Rules and their Authority in the Early Medieval West', *English Historical Review* 105 (1990), 567–94, to which Adalbert de Vogue has replied in 'The Master and St Benedict: A Reply to Marilyn Dunn', *English Historical Review* 107 (1992), 95–103.

For Ireland the reader will find a judicious summary, analysis and translation of early sources in Liam de Paor, *St Patrick's World: The Christian Culture of Ireland's Apostolic Age* (Notre-Dame, IN, 1993). An eccentric volume of value for the patient is David N. Dumville *et al.*, *Saint Patrick, A.D. 493–1993* (Woodbridge, Suffolk, 1993). A charming book with great learning worn lightly is Ludwig Bieler, *Ireland, Harbinger of the Middle Ages* (London, 1963). Still of value is J. Ryan, *Irish Monasticism: Origins and Early Development* (2nd edn; Dublin, 1972). With much profit one should consult Kathleen Hughes, *Early Christian Ireland: Introduction to the Sources* (London, 1972), Richard Sharpe, 'Some Problems Concerning the Organization of the Church in Early Medieval Ireland', *Peritia* 3 (1984), 230–70, H.B. Clark and Mary Brennan (eds), *Columbanus and Merovingian Monasticism* (Oxford, 1981) and the article by Donnchadh Ó Córráin, 'Prehistoric and Early Christian Ireland', in *The Oxford History of Ireland* (ed. R.F. Foster; Oxford, 1992), pp. 1–43 (with a bibliography, pp. 282–5). The Rule of St Columbanus in facing Latin text and English translation can be found in the edition by G.S.M. Walker, *Sancti Columbani Opera* (*Scriptores Latini Hiberniae*, vol. 2; Dublin, 1957). Richard Sharpe's translation of *Life of St. Columba* by Adomnán of Iona is available as a Penguin Classic (London, 1995). Bernhard Bischoff's wide-ranging essays are available in an English translation by Michael M. Gorman, *Manuscripts and Libraries in the Age of Charlemagne* (Cambridge, 1995). For penitentials see J.T. McNeill and H.M. Gamer, *Medieval Handbooks of Penance: A Translation* (New York, 1938) and Ludwig Bieler (ed.), *The Irish Penitentials* (Dublin, 1963). For a later period see Sarah Hamilton, *The Practice of Penance, 900–1050* (Woodbridge, Suffolk, and Rochester, NY, 2001).

3

JUSTINIAN AND MOHAMMED

Two external forces served to shape the Middle Ages: the Byzantine Empire and Islam. More than merely defining the geographical borders of the medieval world, they interacted with it, producing, at times, friction and, at other times, great achievements. As much as any two individuals can effect movements and institutions containing their own inner dynamics, the emperor Justinian and the prophet Mohammed can be said to have shaped the Middle Ages by establishing contexts, limits and opposition to the European West. It was once said (by Henri Pirenne) that 'without Mohammed Charlemagne would have been inconceivable'. Taking a broader view, it may be said that without Justinian and Mohammed there would never have been a Frederick II and Innocent III, i.e., there never would have been a medieval empire and a medieval papacy. It is a proposition worth examining.

Justinian's achievement

Few perhaps expected it at the time, but Justinian (527–65) was the last in a centuries-long line of native Latin-speaking emperors. Although his uncle Justin (518–27) rose to the purple as a military commander, Justinian, Illyrian-born, was educated at Constantinople and played a substantial policy-making role in his uncle's reign. Among the most intellectual of Roman emperors and perhaps the hardest working, Justinian, judged in terms of his territorial aims, must be seen as a failure. His overarching aim was to preserve and perfect the Roman Empire, and, if preservation required restoration, so be it.

The territorial integrity of the traditional empire required Justinian to undertake the reconquest of the West from the German tribes that now ruled those imperial lands. It was a reconquest that was to prove expensive, partial and short-lived. Britain was recognized as lost for ever, but Justinian's ambitions saw North Africa, Italy, Spain and perhaps even Gaul under his effective authority, with the Mediterranean once again an inland Roman sea. Twice his general, Belisarius, returned to Constantinople, bringing defeated German kings with him: the Vandal Gelimer (534) and the Ostrogoth Witgis (540). And when the dust raised by the imperial armies (always containing large numbers of mercenaries) finally settled, Belisarius and other generals had conquered North Africa, most of Italy and a swath across south-eastern Spain. This arrangement was far from permanent and was, at the best of times, tenuous. Although Justinian's armies consigned the Vandals to historical oblivion, the indigenous Berbers by guerilla warfare almost constantly kept imperial rule in North Africa off-balance. The costly and devastating Italian campaigns – Rome was thrice besieged and Milan razed, its entire male population massacred – contained the seeds of its own ultimate failure, for the imperial general Narses recruited forces from the Lombards to fight the Ostrogoths. Within three years after Justinian's death, these same Lombards invaded Italy and seized control over much of the north. And, in Spain, the empire was but one of the players in the century or so before Islam was to transform the history of that peninsula. The reconquest was far from complete and, in the event, short-lived.

Justinian's attempted reconquest of the western provinces was more than a geopolitical move: it was also a religious statement. The term 'crusade', coming as it does from the Latin word for 'cross', belongs to a later period, but, at the risk of anachronism, it may be applied to Justinian's efforts. The Vandals in North Africa, the Ostrogoths in Italy and the Visigoths in Spain were all heretics, whose removal from power the emperor, never having relinquished total claim over the West, saw as a religious act. Justinian viewed his empire as a Christian society and his role as ruler of that Christian society. In 545 he decreed that the canons of the church councils of Nicaea (325), Constantinople (381) and Chalcedon (451) were imperial laws. The *locus classicus* of his view of the place of religion in the empire is found in Novella 6:

> The greatest gifts God has bestowed upon man are the priesthood (*sacerdotium*) and the imperial dignity (*imperium*). The former looks after divine matters and the latter presides watchfully over human affairs. Both proceed from one and the same principle and govern human life.

The word 'caesaro-papism' – the ruler (*caesar*) as also head of the church (*papa*) – has frequently been applied to Justinian's rule, but he would find its usually invidious connotation wholly inappropriate. Justinian did not dabble in theology: he was a trained and exceptionally able theologian. In the East theology was seen as too important to leave solely to the clergy. The many religious divisions in the empire needed remedy, and the taking of the West from heretics was but one means to do this. Justinian, in his own view, was not interfering in ecclesiastical matters: he was merely doing his duty as he saw it.

In the East religious divisions were pronounced and profound. Justinian considered most of Syria and Egypt heretical. Never having fully accepted the pronouncements of the Council of Chalcedon (451), many in those lands professed a belief in the nature of Christ which contemporaries called 'Monophysite'. Rather than believing that the one person, Christ, has two natures, one divine and one human, they believed that Christ has only one nature (*mono-phusus*). Justinian's extraordinary wife, Theodora, was their partisan, and, whatever rumour and snobbery have done to defame her, she stands apart as one of the outstanding persons of the age. Even the fault-picking, salacious Procopius in his *Secret History*, yellow-dog journalism of the time, described dinner-time conversation at the palace, where the fine points of Christological theology were discussed by emperor and empress. Justinian certainly made conciliatory efforts to reconcile the Monophysites to orthodoxy, but, in the end, Monophysite churches endured in Syria, Egypt and Armenia.

A word must be said about the place of the pope – by now the word 'pope' applied only to the bishop of Rome – in the Christian world. From an early date the bishop of Rome claimed a primacy over the other churches not, as one might suspect, because Rome was the capital of the empire but because Rome was the church of Peter, chief among the apostles, to whom Christ entrusted the power of the keys (Matt. 16, 18). From sub-apostolic times, acknowledged with Rome among the great churches of the Catholic world were Alexandria in Egypt and Antioch in Syria. The establishment of a New Rome at Byzantium in 330 meant that the church of Constantinople was to take its place with these others. The Council of Constantinople (381) asserted that Constantinople should be accorded precedence of honour after Rome. Thus, the four great churches (later called 'patriarchates') in the Catholic world were Rome, Constantinople, Alexandria and Antioch. (Jerusalem's rank as a 'patriarchate' had little practical impact and, in fact, was not granted until 451). Justinian in 545 provided his view of church polity:

> The most holy pope of the Old Rome is first of all priests. The most blessed archbishop of Constantinople, the New Rome, has second place after the holy and apostolic see of Old Rome and is to be honoured above all others.

Such a statement did not mean that the emperor held himself above manipulating the pope or, indeed, selecting the pope. At a crucial moment in the Monophysite controversy Justinian sought to replace Pope Silverius with the pope's nuncio in Constantinople, a certain Vigilius. Belisarius, then in control of Rome, had Silverius deposed and reduced to the state of simple monk (537), exiled to an island off Gaeta, where soon he died probably of starvation and mistreatment. Pope Vigilius could not afford to offend his new masters: on one dramatic occasion Justinian's men hauled him from the altar, as he clung to the altar cloth. Thereafter, he echoed the theological views of the emperor. In all this, it should be remembered that the see of Rome was not subordinate to any other see – it was acknowledged as prior to all others – but that the bishop of Rome in the mid-sixth century came close to being a puppet of the Roman emperor, as, similarly, he had been to the Gothic kings and was fairly soon to be to local Roman aristocratic families. The break between East and West – schism, to use the Greek-derived word for 'break' – was in the future, but from the perspective of the sixth century the break is not entirely surprising. The two churches were set on two separate courses: the Greek-speaking East with its future clearly connected with the fortunes of the Byzantine Empire and the Latin-speaking West with its future connected with the Christian descendants of once barbarian invaders.

Justinian and the law

How better to solidify the Roman accomplishment than to reduce to manageable order the unwieldy bulk of laws and legal opinions? Justinian accomplished this task, and it is arguably the crowning achievement of the Roman Empire. The task of codifying existing laws into a systematic body produced in 529 a code, now lost, and, in 534, a revised code, which we have as the Code of Justinian in twelve books, containing 4,652 laws. Book one begins with the title *De summa trinitate* (*On the high trinity*), and the next dozen titles all deal with ecclesiastical matters. Further, Justinian ordered the jurisprudence – the opinions of the learned jurists of the second and third centuries – together with imperial edicts likewise to be organized. In fifty books the best opinions were gathered and given the force of law in the book called the *Digest* (or *Pandects*), issued in 533. Thus, the great wealth of Roman law was contained in the *Code of Justinian* and the *Digest*: they were exclusive collections, which abrogated all other, earlier laws. The later laws of Justinian (and others) were collected in the *Novels*. A textbook for students, the *Institutes*, completed the work of Justinian. These five law books are known collectively as the *Corpus Iuris Civilis* (*Body of Civil Law*), one of the greatest achievements of human civilization.

What strikes the student of the medieval church is the afterlife of the Justinian *Corpus*. Its immediate impact in the West was short-lived, for it perished with the unravelling of the reconquest. Not until the eleventh century did the works of Justinian resurface in the West. The great schools of law that emerged, first at Bologna and later at Montpellier and elsewhere, were essentially based on the great *Corpus*. And, as the church at the same time was devising its own system of laws (canons), it used Roman law as its model. The great collections of canon law issued by the medieval popes bore clear resemblance to the Justinian model, and canon law as studied at the medieval universities relied on the principles of Roman law. Canon law, with its enormous impact on the medieval church, took its shape and, indeed, much of its substance from the law reforms of Emperor Justinian.

Justinian and church buildings

If Justinian had done nothing more than build Santa Sophia (*Hagia Sophia*), he would have had an enduring place in human history. Every subsequent age has sung the glories of this building whether as Christian church, Islamic mosque or, now, state museum. It stands today as Justinian's greatest visible achievement. In the Nika revolt of 532 the previous church, built by Theodosius (376–95), was destroyed. Justinian commissioned Anthemius of Tralles and Isidorus of Miletus, who, in the amazingly short time of five years – Notre-Dame of Paris took nearly two hundred years – completed their task. Neither Justinian nor we know if their building surpassed in beauty the great temple of Solomon – since the latter was destroyed in AD 70 – yet he may have spoken accurately when at Santa Sophia's dedication (27 December 537) Justinian reportedly said, 'Solomon, I have surpassed you.' Problems with supports combined with a minor earthquake in 558 to cause the original dome to collapse. The structure was quickly rebuilt, and it is this rebuilt Santa Sophia of 562–63 that the visitor to Istanbul sees today. The description of the contemporary Procopius hardly exaggerates:

> . . . a spectacle of marvellous beauty, overwhelming to those who see it, but to those who know it by hearsay altogether incredible. For it soars to a height to match the sky, and, as if surging up from amongst the other buildings, it stands on high and looks down upon the remainder of the city, adorning it, because it is a part of it, but glorying in its own beauty, because, though a part of the city and dominating it, at the same time it towers above it to such a height that the whole city is viewed from there as from a watch-tower.

The floor plan shows Santa Sophia rectangular in shape, yet, subtracting the two side aisles, what is revealed is virtually a square area with adjacent areas to the east and west creating an oval shape. The dome – by definition a segment of a sphere – had for some time been used by architects, perhaps the best-known example being the Pantheon in Rome – but these domes covered a round floor area and simply placed the dome atop a drum-like wall built along the perimeter of the circle. The vaulting of a square area with a dome was first accomplished by Justinian's architects. They constructed four large piers at the four corners of the square and joined them with semicircular arches, thus forming four arches above the sides of the square. They then filled in the spaces between the arches, creating pendentives, which were shaped like inverse spherical triangles, rising from each pier to the height of the tops of the arches. The pendentives, of necessity, were somewhat concave. The tops of the four pendentives, when joined, formed a perfect circle, upon which the dome could rest. External buttressing towers on the north and south as well as interior half-domes to the east and west (vaulting high above the floor) served to carry the downward thrust of the dome. In diameter 107 feet, the dome at its centre point reaches a height of 184 feet above the floor. Near its lower part the dome has forty small windows, spaced so closely together that, looking up from the floor, one almost thinks the dome suspended in air. Procopius commented,

> It seems not to rest upon solid masonry, but this golden dome appears
> as if suspended from heaven.

God holding a golden chain that suspends the dome in air above Santa Sophia: it is an image often repeated through the ages.

Not comparable with Santa Sophia architecturally but significant in other ways were the churches built by Justinian in Ravenna in Italy. Situated near the Adriatic Sea south of the mouth of the Po River, Ravenna had become an imperial centre in the West in 402. Belisarius recaptured it from the Ostrogoths in 540, restoring it to its vice-regal status. The church of Sant'Apollinare in Classe, the port of Ravenna, although begun earlier, was now completed and dedicated in 549. The church in Ravenna then called St Martin (but later, as now, called Sant' Apollinare nuovo) had its mosaic decorations completed under Justinian. Also, Ravenna's church of San Vitale, begun before the reconquest, was largely built under Justinian and was consecrated in 547. Octagonal in shape, it contains a programme of mosaics outstanding even in a city renowned for its mosaics. On facing north and south walls above the altar are the figures of Justinian and Theodora, each surrounded by courtiers, each carrying a gift for the Eucharist. The imperial presence in this reconquered city could scarcely be more prominent than in these realistic, non-idealized portraits.

2 Santa Sophia, Istanbul. Reproduced by permission of the Courtauld Institute of Art.

The Lombards

In a sense, the depiction of emperor and empress at Ravenna captured the imperial couple at their most famous moment in time. It was a fleeting moment. A few scant decades later much of Italy fell to the Lombards. In their expansion south these barbarian people bypassed Ravenna, which was virtually an island in a Lombard sea. In 568, less than three years after Justinian's death, the Lombard king, Alboin, led this fierce people from the lower Austrian Danube region into an Italy still suffering the consequences of almost two decades of war. Most of Italy north of the Po River fell to them within a year. They soon crossed the Appennines into the north-western part of the Italian boot. Soon they were in northern Tuscany, and before long duchies were established in the south at Spoleto and Benevento. Shifting territorial boundaries were to occur, but from the time of the Lombard invasions of the late sixth century Italy was divided and remained divided until 1870. The conquering Lombards, as they entered Italy, were largely pagan. The Bavarian princess Theodolinda, a Catholic, became queen to two successive Lombard kings. She and her husband King Agiluf (590–616) made important contacts with the Irish monk Columbanus, to whom they gave land for a monastery at Bobbio. How quickly the Lombards became Catholic, at this distance in time, it is not possible to say, but it seems clear that there was no instant conversion to Catholic orthodoxy, rather, a slow process, mostly hidden from our sight. Paul the Deacon's account of the Lombard conversion is not a particularly reliable source, since he wrote his *History of the Lombards* at the end of the eighth century about events two centuries earlier and he wished to stress the Catholic victory. The conquest of these people by the Franks at papal invitation belongs to the time of Paul and his patron Charlemagne.

The Italy of the end of the sixth century had a Lombard north and also Lombard lands north-east of Rome at Spoleto and south of Rome at Benevento. The remainder – roughly lands around Rome and Ravenna as well as the Greek-speaking deep south (*Nova Graecia*) – were the only places where Justinian's successors could exercise effective control. Viewed from Constantinople, Italy was seen as a remote province at the periphery of their world. Effective imperial power in Italy, now weak where it existed, was soon to disappear and with it the last vestiges of the ancient political structures in Italy. The West and the Western church were to continue on their way now with little reference to the empire to its east, whose people still called themselves Romans ('Ρωμαîοι). Schism and crusades shall bring the East into our focus in later periods, but these were to be but episodes in medieval history. A wall severely limiting contacts was up between East and West, and it is an irony of some relevance that the great thinkers of classical Greece only came to the West in the twelfth century and then not directly but through an intermediary, Islam. It is to Islam that we must now turn.

Islam

In the seventh century a religion of a simple but compelling doctrine took root beyond the edges of the Roman world in Arabia. It was to have a profound influence not only on European history but, indeed, on world history. Mohammed died in 632, and within a hundred years his followers had conquered a wide swath from the Atlantic to the Indian Oceans and far into the Asian interior. The rise of Islam was as unexpected as it was successful. From the desert seas of the Arabian peninsula came a religion, a movement, a political and spiritual force that transformed the context in which the Christian religion lived and developed.

The land of Mohammed

The Arabian peninsula is part of the desert lands which form the Sahara desert and which become the Asian steppeland. The rift valley that created the Red Sea gave Arabia its western border. The Persian Gulf forms its eastern border. Where the Arabian peninsula ends in the north and the Asian mainland begins is not susceptible to precise definition, but the Fertile Crescent and its hinterland (ancient Palestine, Syria and Mesopotamia, the modern states of Israel, Jordan, Lebanon, Syria and Iraq) can be used conveniently for this purpose. The largest peninsula in the world – one-third the size of the Continental United States and almost nine times the size of the British Isles – the Arabian peninsula was and remains not very congenial for human habitation. Only the southern regions (Yemen) between the coastal mountains and the sea receive enough rain for agriculture. The remainder is chiefly arid steppeland and desert. Two vast areas of shifting sand-dunes, the Great Nefud in the north and Rub al-Khali' in the south, the two joined by a ribbon of sandy desert, comprise about one-third of the peninsula's land area. Deep wells helped to create the occasional oasis in this dry land, and desiccated riverbeds called *wadis* were and are used for overland travel.

The Bedouin people, to survive in the interior of Arabia, had to be nomadic, living in tribes or kinship clans, relying on the pasturing of camels and, to a lesser extent, other animals. A life lived vulnerable to the harsh forces of nature led these peoples to stress loyalty within their group and enmity to other groups. Raids were almost a way of life. Bedouin gods were many, usually heavenly bodies thought to inhabit places like trees and rocks. Yet demons, threatening the Bedouins at any moment, perhaps played a larger role in their lives. The town of Mecca, midway along the peninsula's western side, had a special place in the life of the Arabs. The caravan route from Yemen north to the Fertile Crescent was organized at Mecca, and Meccans ran it. The holy place at Mecca, the Kaaba, a shrine for many of their gods, was the centre of a peace zone, where tribal hostilities were put aside. Such a peaceful place provided an ideal climate for commerce. It was into the mercantile class at Mecca in the late sixth century that the future Prophet was born.

The Prophet

For the historian no subject in the history of Islam is more challenging than the life of Mohammed, chiefly because of the nature of the surviving sources. The Koran itself was not gathered together in its present form until many years after the Prophet's death. The *hadith*, traditions accepted by Muslims about the life of Mohammed and the early years of Islam, present more formidable problems for the modern Western historian, who tends towards caution in accepting tradition literature as history. While respecting the religious sensibilities of Muslims who, for reasons that transcend scientific historical methodology, may have deep convictions about these matters, the historian as historian can merely adopt a cautious but not irreverent attitude towards the *hadith* evidence. What, then, can be said of the historic person who is the Prophet to about 750,000,000 of our contemporaries?

Mohammed was born about 570 at Mecca. He may have been involved in the caravan trade, though we know that less certainly than that he married the widow of a wealthy merchant. At some point, at age forty according to tradition, he felt a call to preach the message of a single, transcendent God. Gaining some converts, he felt that opposition in Mecca required him to leave. This he did in 622, when he went to Medina, 220 miles to the north, and this date of the *hejira* ('flight') marks the point at which the Islamic calendar begins. The warring clans at Medina had called Mohammed to mediate. The resulting 'Constitution of Medina' brought peace to Medina and converts to Mohammed, although Jewish groups were to suffer. The refusal of Jews to follow the religion of Mohammed, it is said, led the Prophet to cease facing Jerusalem at prayer and to begin facing Mecca. In 630 Mohammed and his followers marched on Mecca, and the Meccans with little resistance capitulated. Mecca became what it is today the spiritual centre of Islam, its holiest place and the centre of pilgrimage, and the Kaaba became the greatest shrine of Islam. In 632 Mohammed died at Medina.

The central teaching of Mohammed, repeated millions of times daily by pious Muslims, is 'There is no God but Allah, and Mohammed is his prophet'. Belief in but one God – Allah being the Arabic word for God used by Muslims and Christians alike – is the core belief. The so-called Satanic verses of the Koran – which may have once followed sura 53, 19–20 – derive their controversial nature from their being interpreted to mean that Mohammed, in a moment of weakness, allowed rich Meccan merchants to practise polytheism. The opening sura of the Koran provides an exact theological statement of Muslim belief:

> In the Name of God, the Compassionate, the Merciful,
> Praise be to God, the Lord of all beings,
> the All-compassionate, the All-merciful,
> the Master of the Day of Judgement.
> Thee alone do we serve; to Thee alone do we pray
> for help.

Guide us in the straight way,
the way of those whom Thou hast blessed,
not of those who have incurred Thy anger,
nor of those who are now astray.

The only God is the God of all peoples, not merely the national god of their own people (as the early Hebrews believed their god Yahweh to be only their god). The two qualities, mentioned in this sura and repeated before the recitation of each sura, were compassion and mercy. On the Day of Judgement God's justice will separate the good and the evil. It is to this God, merciful yet just, to whom humans should turn for help and guidance so that they may live holy lives.

Throughout the Koran the word 'unbelievers' means those who refuse to believe in the one God. The people of the book – Jews and Christians – are not unbelievers, but the Jews have been unheeding of their prophets and the Christians seem to believe in three gods. Unlike the Christian belief in Jesus – that he is the Son of God – the Muslims steadfastly refused to make any claims of divinity for Mohammed: he is human like other men. He traced himself in a line of prophets that included Jesus and Moses and, ultimately, Abraham. Later Muslims were to call him prophet and seal, meaning that he was the last of the prophets.

Life after death and a redressing of the balance of justice, so obviously unbalanced in this life, are essential features of Islamic theology. The evil will be punished by eternal fire in Gehenna and the good will live in a verdant paradise where there flow cooling streams that will never dry up. What a most inviting prospect paradise must have held out for desert nomads. The bearing of life's transitory troubles in submission to God would lead believers to a most rewarding heaven where life's deficiencies will be fully compensated for – and then some – by a merciful and just God. It was a potent message, which in human terms – the historian has no other – proved compelling, first to the tribesmen of Arabia and then to millions elsewhere.

The Koran

To the Muslim, the Koran was not written by Mohammed: he was merely the voice that recited – Koran means recitation – the word of God as revealed to him through the Angel Gabriel. In trance-like states Mohammed spoke, and his words were written down by others on whatever was at hand, even a mere scrap. The process whereby these recitations were collected to form this holy book is largely hidden from our eyes. In a pre-literate culture memorizers played a prominent role, and memorizers committed to memory with an exactness that amazes us in the twenty-first century. In Arabia we may assume that memorizers knew and repeated Mohammed's recitations and taught others. A network of reciters might soon have appeared. By the time of Mohammed's death in 632 it is just possible that there was a written collection of this oral tradition. Accounts vary about what happened next. It was once widely held that an official version was produced within two years of the Prophet's death, during the time of the Caliph Abu-Bakr (632–34). More likely, the next Caliph but one, Uthman (644–56), was responsible for the collection of the recitations in the number and order of the received text. Even allowing for the possibility of later insertions, the text of the Koran as we have it is substantially a very early witness of Islamic belief. It is more reliably closer to the time of Mohammed than the earliest Christian gospel is to the time of Christ.

The first-time and, indeed, the many-time Western reader of the Koran is struck by the frequency of biblical references. We meet Adam, Noah and Abraham as well as Moses, Saul, David, Solomon and several of the Old Testament prophets. John the Baptist, Jesus and Mary (conflated with Miriam, sister of Moses) appear frequently. Questions arise about the Koran's dependence on the Bible or, at least, on biblical stories. Since Islam was not a rejection of Judaism or Christianity but saw itself in the line of Abraham and acknowledged the prophets, including Jesus, the inclusion of familiar biblical incidents and characters should not be such a great surprise. Traditions about the young Mohammed meeting Jews and Christians along caravan routes do not command historical assent. Indirect rather than direct access to biblical accounts should probably be assumed, and attempts to identify the sources tend to point to Jews and dissident Christian people living in Arabia.

The arrangement of the 114 suras of the Koran, ordered by Uthman, follows no chronological order. After the opening sura (quoted above), there follows the longs sura ('Cattle'), which, in turn, is followed by suras in declining length, with the shortest suras coming at the end. Official translations of the Arabic Koran have not been permitted until the twentieth century and then only in favour of Turkish. The language of the Koran – its cadences and sonorities – are integral to its understanding. Westerners can gain some small sense of this by listening to recordings. That the language of the Muslim holy book was so integral to Islamic religion meant that converts would learn Arabic. In time, they would become Arabic speaking. The Arabization of the conquered peoples owed much to the language of the Book.

The Koran became a code of living, reflecting the total integration of life. Religion was not compartmentalized, even if that compartment had the loftiest place: nothing could be more antithetical to the Muslim view of life. 'Islam' means submission, a total submission, to God. Hence, social behaviour and customs are spelled out. Rules of inheritance are given in some detail (e.g., sura 4, 8–16). Dietary regulations introduce a sense of restraint and discrimination:

> Forbidden you are to eat
> putrifying flesh, blood, the flesh of pigs,
> what has been offered to other than God,
> the flesh of animals strangled, beaten down,
> animals dead from a fall or from being gored,

animals disturbed by beasts of prey
and also food sacrificed to idols.

(Sura 5, 4)

Slavery was not forbidden (nor was it forbidden in the West for well over a millennium later), but to free slaves pleases God:

> Emancipate those you own
> who wish to be free,
> if you see good in them,
> and give them of the riches God
> has given you. And force not
> your slave girls into prostitution for your profit, if they
> desire to live chastely.

(Sura 24, 33)

The status of women was greatly elevated by the Koran, their protection from the injustices of society a frequent theme in its pages. Polygamy (four wives) was allowed, among other reasons, to give a place in society to spinsters and widows, who were among the most vulnerable persons in society. Divorce was allowed, but a woman could not be merely ejected from her husband's household. She was entitled to the wedding gifts without deduction. The mandatory three-month waiting period would determine if she was pregnant, in which case divorce could not occur until after birth of the child; the waiting period also gave scope for a possible reconciliation. A divorced woman was free to marry and even to remarry her former husband. Women could also hold property. The improvement in the status of women is one of the greatest achievements of the teachings of the Koran. Modern critics who ahistorically impose modern ideals on early history and, thus, harshly criticize these provisions of the Koran rip history from context and would do well to reflect on the fact that in the seventh century the most enlightened attitudes towards women and slavery were among the followers of Mohammed. Christian Europe lagged behind.

The high ethic of the Koran may be best seen in a passage reminiscent of the Christian gospels (Matt. 25, 34–46):

> Be kind to your parents and your kinsmen,
> to orphans and to the needy,
> to neighbours who are of family and those who are not,
> to those who travel with you and to the traveller you meet on the
> way
> and to your slaves.
> God has no love
> for the arrogant and boastful,
> who are miserly and encourage others

also to be miserly, while themselves concealing
the wealth with which God has favoured them.

(Sura 4, 40–1)

It was this book the men from the Arabian peninsula took with them as warriors.

Conquests

The prophet died in 632, and a hundred years later the religion of Islam stretched from the Atlantic coasts of North Africa and Spain in the west to the area beyond the Oxus River in central Asia. History knows no equal to the extraordinary spread of Islam, not even Christianity, which for several hundred years after its founder's death was still a minority religion in the Roman world. The stages in the remarkable expansion of Islam can be easily sketched, although tantalizing gaps exist in our knowledge.

The death of Mohammed left a leadership vacuum. No provisions had been made for his succession. He had no surviving sons, but, even if he had, tribal chiefdoms were not necessarily hereditary. Whatever the exact nature of the consultation, Abu-Bakr, father-in-law of Mohammed and an early convert, was chosen. He was called 'Caliph', i.e., deputy or successor, but not successor to Mohammed's prophetic office; the caliph served as a political leader, one might say, as sheik of the 'Islamic tribe'. First of the four Orthodox Caliphs, Abu-Bakr, who ruled for less than two years, did so from Medina as did his successors: Umar (634–44), Uthman (644–56) and Ali (656–61), husband of Mohammed's daughter Fatima. The immediate need after Mohammed's death was to recover so-called apostate peoples, those who had withdrawn their loyalty and their tax payments. Abu-Bakr recovered the secessionist tribes and also succeeded in bringing other Arabic peoples under the sway of Medina. By the time of his death Abu-Bakr controlled the entire peninsula. The second phase, the breaking out of the Arabian peninsula, took place under his successor Umar. A powerful military force was in place and, having succeeded in internal conquest, was restless. The largely Bedouin army craved the rich lands of the Fertile Crescent. Mass movements have their own inner dynamic, that mixture of greed and idealism and shifting ambitions born of events as they occur. The great Muslim expansion was no exception. Whatever else it was, this great expansion was not a religious movement intent on converting the world to Islam. (The process of conversion will be seen shortly.) Historians, looking for causes which they can analyse, cannot affirm the providential workings of God but can only see human beings moved by forces complex and largely hidden from us. And booty was clearly among them.

The second step, then, in the expansion of Islam saw the Fertile Crescent and Egypt submit to the Arabs. Raiding attacks in the time of Abu-Bakr revealed lands militarily weak and peoples with little loyalty to their Byzantine masters. These lands were ruled by the emperor at Constantinople, but poor administration,

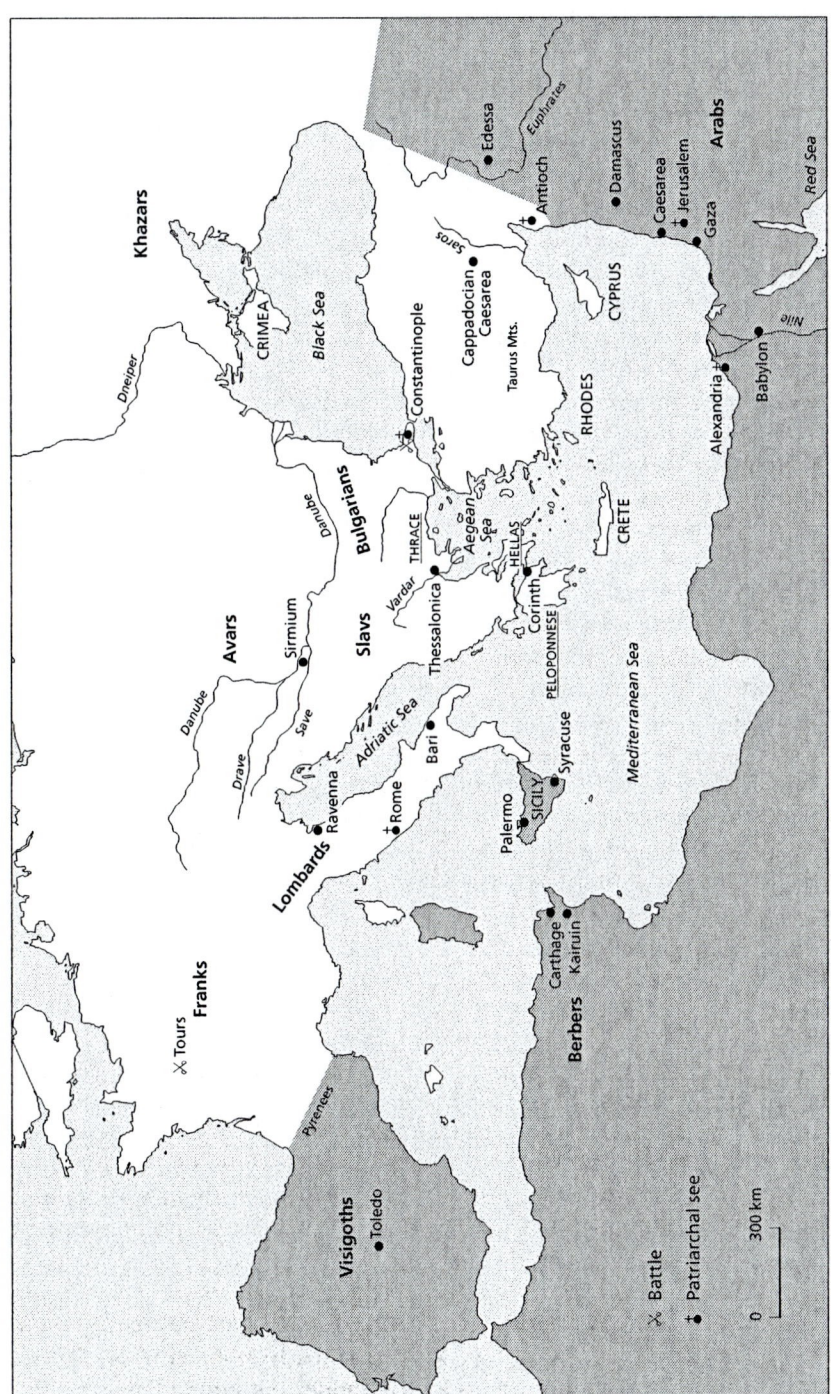

Note: Shaded areas are 'Islamic' lands

Map 4 Byzantium and the expansion of Islam in the Mediterranean region (seventh to ninth centuries).

overburdening taxation, strong local loyalties and theological differences had drained the populations of any sense of allegiance to their foreign oppressors. To say the Arabs were viewed as liberators would overstate the case, yet a later Christian writer in Syria was to say, 'The God of vengeance has delivered us from the hands of the Romans by means of the Arabs.' In 635 Damascus (Islam's future capital) and in 637 Jerusalem (from which Muslims believe the Prophet ascended to heaven) were in their hands. The Persian Empire lay to their east, a once mighty empire, now weak and vulnerable to the attacks of Arab warriors. Soon Ctesiphon fell (637), and in a great battle in 642 the Persians were defeated, and with them fell their ancient empire. In 639 under other generals Arab armies entered Egypt. Their success was quick and with it the rich valley of the Nile and the great harbour of Alexandria as their prizes. They controlled Egypt by 642 and built a navy, which soon challenged the great Byzantine fleet and, in 649, captured Cyprus.

After these immediate conquests, the third stage could occur. To the east from the Taurus Mountains at the northern edge of Syria they could raid and conquer Armenia, Georgia and Azerbaijan. Then on to the Oxus River in central Asia, the border between Persians and Turks. These events and their consequences go well beyond the confines of this book, yet they signal to us the breadth and depth of the neighbour of medieval Europe to its south and south-east. More relevantly, the Arab armies in Egypt found no opposition to their immediate west in the vast Western Desert and along the Libyan coast beyond Tripoli. They halted at the border of Tunisia, short of Carthage. By now the Orthodox Caliphs had passed from the scene after serious civil wars at home, and the Umayyad Caliphs (616–750) soon moved the capital from Arabia to Damascus, where it was to remain until it was moved to Baghdad in 762. When the campaigns continued, the Muslims took Carthage and, with the support of the North African Berbers, made their way across modern Morocco to the Atlantic.

Standing at Africa's northernmost point, they could see Spain a scant eight miles across the straits. In the spring of 711 Tariq Ibn Ziyad landed at the massive rock jutting into the Mediterranean Sea, a pillar of Hercules, and gave it his name 'Jabal Tariq' (i.e., Tariq's mountain), which by corruption became 'Gibraltar'. At a crucial battle on 19 July 711, Tariq and his Berber warriors defeated the Visigothic forces of King Roderick. The country lay before them. Bypassing Seville, the Muslims headed north for Toledo, the Visigoths' capital, which they quickly took. By summer's end Tariq controlled half of Spain, including the towns of Archidona, Elvira, Malaga and Cordova, their future capital. Musa, the Arab general who had led the recent African campaigns, arrived with 10,000 Arab troops to join the Berbers. He besieged Seville, which, in June 713, succumbed. With the fall of Saragossa in that same year, the conquest was virtually complete, and Musa, accompanied by Tariq, led a triumphal procession with eighty Visigothic princes and thousands of other prisoners across North Africa and entered Damascus in February 715. The mopping-up continued and in 719 the conquest was complete save for a Visigothic Christian enclave in the north-west (Asturias). A small splinter group of the Muslim army crossed the

Pyrenees and was defeated by Charles Martel near Tours in 732, a minor incident in this whole story and, in no way, the turning point in European history as it has sometimes been portrayed. The lines were too long, and a major Muslim assault north of the Pyrenees was impossible. In a brief eight years the great Visigothic kingdom had fallen and Spain was now ruled by Muslims. It was not till 1492 that the last vestige of Muslim rule disappeared, when Catholic monarchs entered Granada.

In Spain and elsewhere the Muslim conquerors did not convert the defeated peoples by the sword. Unlike Charlemagne, the Christian king of the Franks (768–814), who gave Saxons the choice between baptism and death, the Arabs allowed their subjects the tolerance necessary to practise their religions. The non-Muslims paid a tribute, but often considerably less than what they had paid to the Byzantine emperor. The process of conversion to Islam was a slow process, taking several hundred years and even then leaving pockets of Christians.

For the student of the medieval church what Islam accomplished was to demarcate the southern boundary of medieval Christian Europe. The world of Islam began at the Pyrenees and extended far to the east. Even Sicily and parts of southern Italy came under Muslim rule. Two walls now existed. The Mediterranean was a wall which separated Christian Europe on its north from an alien culture to its south. Another wall, this a north–south wall, separated Latin Christians from Greek Christians. To the north and west of these walls Europe of the Middle Ages was to live its life. It is this European world of Latin Christianity, often called Western Europe, whose story we now follow.

Further reading

On Justinian good places to begin are John Moorhead, *Justinian* (London, 1994) and J.A.S. Evans, *The Age of Justinian: The Circumstances of Imperial Power* (New York, 1996). Robert Browning, *Justinian and Theodora* (rev. edn; London, 1987) is also useful. About questions of *imperium* and *sacerdotium* see Francis Dvornik, *Early Christian and Byzantine Political Philosophy: Origins and Background* (2 vols; Dumbarton Oaks Studies 9, Washington, DC, 1966) and John Meyendorff, 'Justinian, the Empire and the Church', *Dumbarton Oaks Papers* 22 (1968), 45–60. On Santa Sophia see Rowland J. Mainstone, *Hagia Sophia: Architecture, Structure and Liturgy of Justinian's Great Church* ([London], 1988) and Robert Mark and Ahmet S. Cakmak (eds), *Hagia Sophia from the Age of Justinian to the Present* (Cambridge, 1992). *The Buildings* by Procopius, which provides a contemporary description, is available in Loeb Classics series as vol. 7 of the works of Procopius (Cambridge, MA, 1961). His *Secret History* may be conveniently used in the translation by Richard Atwater (Ann Arbor, 1961). Sensible and immensely informative is Averil Cameron, *Procopius and the Sixth Century* (London, 1985). The texts of the law books in their original language comprise the *Corpus Iuris Civilis* (3 vols; Berlin, 1872–95). An English translation of all the law texts can be found in *The Civil Law* (tr. S.P. Scott; 17 vols; Cincinnati, 1932). More accessible is the translation of *The Digest of Justinian*, edited by Alan Watson (Philadelphia, 1985; paperback, 1998).

Several general works are available on Islamic history. Among them are Bernard Lewis, *The Arabs in History* (6th edn; Oxford, 1993), W. Montgomery Watt, *A Short History of*

Islam (Oxford, 1996) and Malise Ruthven, *Islam in the World* (2nd edn; Cambridge, 2000). Older but still quite useful are G.E. von Grunebaum, *Classical Islam: A History, 600–1258* (tr. Katherine Watson; London, 1970); Philip K. Hitti, *History of the Arabs from the Earliest Times to the Present* (10th edn; London, 1970) and *The Arabs: A Short History* (5th edn; London, 1968). Of particular interest is Hugh N. Kennedy, *The Prophet and Age of the Caliphates: The Islamic Near East from the Sixth to the Eleventh Century* (London, 1986). The standard reference work is *The Encyclopedia of Islam* (new edn; London, 1960–). The historian will learn much from R. Stephen Humphreys, *Islamic History: A Framework for Inquiry* (rev. edn; Princeton, 1991). Many translations of the Koran are available: Arthur J. Arberry's *The Koran Interpreted* (London, 1964) attempts to provide something of the rhetorical and rhythmic patterns of the original Arabic.

4

THE SCENE IS SET

St Gregory the Great to St Boniface

The years from the accession of Gregory the Great as pope (590) to the death of St Boniface (754) witnessed the fashioning of the set on which would be played out the story of the church in the Middle Ages. To suggest this does not imply that no dynamics followed. On the contrary, dynamics there indeed were aplenty, but the general context had been established by the middle of the eighth century: an active papacy, allied with the Frankish kings, and a Christian population throughout all Western Europe except Scandinavia. Saving the place of the Frankish kings, which will be treated in the next chapter, here we shall see the development of papal power, the northward movement of Christianity into the islands off Europe's north-west shores and from there back to large parts of the Continent, and the role which learning played. No better starting place than with Pope Gregory I.

Gregory the Great

It might seem idle to raise the question, Who was the greatest pope of the Middle Ages? Many candidates will appear in these pages, yet the historian knows that the measure of greatness reveals something of the historian's own values, and, in any case, different times require different human qualities of leadership. That having been said, a strong case might be made that at the head of any such list should be the name of Pope Gregory the Great (590–604). A near contemporary description of Gregory is unique for popes of the early Middle Ages. A picture of him was made at his death, and it was described by John the Deacon, who saw it in the ninth century:

> His figure was of ordinary height and was well made. His face was a happy medium between the length of his father's face and the roundness of his mother's face, so that with a certain roundness it seemed to be of very comely length. His beard was like his father's, of a rather tawny colour and of moderate length. He was rather bald, so that in the middle of his forehead he had two small, neat curls, twisted towards the right. The crown of his head was round and

large, his darkish hair being nicely curled and hanging down as far as the middle of his ear. His forehead was high, his eyebrows long and elevated. His eyes had dark pupils and, though not large, were open, under full eyelids. His nose from the starting point of his curving eyebrows was thin and straight, broader about the middle, slightly aquiline and expanded at the nostrils. His mouth was red, his lips thick and subdivided. His cheeks were well-shaped, and his chin of a comely prominence from the confines of the jaws. His colour was swarthy and ruddy . . . His expression was kindly. He had beautiful hands with tapering fingers, well suited for writing.

A modern artist might indeed be able to reconstruct a fair likeness of one of only two popes to whom history has given the sobriquet 'the Great'.

Gregory came from a distinguished Roman family, influential in affairs civil and ecclesiastical. His great grandfather was Pope Felix III (483–92) – so much for an early rule of priestly celibacy – and he was collaterally related to Pope Agapitus I (535–36). Responding to the exigencies of the time, Gregory, as a young man of the aristocratic class, served in the civic administration of the city of Rome, almost certainly becoming prefect in 572. When his father died in 574, he used what must have been a substantial inheritance to found six monasteries in Sicily and turned the family home on the Caelian Hill in Rome into a monastery dedicated to St Andrew. There, at the monastery of St Andrew, Gregory became not abbot but monk-founder. The near crippling circumstances of the times did not allow him the quiet life of a monk. The pope made him a deacon and his closest adviser. Gregory adopted the title 'servant of the servants of God' (*servus servorum dei*), a title which he later used as pope and which has been used by popes ever since, if not always with the same appropriateness.

A few words must be said about the state of Italy at the time of Gregory. It will be recalled that Justinian's wars against the Ostrogoths were prolonged (535–54) and left in their wake widespread devastation. Rome itself was besieged three times in 546. Milan was almost entirely levelled. At war's end a Pragmatic Sanction was imposed by Justinian: Italy would now become a province of the empire ruled from Constantinople by an exarch at Ravenna (not Rome). Before the details of this settlement could be worked out, the Lombards took over much of Italy, establishing themselves in the north and in the two southern duchies of Spoleto and Benevento. The results left the city of Rome and its environs connected only by a narrow corridor (the Via Flaminia) to the territory held by the exarch in the north-east. In a fluid situation with the Lombard lust for land far from satisfied and boundaries far from fixed, the parts of Italy still under imperial control stood in dire peril from the Lombard invaders. With the meagre imperial forces largely concentrated along the corridor, Rome itself was left with sparse defences.

In this situation the pressing need of assistance from the empire was clearly seen, and Pope Pelagius (579–90), whose predecessor died while Lombards had the city under siege, almost immediately upon his election sent his deacon Gregory, the future pope, to Constantinople with a message pleading with the emperor to come to the help of ancient Rome:

> So great are the calamities and tribulations we suffer from the perfidy of the Lombards, in spite of their solemn promises, that no one could adequately describe them . . . The Empire is in so critical a situation that, unless God prevails on the heart of our most pious prince to show his servants the pity he feels and to grant them a commander or general, then we are lost. For the territory around Rome is completely undefended and the exarch writes that he can do nothing for us, being unable himself to defend the region around Ravenna. May God bid the emperor to come to our aid with all speed before the army of that impious nation, the Lombards, shall have seized the lands that still form part of the Empire.

Gregory's mission failed, not least because the emperors, stretched almost beyond their resources in the East, were simply unable to provide much help. In 582 the new emperor, Maurice (582–602), sent as exarch the able Smaragdus to reorganize defences and to try for an alliance with the Franks against the Lombards. When Gregory returned to Rome in 586, he again served as deacon to Pope Pelagius. But the difficulties of the city were soon compounded by the affliction of the plague that had been present in the Mediterranean basin since the time of Justinian. Concurrent flooding of the Tiber, reducing much of the city to marsh, heightened the human tragedy and sense of Armageddon. Pelagius himself died, a victim of the plague. Without waiting for imperial consent the Romans elected the deacon Gregory as pope. Viewing the ancient capital of a once great empire, the new pope lamented:

> We see what has happened to her. She who was once the mistress of the world has suffered misfortunes incalculable in number and intensity: her people are desolate and threatened by external enemies. Everywhere there is only ruin, nothing but ruin . . . We, the remnant, are menaced by the sword and by trials without number . . . We no longer have a Senate, no longer a people. For those still living only sorrows and tears . . . Rome is deserted and in flames.

The Roman Gregory found not only his city in anguish, but Italy had 'its cities destroyed, its fortifications in ruins, its countryside depopulated and the earth a wasteland'.

This pope, who, as legate, in Constantinople had lived like a monk and who now, as pope, turned the Lateran Palace virtually into a monastery, undertook the task of saving Rome and Italy from the threats to its civil and religious life. His register survives, containing 854 letters, which show his efforts to manage

– almost, at times, to micro-manage – this task. When the Lombard duke of Spoleto threatened Rome, it was Gregory who took control, dispatched troops and tactical advice to the imperial commander in the field. When in 592 the exarch refused to appoint commandants at Lepe and Naples, which were key to the imperial defences of Rome, it was Gregory who sent Leontius and Constantius to take charge of the imperial garrisons. When, at the same time, the garrison in Rome was near mutiny for lack of pay, it was Gregory who paid them from the church's treasury. When the Roman defences proved inadequate, it was Gregory who bought peace by paying 500 pounds of gold from church funds. When the civil authorities were unable to feed the Romans, the pope did. When the exarch Romanus appeared uninterested and even indifferent to securing a general peace with the Lombards, it was Gregory who negotiated with the Lombard king but, refusing to make a separate peace, waited until 598, when the new exarch agreed. In addition, the Patrimony of Peter, the lands held by the popes, now enlarged by the acquisition of the estates of the Arian churches after the defeat of the Ostrogoths, enabled Pope Gregory to relieve the sufferings of people in Italy and in Sicily. Not even the harshest critics of the medieval popes suggest that Gregory took advantage of the situation to enlarge the power of the papacy. On the contrary, it was a reluctant Gregory who stepped in to insure public order in the most desperate of circumstances. Of other medieval popes whom we shall meet in this history it can be said that they made power plays with little spiritual justification, but not of the monk-pope in the Lateran Palace. This extension of papal authority into civil matters and far beyond the city of Rome, the result of exigencies of the late sixth century, meant that the popes had become secular rulers, one of the defining characteristics of the medieval papacy. In time, the area over which the popes de facto ruled would grow and become known as the Papal States. Gregory's tomb in St Peter's bore the inscription, 'Consul of God' (*consul dei*).

Living at the end or, indeed, after the end of the period of classical culture, Gregory was not, as is sometimes said, its opponent. He did chastise the bishop of Vienne for teaching boys the pagan classics, and he showed no interest in learning either to speak or read Greek, although he lived in Constantinople for six years. The latter can be explained by the superior attitude of educated, aristocratic Romans towards things Greek. Classical learning was a separate matter. Not its enemy, Gregory, living in the most turbulent of times, thought that classical learning should be used to serve the Christian faith. His own Latinity knew neither the subtlety nor sonority of classical Latin. It was practical, direct, unnuanced. A staple part of the medieval library was to be his book *Pastoral Care* (*Regulae liber pastoralis*). Although intended for bishops, it became a classic guide to the spiritual life and care of souls, its impact impossible to measure. King Alfred had it translated into English in the late ninth century and sent copies to all his bishops. This treatise and other works attributed to Gregory, particularly a collection of miracle stories of Italian saints (called the *Dialogues*), caused Gregory the Great's name to be placed with Ambrose, Augustine and Jerome as a Father of the Church, the fourth and last in the West. That his name has been wrongly associated with Gregorian chant since the ninth century diminishes in no way his place in history.

Conversion of the Anglo-Saxons

The story was told in England in the early eighth century about the motivating reasons that impelled Gregory the Great to send Christian missionaries to England. In its earliest form (*c.*710) the story by an anonymous monk or nun of Whitby Abbey in the north of England runs that, before he became pope, Gregory was eager to see fair-skinned and light-haired boys or youths who had come to Rome. He asked them what people they belonged to.

> They answered, 'The people we belong to are called Angles.'
> 'Angels of God', he replied.
> Then, he asked, 'What is the name of the king of that people?'
> They replied, 'Aelli.'
> Whereupon Gregory said, 'Alleluia. God's praise must be heard there.'
> Then he asked the name of their own tribe. They answered, 'Deire.'
> Gregory replied, 'They shall flee from the wrath (*de ira*) of God to the faith.'

A charming story, and probably nothing more. But what lies behind it is probably an incident found in Gregory's own letters. In September 595 Gregory ordered his administrator in Gaul to buy English boys of seventeen or eighteen years of age on the slave market so that they could be brought to Rome and taught in monasteries, quite possibly with a view of sending them on a future mission to their own people. It is easy to see how this historical episode, well grounded in fact, could have been elaborated, distended and even distorted during the next century till a writer at Whitby gave this version. Within three decades of the telling of the story, a monk from the north of England, Bede of Wearmouth, told the same story in a slightly different version. These later tales, hardly historical, nonetheless witness the English devotion to the pope who first sent missionaries to their people and who, in the words of the Whitby writer, 'will present the English people on the Day of Judgement'. More generally, it should be said that these latter tales err in exaggerating the mission of Augustine, a monk of Gregory's monastery on the Caelian Hill, who in 597 was sent by Gregory to England, and in thus belittling the historical significance of other Christian missionaries to Britain.

The island to which the Italian missionaries came had had Christian inhabitants for hundreds of years. The Romano-British Christians must have formed a considerable part of the population, when, in the early fifth century, pagan, barbarian, Germanic peoples came from Frisia and more remotely from lands near the Jutland peninsula as peaceful inhabitants of the so-called Saxon Shore, coastal areas along the east and south coast of Britain. Later, the Saxons were joined by kindred but less peaceful peoples, and, in the first half of the fifth century, the Romans abandoned the Britons to their own devices. Centuries of hostilities followed between Britons and Anglo-Saxons, the fortunes of war fluctuating from one side to the other. The mingling of peoples no doubt occurred, but the hostilities were far from over at the time of Augustine's mission to Kent in 597. The picture of the Celtic Britons pushed to the west – to Cornwall, Wales and Strathclyde – belongs to a future time. In the 570s, shortly before Augustine's arrival, the pagan West Saxons were fighting the Christian Britons for Gloucester, Cirencester and Bath and continued campaigns for some time in the upper Thames, Severn and Avon valleys. To the west, the lands of Dorset and Somerset were still controlled by British princes. In the very year of Augustine's coming, 597, a new pagan king of Wessex took power, and he continued the struggle of the pagan West Saxons against the Christian Britons. The situation in other parts of the country was also fluid, and in Northumbria the British presence was to remain a factor for some time, its importance difficult to measure.

Augustine arrived in Kent not unexpectedly. Pope Gregory, in 596, had written to two Frankish princes that 'it has come to our ears that by the mercy of God the English race earnestly desire to be converted to Christianity.' In Kent, the Christian Bertha, a former Frankish princess and now wife of the local king, lived at Canterbury and worshipped in a church once used by Romano-British Christians, almost certainly the present St Martin's church or another church on the same site. The dramatic meeting of Augustine with King Aethelbert on the Isle of Thanet, held at the king's insistence in the open air lest the visitors unleash evil spirits, may have been merely part of a carefully choreographed ritual. In Kent conversions followed swiftly. Gregory the Great wrote in July 598 to the patriarch of Alexandria that

> the English race, who live in a corner of the world, have until now remained, unbelieving, worshipping sticks and stones, but, aided by your prayers and prompted by God, I decided that I ought to send a monk of my monastery to preach to them. With my permission he was made a bishop by the bishops of the Germanies and with their help he reached their people at the end of the world, and now letters have just reached me about his safety and his work . . . At the feast of Christmas last . . . more than 10,000 Englishmen are reported to have been baptized by our brother and fellow bishop.

The precise figure of 10,000 should be understood not literally but as meaning a very large number. The date of King Aethelbert's conversion is not known, but by 601 he was almost certainly a Christian. In England, as elsewhere, the

3 St Martin's Church, Canterbury. Reproduced by permission of the Courtauld Institute of Art.

conversion of the king was generally followed by the conversion of the tribal aristocracy.

This initial success in but one, small part of the country emboldened the pope in 601 to reveal his organizational plan for the English church. The principal see was to be at London, and Augustine could consecrate twelve other bishops. In addition, a bishop could be sent to York, and, if successful, he could create twelve bishops for his province. This stress on organization at such an early stage in the conversion process was indeed premature. Never did the archbishop of York have twelve subordinate bishops. More importantly, the choice of London must have been based on a recollection of its significance in Roman times, for at this time the Roman city of London was desolate and a small Anglo-Saxon settlement stood to its west. The later importance of London as a national capital should not be read back into the seventh century. And, most importantly, the Gregorian plans for church polity were premature, because within a generation of the coming of Augustine the mission came within an ace of failing. Aethelbert's son, who succeeded his father in 616, reverted to paganism. At about the same time the three pagan sons of the late king of the East Saxons, who had converted, were openly hostile to Christianity. Meanwhile, Raedwald, king of the East Angles, who had been baptized in Kent, hedged his bets and kept in his place of worship one altar to offer sacrifice to Christ and another altar to offer sacrifice to the old gods. He died *c*.625, and, if the Sutton Hoo burial ship was associated with him, as seems quite likely, it bears no sign of the Christian faith save two silver spoons with SAUL and PAUL inscriptions and possibly silver bowls with cross designs, and it lies in a field of pagan burials. With Kent, Essex and East Anglia reverting to paganism, the three remaining Christian bishops – Laurence of Canterbury, Justus of Rochester and Mellitus of London, the latter expelled from London – decided to leave. Justus and Mellitus fled to Gaul, there to await events. Laurence lingered at Canterbury, where (the historian Bede tells us) by a miracle Kent's new pagan king accepted baptism, and the two other bishops were recalled. Progress thereafter was slow, and the Christian inroads to other regions of the Anglo-Saxon settlements came not from Canterbury and the successors of Augustine but from other sources and over a period of many decades in the seventh century. Yet before they can be visited, two comments need be made about the Augustinian mission.

In the first place, there exist detailed instructions from Pope Gregory to his missionary about the process of acculturating pagans to a Christian way of life. The temples need not be destroyed – only the pagan shrines – but even they can be converted to Christian use. Do we hear here not only the voice of the shepherd of souls but also the practical voice of the former Roman civil official? Substitute, he said, the sacrifice of oxen to devils with some other festivals, Christian feasts, at which they may kill animals in thanksgiving to God for generous bounty.

> It is certainly impossible to eradicate all errors from obstinate minds at one stroke. The highest peaks are reached not by leaps but gradually step by step.
>
> (Bede, *Ecclesiastical History*, bk 1, ch. 30)

Gregory sounded this early note of caution and respected the process by which religious belief and practice were translated into cultural forms.

The second point that needs be made about the Augustinian mission concerns the treatment by Augustine of the native British church. To say his attitude was tainted by hubris and condescension would be putting a gentle gloss on this embarrassing aspect of his mission. The crucial episode bears telling if for no other reason than to illustrate the human problems which got in the way of the spread of Christianity. The Romano-Britons were not recent converts but bearers of the Christian name for centuries. They had withstood the attacks of the pagans for nearly two centuries before the Roman Augustine arrived on their shores, rebuking them for not converting their enemies. He insisted on a meeting, and one was held at the border of the British and English peoples, probably in the

Severn valley. Augustine reproved the Britons for celebrating Easter at a different date from the Romans (although, as we now know, the Roman date had been adopted at Rome only fairly recently). The story that reaches us from the English historian Bede, almost certainly via a Kentish source, recounts how the Britons refused to yield to Augustine in this matter. Let the matter be settled by a sign from heaven, they both agreed. And then a blind man was cured not by the Britons but by Augustine. That this blind man was an Englishman may have made Augustine's deed less impressive to the Britons. In any case, they could not alter so significant a custom without consulting the British people. Another meeting was planned. Seven bishops and many learned men of the Romano-British church were to attend. On their way to the meeting, they consulted with a holy anchorite. His advice was that they must follow Augustine if he is truly a man of God. How are we to determine this, they asked. Arrive at the meeting place after Augustine's party, and, if he rises upon your arrival, know that he is of God, for he is 'meek and humble of heart'. When they arrived, Augustine refused to rise, and the British believed him not of God and spurned his demands. In what must have been considerable anger, Augustine prophetically threatened them with destruction. And Bede, the Northumbrian monk, writing over a century later and apparently revealing his own anti-British feelings, seemed to take delight in the fulfilment of Augustine's prophecy of doom against this 'nation of heretics', when he recounted that hundreds of unarmed British monks of Bangor were ruthlessly slaughtered. Whether Augustine walked with the swagger of a colonial officer we shall never know, yet his attitude, told by friendly sources, reveals an unattractive sense of superiority in a Christian missionary whose disciples and immediate successors, in the face of reversals, all but abandoned their mission.

If the final judgement must be that Augustine's mission was less than successful – the reversion to paganism after his death and his alienation of Romano-British Christians are persuasive indications of this – he did establish a Roman connection, and the Augustine myth itself became established in the firmament of English Christianity. It must be further emphasized that much of the conversion in southern England was independent of Canterbury and Augustine's mission. For example, when Christianity came to East Anglia, it came from Gaul, where an exiled English king had been baptized, and the first bishop of the East Angles came from Burgundy. And the ascetic tradition of the East Angles derived from the Irish monk Fursey. Christianity came to the West Saxons, again, not through Canterbury but through the missionary Birinus, probably of German origin, who baptized the king in 635 and who took his episcopal seat at Dorchester on Thames. Even there in Wessex, mass conversion did not immediately follow the king's conversion but was the work of time, to be measured not in years but in decades. This slow, almost hidden process best describes the spread of Christianity in the south of England. In the north there was a very different story.

Two stages marked the coming of Christianity to the north, the first a mission from the south, which was largely unsuccessful, and the second a mission from

Ireland, which had astonishing success. In 625 the pagan king of Northumbria – i.e., the lands north of the Humber – married a Kentish princess, who was a Christian. She brought with her to the north a certain Paulinus, an Italian missionary sent to Canterbury by Gregory the Great in 601. Now consecrated a bishop, Paulinus met with almost immediate success. King Edwin accepted baptism at York in 627, and a member of his council, the high priest, said that 'the temple and altars which we have dedicated to no advantage should be immediately desecrated and burned'. Paulinus, at one time, was said to be staying at the royal palace, spending his long days teaching the crowds who came to him and baptizing them in the River Glen. We also can see Paulinus baptizing in the River Swale, near Catterick. Almost six years of remarkable effect, then the Paulinus mission, closely allied to the person of the Northumbrian king, ended abruptly in 632 with the death of King Edwin in battle. Paulinus fled south, abandoning the infant church of Northumbria. It must be emphasized that the Paulinus mission was to the English in Northumbria, for there was clearly a British population there, its size difficult to estimate. While Paulinus was baptizing in the Glen, there may indeed have been villages of Christian Britons in other nearby valleys.

The more enduring mission to the north came from Irish monk-missionaries, and it is a story with an ending edged in sadness. When King Edwin's enemies were overthrown, the English kingdom of Northumbria was re-established with Oswald as king. During Edwin's time, Oswald, then heir to English opponents of Edwin, lived in exile (c.617–34) in the far north, where he received baptism from Irish monks. Now king, Oswald almost immediately sent to Iona, the monastery founded by Columba on an island off the Ross of Mull, for assistance so that 'his people might learn faith in the Lord'. What Oswald got in response, in 635, was the remarkable Aidan, whom Bede was to call 'a man of outstanding gentleness, devotion and moderation'. Aidan knew that he must first offer the people 'the milk of gentle teaching, and gradually, as they grew strong on the nourishment of God's word, they could live more perfectly and grasp the more sublime aspects of God's commands'. King Oswald established the newly consecrated bishop Aidan on the high-tide island of Lindisfarne (known since the twelfth century as Holy Island), about five miles across the bay from the king's chief seat at Bamburgh. One can see vividly (through Bede's account) the picture of the Irish monk preaching the gospel to Oswald's men with the bilingual king himself acting as interpreter. And other Irish missionaries came after Aidan to preach in Oswald's kingdom. The enduring conversion of the north was being accomplished by Irish monks and a pious king. And it was from the nascent Northumbrian church that missionaries went south in 653 to convert the still pagan Mercians, whose first bishop was one of these Irish monks.

A major problem loomed. The ascetic and learned Irish monks had customs different from the customs brought from the Continent by other missionaries. Three major differences stood out: they concerned the date of Easter, the form of the tonsure and the rite of baptism. Nothing of detail is known about the third.

Tonsure, the form of shaving of the head of monks and clerics, was indeed slightly different, but this was not the matter of major moment. What mattered was the date of Easter, the principal Christian feast, which, since it was movable (based on lunar months), determined much of the church calendar. The dispute over Easter was neither new nor confined to Britain. It had deeply divided East and West for some time and had been addressed at the Council of Nicaea (325). From very early times it had been agreed that the Christian celebration of Christ's resurrection should not be held on a weekday but on a Sunday. The question in dispute was quite simple: when the Jewish feast of Passover fell on a Sunday, should that Sunday be Easter or should Easter be celebrated on the next Sunday? The Irish held to the former, the Romans to the latter, but it was a Roman practice of only recent origin. Why this matter was raised in 664 at a 'synod' convened at Whitby is not clear. The discrepancy in the celebration dates of Easter between the Christians converted by the Roman mission and the Christians converted by Irish missionaries was nothing new. Differences had quite simply been lived with. But in 664 the tolerance ended, and two figures appear as the principal players in support of the Roman cause in the confrontation at Whitby. Ealhfrith, sub-king of Deira, was the ambitious son of King Oswy of Northumbria, and was eager to assert himself. The other figure, Wilfrid, had lived at Lindisfarne at the time of Aidan but later spent a year in Kent, several years at Lyons in Gaul and some time in Rome. He had returned to Northumbria as a convert to the Roman Easter. He met Ealhfrith, who quickly dispatched the Irish monks from Ripon and gave the monastery to his new friend, Wilfrid. Ealhfrith's political ambitions and Wilfrid's paschal convictions coincided. It seems likely that Ealhfrith's purpose was to gain a degree of independence from his father and that Wilfrid's purpose was to impose the Continental customs. It was, then, Ealhfrith and Wilfrid who led the party in favour of the Roman usage. The Celtic party was led by the holy Colman, the Irish bishop of Lindisfarne, and the noble Hild, abbess of Whitby and one of the highborn women then ruling monastic communities made up of both men and women. The meeting at Whitby – which Bede called a 'synod' – was presided over by King Oswy; it was not national in scope but Northumbrian. Oswy's own wife was a Kentish Christian, and, it was said, in years when the Irish and Roman Easters did not concur she was still fasting while her husband was feasting. To speak of the Irish tradition and the Roman tradition is probably to misspeak, for in 664 the southern Irish had already accepted the so-called Roman tradition as had the British monks at Bangor in Wales. What was at issue at Whitby was the Iona tradition, established by Columba and brought to Lindisfarne by Aidan and now defended by Colman. And what was called the Roman tradition was only a recent usage at Rome. In any case, Whitby did not signify an attempt by Rome to bring the Celtic church into its jurisdiction. Given the extremely passive exercise of papal jurisdiction at this time, a jurisdiction not rejected in Ireland, the event at Whitby should be seen as the local issue it was. The decision at Whitby in favour of the so-called Roman tradition was made not by a show of hands of the clergy present but by the king, who, it was said, preferred the tradition of Peter, holder of the keys of the gates heaven, to the tradition of the apostle John, who held not those keys, whose tradition passed down through Columba. The story of the 'synod' ends with Colman, unable to comply, sadly leaving, a man of simple and austere life, a Francis of Assisi before his time, who walked the dusty trackways back to Iona. His simplicity and humility were not lost on the straightforward English monk-historian Bede.

> How frugal and austere he and his predecessor had been, the place itself [Lindisfarne] over which they ruled bears witness. When they left, there were very few buildings there except for the church, in fact only those without which community life was impossible. They had no money from the rich; they promptly gave it to the poor. They had no need to collect money or to provide dwellings for the reception of worldly and powerful men, since these only came to the church to pray and to hear the word of God . . . The priests and the monks visited the villages for no other reason than to preach, to baptize, and to visit the sick, in brief, to care for their souls. They were so free from all taint of avarice that none of them would accept lands or possessions to build monasteries, unless compelled to do so by the secular authorities.
>
> (Bede, *Ecclesiastical History*, bk 3, ch. 26)

A generous epitaph to a simple form of the Christian faith, little bothered by matters of organization and power, committed to an uncomplicated understanding of the gospels. In contrast to his description of Colman, Bede's cool, almost detached, words about Wilfrid leave little doubt in the mind of the reader who Bede thought was more Christ-like.

What the 'Synod' of Whitby meant on the broad canvas of the history of the church is a question with a range of answers. The participants saw the issues in terms of the debate about Easter and the subsequent departure of the Irish monks. Bede, writing two-thirds of a century later, gave it considerable attention, but his focus was largely on the computistics of the date of Easter, a subject which he raised to an essential sign of the unity of the church. What is clear to us, at our remove from the events, is that the English church was to become organized in the Roman fashion. Bishops with territorial dioceses would replace bishops of specific peoples. In 672 the Council of Hertford made clear the territorial nature of a bishop's diocese, although some decades would pass before the system was fully in force: by 737 there would be four dioceses in the north and thirteen in the south. It is also clear that England was now firmly in the Roman orbit, not that the pope consistently exercised active jurisdiction over the internal affairs of remote places such as England. Yet, when English missionaries, as we shall soon see, went to the Continent, it was under papal authority, and there they established a diocesan organization.

The transmission of learning

In 782, Charlemagne, king of the Franks and soon to be 'emperor', invited to join his court and to advise him on educational matters the deacon Alcuin from York in the far-away English kingdom of Northumbria at the edge of the known world. Why did Charlemagne turn to Northumbria? What events lay behind this extraordinary selection? How to explain that, within two hundred years of the advent of Christianity among the English, their school at York helped to reintroduce learning to the European mainland?

When Augustine arrived at Canterbury in 597, he came as a missionary of the Christian gospel, not as a scholar intent on establishing a school. He and his fellow monks brought very few books with them, and these almost certainly were liturgical books needed to conduct ceremonies of Christian worship: Mass books, psalters, etc. His mission, it is widely agreed, was purely evangelical in nature and did not advance the cause of learning. From where did the learning of the West come to the English?

There were two distinct streams meeting to make England one of the foremost centres of scholarly learning in eighth-century Europe, although we may not be able with precision to weigh their relative contributions. Both were significant, and the diminution of one or the other imperils our historical understanding. One stream came from Ireland, the other from the Continent, particularly from Rome. Together they produced a vibrant intellectual climate that fostered serious learning, making England, particularly Northumbria, arguably the pre-eminent centre of scholarship in Western Europe and creating a decisive moment in the history of the Christian church. The details need to be seen.

The most obvious line of development came from Rome to Canterbury and thence to Northumbria. In 669, the new archbishop of Canterbury, Theodore of Tarsus, a Greek biblical scholar, arrived from Rome, with the learned Hadrian, a North African abbot, who like Theodore had long lived in Italy, and the Northumbrian noble Benedict Biscop, who had been a monk on the island of Lerins off the south coast of Gaul. A school in the sense of a centre of learning was quickly established at Canterbury. No inventory of books survives for any of the English centres of learning tracing their descent from Theodore's Canterbury, but the library at Canterbury must have contained the Bible, works of grammar and rhetoric as well as epitomes of classical and patristic learning. Aldhelm, one of his students at Canterbury, complained that, as a student, he had not enough time to learn everything he wanted to learn: law, prose and poetic literature, music, arithmetic and the mysteries of the heavens. He described Theodore 'like an angry boar surrounded by a pack of smirking hounds'. More measuredly, Bede wrote of the school of Theodore and Hadrian at Canterbury:

> They were both extremely learned in both secular and sacred literature and thus attracted a crowd of students into whose minds they daily poured the streams of wholesome learning. They gave

their hearers instruction not only in the books of Holy Scripture but also in the art of metre, astronomy and ecclesiastical computation. As evidence of this, some of their students still survive who know Latin and Greek just as well as they know their native tongue.

(Bede, *Ecclesiastical History*, bk 4, ch. 2)

Erudite teachers, a broad curriculum, eager students and learned books provide the essentials of any school, and these were all present at Canterbury in the last decades of the seventh century.

His name 'Biscop' might suggest that Benedict Biscop was of a priestly family, but, in any case, he was certainly from a noble, wealthy Northumbrian family. During the course of his life he travelled six times to Rome, the latter four journeys while he was involved with establishing new English schools. Among the founders of the school at Canterbury in 669, Biscop, after perhaps three winters there, undertook a journey to Rome: it was to set in motion events of far-reaching significance. Unlike his previous journeys, this was a journey in search of books, pictures and relics, but mostly books. At Rome he acquired a substantial number of books and, on his return journey, he collected a large number of books at Vienne, which he had asked friends to collect for him. His intentions seem clear: to return to England and establish a new monastery with relics for its altar, pictures for devotion and books for learning and liturgy. It was to his native Northumbria, from which he had been absent for twenty years, that Biscop went to found his monastery on land given him by the king of Northumbria on the north banks of the Wear River near its mouth. The Wearmouth foundation, in 673, was followed by a foundation, in 681, at Jarrow, overlooking the mud flats where the Don enters the Tyne, only a few miles from Wearmouth. Dedicated to SS. Peter and Paul and for some time a single community under one abbot, Wearmouth and Jarrow became key centres of learning in Western Europe, producing in the first generation the Venerable Bede, considered the most learned man of his times.

Often forgotten in this run of events from Biscop to Bede was the great figure of Ceolfrid, who became first abbot of the combined monasteries in 688. Ten years earlier he had accompanied Biscop on the latter's last trip to Rome. During his abbotship the library collection was doubled, and the number of monks, almost incredibly, rose to over 600. It was a long abbotship of twenty-eight years and ended not with Ceolfrid's death but with his retirement in June 716, when, laden with gifts, he left for Rome, never to see his native land again. He never arrived in Rome. Age and a difficulty journey combined to weaken his physical strength, and in Burgundy on 25 September 716 Ceolfrid died. Some of his companions continued their way to Rome, where they presented Pope Gregory II with their gifts from Tyneside. Among them was a truly exceptional book: the Codex Amiatinus, so-called from the monastery of Monte Amiata, where it resided in the early modern period before finding its present home in the Laurentian Library in Florence. It is considered one of the most important manuscripts surviving from early medieval Europe. To the paleographer, who studies handwriting, it may provide links between the scriptoria of southern Italy and northern England, but to the cultural historian it is more: it is the earliest surviving complete Latin Bible and a clear window into the age in which it was made. The dedication reveals much. It is a poem in praise of the Petrine headship of the church written by Ceolfrid, this abbot from remotest Northumbria. He called himself 'Ceolfridus Anglorum extremis de finibus abbas' ('Ceolfrid, abbot, from the outermost parts of the English'). An enormous book (or codex) for its time and, indeed, for most times, it has over 1,000 folios (i.e., leaves), and each folio measures about 20 inches high by about 13 inches wide. Some consider that this book represents the greatest achievement of Northumbrian learning.

The other towering achievement of Northumbrian scriptoria, the Lindisfarne Gospels, was a very near contemporary of the Codex Amiatinus. There may be some doubt whether this book of the gospels was produced at the island monastery of Lindisfarne, yet its Northumbrian origin is assured. It rivals the later Book of Kells for the splendour of its artistic decoration. Each of the four gospels is preceded by a 'carpet page' (a full page of decoration, carpet-like, fashioned largely of skilfully interlaced coloured ribbons) and a page with a portrait of the evangelist. Besides, virtually every page has decorated initial letters and border designs, and many pages contain miniatures, so called not because they are small but because they are coloured (from *miniare*, to colour). The Lindisfarne Gospels is now on permanent display at the British Library in London.

While these two great books were being fashioned, the north of England produced the greatest scholar of the age. Bede (*c.*672–735) was born on the estates of Wearmouth and at age seven was presented by his parents to the monastic community. When Jarrow was founded in 681, he went there, and there he remained for the rest of his life, using the library developed by Biscop and Ceolfrid. Travelling little if at all outside his monastery, Bede composed a flood of works: twenty books of scriptural exegesis and six works on chronology as well as homilies, saints' lives, histories, hymns, prayers, letters and much more. In short, he was a genius. The great twentieth-century historian Sir Richard Southern observed that Bede was 'the first scientific intellect produced by the German peoples of Europe' and that in Bede's lifetime Jarrow had become 'the chief centre of Roman civilization in Europe'. Bede is best known – perhaps unfairly to his other works – for his *Ecclesiastical History of the English People*. Its preface has almost a modern ring to it, as he describes there his efforts to get reliable evidence for his historical account. For him history is not the retelling of old stories, the passing along of traditional accounts. For Bede history is the attempt to recount the past as accurately as possible, acknowledging that to do so is the essential task of the historian.

The line which we are tracing from Theodore and Hadrian and Biscop and Ceolfrid does not end with Bede. Among Bede's students was the son of the Northumbrian royal family, Egbert, who about 732 became archbishop of York. There at York he established a school, which would surpass even the school of his own training. To it would come the sons of the great northern families and books and even more books. Under Aethelbert (*c.*766–79), Egbert's successor, the school at York had probably the best library in Western Europe. Also under Aethelbert the school had its greatest student, Alcuin. Hence, it was in light of these events of a century or more in England that we should see Charlemagne in 781 inviting Alcuin from York in the north of England to the royal palace at Aix-la-Chapelle (Aachen).

This line of descent, just described, from the coming of Theodore to Canterbury in 669 to the going of Alcuin to the Frankish court in 783 might seem clear enough and might even be drawn as follows:

Theodore/Hadrian > Benedict Biscop > Ceolfrid > Bede >
Aegbert > Ethelbert > Alcuin.

Yet such a straight, unambiguous line gives an inaccurate picture, for it tells only part of the story and assumes (wrongly) a single line of cultural transmission. There was another line that originated in Ireland, which is overlooked at the peril of historical distortion. From the early days of Christianity in Ireland an emphasis was placed on the value of learning, and great efforts were made to introduce biblical, patristic and even secular works into Irish monasteries. The influence of the Irish foundation at Lindisfarne in 635 continued long after the withdrawal of Colman in 664. The foundation at (Old) Melrose by Eata, a pupil of Aidan, was Irish in culture, and it was there that Cuthbert entered as a novice. When, in 664, Eata came to replace Colman as abbot of Lindisfarne, he brought with him Cuthbert as his prior. There they continued the Irish monastic traditions of Aidan and Colman. In a curious twist, when Colman left Lindisfarne after the 'Synod' of Whitby, thirty English monks went with him and soon established their own monastery on an island off the west coast of Ireland, which, when Bede wrote his *Ecclesiastical History* (731), was a flourishing community of English monks following the Irish ways. Yet they were not the first English monks to make such a journey. A large number (*multi*) of English monks in search of learning and an ascetical life had already gone to Irish monasteries, where, in Bede's words, 'they were most gladly welcomed by the Irish and given food, books and instruction without any payment'. Bede names eleven of these; other sources name still others. There was, for example, the young Northumbrian noble Aethelwine, who after studying in Ireland returned to England and became a bishop. A brother of the great Abbot Ceolfrid of Wearmouth–Jarrow went to Ireland to study the scriptures, and he was among the many English monks in Ireland who fell victim to the plague of 664. Other English monks formed a community at Clonmelsh (in modern Co. Carlow), from which the successful mission of Willibrord to the Frisians set out.

Moreover, Irish influences were not limited to Northumbria. In East Anglia (*c.*630), the Irish monk Fursey established a monastery, again in Bede's words, 'in order to devote himself more freely to sacred studies'. In Wessex, Aldhelm, whom we have already met at Canterbury, had been taught by the Irish masters at Malmesbury, where he later (*c*.675) became abbot. Sir Frank Stenton has called him 'the most learned and ingenious western scholar of the late seventh century'. At about the same time that Aldhelm was studying at Malmesbury, there came to Wessex Agilbert, who, although born in Gaul, had studied the scriptures in Ireland; he soon became bishop. And, again, in the 650s, Diuma, an Irish monk from Lindisfarne, became the first bishop of the Mercians. His successor was Irish born and trained. His successor, in turn, was English but Irish-trained. There, among the Mercians, in three generations the process of assimilation can be seen taking place.

The Irish line, in all this, is clearly unmistakable. The historical reality reveals that the glory of late seventh- and eighth-century English learning derived from two sources: one continental and one Irish. The two combined like the interlacing in the manuscript illuminations, the two so closely interwoven that one attempts to separate them at one's peril. The historian, faced with this complexity, should perhaps be content to describe this culture and learning as 'insular', thus giving credit to undoubted Irish and continental influences and to native English genius. The further danger is that the historian, trying to separate these strands, might lose sight of what truly happened in England in the seventh and eighth centuries: the civilizing of the barbarian English by reason of their conversion to the Christian religion. It was the Christian missionaries, whatever their origins, who brought literacy, book learning, scholarship – the framework for a civilized society – to England. As it was to be elsewhere, Christianity was in England the means of introducing barbarian peoples to the civilizing effects of learning.

English mission to the Continent

Two names stand out in the story of the conversion of the Germanic peoples east of the Rhine to Christianity. They are Willibrord and Boniface, two English monks, who under papal authority set out on their missions. What is particularly striking is that it was from the English, themselves recently converted and with recent memories of paganism, that this general mission came to the Continent of Europe. It was led by monks, products of monasteries, where Latin was taught and the scriptures studied. With the waters of baptism scarcely dry on their brows English missionaries undertook the conversion of large parts of the Germanic peoples. How did this come about?

It was not by a grand design that English monks went to the Continent as missionaries. It was almost by accident, at least in the beginning. The irascible Wilfrid, whom we have already met at the 'Synod' of Whitby (664), his enormous northern diocese having been divided and he deposed by Archbishop Theodore, decided to go to Rome to appeal and, in 678, set out on his journey. Something unplanned happened on the way. The direct route across the Dover Straits was closed to him, and so he sailed to the delta of the Rhine, in the modern Netherlands, then the lands of the heathen Frisians. He stayed there during the

Map 5 Conversion of the Germanic peoples (*c.*350–*c.*750).

winter months of 678–79 and preached the gospel, gaining some converts. It was but a brief episode in a busy life, and, in any case, the converted Frisians soon reverted to paganism. In the next century Bede and others, no doubt wrongly, attributed to Wilfrid the origins of the Continental mission. His was but a passing adventure, remembered more for his self-inflated image as a churchman than for its real effect. The true origins of the English mission are not to be found in England but in Ireland at the English monastery at Clonmelsh (Co. Carlow). The Northumbrian Egbert – to be distinguished from the later Egbert, archbishop of York – was in Ireland as a *pilgrim*, a voluntary exile, in 664, when the plague struck Ireland. He was spared, vowed never to return to England and died among the Irish sixty-five years later, in 729, at the age of ninety. If we can trust the details of our sources, Egbert, while abbot of Clonmelsh, planned to go as a pilgrim-missionary to the Frisians. His motivation for the mission made no mention of Wilfrid: it was as a *German* that Egbert was moved to bring the Christian message to other German peoples. In the event, he never went. It was in 690 that the effective English mission began, when Willibrord and other English monks left Clonmelsh. The English mission thus originated in Ireland.

The part of continental Europe to which these English missionaries sailed lay just beyond the political control of the Franks in what was a fluid political situation. By the late seventh century the Merovingian kings, descendants of Clovis, their power now emasculated, were mere *rois fainéants*, do-nothing kings. Real power lay elsewhere, particularly in the hands of the mayors of the palace of these kings. The political dust was still in motion when Willibrord arrived in Frisia. Pepin II, a mayor of the palace (d. 714), had control over most of Francia and now also controlled western Frisia, including Utrecht, and he had the ambition to expand his power further north. Among the German peoples beyond Frankish control were not only the Frisians but also the Saxons, both of whom were still pagan. Even within the Frankish kingdom, where Irish monks had been active for a hundred years, there still existed pockets – even large pockets – of heathenism. It was into this volatile situation that, in 690, Willibrord and eleven other English monks came from Ireland to preach the Christian gospel.

The missionaries, probably well informed of the political situation, arrived in Frankish-controlled Frisia, and it was under the protection and with the support of Pepin II that the mission was to thrive. Willibrord went almost immediately to Rome to get papal sanction for his mission. This readily given, he returned to Frisia, with relics in his bags to replace the idols of his converts. Success was immediate: Bede says that many Frisians were converted in a short time. Are we to believe that these English monks could preach in the language of the Frisians? The support of Pepin must have been a major ingredient in all this. In retrospect, the decision made by Pepin and his council in 695 was to have far-reaching consequences in European history. In that year Pepin sent Willibrord to Rome to get authority to establish an ecclesiastical province. Authority was quickly given, and Willibrord became archbishop to the Frisians with his see at Utrecht and with the power to create subordinate dioceses and to consecrate bishops.

With these events is marked a turning point in that relationship which was to be central to medieval history, the relationship between the Franks and the pope. A small enough turning, perhaps, but a precedent to be followed and to be enlarged by Pepin II's son (Charles Martel), his grandson (King Pepin) and his great-grandson (Charlemagne).

Willibrord's commission was clear: to establish Christianity among the Frisians. He is said to have preached widely, gained numerous converts, appointed subordinate bishops and established churches and monasteries. His successes were in west Frisia, in the lands between the Lek River and the Zuider Zee, leaving much of Frisia beyond his reach. Yet Willibrord, at one point, had the hopes of converting the Danes and even visited their land, bringing back with him thirty boys to train. It all came to nothing, but the incident indicates something of the scope of Willibrord's intention. Puzzling in this context was his founding of a monastery at Echternach, c.697, very shortly after his return from Rome as archbishop to the Frisians. Over 200 miles from Utrecht, Echternach cannot be associated with a Frisian mission. Willibrord's secular supporters provided him with land (in modern Luxembourg), where the new monastery was built. Willibrord may have used Echternach as a place of retreat; it was there that he spent his final years and where he died, aged eighty-one, in 739, almost fifty years after his arrival on the Continent. The scriptorium at Echternach from very early in its history produced illuminated books of very high quality: the Echternach Gospels rivals the Lindisfarne Gospels and the Book of Kells. Once thought to have been brought from Northumbria, the Echternach Gospels is now recognized (by its use of goatskin) as continental, undoubtedly a product of the scriptorium at Echternach, the work of monks trained in the traditions of their monastery at Clonmelsh in Ireland. The accomplishments of Echternach are not to be confused with the principal mission of Willibrord, which was to convert the heathen Frisians. He was successful in doing this at least among those Frisians subject to Frankish rule and in establishing an infrastructure of churches, monasteries and clergy to nurture the new Christian life. He did this with the assistance of secular Frankish rulers and under the authority of the pope, two elements essential also to the mission of St Boniface.

The man whose name was changed by the pope to Boniface was born Winfrid in the south-west of England, in Wessex, c.675. He stands out as the single most significant fashioner of the direction of the church in the eighth century. And there are historians who, with some persuasion, would make even grander claims. The name of Boniface is synonymous with the conversion of the Germans, although the nature of his role in this conversions needs close examination.

Whatever else must be said about Boniface's mission to the Germans – and there is much – it has to be emphasized that his was a papal mission. From the very beginning he sought papal approval: he traversed the Alps in 719 to ask – and receive – Pope Gregory II's permission to preach to the Germans. He returned to Rome to be consecrated a bishop in 722, when he took the oath of fidelity to St Peter and his successors. The oath was in the form used by bishops within the immediate jurisdiction of the pope in central Italy. It was unusual and, indeed, novel for a bishop of a far-away mission to swear in this way. Ten years later Pope Gregory III made him archbishop and sent him the pallium, the short woollen, scarf-like vestment which was the sign of authority over a province of the church. A reader of Boniface's remarkable correspondence will encounter Boniface asking the pope's advice, sending reports of his activities and humbly giving his loyalty to each new pope. Boniface was called *missus sancti Petri* ('the legate of St Peter'). Hitherto, papal primacy, accepted as it was in the West, did not imply an active exercise of papal authority. The mission of St Boniface under the direct supervision of the pope transformed the role of the papacy from a mostly passive to a now much more active role in the leadership of the church in the West. If Boniface had done nothing else, he would still be considered a major figure in medieval history. But he did much more.

To us, the mission of Boniface is both clear and vague. It is clear in that it was a mission to the German peoples living east of the Rhine and north of the Danube. It is vague because he had no diocese, not even after he became an archbishop with a pallium, at least until very late in his life, when a see was established for him at Mainz. His was a roving commission to a people. From our vantage point, we can see that his activities were generally confined to the lands of Hesse and Thuringia. The leaders of Hesse had embraced Christianity only superficially, and their people were still heathen. The Thuringians had been converted to Christianity at an earlier time, but the lack of continued instruction allowed pagan practices to reassert themselves. Boniface's challenge, then, was to convert and reconvert. With what must have been exceptional physical vigour and driving motivation he had quick success. Thousands, we are told, accepted Christianity. Of course, he had companions and, equally of course, he had reinforcements from Britain: 'an exceedingly large number of holy men came to his aid, among them readers, writers and learned men trained in the other arts' (Willibald's *Life of St Boniface*, ch. 6). Monasteries of men and of women began to dot the countryside. Tauberbischofsheim, where his cousin Leoba was first abbess, became the nursery for abbesses of other houses. At Kitzingen on Main another English lady became abbess. Boniface's countryman Wigbert was placed as the first abbot of Fritzlar. And near Marburg Boniface established an influential monastery at Amöneburg, and near Gotha the monastery of Ohrdruf. And the list goes on, ending with the crown in Boniface's foundations, the monastery at Fulda (744), a monastery exempt from all local jurisdictions and subject directly to the pope. It was at Fulda that Boniface was to be buried and where within eighty years of his death there were over 130 monks.

Boniface, the missionary, faced the problems encountered by most missionaries, and he sought advice from the pope and from brother bishops. Bishop Daniel of Winchester wisely counselled him,

> Do not begin by arguing with them about the origins of their gods,
> false as those are, but let them affirm that some of them were begotten

by others, through the intercourse of male and female, so that you may at least prove that gods and goddesses born after the manner of men are men and not gods, and, since they did not exist before, must have had a beginning . . . These and many similar things you should put before them, not offensively or so as to anger them, but calmly and with great moderation.

(Letter no. 15)

Pope Gregory II took a sensible approach in advising Boniface about marital matters. Within what degrees of kinship is marriage forbidden?

Since moderation is better than strictness of discipline, especially towards so uncivilized a people, they may contract marriage after the fourth degree [i.e., beyond first cousins].

The pope went on to deal with Boniface's question about a man whose wife, owing to disease, was unable to have sexual intercourse with him:

It would be better if he could remain in a state of continence. But, since this is a matter of great difficulty, it is better for him who cannot refrain to take a wife. He may not, however, withdraw his support from the one who was prevented by disease.

(Letter no. 18)

Boniface worried about the validity of baptisms performed by bad priests or in an unacceptable form (e.g., without invocation of the Trinity). To which the pope responded, that in such cases he was to follow the ancient custom of the church, for he who has been baptized in the name of the Father, Son and Holy Spirit may on no account be baptized again' (Letter no. 18). Boniface's scruple even extended to baptisms performed by priests who, in their ignorance, used wrong Latin case endings, and the pope corrected him for needlessly rebaptizing in such cases (Letter no. 54).

The extermination of pagan practices proved not an easy task. Boniface's biographer comments,

Some continued secretly, others openly, to offer sacrifices to trees and springs, to inspect the entrails of victims; some practised divination, magic and incantations; some turned their attention to auguries, auspices and other sacrificial rites.

(Willibald, *Life of St Boniface*, ch. 6)

One can picture Boniface, axe in hand, at Geismar, confronting a giant oak tree (the Oak of Jupiter), long the object of pagan worship, while a host of pagan worshippers angrily watched. He made a mere superficial cut, his biographer tells us, when a mighty wind toppled the sacred oak, and it landed divided in four equal parts, trunk to top. And the amazed onlookers accepted Christianity.

Unlike Wilfrid's mission, Boniface's had lasting consequences because he established a clear institutional structure which would ensure its continuation long after he and his fellow missionaries had passed from the scene. When he was made archbishop in 732, he neither had a diocese of his own nor any bishops under him. As late as 739 he was without bishops, but by 741 Boniface had eight suffragans. Four were in Bavaria, where, at the request of the local duke, he created territorial dioceses at Passau, Regensburg, Salzburg and Freising. Boniface was their metropolitan (i.e., archbishop). Also, he had suffragan bishops with territorial jurisdiction at Buraburg in Hesse, at Erfurt in Thuringia, at Würzburg on the Main and at Eichstätt in Franconia. Of these latter four bishops, three were fellow countrymen of Boniface. In 739 Pope Gregory III had warned him, 'You are not at liberty to linger in one place when your work is done there.' Perhaps as a concession to his age, then nearing seventy, Boniface in 745 was made archbishop of Mainz, metropolitan of the 'German church' which he had created. With the cooperation – always – of the secular rulers he held synods of bishops to address the practical matters among German Catholics. The matters, important though they were, were less important historically than the establishing of the mechanism for dealing with them. A hierarchical structure was in place, and it marked the post-missionary phase in the history of these peoples.

As a final witness to his sense of vocation, Boniface in his old age left Mainz – provision for his successor assured – and returned to the mission field. In 753 he and companions journeyed to Frisia to preach in the lands beyond the Zuider Zee. Thousands apparently were converted, but, in June 754, Boniface and fifty-three others were slaughtered by heathens seeking booty. To the title of bishop, archbishop and legate were added martyr and saint.

A dispassionate view of the English missions to the Continent in the eighth century cannot escape concluding that they gave a shape and direction to the future history of the church. A strong church among the Germanic peoples and a firm link of these peoples to the papacy, with consequences, friendly as well as hostile, were to be hallmarks of the medieval church.

Further reading

On Gregory the Great the reader will find very useful Jeffrey Richards, *Consul of God: The Life and Times of Gregory the Great* (London, 1980). Other studies include Pierre Batiffol, *Saint Gregory the Great* (tr. John L. Stoddard; London, 1929); G.R. Evans, *The Thought of Gregory the Great* (Cambridge, 1986); Carole Straw, *Gregory the Great: Perfection in Imperfection* (Berkeley, CA, 1988); and Robert A. Markus, *Gregory the Great and his World* (Cambridge, 1997). An interesting text is an early life of Gregory: Bertram Colgrave (ed. and tr.), *The Earliest Life of Gregory the Great by an Anonymous Monk of Whitby* (Lawrence, KA, 1968). About Gregory's authorship of the Dialogues see Francis Clark, *The Pseudo-Gregorian Dialogues* (2 vols; Leiden, 1987), a view not unchallenged: see Paul Meyvaert's rebuttal in *Journal of Ecclesiastical History* 39 (1988), 335–82. On broader issues see T.S. Brown, *Gentlemen and Officers: Imperial Administration and Aristocratic Power in Byzantine Italy, A.D. 554–800* (Rome, 1984) and Jeffrey Richards, *The Popes and the Papacy in the Early Middle Ages* (London, 1979).

On the English mission one should begin with Henry Mayr-Harting, *The Coming of Christianity to Anglo-Saxon England* (3rd edn; London, 1991), and with Frank Stenton, *Anglo-Saxon England* (3rd edn; Oxford, 1971). For the pre-mission period see Charles Thomas, *Christianity in Roman Britain to A.D. 500* (Berkeley, CA, 1981). On St Augustine see the essays in Richard Gameson (ed.), *St Augustine and the Conversion of England* (Stroud, Glos, 1999). A thorough analysis of the issues involved in the Easter controversy is Maura Walsh and Dáibhí Ó Cróinín (eds), *Cummian's Letter De controversia Paschali, Together with Related Irish Computistical Tract De Ratione Computandi* (Toronto, 1988). On the dispute about tonsure see Edward James, 'Bede and the Tonsure Question', *Peritia* 3 (1984), 85–98. About the early schools see Michael Lapidge, 'The School of Theodore and Hadrian', *Anglo-Saxon England* 15 (1986), 45–72. The modern controversies about the putative Lindisfarne scriptorium can be followed in the journals *Peritia* and *Anglo-Saxon England*. On the Codex Amiatinus see the scholarly article by Karen Corsano, 'The First Quire of the Codex Amiatinus and the *Institutiones* of Cassiodorus', *Scriptorium* 41 (1987), 3–34. An excellent introduction to an allied manuscript is Janet Backhouse, *The Lindisfarne Gospels: A Masterpiece of Book Painting* (London, 1995). On Bede the literature is vast. One will find helpful such items as R.W. Southern, *Medieval Humanism and Other Studies* (New York, 1970), ch. 1; Peter Hunter Blair, *The World of Bede* (London, 1970); George H. Brown, *Bede the Venerable* (Boston, 1987). Nothing can replace reading the actual text of Bede's history, which exists in many English translations, for example, Bertram Colgrave's *Ecclesiastical History of the English People*, edited by Judith McClure and Roger Collins (Oxford, 1994), and Leo Sherley-Price's *A History of the English Church and People*, a Penguin paperback (Harmondsworth, Mddsx, 1955).

Essential to a study of the English mission to the Continent is W. Levison, *England and the Continent in the Eighth Century* (Oxford, 1946). The remarkable correspondence of Boniface is accessible in several English translations, most notably in Ephraim Emerton's frequently reprinted *The Letters of Saint Boniface* (New York, 1940). C.H. Talbot (tr. and ed.), *The Anglo-Saxon Missionaries in Germany: Being the Lives of SS. Willibrord, Boniface, Sturm, Leoba and Leben* (London and New York, 1954) has valuable texts. For the role of women in the conversion process see Rosamond McKitterick, 'Anglo-Saxon Missionaries in Germany: Personal Connexions and Local Influences', in her collected papers, *Books, Scribes and Learning in the Frankish Kingdoms, 6th–9th Centuries* (Aldershot, Hants, and Brookfield, VT, 1994).

5

CHURCH, CAROLINGIANS
AND VIKINGS

It might be thought that the word 'Carolingian' derives from the greatest person of that dynasty, Charlemagne (*Carolus magnus*, Charles the Great), but such is not the case. The word 'Carolingian' derives from Charles Martel, whose son Pepin became the first king of the dynasty. At the height of their power under Charlemagne, the Carolingians controlled a vast area of Western Europe, not just the area of modern France nor even of Napoleonic France. The Frankish campaign into Spain famously failed at Roncesvalles (778), giving us the epic Song of Roland (*Chanson de Roland*) and fixed the south-western border of their lands at the Pyrenees. Yet their south-eastern lands extended deep into central Italy. And their power extended from the western sea well into central Europe, including Saxony, Thuringia and Bavaria, thus neutralizing the Avar threat to the eastern borders. In the north, Carolingian dominion stopped only at the inhospitable Danish march. Europe was not to see such massive territorial control by one power until the time of Napoleon in the eighteenth and nineteenth centuries and Hitler in the twentieth century. It was in the context of this Frankish aggrandizement that the church was to play a major role. The relation-ship of the kings of this dynasty, particularly Pepin III (751–68), Charlemagne (768–814) and Louis the Pious (814–40), with the papacy profoundly influenced that institution and the Christian religion more generally. It was a dynasty too soon, a dynasty too ambitious in its aims and too weak even at its strongest moment to survive long. Within ninety years from the coronation of Pepin (751) the Frankish lands, the new 'empire', were divided into three parts and soon into even more parts as centrifugal forces left it in pieces. Yet, on that account, its accomplishments should not be denied: they were considerable, like nothing before, and they touched the church on many levels and in many ways that continued long after the grandsons of Charlemagne were engaged in unseemly fratricidal warfare.

Franco-papal alliance

Events in Italy and Francia combined to form the central political alliance of the Middle Ages. More than political and, indeed, more than an alliance, the relationship of pope and emperor provided one of the most significant themes in medieval history; some would say the central theme. With Charles Martel ruling Francia as mayor of the palace and not as king and with Pope Gregory III being harassed by the Lombard kings, the scene was set in 739 for the first approach by the papacy – which was not acted upon – to obtain Frankish military assistance. Other approaches would be made and with much greater success. The papal concern was for security of the republic of Rome (*respublica romana*), over which the pope had de facto authority, against the threats of the Lombards, not only from the northern centre of the Lombard kingdom but also from the two Lombard duchies (Spoleto and Benevento) separated geographically from their northern brothers. At issue also was the fate of the exarchate of Ravenna, now without an effective Byzantine presence.

The events of 751–54 may be central to the developing situation. By 750 Charles Martel's son Pepin, the third of that name, had become mayor of the palace. The king was Childeric III, a mere figurehead, who, in fact, had been appointed by Pepin in 743. For reasons not altogether clear to us, Pepin found his situation intolerable. According to the Royal Frankish Annals, written after the events, Pepin, in 751, asked Pope Zachary the famous question: Who should be king, he who has the title but no power or he who has the power but not the title? The annals state that the pope answered that he who has the power should be king. If this is true, then Pope Zachary would have been involved in the creation of a new Frankish dynasty. Exactly what happened we may never know. Perhaps the account in the annals is unreliable and Pepin became king merely by the assent of the Frankish nobility with no papal involvement. The scenario of the annals, however, was taken up by others and became widely accepted. If its account is precise and correct, then the pope had done what no earlier pope had done: popes had never before created a monarch or even claimed the right to do so. It should not be lost on the observer that, in 751, Pepin was not only crowned but also anointed with holy chrism by the Frankish bishops: the office of king had a sacramental element to it that gave the anointed king a place and a function in the church with duties, responsibilities and privileges to be spelled out in time but there in seed at Pepin's anointing in 751. About two years later the pope (now Stephen II) crossed the Alps to Francia, and there at Ponthion met King Pepin, who acceded to the pope's request for military assistance to thwart Lombard aggression against papal lands. While in Francia, Pope Stephen anointed King Pepin at the church of St Denis outside Paris; he also conferred on Pepin the title 'Patrician of the Romans', the meaning of which still exercises the minds of historians, although it was not as significant as once thought. In the spring of 755 Pepin led a small army into Italy and quickly defeated the Lombards. One need scarcely be cynical to ask whether there was a *quid pro quo* in all this: if the pope in 751 agreed to legitimize Pepin as king – and it would be prudent to have some doubt about this – did he do so in return for a promise of military assistance from the Franks, a promise fulfilled by the Frankish expedition of 755? An alliance with the pope had been struck, whether in 751 or in 755 or at some point in between. Pepin marched against the Lombards, in 756, and not only defeated the Lombards but took the keys to twenty-two cities and had them sent to Rome. To call this act the Donation of Pepin would be to misconstrue the meaning. Pepin did not conquer Lombard cities and then grant the pope authority over them. The cities in question were not Lombard but were in the exarchate and duchy of Rome and had been only recently held by the Lombards.

Another donation of far greater moment came to light at about this time: the Donation of Constantine. A precise date cannot be given to this forgery, but the document was drawn up at the papal palace (the Lateran Palace) quite possibly in the early 770s. It took the form of a fourth-century grant by the Emperor Constantine to Pope Sylvester I, which gave the pope authority over the city of Rome and over all the provinces, districts and cities of Italy and the Western regions. This claim of the papacy to temporal rule over the West dazzles the mind in its sheer audacity. Whoever drew up the Donation of Constantine might have been concerned more with Byzantine emperors than with Germanic kings, since it seemed to refute the emperors' claims over Italy. No evidence exists that it was trotted out in the eighth century against either emperors or kings. It was to figure in later time as a prima facie indication of papal supremacy in the West, yet, even then, there is no indication that these later popes knew it was a forged document. Only in the fifteenth century did Lorenzo Valla prove it a forgery.

The coming of Charlemagne to power in 768, a power shared with his brother till the latter's death in 771, promised a continuation of the policy of papal alliance but in ways beyond imagining. The rift between the Franks and Lombards was seen as healed when, in 770, Charlemagne agreed to marry the daughter of the Lombard king, yet within a year he rejected her, with or without having married her is not clear. What is clear is that any *rapprochement* with the Lombards had ended. As his father had done, Charlemagne led an army into Italy and defeated the Lombards, but, unlike his father, Charlemagne sent the Lombard king to a monastery and made himself king of the Lombards. During 774 Charlemagne went to Rome, and at Easter time he and Pope Hadrian I went to St Peter's Basilica, where they swore mutual oaths, thus confirming the alliance of Charles's father with the papacy. The meaning of the alliance was spelled out by Charlemagne in a letter to Pope Leo III in 796:

> It is our part with the help of divine holiness to defend by armed strength the holy church of Christ everywhere from the outward onslaughts of the pagans and the ravages of the infidels and to strengthen within the knowledge of the Catholic faith.
>
> It is your part, most holy Father, to help our armies with your hands lifted up to God like Moses, so that, by your intercession and by the leadership and gift of God, the Christian people (*populus christianus*) may everywhere and always have victory over the enemies of his holy name and that the name of our Lord Jesus Christ may be glorified throughout the world.

4 Throne of Charlemagne, royal chapel, Aachen. Reproduced by permission of Foto Marburg.

Here is a vision of a seamless Christian society, to whose well-being both king and pope were bound together in a common effort.

Four years after this statement, at Christmas Mass in St Peter's Basilica, Pope Leo crowned Charlemagne Roman emperor. This barbarian king of a Germanic people received the title of emperor in an event whose full meaning still challenges modern scholarship. There had been no Roman emperor in the West since 487; the only emperor was the woman Irene, ruling the remnant of the old Roman Empire from Constantinople. Four comments can be made about this extraordinary happening in St Peter's. In the first place, whatever the internal confusion of Roman politics and the difficulties experienced by Pope Leo, the conferral of the imperial title had to have been Charlemagne's idea, and the tale told by his biographer decades later of a reluctant, surprised Charlemagne carries no conviction. Second, the conferral of this title by the pope may have followed the precedent of a pope fifty years earlier possibly conferring the title of king on Charlemagne's father. Third, an empire was not created that Christmas Day. The lands held by the Franks, considerably augmented as they had been by the Carolingians, did not now form an empire with imperial administration. What the Franks had held they continued to hold in the same way: a series of holdings each with its own structure of government, not unlike the Hapsburg holdings in the early modern period. And, fourth, the coronation of Charlemagne as emperor, as it were, crowned the alliance between the papacy and the Franks. It was further confirmed by his son Louis the Pious (814–40), when he met with Pope Stephen IV in Francia in 816 and entered into a 'pact of confirmation' (*pactum confirmationis*). Pope Stephen reanointed Louis much as an earlier pope had reanointed Pepin.

What needs to be emphasized amidst all these dates and events is that the Frankish kings took it as a *religious* responsibility to defend the papacy. That there were also political considerations few would deny, but these anointed figures from north of the Alps, themselves not many generations removed from worshipping trees and winds, defined their office as having a spiritual dimension. With reason did those at Charlemagne's court call him 'David'.

As an active, formal, treaty-based relationship, the Franco-papal alliance did not survive the collapse of Carolingian power. When the Carolingian lands were divided in 840 between the three sons of Louis the Pious, there began the process of dismemberment. One of these sons died in 855, and his kingdom was subdivided into three kingdoms. The process of dissolution and decline was well under way. The power of the local nobles, which was held under control by Charlemagne, now reasserted itself. The office of emperor was to be held by increasingly weak and insignificant descendants of Charlemagne. A meaningful alliance could not survive such shifts of political power.

The Carolingians and church practice

Einhard, in his biography, describes Charlemagne as a devout Christian:

> Charles practised the Christian religion with great devotion and piety,
> for he had been brought up in this faith since earliest childhood . . .
> As long as his health lasted he went to church morning and evening
> with great regularity, and also for early-morning Mass and for the
> late-night hours.
>
> (Bk 3, no. 26)

It is at the risk of the charge of moral arrogance that a historian would sit in judgement on the sincerity of Charles's religious practices or the depth of his spiritual life. Such knowledge lies beyond the reach even of the most imaginative among us. Yet the policies of the Carolingian state, shaped by its kings, affected the way in which the Christian religion was lived in the Frankish lands.

The consecrated kings of the Franks issued capitularies (each a series of chapters, *capitula*), which regulated both secular and religious matters, the two frequently mixed in the same capitulary. This concern for the state of religious practice can be seen most vividly in a capitulary of 789, generally referred to as *Admonitio generalis*, echoes of whose provisions can be heard in later legislation. It was directed entirely to religious affairs, the first such capitulary of Charlemagne's reign. We should back up fifteen years, to 774, when Charlemagne, while besieging the Lombard capital of Pavia, received from Pope Hadrian a collection of canon law. Essentially the collection which had been made by Dionysius Exiguus in the early sixth century, to which other canons had been added, it is now generally referred to as the *Dionysio-Hadriana*. Without doubt it was the basic collection of canon law used at Rome and, indeed, in other places as well. It became the basis of such law in the Frankish lands, and we are to find much of it in the *Admonitio generalis* of 789. The first sixty of the eighty-two articles that comprise this capitulary were drawn from the *Dionysio-Hadriana* and, in Professor McKitterick's words, form 'the basic outlines for the administration of the Frankish church'. The first chapter deals with excommunication, citing early general councils. The capitulary moves on to other matters. Bishops are told to investigate candidates for orders. Priests who say Mass and do not themselves receive communion act wrongly. Monks and clerics should not enter taverns to eat or drink, nor should they engage in business. No money should pass hands in the ordaining of bishops or priests. No one should become a bishop before his thirtieth year, because the Lord Jesus did not preach before his thirtieth year. Bishops should not admit slaves to the clerical state without the permission of their masters. And so it runs, directives applying to bishops, clergy and laity, all drawn from Hadrian's collection and applied to a Frankish setting. Yet there is more.

An additional twenty-two chapters reveal something of the Carolingian genius for originality and invention, perhaps as close as we can come to a Carolingian programme of church discipline and reform. The emphasis is clearly pastoral. Baptism and outward acceptance of Christianity is not enough: a knowledge of that faith is necessary in order to give it depth. Schools should be established at every monastery and every cathedral, where boys should read the psalms and books about grammar and music and numbers as well as 'Catholic books' (the scriptures) and where experienced copiers should prepare copies of the gospels, psalter and missal, if this is necessary. Priests should explain the Lord's Prayer to the people so that they will know what they are asking of God. Sunday was singled out in detail as a special day, a day free from usual occupations. On that day men should not work in the fields or vineyards or woods; nor should they sue pleas or hunt animals or build houses or tend their gardens. They may take bodies to be buried. Prohibitions also reveal much of what women did on the other days of the week: on Sundays they should not engage in weaving, making clothes, embroidering, carding wool, beating linen or doing laundry in public. Sunday should be an honoured day, a day of rest, when Christians go to Mass and praise God. And priests must instruct their people by preaching: how God is one and three, how God became man and will judge the dead, sending the wicked into eternal fire with the devil and the just into eternal life with Christ and the angels. They are to preach love of God and love of neighbour, faith and hope in God, the virtues of chastity and continence, kindness and mercy, concern for the poor, admission of one's sins and forgiveness of others, 'for it is by living in such a way that they will possess the kingdom of heaven'. A modern syllabus of sermon subjects could scarcely improve on this list issued by Charlemagne in 789.

Canon law was thus established as an element essential to the life of the Christian community. Ideals, expectations, *desiderata* are expressed in the canons. That they were always observed need hardly be believed, yet they stood as expressions of the order needed in a community of Christian believers and of the ideal that external behaviour conform to inner beliefs. In the generation after Charlemagne there was produced in the Frankish kingdom the most famous canonical collection of the period, and it was a forgery, known to us as the Pseudo-Isidorian Decretals. To say it was a forgery is to tell only part of the story. In fact, the collection is a patchwork of authentic laws and made-up laws, and the whole was taken for authentic. It contained real canons from real councils and real provisions from real papal decretals, but about a hundred decretals were falsely attributed to early popes and were the creation of the forger or, more likely, of a workshop of forgers, who produced the collection. It also provided the means by which the Donation of Constantine became known to subsequent centuries. Pseudo-Isidore was the creature of disputes in Francia between bishops and their metropolitan archbishop in the middle of the ninth century. Fingers can be pointed at the suffragan bishops of Hincmar of Rheims, the powerful, self-assertive, not wholly attractive metropolitan of that region. The collection may have arisen in an attempt of suffragan bishops to assert their own role as pastors of souls and, by asserting a direct connection with the pope, to try to thwart the attempts of the metropolitan to interfere in their dioceses.

Sections of Pseudo-Isidore were to have a long life when they were taken up by reforming popes in the eleventh century, particularly Urban II (1088–99), and by canonists then and later, who incorporated 'false decretals' in their collections of canons. The formative collection of Gratian (*c.*1140) contains 375 chapters drawn from this source. It should be quickly added that there is no reason to suspect that popes or canonists knew that they were dealing with forgeries. In any case, no matter what their origin, they were clearly used as instruments to support papal power.

The form of life for monks and clerics was seriously affected by the actions of the Carolingian kings. A variety of styles of monastic life gave way to an almost universal adoption of the Rule of St Benedict. Charlemagne was influential in the adoption of St Benedict's Rule in many monasteries east of the Rhine and in southern Gaul. Elsewhere monasteries tended to follow a mixed rule. It was not until the reign of his son Louis the Pious that the Rule of St Benedict won out. Central to Louis's efforts was another Benedict, Benedict of Aniane. Brought to Aachen by the new emperor-king, he presided over two meetings of abbots, in 816 and 817, which produced the Monastic Capitulary. Essentially this capitulary was an endorsement of the Rule of St Benedict; it ordered that this rule and only this rule be observed in monasteries. Imperial officials visited monasteries to insure that the capitulary was being obeyed. Yet, for all of Benedict of Aniane's strictures about observing St Benedict's Rule, what in fact emerged was Benedict's rule altered in ways that changed the simple form of life of pure Benedictinism. Now, thanks to the second Benedict, prayers were added to such an extent that monks spent vast amounts of time in choir and were consequently unable to perform the manual labour which was clearly part of St Benedict's vision of a monk's life. The balance of work and prayer was lost, and the liturgy was henceforth to dominate monastic life. The Monastic Capitulary was promulgated by the emperor in 817. Since its aim was to gain observance of the Rule by all Frankish monasteries, all abbots were ordered to have copies of the Rule made and to have the Rule read to their monks. The result was the emergence of the Benedictine form of monasticism as the standard in Western Europe.

In another way the life of monks was seriously changed. Hitherto the vast majority of monks were not priests and generally one conventual Mass would be celebrated daily for the community by a monk-priest. Now, however, two matters intersected. In the first place, more monks became priests and, secondly, in another innovation, each priest wanted to say Mass each day. Mass as private devotion was at odds with Mass as corporate worship, and with this innovation a corner had been turned in the history of Christian worship. And there were architectural consequences. Since not only the priest but also the altar had to fast before Mass, a multiplication of altars occurred in monastic churches, a phenomenon also occurring in other, non-monastic churches.

The mention of priests living in non-monastic churches brings us to the clergy living in the world (the 'secular' clergy). Their ministry was to care for the pastoral needs of the Christian people, and this they did in ways that are mostly hidden from our view. Some of the secular clergy lived in remote places in the country-side, baptizing, preaching and saying Masses in churches usually provided by the local lord. In English these churches are called proprietary churches and in German *Eigenkirchen*. It was from these that parishes would eventually develop; it was also from this practice of the local lord appointing the priest for his church that, in time, would lead to disputes about the lay appointment of priests and even bishops. Other members of the secular clergy lived in towns in communities gathered about principal churches, and some of these in cathedral cities where they lived with the bishop in his household. Chrodegang, bishop of Metz, *c.*755, drew up an influential rule for his household clergy. They were to live a common or conventual life, eating and sleeping in the same house, joining together for daily prayers, yet, not bound by a vow of poverty, they could own property. They were said to live according to the ancient canons and were thus called 'canons', and, since each day they would gather to hear the reading of a chapter of sacred literature, their community became known as a chapter. Other chapters of secular canons following Chrodegang's rule speedily appeared not only at other cathedrals but also at large churches like St Denis outside Paris. We are to hear more of this rule in the twelfth century. Chrodegang is also credited with introducing the Roman liturgy, especially Roman chants, into Metz.

It was the relationship of Charlemagne and Pope Hadrian that greatly influenced liturgical development. 'Sacramentaries' (i.e., books used by priests to celebrate Mass and to perform other rites) were commonplace in Francia at this time, but no uniform usage prevailed. About 786, in response to Charlemagne's request for an authentic text, Hadrian sent him a deluxe sacra-mentary, which probably reflected contemporary Roman usage. A supplement was added to the text to suit Frankish needs, quite possibly by the learned Alcuin of York. This text contained the text and rubrics for the Mass, the central liturgical act of the Christian religion, a re-enactment of the Last Supper, when Catholics believe that Jesus transformed bread and wine into his body and blood. In a quirk of history, in the course of the tenth century this Hadrianic text as supplemented by Alcuin or someone else and as refined by usage in Francia was introduced into Rome and became the historic Roman Rite, which remained in use with little change until the 1960s.

Lest one think that the Carolingian kings, particularly Charlemagne, always acted according to the high principles of Christian teaching, which they openly supported, this section must conclude with the sad tale of the forced conversion of pagan Saxons by the Christian king of the Franks. Attempts by the Franks to conquer the Saxons long predated the reign of Charlemagne (768–814) but invariably met with frustrating failures. To acquire Saxony made much strategic sense to the Franks. It would give them the lands north of Thuringia and east of the Rhine and would stop once and for all the Saxon raiding on their borders. It would also lead to the extension of Christianity to these heathen people. The campaigns began in earnest in 772 and continued with almost annual regularity for over thirty years, ranging from major military efforts to punitive raids. At war's end, the victorious Franks had extended their border to the Elbe River, even to its further bank. In one incident in 782 Charles, furious at the outcome of an earlier engagement, beheaded 4,500 Saxon prisoners in a single day. Although the figure should not be taken exactly, the chronicler is telling us that there was vast slaughter of unarmed prisoners ordered by the anointed king of the Franks. Massive deportations followed after subsequent campaigns. In a celebrated capitulary possibly of 782 death was decreed as the penalty for any Saxon who refused baptism: *morte moriaturus* ('he will die the death'). The same penalty applied to Saxons not only for burning the dead, for cannibalism and for human sacrifice but also for such sins as not observing the Lenten practice. In times of war only the rare voices of the very courageous are raised against the outrages of their own country. So it was in Francia during the Saxon wars. One might think Alcuin of York the consummate insider, the perfect bureaucrat, who combined intelligence, a worldly wisdom and a sensitivity to the words and wishes of his superiors, yet it was he who spoke up. Appalled at Charlemagne's treatment of the Saxons, he wrote for the emperor's attention:

> Faith must be voluntary not coerced. Converts must be drawn to the faith not forced. A person can be compelled to be baptized yet not believe. An adult convert should answer what he truly believes and feels, and, if he lies, then he will not have true salvation.

The conversion of the Saxons, not the happiest chapter in the history of the Franks, bears witness to what contemporary theologians would have called the universality of original sin and what moderns might describe as the dark side of our human nature.

The Vikings

A profound influence on historical Christianity was had by the warrior-seamen who left the islands and peninsulas of Scandinavia for overseas adventures and who gave their name to an epoch, the Viking Age. Out of fjords and viks (inlets) in their homelands, they sailed westward to the British Isles and further west to Iceland, Greenland and the shores of North America. They sailed southward, coursing through the river systems of the modern Low Countries and France. And they sailed eastward across the Baltic Sea and by river and portage reached deep into Russia. They sailed as pagans, as worshippers of anthropomorphic deities like Thor, the thunder god, Odin, the god of the spear, and Frey, the god of sexual pleasure. Unexpectedly, in the years surrounding 800, Vikings first appeared, raiding the coast of the British Isles and the north-western continental mainland. The reasons lying behind this sudden eruption of these forces from the far north still divide historians, but an explanation that includes a population factor has much to commend it. In a culture with massive polygamy a crisis of population can occur within even one generation. Much evidence exists that at

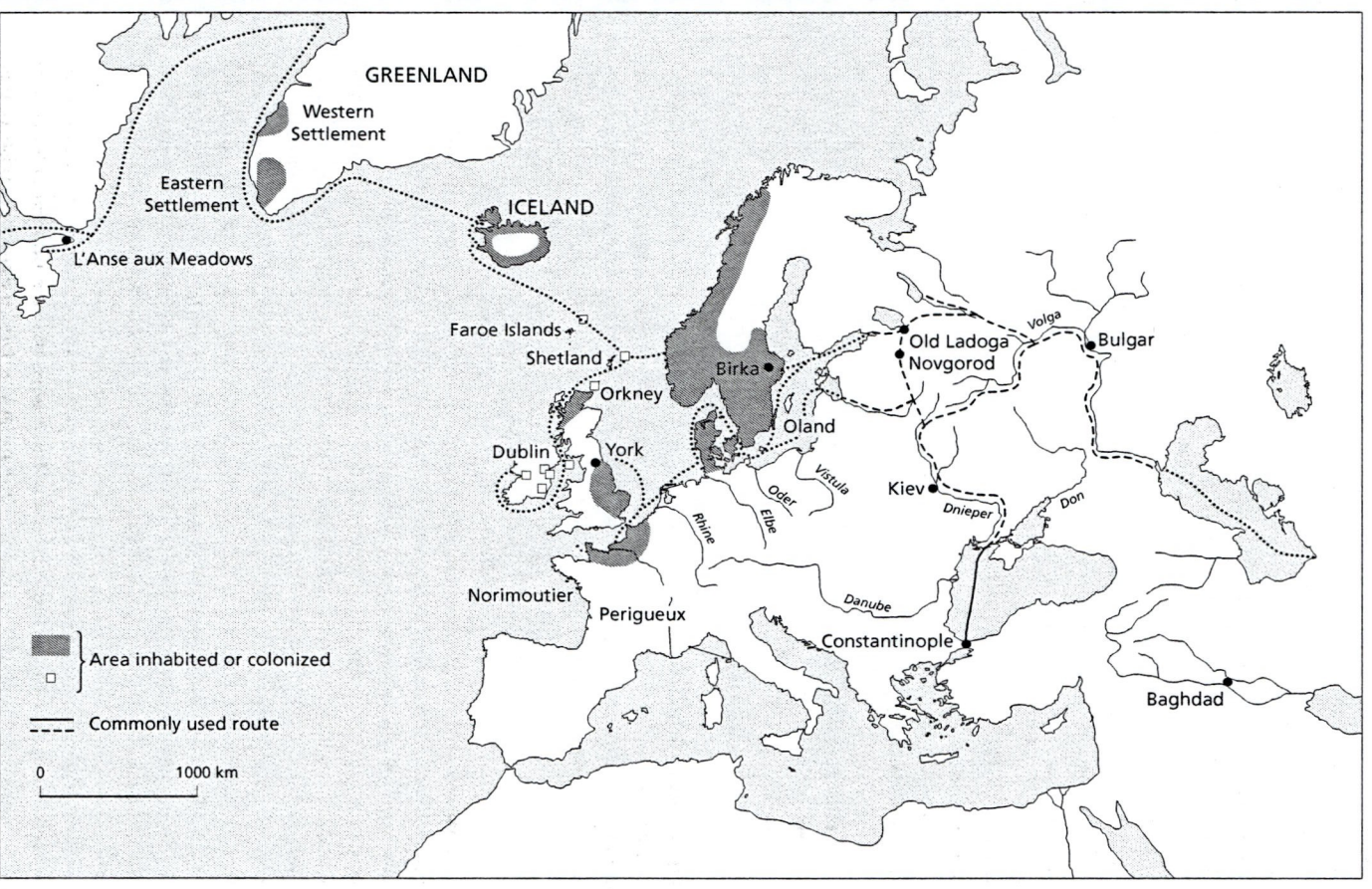

Map 6 Vikings.

this time land in Scandinavia was being used increasingly for crops intended for human consumption and that marginal lands were being cultivated, both fairly clear indications of a growing human population. A population crunch may have occurred at the turn into the ninth century. Whatever the reasons, these peoples of the sea soon took to the seas in search of land. Except in Iceland and Greenland, it was already largely occupied land which they wanted and which they took only after violent encounters with native inhabitants, who were almost invariably Christians.

It is not without significance that among the very first known attacks was the fierce Viking raid on the monastery at Lindisfarne in Northumbria, defenceless and open to the seas. Under the year 793 the *Anglo-Saxon Chronicle* reports:

> Dire portents appeared over Northumbria and sorely frightened the people. They consisted of immense whirlwinds and flashes of lightning, and fiery dragons were seen in the air. A great famine immediately followed these signs, and later in the same year, on 8th June, the ravages of heathen men miserably destroyed God's church on Lindisfarne with plunder and slaughter.

A later writer, using near contemporary sources, likened this attack on Lindisfarne to 'stinging hornets' and 'ravenous wolves' and recounted that the Vikings slew priests and nuns and destroyed everything in sight, including holy relics, and took with them some monks as slaves. Even the far-off Alcuin, the native Northumbrian by then in Francia, wrote seven letters in response to news of this raid. In the following year the Vikings were at Jarrow. Yet these were but incidents in larger movements. The Vikings were soon in the Orkney and Shetland islands and sailed down the west coast of Britain. In 794 they attacked the Hebrides and the famous island monastery at Iona. In the next year – these were summer raids – they attacked Iona again and the island of Skye and, across the Irish Sea, the island of Lambay, just north of Dublin, and even islands off the west coast of Ireland. Iona was attacked yet again in 802 and 806, and in the latter raid sixty-eight Irish monks were slain and the survivors abandoned Columba's monastery for Kells on the Irish mainland. And so the raids on Ireland continued not always against monastic sites but with a chilling regularity. In 823 they attacked Skellig Michael, the monastic sanctuary perched on rocks eight miles off the Kerry coast, and, at the other end of the island, the monastery at Bangor, Co. Down, where the relics of St Comgall were desecrated. In 832 alone the monastery at Armagh was attacked three times in one month. At about this same time Vikings gained access to the Irish heartland, sailing up the River Shannon, attacking the monastery at Clonmacnois. In 839 they burned the monastery at Cork. Such raids – and many others could be added to this litany of devastating attacks – were not against monasteries as monasteries (i.e., as places of Christian worship) but against monasteries as keepers of gold and silver vessels and as places containing prominent men, who could be held for ransom. Undefended monasteries were obvious targets. Both in Ireland and in England the Vikings were frequently referred to simply as 'heathens'.

Attacks by these 'heathens' were not confined to the British Isles. By 834 they were attacking in large numbers at Dorestad, the great entrepot situated where the Rhine and Lek then met, at the modern Wijk in the Netherlands, and they were there again in each of the next three years. The Vikings were soon penetrating the river systems of modern France and the Low Countries. Viking ships sailed up the Schelde in 836 and set fire to Antwerp. Their ships sailed into the Loire in 834, attacking the monastic island of Noirmoutier at the river mouth. They soon used it as a base for raids upriver: in 843 they reached Nantes, where, on the feast of St John the Baptist (24 June), they seized the bishop and slew him at the altar of his cathedral. And it was at Nantes, if we can believe later chronicles, that a scene of utter barbarity ensued. The Vikings killed whom they willed in a butchery of epic proportions, stopping only when, dripping with blood and laden with bloodied jewels, they returned to Noirmoutier. Other Vikings sailed up the Seine, where, in 841, they attacked Rouen and then the monastery of Jumièges, before seizing the monastery of St Wandrille and holding it for ransom. They harassed Paris and, later, in the 880s, besieged the town for a full year. And they were in other rivers: the Meuse, Scheldt, Somme and Dordogne. One contemporary lamented

> The fleets grow larger and the Vikings themselves grow and grow in number. On all sides Christian people suffer massacre and burning and plunder . . . The Vikings crush everything in their path: there is no defense. They capture Bordeaux, Périgeux, Limoges, Angoulême and Toulouse. They destroy Angers, Tours and Orléans . . . Ships beyond counting sail up the Seine, where evil prevails. Rouen is attacked, pillaged and burnt; Paris, Beauvais and Meaux are seized; the stronghold of Melun is razed; Chartres is occupied; Evreux and Bayeux are pillaged; and all the towns are attacked.

Monks, unprepared for such attacks, fled from such monasteries as St Maixent, Charroux, St Maur-sur-Loire and St Martin of Tours. For two generations fleeing monks could be seen on the roads leading to Burgundy, the Auvergne and Flanders, taking with them their 'saints', the canons of Tours carrying away the body of St Martin at least four times from the attacking heathens.

When peace was made with the Vikings, it was everywhere accompanied by the conversion of the heathens to Christianity. After the defeat of the Danes by King Alfred at Edington in 878, Guthrum, the Viking leader, whose army was still intact and still a threat, accepted baptism, and the conversion of his followers no doubt followed. When, in the following year, these Vikings crossed the country to 'share' out East Anglia, they did so as Christians. And, in the north of England, when the Viking king Guthfrith died c.895, he was buried beneath York Minster with full Christian rites. Integration in England was fairly swift. For example, Oda, archbishop of Canterbury (941–48), was the son of a Danish settler who had converted to Christianity. Thus Oda's nephew, St Oswald, the great monastic reformer, was the grandson of a pagan Viking. Three generations from hammer to cross: by any measure a rapid assimilation.

In Ireland, the tale that Brian Boru's Irish Christian army defeated the Viking pagan army at the Battle of Clontarf on Good Friday, 1014, and that the defeated Vikings accepted Christian baptism has much of fancy about it. There was a Battle of Clontarf on that day, but it was not between the Irish and the Vikings, between the Christians and the heathens: the battle was between two Irish factions, each of which had Viking contingents in its army. The process of assimilation in Ireland had already begun in the late ninth century with the intermarriage of some Viking leaders and Irish princesses, accompanied by the Vikings' conversion. Such marriages became more frequent from *c.*950 and continued apace both before and after Clontarf. In 1169, when other strangers came, they could not identify the Vikings, so complete was their assimilation: they were indistinguishable from the native Irish Catholics.

The situation in Francia warrants close examination. At least three attempts were made by the Vikings to establish permanent settlements. Only one was successful, in the lower Seine, and it is this part of Francia that still bears their name, Normandy. The exact date is not clear, but it was probably in 911 that the West Frankish king, Charles the Simple, made an agreement with the Viking leader, Rollo. The latter was allowed to settle that probably underpopulated region, and, in return, he became a Christian and promised to defend the lower Seine from future attacks, apparently from the Bretons and from other Vikings. Intermarriage between newly baptized Viking men and Christian Frankish women must have quickly followed. The Vikings took new, Christian names: Rollo became Robert; his daughter Geloc became Adèle; Thurstein of the Contentin became Richard; Stigand of Mézidon became Odo; and so forth. The son of Rollo, William Longsword, became so fervent a Christian that he had to be restrained from becoming a monk so that he could succeed his father. He married a Christian princess and his sister married a Christian prince. So swift was this integration that William's son (Rollo's grandson) had to be sent from Rouen to Bayeux to learn Viking ways. Thus in less than twenty-five years the Viking capital at Rouen was a French-speaking city. The younger sons of Norman lords who were to land in southern Italy and Sicily in the decades after 1016 were French, as was the Norman duke who was to sail with his army to England in 1066. The lords of Normandy were to establish monasteries, to lead the reforming movements of the eleventh century and, later, to be in the front ranks of Christian warriors who went to the Holy Land on crusade. The conversion and assimilation of the northmen in Francia proved to have a significant impact on the future of the medieval church.

An appraisal of the Vikings that stops here would tell only part of the story. Perhaps the most fascinating aspects of their achievements took place far, far west from the Seine estuary. Beyond Ireland and Scotland and the islands to the north,

Viking sailors discovered the empty land they called Iceland, empty, that is, except for Irish monks who lived in the south-west during summer seasons. Settlement on this land, the size of Ireland, followed almost immediately, and in the sixty years from 870 to 930 a substantial migration took place, principally from Norway itself but also from Norse settlements in the nearer Celtic lands, including some Celts, many of them slaves. It was a migration numbering in the tens of thousands, perhaps near 30,000. There was no assimilation needed, and their Christianization came from their Norse homeland. Tales were told that a sudden volcanic eruption in the year 1000 led the settlers to accept Christianity. More prosaically, mass conversion did take place in the year 1000 but came through two Icelandic chieftains, who had been converted at the court of King Olaf, who, as a Christian, had become king of Norway in 995. They were sent back to Iceland to establish Christianity as the official religion of the land. And, so, Gizur, a converted chieftain missionary, attended the general assembly held at their outdoor meeting place, the Law Rock. He and his supporters demanded official acceptance of the Christian religion. For twenty-four hours the Law Speaker pondered the issues and decreed that there should be but one religion in Iceland. All people should be baptized and should publicly be Christians, but, if they wished, they could privately be heathen. Heathenism soon faded away. Bishops were appointed at Skalholt (1056) and at Holar (1106). A codification of canon law was made in 1123, seventeen years before Gratian produced his Decretum at Bologna.

Beyond Iceland to the west the Vikings sailed, and not far behind them came the Christian religion. From western Iceland in 985 Eric the Red set sail westward for almost 450 miles, when he caught sight of an enormous land mass with imposing glaciers reaching to a height of 1,900 metres. He turned south, following the coast around Cape Farewell, east of which he found green, rich-looking land on deep fjords, reaching out from the mountains, a sight clearly reminiscent of Norway. Two settlements were made: one in the extreme south-west (the Eastern Settlement) and the other four hundred miles further north along the western coast (the Western Settlement). In a practice not unknown to modern land developers, Eric called this glaciered land 'Greenland'. In truth, the land in the south-west where the settlements lay was verdant and warmer then than now. Greenland's conversion to Christianity came as a result of the conversion of Iceland and, also, about the year 1000. The *Eric Saga* relates,

> Eric was loath to leave the old religion, but his wife, Thjodhild, was converted at once and had a church built at a distance from the farmstead, which was called Thjodhild's church. It was there that she and other converts would go to pray. Thjodhild refused to live with her husband after her conversion, and this greatly displeased him.

His displeasure might have abated as, in time, Eric too probably became a Christian. The Christian church flourished in Greenland. A diocese with a cathedral and a resident bishop was established at Gardar near Eiriksfjord in 1126, and bishops from Greenland travelled to Europe for ecumenical councils. A monastery of Augustinian canons and a nunnery of Benedictine nuns were both founded in the twelfth century. A total of twelve parish churches in the Eastern Settlement and four parish churches in the Western Settlement are signs of a vital, if small, Christian community. A thirteenth-century Norse book (*King's Mirror*) commented,

> The peoples in Greenland are few in number, since only part of the land is free enough from ice for human habitation. They are a Christian community with their own churches and priests. By comparison to other places it would form probably a third of a diocese: yet the Greenlanders have their own bishop owing to their distance from other Christian people.

For over four hundred years these two settlements were the westernmost part of the medieval, European, Christian world. And it ended sometime before 1500 without witnesses, its demise a historical puzzle. An explanation stressing severe climatic cooling and hostile relations with displaced native peoples might be near the mark. Writing in 1492, Pope Alexander VI spoke of a dimly remembered outpost of Christendom:

> The diocese of Gardar lies at the ends of the earth in the land called Greenland . . . It is reckoned that no ship has sailed there for eighty years and that no bishop or priest has resided there during this period. As a result, many inhabitants have abandoned the faith of their Christian baptism: once a year they exhibit a sacred linen used by the last priest to say Mass there about a hundred years ago.

The Vikings also reached into areas to the east of their northern homelands, but that story runs beyond the limits of this book.

Ironically more is known about the conversion process of Vikings who journeyed abroad than about the conversion of their kinsmen who stayed home. A few mileposts can be seen, but much of the northern landscape lies in a historical mist. Denmark was visited in the eighth century by Willibrord (above, pp. 65–6) with no success and in the ninth century by Ansgar only with limited success. The conversion of the Danish people occurred through the conversion of their king, Harald Bluetooth (*c*.960–*c*.987). His mother was Christian but his father a resolute pagan. It was probably upon becoming king that Harald accepted baptism. An early legend has it that a German missionary came to his court and a debate ensued. The Danes would accept Christ in their pantheon of God, it was argued, but just as one of many gods and as a god decidedly inferior to the chief gods. The missionary asserted one God and three divine persons. One might wonder how the theological subtleties of the doctrine of the Trinity sounded to Danish ears. In any case, the story runs that the missionary would be believed if he could pass the ordeal of fire. He placed his bare hand in a glove heated by fire. When he withdrew his hand, it was seen to have been unaffected by the ordeal, and Harald thereupon took baptism and decreed that Christianity was to be the sole religion of his kingdom. It is not only the cynical who can see here in the conversion of Harald a possible political motivation – a smoother relationship with the German emperor Otto. At Jelling, midway up the Danish peninsula, two remarkable stones stand as witnesses to the conversion of Denmark. One, the smaller, was erected by Gorm (Harald's father) to his wife; it bears the inscription: 'King Gorm did this in memory of his wife, Thyri, glory of Denmark.' No mention of her being a Christian and certainly no Christian symbols. The other, a larger stone about eight feet tall, contains a large figure of Christ and this inscription: 'King Harald had this stone made in memory of his father, Gorm, and his mother, Thyri, the same Harald who conquered all Denmark and Norway and who made the Danes Christian.' A simple act of state and the Danes were officially Christian, but the pastoral process of instruction in the new ways lies beyond our view.

Norway's conversion followed in the first third of the eleventh century, and, again, a king was involved or, rather, two kings, each called Olaf. The first, Olaf Tryggvason, fought in England in the last wave of Viking attacks, which began in the 990s. There in England, in 994, he became a Christian, the Anglo-Saxon Chronicle tells us, as part of a peace settlement after extensive raids in south-eastern England, and the English King Etheldred stood sponsor at Olaf's confirmation. Olaf returned home, probably in 995, intent on seizing the crown of Norway and converting his people to the Christian faith. He succeeded in the former and ruled Norway until 1000, but he only partially succeeded in the latter, and this success, as we have seen, was felt as far west as Iceland and Greenland. It was another Olaf – Olaf Haraldsson (1025–30), known to history as St Olaf – who made Norway Christian. Saint though he may be, his methods were far from benign: in Professor Jones's words, 'he executed the recalcitrant, blinded or maimed them, drove them from their homes, cast down their images and marred their sacred places.' Olaf organized a church which, at first, was to have bishops subject to the archbishop of Bremen, but, in time, Norway had its own archbishop at Trondheim, site of St Olaf's tomb, and the archbishop's jurisdiction extended as far west as the tiny diocese of Gardar in Greenland.

What happened in Sweden cannot be described in terms similar to those used to describe the conversion process in Denmark and Norway, namely, a king's conversion followed by his people's conversion. Sweden was different. It is true that a Swedish king called Olaf received baptism at the hands of an English missionary in 1008 and that his daughter married the converted King Olaf of Norway. Yet the conversion of the Swedish people did not follow. A long process of at least a century followed. Large areas of Sweden remained loyal to old gods and old ways. At Uppsala, site of a great pagan temple, worship and sacrifice (even human sacrifice) continued into the next century. Writing c.1075, Adam of Bremen recounts,

> It is customary to solemnize in Uppsala, at nine-year intervals, a general feast of all the provinces of Sweden. From attendance at this festival no one is exempted. Kings and people all and singly send their gifts to Uppsala and, what is more distressing than any kind of punishment, those who have already adopted Christianity redeem themselves through these ceremonies.

A diocese was established at Sigtuna, but in 1060 the bishop was driven out. Twenty years later the Christian King Inge refused to worship at Uppsala and had to flee for his life. In the opening years of the twelfth century the temple of Uppsala was destroyed and a Christian church, still surviving, rose on its site at what is now Old Uppsala.

Our story has taken us far into the future, beyond our general narrative. It is time now to return there to look at the state of the Christian religion more generally at the time of the break-up and, indeed, breakdown of the Carolingian synthesis and after. Back to Europe of the mid-ninth century.

Further reading

A general work containing several essays relevant to this subject is Rosamond McKitterick (ed.), *The New Cambridge Medieval History*, vol. 2, *c. 700–c. 900* (Cambridge, 1995). Three other studies by Professor McKitterick can also be profitably consulted: *The Frankish Church and the Carolingian Reforms, 789–895* (London, 1977), *The Frankish Kingdom under the Carolingians* (London, 1983) and 'Nuns' Scriptoria in England and Francia in the Eighth Century', in *Books, Scribes and Learning in the Frankish Kingdoms, 6th–9th Centuries* (ed. R. McKitterick; Aldershot, Hants, 1994). Also, the general subject is treated in Heinrich Fichtenau, *The Carolingian Empire* (tr. Peter Munz; Oxford, 1957) and J.M. Wallace-Hadrill, *The Frankish Church* (Oxford, 1983). An excellent discussion of the Franco-papal alliance is Thomas F.X. Noble, *The Republic of St Peter: The Birth of the Papal State, 680–825* (Philadelphia, 1984). An important article which questions the traditional view of the events of 751 is Rosamond McKitterick, 'Illusion of Power in the Carolingian Annals', *English Historical Review* 115 (2000), 1–20.

Lives of Charlemagne can be found in convenient English translation; for example, Einhard and Notker the Stammerer, *Two Lives of Charlemagne* (tr. Lewis Thorpe; Harmondsworth, Middlesex, 1969). Translations of key documents (e.g., the Donation of Constantine) can be found in S.Z. Ehler and J.B. Morrall (eds), *Church and State Through the Centuries* (London, 1954).

The best general work on the liturgy remains Joseph A. Jungmann, *The Mass of the Roman Rite: Its Origins and Development (Missarum Sollemnia)* (Eng. tr.; London, 1959). See also H.A. Wilson (ed.), *The Gregorian Sacramentary under Charles the Great* (Henry Bradshaw Society, vol. 49, 1915).

For general works on the Vikings see Gwyn Jones, *A History of the Vikings* (2nd edn; Oxford, 1984), F. Donald Logan, *The Vikings in History* (2nd edn; London, 1991) and Peter Sawyer (ed.), *The Oxford Illustrated History of the Vikings* (Oxford, 1997). A useful work of reference is Phillip Pulsiano (ed.), *Medieval Scandinavia: An Encyclopedia* (New York, 1993). For Iceland the standard work is Dag Strömbäck, *The Conversion of Iceland:*

A Survey (Viking Society for Northern Research, 1975), to which should be added Jenny Jochens, 'Late and Peaceful: Iceland's Conversion through Arbitration in 1000', *Speculum* 74 (1999), 621–55, and Orri Vésteinsson, *The Christianization of Iceland: Priests, Power, and Social Change, 1000–1300* (Oxford, 2000). For Greenland two works stand out: Finn Gad, *The History of Greenland*, vol. 1, *Earliest Times to 1700* (London, 1970), and Kirsten A. Seaver, *The Frozen Echo* (Stanford, 1996). A book of much helpful detail is Tore Nyberg, *Monasticism in North-Western Europe, 800–1200* (Aldershort, Hants, and Burlingon, VT, 2000).

6

THE CHURCH IN DISARRAY,
c.850–*c*.1050

The disintegration of the Carolingian Empire had serious consequences for the church. When the three surviving sons of Louis the Pious (d. 840) divided the so-called empire – it never did have a unified imperial structure – into three parts, it presaged further divisions. The holdings of one of these sons were soon divided into three parts, and so it went on. Internecine rivalries, outright civil war, Frankish inheritance customs – all contributed to the centrifugal force that destroyed the Carolingian political structure. Whatever there was of central government died with Louis the Pious. The title 'emperor' continued to be used by men with less and less power until it was held by such deservedly obscure petty Italian kings as Wido (891–94) and Berengar (915–24). With the death of the latter, the title ceased to be used, and almost no one noticed. The Carolingian dynasty that had produced great leaders such as Pepin, Charlemagne and even Louis the Pious was reduced to small men with embarrassing sobriquets: the Bald, the Stammerer, the Fat, the Simple and the Child, to which one is tempted to add 'the Irrelevant'. In what was to become Germany real power rested in the duchies. In what was to become France real power was in the hands of local strongmen.

This atomization of political power was true not only in the Carolingian orbit but even beyond. England was little more than a geographical expression to describe where the Anglo-Saxons lived, themselves organized into many kingdoms, and the man called Alfred the Great (d. 899) was great only in the kingdom of Wessex, although it is true to add that by the 950s England appears as a fledgling political unit. Ireland, Scotland and the British parts of Britain continued to have tribal structures of government. Personal safety and security were not to be had from far-away men with titles but, rather, from local lords with local interest and, above all, with effective power. Europe was in pieces.

Local, too, was the governance of the Christian church. The overarching juris-diction of the bishop of Rome as pope was not consciously challenged by local bishops. Yet, in the environment which saw the weakening of the power of the kings, the stressing of local connections and, indeed, the difficulties encountered in communications, the papacy, particularly after the death of Nicholas (d. 867),

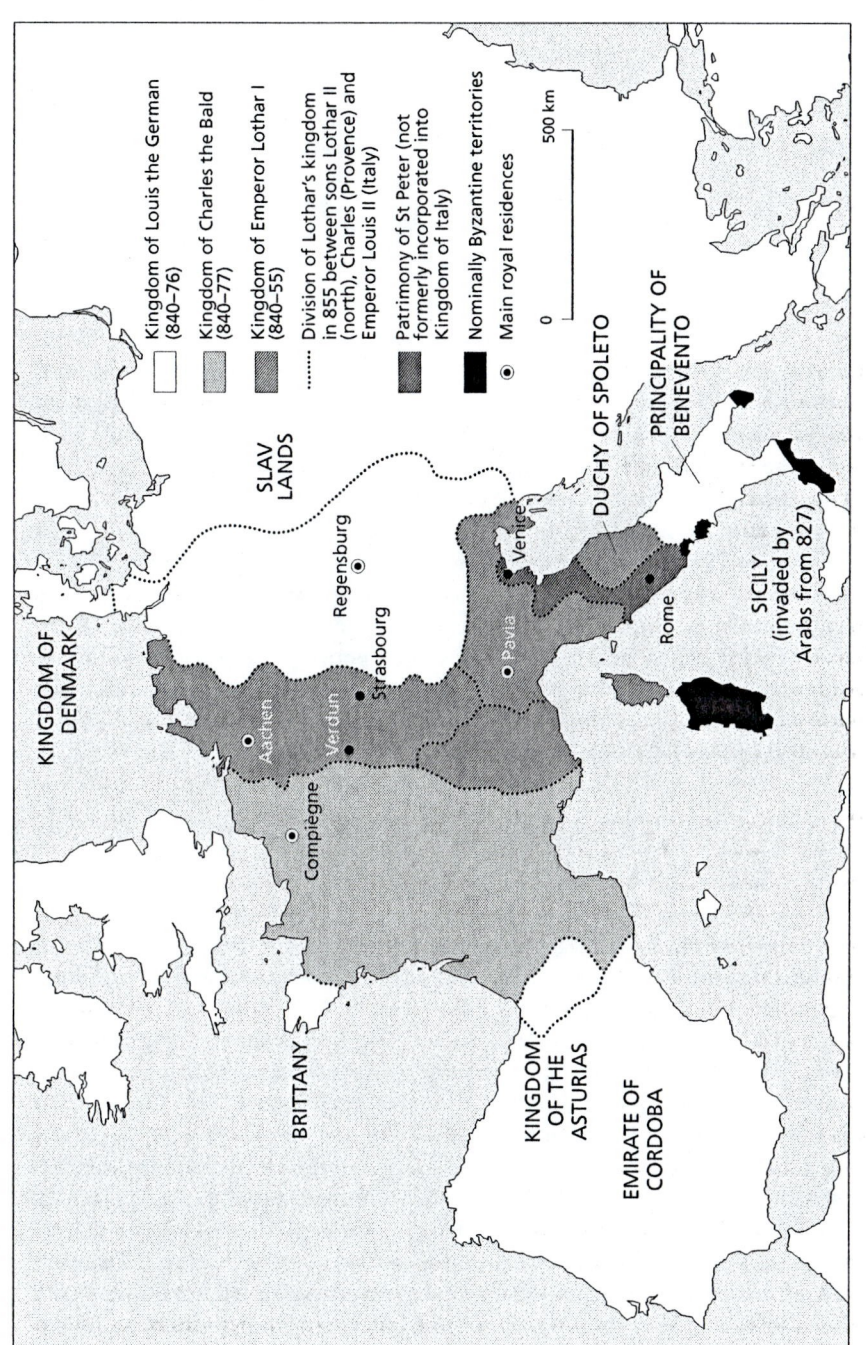

Legend:

- Kingdom of Louis the German (840–76)
- Kingdom of Charles the Bald (840–77)
- Kingdom of Emperor Lothar I (840–55)
- Division of Lothar's kingdom in 855 between sons Lothar II (north), Charles (Provence) and Emperor Louis II (Italy)
- Patrimony of St Peter (not formerly incorporated into Kingdom of Italy)
- Nominally Byzantine territories
- Main royal residences

0   500 km

KINGDOM OF DENMARK

SLAV LANDS

Regensburg

Strasbourg

Aachen

Verdun

Pavia

Compiègne

BRITTANY

Venice

DUCHY OF SPOLETO

Rome

PRINCIPALITY OF BENEVENTO

SICILY (invaded by Arabs from 827)

KINGDOM OF THE ASTURIAS

EMIRATE OF CORDOBA

Map 7 Carolingian lands after division, 843.

can be described as passive, rarely taking the initiative to involve itself in remote churches, even in Italy. Although it may be going too far to speak of a 'federal church', it is eminently clear that local churches looked to their own affairs, and tensions frequently became evident between local bishops and their metropolitans. In Rome the weakened papacy became the plaything of local Roman political factions. If Europe had fallen apart, so too had the church.

No attempt will be made here to tell in narrative form a connected story of the church in these dark centuries. The surviving documention is so exceedingly thin and fragmented that an adequate narrative is close to impossible and could give the impression that there was order, when in reality there was considerable disorder. While other approaches could be profitably taken, here we shall take as examples of the general disarray of the church four popes, who ruled at various times in this darkest of periods for the church. It will not be a continuous story of the popes. Instead, there will be recounted the pontificates of popes who ruled at various points in this period: through them we can see some of the issues facing the church in general, and, further, they can show dramatically the descent of the papacy in power and influence from the height of Nicholas I to successors who were frequently little more than the puppets of local Roman strong men and women. Those historians who would plot the history of the papacy on a chart would almost all agree that, whatever other low points there were in the history of that institution, the absolute nadir would be the period from the late ninth century to the middle of the eleventh century. The papacy was not the church, but we may let these four popes serve for us as prisms through which we can get a partial and admittedly inadequate view of the church in its sorriest days since the early Roman persecutions.

Pope Nicholas I (858–67)

An argument could be made that Nicholas I was the greatest pope between Gregory the Great (590–604) and Gregory VII (1073–85). Nicholas was to live out his pontificate on a large stage, the last of the popes to do so for well over a century and a half. He is better seen as the last in a series of strong popes beginning with Gregory the Great rather than as the harbinger of the powerful popes of a later period. Like Gregory the Great, he was son of a senior Roman official. Associated with the three previous popes, Nicholas, still a deacon, was elected pope at the age of about thirty-eight. At that time (858) Louis II bore the title 'emperor', but his real power was limited to only one part of the central kingdom carved out for his father in 843. Yet Louis exercised influence in Rome and had hastened to Rome when he learned of the death of the late pope. The extent of his influence on Nicholas's election is difficult to measure, but it is safe to say that Nicholas would not have been elected by the clergy and nobility of Rome had Louis opposed it. Quickly ordained a priest, Nicholas was consecrated bishop of Rome and, thus, pope, on 24 April 858. Two days later at a solemn banquet he and the emperor embraced.

Almost at once Nicholas faced a serious problem in one of the Frankish kingdoms. The emperor's brother, King Lothar II of Lotharingia (or Lorraine), the Middle Kingdom between the East and West Franks, renounced his queen, Theutberga, claiming that she had committed incest with her own brother and then aborted the foetus conceived of their coitus. She was banished to a nunnery, and the king married his lover, Waldrada, who had borne him a son. The exiled queen escaped from the nunnery and appealed to the pope. Nicholas sent legates to Metz in Lotharingia to resolve the matter. Possibly under the influence of bribery, they found for the king. When the two great archbishops of the kingdom (Cologne and Trier) brought this decision to Rome, Nicholas deposed and excommunicated them. Lothar's brother, the 'emperor' Louis, supporting Lothar, marched on Rome in 864, and his troops violently assaulted the clergy entering St Peter's in procession and threw to the ground the great relic of the holy cross. The attack failed to sway the pope, and Lothar, in 865, bowing to circumstances, reconciled with Theutberga, although she later pleaded with Nicholas unsuccessfully to annul the marriage. Nicholas's successor had to deal with both Theutberga and Waldrada, but the death of Lothar followed by the entrance of both women into convents, ended this sorry affair. Lothar had been opposed in this matter by two of his uncles, kings of the lands to his east and west, who may have desired to carve out large chunks of Lothar's middle kingdom, and, in this reading, the pope was a player, himself calculating the place of the papacy in a new political order and, in turn, getting a lesson in late Carolingian politics.

Two great archbishops of the Western church challenged the authority of Nicholas I and with no more success than the Frankish rulers. Hincmar, archbishop of Rheims, the most powerful churchman in the kingdom of the West Franks, then ruled by Charles the Bald, and a man of considerable learning, particularly in the law, had supported Lothar in his marital concerns. Hincmar came into more direct conflict with the pope over his treatment of Rothad, his suffragan bishop of Soissons. In 861, the archbishop restored an adulterous priest of Soissons, whom Rothad had deposed, and imprisoned his replacement. Rothad strongly objected to what he considered the metropolitan's interference and appealed to the pope. At Hincmar's instigation a synod at Soissons summoned Rothad, who, citing his appeal, rightly refused to appear; he was summarily dismissed as bishop, imprisoned and replaced by another bishop. The matter was joined. Nicholas became indignant, firing off letters to Hincmar, Charles the Bald and others. Hincmar must either reinstate Rothad or appear at Rome either personally or by a representative; failure to do so would result in the archbishop being suspended from saying Mass. The archbishop released Rothad but delayed in restoring him. New papal letters went to Hincmar, who finally capitulated and restored the aged Rothad to the bishopric of Soissons. In Hincmar's words, 'What Nicholas has decided I have not contradicted, but, as he commands, I have diligently obeyed.' Nicholas prevailed over Hincmar, Rome over Rheims.

Nicholas was also much preoccupied with another archbishop, and whether he won a moral victory or merely a political victory the reader may judge. The dispute concerned the archbishop of Ravenna. Ravenna had been made the capital of the empire in the West in 402 and, after its recapture from the Lombards by the forces of the Byzantine emperor, its power became restricted mainly to the area of the exarchate (around Ravenna) and to parts of Sicily and southern Italy. By the time of Nicholas I Ravenna had long since fallen to the Franks, and the archbishop's pretension of a special place supposed a political order no longer existing. Such pretensions collided with the claims of power of the bishop of Rome. At least, that was the spin put on events by contemporary papal historians. Archbishop John VIII of Ravenna, like his predecessors, enjoyed more than the usual archiepiscopal independence of Rome, to which must be added that he also enjoyed a close relationship with Emperor Louis II. Papal agents at Ravenna were allegedly mistreated by the archbishop and papal property there seized. Whether theological issues really mattered or whether the matter really concerned papal muscle-flexing we cannot tell, but charges of heresy were made against the archbishop, who was said to believe that, when Jesus suffered on the cross, he suffered as God and that baptism did not have the same effects on all who received it. Archbishop John was summoned to Rome in 861 to answer these and other charges. He refused to go and was excommunicated. Pope Nicholas, in an extraordinary move, journeyed to Ravenna to remonstrate with the archbishop face to face, but, wisely, John fled to the comfort of the imperial court at Pavia. Yet, now excommunicate, John found his position perilous even there. Virtually abandoned by Louis II, he went later that year to Rome for a humiliating submission. More significant than alleged theological aberrations – after all, the soaring rhetoric of a preacher might not always pass doctrinal scrutiny – was the matter of John of Ravenna's relations with his suffragan bishops. Four further charges surfaced at Rome: (i) that he had interfered in episcopal elections, (ii) that, when on visitations, he would come with 500 men on horseback, demanding provisions for their needs, and would not leave until bribed to do so, (iii) that he claimed jurisdiction over monasteries in their dioceses and (iv) that he prevented his suffragan bishops from visiting Rome. The council that reconciled the archbishop formally forbade him from indulging in such practices. There the matter seemed to end.

The presence of strong regional archbishops at Rheims and Ravenna did not eclipse the authority of Pope Nicholas, nor should the power and influence of these metropolitans inflate, for us, their roles in contemporary events. They were major players but only in a secondary way: centre stage had only room for Nicholas. Hincmar and John were regional figures in a fragmented world. Some may say that Hincmar and John were but big fish in small ponds, which would be unfair particularly to Hincmar, who would almost certainly be considered a great churchman in any age. Yet Nicholas's world was much, much larger.

It is for his relations with the Eastern Church, if for nothing else, that Pope Nicholas will be remembered. The ancient patriarchates of Antioch, Alexandria and Jerusalem were by now in Muslim hands. Only the patriarchate of Constantinople remained powerful, its patriarch closely allied with the Byzantine emperor. The patriarch's attitude to Rome was characterized by theoretical deference but practical independence. Under Nicholas I a crisis occurred, for which the pope bears much of the responsibility. In the shorthand way in which we deal with historical events, historians have traditionally called this crisis the 'Photian Schism'. We shall soon see how inappropriate this label is.

Events in the East drew the pope into this dispute, not inevitably, for Nicholas could have remained in dignified aloofness to these events, but he chose not to. When Michael III became Byzantine emperor in 842, he was but three years old, and his mother, Theodora, ruled as regent. In 847 she appointed a new patriarch without observing the formalities of an electoral synod. The new patriarch was Ignatius, son of a former emperor, who, at his father's death, had been castrated and sent to a monastery. His fate was tied to that of Theodora. When Michael III asserted himself in 857, he banished his mother to a nunnery and his patriarch into exile. Forced to resign, Ignatius was to remain not far off stage while events were played out. A synod met and elected the learned layman Photius as patriarch. Breaking with recent custom, Photius wrote to Pope Nicholas, informing him of his election. A more diplomatic pope might have answered with gracious words to the new patriarch, but, for reasons not fully clear to us, Nicholas's response was hostile and provocative. Why was he not consulted about the deposition of Patriarch Ignatius? And why was a layman selected as patriarch? Two papal legates were sent East to protest at these matters. Without waiting for further instructions from the pope, once in Constantinople in 861, they agreed to act as mediators between Photius and Ignatius. Although they were later charged with having acted beyond their briefs, they found that Ignatius was validly deposed and that Photius was the true patriarch. Pope Nicholas, furious at the legates' action, held a synod at Rome in 863, at which Photius was deposed and deprived of all his ecclesiastical dignities. Two years later, in response to a letter from the emperor, Pope Nicholas wrote a letter, which, in Professor Dvornik's words, 'was destined to be one of the most important documents in the evolution of the papacy'. A forceful, exuberant, even belligerent letter, it began ominously by addressing the emperor as 'our son'. There followed an assertion of the divinely given universal powers of the Roman church.

> The privileges of the Roman church came from the mouth of Christ, who conferred them on Blessed Peter. They can in no way be diminished, infringed upon or changed, because what God has established man cannot change . . . These privileges existed before you became emperor and will remain after you . . . They were given to the holy church by Christ and not by synods . . . We are constituted princes over every land, that is to say, over the church universal.

It concluded by telling the emperor not to meddle in ecclesiastical affairs. Echoing statements of earlier popes such as Leo I (440–61) and Gelasius (492–96), the words of Nicholas I were to have a long life as they were to be adopted by later canonists to describe papal power. As an attempt to heal the growing division, the papal letter not surprisingly failed. And other events added to the brewing discord.

History like life can have its complications, and here, in this dispute, the complication was Bulgaria. The Bulgars, a people of Turkic, Asian origin, had migrated from north of the Black Sea to the lands south of the lower Danube and had by the late ninth century become largely Slavic in language and culture through the twin forces of subjugation and intermarriage. In the 860s their king, Boris (852–89), felt the attractions of Christianity. His motives may have been exclusively political, although a story relates that he was deeply moved by a painting of hell on his wall, the work of a Byzantine monk, and, in fact, he did retire to a monastery three years before his death. Peace with the great Christian powers was also a strong motive. Whatever the reasons, in 864 Boris was baptized by the Byzantine patriarch, Photius, with the emperor as his godfather. (It is ironic that only half a century earlier one of Boris's predecessors had slain an emperor and made a drinking-cup of his skull). When the Byzantines refused to appoint a patriarch for the Bulgars, Boris, already fearful of his Byzantine neighbours, turned to Rome and to Pope Nicholas I. The bishop of Porto, Formosus, was quickly dispatched to Bulgaria, bearing with him 106 papal answers to questions of a pastoral nature proposed by King Boris. Had the Roman mission been successful, these answers might have become as famous historically as Gregory the Great's responses to Augustine of Canterbury and the papal responses to Boniface in Germany. As it is, they are but footnotes, known principally by the inclusion of some parts in later canon-law collections. This mission from Rome to Bulgaria greatly exercised emperor and patriarch in the East: the Eastern church had received Boris as a Christian, and the Bulgars were immediate neighbours. The Roman mission was viewed from Constantinople as a mischievous intervention. As a result, relations between Rome and Constantinople, already bad, were made worse. Pope Nicholas refused Boris's request that Formosus be made archbishop of the Bulgars. For this reason and for other reasons the Roman mission to Bulgaria failed, and Bulgaria entered the world of the Eastern church, where it has remained ever since. This short-lived crisis over Bulgaria served to intensify the growing tensions, suspicions and animosity between Rome and Constantinople, between Pope Nicholas and Patriarch Photius.

In this atmosphere, Photius presided over a synod in Constantinople during the summer of 867, the business of papal involvement in Bulgaria now added to the boiling cauldron of Byzantine discontent with Nicholas. The synod condemned, excommunicated and deposed Pope Nicholas. We have now all the ingredients for a major break (or schism) between the Christian churches of the East and West – the pope and patriarch each excommunicating and deposing the other – yet a schism did not occur. Two deaths prevented it. Emperor Michael III was assassinated on 24 September 867. The new emperor deposed Photius and, on 3 November, reinstalled Ignatius. Pope Nicholas I died on 13 November without learning of his condemnation by the synod of Constantinople or of the death of the emperor and reinstatement of Ignatius. Thus, by the time of Nicholas's death the synod's actions had been reversed by a *coup d'état*. Yet, even after Nicholas's death, events in the East continued to percolate, and these underline the historical inappropriateness of the expression 'Photian Schism'. When Ignatius died in 877, he was succeeded as patriarch by none other than Photius, whose election was blessed by the pope of the day. There then followed a return to the status quo which had existed before Nicholas I, a relationship with its almost inevitable rivalries and disagreements. The real break was not to occur until the middle of the eleventh century.

Paradoxically, while Nicholas was disputing with Photius about Bulgaria and other matters, he took an interest in the work of two Byzantine missionaries to the Slavic peoples. The brothers Cyril (originally Constantine) and Methodius had been sent by Emperor Michael III and Patriarch Photius to preach to the Slavs in central Europe. In fact, Methodius was a protégé of Photius. Nicholas I, in 867, invited them to Rome. They arrived only after Nicholas's death, and his successor consecrated Methodius as an archbishop and Cyril died in Rome. They had already translated the Bible and liturgical books into Slavonic (i.e., Old Church Slavonic) and disputed with clerics, East and West, about the appropriateness of a vernacular liturgy. Cyril said, 'If I pray in a language that I do not understand, I am prayerful only in spirit and not in understanding.' (The Latin church sanctioned a vernacular liturgy only in 1963.) Their mission, in a sense, failed, but they succeeded in being the principal architects of Slavic as a written language with its own alphabet. The conversion of the Slavs was to come through the conversion of the Slavs in Bohemia and through their missionary efforts, led by their nobles, most notably Duke (and Saint) Wenceslaus, but it was not until 973 that a bishopric was established at Prague. Owing to a marital arrangement with a Bohemian princess, the king of Poland was baptized in 966 and his nation became the easternmost part of a Western, Latin church.

The death of Pope Nicholas I in 867 saw the departure from the scene of the strongest pope of the ninth century, whose interests went far beyond Italy and the remnants of the Carolingian Empire. He had a grander view of his role. He spoke with kings and wrote to emperors and patriarchs and dealt with strong archbishops. Bulgars, Slavs and Greeks were part of his vision of his office. His place in history is diminished because of what happened to the papacy in the next century and a half, glimpses of which we shall see presently, and they provide a stark contrast.

Formosus (891–96)

The first and, for reasons that will soon become clear, the last of that name, Formosus is more remembered today for his posthumous life than his real life. He has been met already as the bishop of Porto dispatched by Pope Nicholas I to Bulgaria. After his return to Italy, as bishop of Porto, Formosus served several popes as an adviser until a moment in the pontificate of the hapless Pope John VIII (872–82), when he was excommunicated and stripped of his office by the pope himself. The intrigues that produced this state of affairs are unknown to us, but Formosus, the now ex-bishop of Porto, fled to France. When John VIII went north and convened a synod at Troyes, Formosus was brought before him and made to swear that he would never attempt to regain his office nor would he ever return to Rome. In 882, one of Pope John's relatives apparently failed in an attempt to poison the pope and then proceeded to bludgeon him to death with a hammer. His successor (Marinus I, 882–84) absolved Formosus of the oaths taken at Troyes and restored him to his bishopric at Porto. When the papal see fell vacant in 891, Formosus was chosen, apparently by the clergy and people of Rome without any outside influence. That he was already a bishop was later to prove a source of controversy. The custom of both East and West held a bishop to be 'married' to his bishopric, from which there could be no divorce. The transfer (or *translation* to use the legal word) of bishops from one diocese to another was virtually unknown. Before the accession of Formosus in 891 only one pope is known to have been previously bishop of another see and translated to Rome: Pope Marinus I, when elected in 882, was bishop of Caere (modern Cerveteri) in Etruria, but his was a short reign – of perhaps less than a year and a half – and was without incident. The matter of the translation of Formosus from Porto to Rome was to pursue Formosus beyond the grave.

Once elected and installed on the papal throne, Pope Formosus found himself involved in the petty political squabbles in Italy. The dukes of Spoleto had desired the imperial title, and the previous pope had crowned Duke Wido as emperor. The ruling family of Spoleto prevailed on Formosus within months of his election not only to recrown Wido but also to crown Wido's son Lambert as co-emperor. To relieve this pressure from Spoleto, Formosus, in 893, invited Arnulf, the Carolingian king of the East Franks (which we can now call Germany), to come to Italy to deliver Italy from 'bad Christians' (the Spoletans). In early 894 Arnulf's invasion fell victim to fever. Shortly thereafter Wido died and Lambert became sole emperor, but the real power lay with his mother, Agiltrude. It was she who, in October 896, took control of the defence of Rome against another invasion by Arnulf. He marched on Rome only to find that Agiltrude had imprisoned the pope and closed the gates to the city. The German army battered their way through the gates, scaled the city walls and soon liberated Rome and freed Pope Formosus. The pope led the German king into St Peter's Basilica and there placed the imperial crown on his head, calling him 'Caesar Augustus'. On his way home the newly crowned emperor died, and, before news of his death reached Rome, Formosus himself had died.

There the story might end, another mediocre pope, ruling the church in troubled times, a pope little different from his immediate predecessors and successors. But the story does not end there. In the next eight years there were nine popes. Formosus's immediate successor, Boniface VI, a man already twice degraded for immoral behaviour, lived only two weeks. It is to Boniface's successor, Stephen VI, that we must look for the sequel of the story of Formosus. With Arnulf and Formosus both dead, Lambert and his mother, Agiltrude, retook Rome. It is difficult to view the new pope as anything but their puppet, and he would exact for them their revenge against Formosus. Pope Stephen ordered the grave of Formosus to be opened and the body exhumed. By then, nine months or so after his death, the body, although intact, exhibited to the senses all the indications of a corrupting cadaver. The pope ordered the body to be clad in the full vesture of a pope and set on a chair in the basilica of St John Lateran, where a Roman synod in January 897 sat in judgement. Two charges were made against 'him': first, he had broken the oath taken at Troyes, and, second, he had illegally moved as bishop from one diocese to another. Unable to speak in response, Formosus was represented by a callow deacon, whose arguments lacked persuasion. Formosus – or, rather, the body of Formosus – was condemned, and he was literally defrocked as the vestments of his office were one by one torn from his decaying body. The fingers of his right hand used in blessing were hacked off and his body thrown into a common grave. Contemporary sources bear unanimous testimony to these macabre events. But the body of Formosus had not yet found rest. It was disturbed apparently by grave robbers, who, seeing this fresh grave, dug it open in the hope of finding treasures. Instead they found a mutilated, unadorned body. In disgust, they cast it into the Tiber River. One contemporary relates that torrential rains that very night caused a flooding of the Tiber and that the body of Formosus was carried downstream, coming ashore at Porto. It was said that a monk, following the instructions given him in a vision, found the body and secretly buried it at Porto. Meanwhile, back at Rome, Stephen VI had been seized by his enemies, put in chains, placed in prison and strangled to death. At about this time an earthquake caused the roof of St John Lateran, scene of the trial, to fall in. The new pope, Romanus, lived only two months, dying in November 897. The next reign was even shorter – the twenty-day reign of Theodore II – but it was long enough to effect the rehabilitation of Formosus. Pope Theodore learned what had happened at Porto and ordered the body to be again exhumed. With reverence and, finally, dignity the body was solemnly returned from Porto to Rome. There it was reclad in papal vestments and, with solemn obsequies, replaced in its original tomb in St Peter's, where it still rests.

Not only the body of a pope but the papacy itself suffered in these unedifying doings, and the papacy was to persist for a dozen decades and more in this unhealthy state. The political context contributed to this condition. The power and even the title of emperor in the West did not exist. Italy, like much of the rest of Europe, was ruled by local factions. And the local faction that ruled Rome ruled the papacy. The Crescenzi, the Theophylact and the Tusculani families were chief among the contesting powers, seeking control of Rome. They made popes even from their own families, the papacy little more than an adjunct to their power base. Tension and its attendant violence were never far away. When, for example, Leo V became pope in 903 he was almost immediately overthrown and cast into prison by a priest, Christopher, who then called himself pope and whom history calls an anti-pope. Very soon a bishop named Sergius descended on Rome with an armed force, cast Christopher into prison, murdered both Leo and Christopher and declared himself Pope Sergius II. So closely connected with the Theophylact family was Sergius that he fathered a son by Marozia, the fifteen-year-old daughter of that family, a son who, in 931, was himself created pope (John XI) by his own mother. The papacy was at its lowest point ever in the century and a half after the cadaver synod that condemned the rotting bones of Pope Formosus.

Pope John XII (955–64)

In 955, a teenager became pope: a certain Octavian, who, among the first to do so, changed his name and became John. His grandmother was the same Marozia whose papally sired son had become Pope John XI. Octavian's father, half-brother of John XI, was Marozia's legitimate son, and by the 950s he was ruler of Rome. On his deathbed he coerced the (willing) Romans to promise to elect his son Octavian pope at the next vacancy. In the event, only months elapsed before the papal see became vacant, and 'the people and clergy of Rome' did his bidding. No matter that Octavian was only eighteen years old. No matter too that he was notorious for his debauched behaviour and for his lack of spiritual feeling. He was a cardinal deacon and promptly became priest and bishop of Rome, all within days. And, in a short time, if we can believe his enemies – and here perhaps we should – he had turned the papal palace into a bordello. That was but one of the many charges against him. In addition, it was said, he celebrated Mass without

5 Investiture of Pope John XII, 955. Seventeenth-century painting of tenth-century mosaic (since destroyed) at the Basilica of St John Lateran, Rome. Reproduced by permission of The Royal Collection © Her Majesty Queen Elizabeth II.

taking communion; he ordained a deacon in a stable; he consecrated a ten-year-old boy as a bishop; he invoked the pagan gods, while playing dice; he hunted publicly; he struck and mutilated men; he was guilty of arson and adultery. Foreign women were said to fear coming to Rome as pilgrims because of the lustful ways of the pope. And he died in 964 when he reputedly suffered a stroke while in bed with a married woman, dead in his late twenties. This list of scandalous behaviour, even if trimmed a bit for exaggeration, must leave a remote modern reader in wonder at the depraved state to which the see of St Peter had fallen. Yet, remarkably, there was another side to this sorry pontificate.

John XII is said to have revived the Holy Roman Empire in the West. Although he himself saw little beyond the needs of the day, the empire which he restored was to last into the nineteenth century. It was a local crisis that prompted the pope to invoke the military aid of a German king. In the early tenth century, Germany, like most of Western Europe, knew no central government. In fact, the use of the word 'Germany' might be premature for this period: it may be more accurate to speak of the lands of the East Franks and Saxons. There did exist an extremely weak, loose confederation of German-speaking duchies: Saxony, Franconia, Swabia, Bavaria and Lotharingia. Otto I, who was to become emperor in 962, followed his father as duke of Saxony and, nominally, as king. Otto was not satisfied with a nominal kingship and quickly exerted greater authority over the other duchies with the support of bishops, many of whom were members of his family, placed in such great archbishoprics as Cologne, Mainz and Trier. No overriding principle of emperorship guided the pope in this whole matter. He felt the need of armed help against the so-called king of Italy, who had some control in northern Italy and wished to extend his power further south. King Otto, ambitious for the title of emperor, marched to Rome, where on Candlemas Day (2 February) 962 in St Peter's Basilica the youthful pope crowned him emperor. The emperor, in turn, confirmed the previous donations of lands to the papacy, to which he added his own donation, leaving the popes with a claim to most of Italy, yet only a claim. Otto then began to bring order to Italy, but, in doing so, he alarmed the pope, who began to intrigue with Otto's former enemies against the newly crowned emperor. Word of this treachery reached Otto, who returned to Rome to find that John XII had fled to Tivoli. When the pope refused to return to face a Roman synod, he was excommunicated and deposed by it, and another pope was elected. Within six months John was dead in the circumstances already described.

To call the coronation of the German king Otto as emperor the 'Ottonian Revival' is to invest what happened in 962 with more significance than it had at the time and runs the risk of reading history backwards. What was 'revived' was not the empire but the imperial title, which had been last used in 924 by a minor Italian prince. Yet, a long look beyond 962 sees the development of one of the key institutions in European history. Three points need stressing about the coronation of 962. The first is the most obvious: the German king recognized that it was the pope and only the pope who could confer the imperial title, a papal right to be unchallenged for centuries. Second, the imperial title became associated with the German kings. For nearly a millennium thereafter the man to be crowned emperor by the pope was a German king. And, third, the emperor, in his turn, accepted obligations towards the church. Otto himself promised that, after he defeated the pope's enemies in Italy, he would return to Rome to see to the moral improvement of the pope. This obligation to the church undertaken by papally crowned emperors could be viewed by popes, at times, as unwarranted interference, but, when the papacy rose from the great depths to which it had sunk, it was largely because of the 'interference' of the German kings in the years in the middle of the eleventh century. In 962, John XII, the debauched pope, had little idea what he had done.

Pope Benedict IX (1032–45; ?1047–48)

With the close of the pontificate of Benedict IX the worst days in the long history of the papacy came to an end. He was the third member of the Tusculum family who, one after another, became popes in the first half of the eleventh century. Tusculum, an ancient site, stood atop the Alban Hills, above modern Frascati, fifteen miles from Rome. How the counts of Tusculum rose to such power we do not know, but it seems certain that they derived from the Theophylacts, whom we have already met. When the millennium dawned, a certain Gregory was head of the Tusculum family, and it was he who controlled the area of Rome and its environs. He had three sons: Alberic, who was to succeed his father as count; Theophylact, who became Pope Benedict VIII (1012–24); and Romanus, who became Pope John XIX (1024–32). The eldest son, Alberic, had two sons: Gregory, who succeeded his father as count, and another Theophylact, who became Pope Benedict IX in 1032, thus succeeding his uncle.

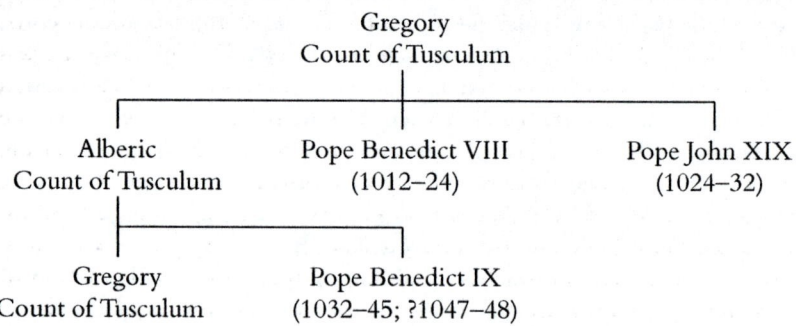

One contemporary, if not wholly reliable, account relates that Benedict IX at the time of his accession was not yet twelve years old. This allegation seems exaggerated, for Benedict was soon charged with behaviour which assumes that he had reached the age of puberty. The sources are exiguous, but they seem to show that, in 1036, political opponents of the Tusculums attempted to kill Benedict in St Peter's Basilica and that the pope escaped and fled into exile. He was restored by the German emperor, Conrad II. Little has been left to us by which we can judge the next seven years, and surviving contemporary sources speak generally of how he stole, murdered and committed other, unspeakable deeds. Unable to bear his behaviour any longer, the people of Rome (we are told) drove him from the city. The truth was probably that a rival faction seized his misconduct as an excuse to rid Rome of the Tusculums. This faction, in January 1045, raised the bishop of Sabina to the papacy as Sylvester III (traditionally listed as an anti-pope). Before the end of March the Tusculums had re-entered Rome and replaced their pope on the seat of St Peter. Sylvester was sent back to Sabina, but he will be heard from again.

The feckless Benedict IX, now restored, decided to resign the papacy for reasons that are confusing (to us) and, indeed, they may have been several. In the first place, it was said that Benedict had a tormented conscience and, thus, wanted to be relieved of the papal office, which had been thrust upon him by his family. In addition, he wanted to marry his cousin, whose father was unwilling for his daughter to marry a pope. This sounds rather like his enemies speaking. Yet another factor entered the picture. Benedict agreed with his godfather, archpriest John Gratian, to resign the papacy in favour of John Gratian in exchange for an enormous sum of money, and this he did on 1 May 1045. Truth being stranger than fiction, Benedict's cousin now refused to marry him, apparently reluctant to marry an ex-pope, and Benedict also will be heard from again.

John Gratian, who took the name Gregory VI, was soon confronted with two opponents: Sylvester III, still clinging to his claim to the papacy, and the hapless Benedict IX, disappointed in love and now anxious to be pope again. With three claimants to the papacy the moment was ripe for the protector of the church, the emperor, to descend on Rome to sort matters out. Henry III (1039–56), perhaps the greatest of the Ottonian line of German kings who became emperors, called a synod, which was held in 1046 at Sutri, near Rome. Sylvester III was degraded and sent to a monastery; Benedict IX was recognized as a resigned pope; and Gregory VI resigned. The slate was now clean for a new pope to be elected, but, alas, the new pope, Clement II, died within ten months. Seizing the moment (8 November 1047), Benedict left his mountain citadel at Tusculum, entered Rome and claimed the papal throne. He held it for about eight months, only to leave (for the last time) at the advance of troops under imperial orders, and a new pope, Damasus II, was enthroned. His reign ended by poison or malaria in twenty-one days, and the way was then open in 1049 for real reform. Benedict IX quite possibly finished his days as a penitent at the monastery of Grottaferrata in his ancestral Alban Hills (d. 1055), perhaps ill-served by the reformers who wrote his story.

The tenth century was not all gloom and doom, and reforming movements were taking shape, particularly north of the Alps, which would have a profound effect on the life of the church. It is to this reform that we shall now turn.

Further reading

An excellent account of the tenth-century church with an emphasis different from that given here is Rosamond McKitterick's essay in *The New Cambridge Medieval History*, vol. 3 (ed. Timothy Reuter; Cambridge, 1999).

An essential book of reference is *The Oxford Dictionary of Popes* (Oxford, 1986) by J.N.D. Kelly. Old but still of considerable use, particularly for its reference to contemporary sources, is Horace K. Mann, *The Lives of the Popes in the Early Middle Ages* (18 vols; London, 1902–1932). Compelling, if not always conventional, is Geoffrey Barraclough, *The Medieval Papacy* (London and New York, 1968). More recent surveys include Eamon Duffy, *Saints and Sinners: A History of the Popes* (London and New Haven, 1997) and Richard P. McBrien, *Lives of the Popes: The Pontiffs from St Peter to John Paul II* (San Francisco, 1997).

Chief among the contemporary sources available to us in English are the translations of the *Liber Pontificalis* prepared by Raymond Davis: *The Book of Popes (Liber Pontificalis): The Ancient Biographies of the First Ninety Roman Bishops to AD 715* (Liverpool, 1989), *The Lives of the Eighth-Century Popes* (Liverpool, 1992) and *The Lives of the Ninth-Century Popes* (Liverpool, 1995). Two valuable chronicles are easily accessible: *The Annals of St-Bertin* (tr. Janet L. Nelson; Manchester, 1991) and *The Annals of Fulda* (tr. Timothy Reuter; Manchester, 1992).

On the Lotharingian divorce case see Stuart Airlie, 'Private Bodies and the Body Politic in the Divorce Case of Lothar II', *Past and Present* 16 (1998), 3–38. On Hincmar see J.M. Wallace-Hadrill, *The Frankish Church* (Oxford, 1983), and Janet L. Nelson, *Charles the Bald* (London and New York, 1992). On the Ravenna dispute see R.F. Belletzkie, 'Pope Nicholas I and John of Ravenna: The Struggle for Ecclesiastical Rights in the Ninth Century', *Church History* 49 (1980), 262–72. On the issues between the Eastern and Western churches see Francis Dvornik, *The Photian Schism: History and Legend* (Cambridge, 1948) and *Byzantium and the Roman Primacy* (New York, 1966) and Steven Runciman, *The Eastern Schism* (Oxford, 1955).

7

REFORM, THE EAST, CRUSADE

The seventy-five years from the middle of the eleventh century witnessed crucial events in the long history of the church. Forms were cast that would shape integral features of the Christian church as it lived its life in the centuries to come. The papacy, long in scandalous decline, woke up or, rather, was awakened to assume a role of active leadership. In the exuberance of its new awakening the popes disastrously but effectively severed the church from the Christians of the East, as disagreement became schism, and schism became permanent, yet not so permanent that, when threatened by Turkish invaders, Eastern Christians would not call upon the West for help. That help was the First Crusade. A church with a strong papacy, often in struggle with secular rulers, a church separated from its Greek-speaking brethren and a church embracing an ideal of war against the infidels – these were henceforth to be benchmarks of the medieval church.

Eleventh-century reform

The need to renew the Christian ideal, to reaffirm the essential meaning of Christianity, to revive the human spirit by a return to the pristine elements of Christian living was not limited to any one period in history and was as old as Pentecost and the early church. Ideals of their nature are goals never attained yet striven for, the horizon never reached yet still the destination one heads towards. A central belief of the Christian religion is the universality of the effects of original sin: human nature, while not depraved, was seriously weakened by the sin of Adam. The frailty of human nature, in this schema, excepted neither pope nor bishop nor priest. It was a church of men and women, children of Adam and heirs to his weakened humanity. In such a world, failure was a constant fear and a frequent reality. Almost integral to the Christian religion as it was lived was the need of reform, renewal, revival – the terms are really synonymous – which, at times, became so intense and so widespread as to constitute a movement. Such a movement occurred in the eleventh century.

Traditional historiography has labelled this movement as either the 'Gregorian Reform' or the 'Hildebrandine Reform.' Both names refer to Pope Gregory VII (1073–85), who, before he became pope, was called Hildebrand. These are inappropriate names. Two dangers lurk behind this usage. First, it assumes that this was a papally led reforming movement, which, only partially true, distorts the historical reality. Secondly, it gives to Pope Gregory VII the central role in the movement, a role it would be difficult to sustain by the historical record. The 'Eleventh-century Reform' better describes the variegated and complex forces at play throughout that century and into the first quarter of the next.

A brief outline might be useful. It can be said that the eleventh-century reform had two general periods. The first was the period up to 1049, when the papacy was corrupt and the plaything of local strongmen (see preceding chapter) and when reform was in the hands of local bishops, abbots and secular rulers outside of Rome. With the coronation of Pope Leo IX (1049) the papacy began to take control of the movement, yet with the pontificate of Gregory VII (1073–85) a clear shift took place. Leo IX and his immediate successors used papal power as a means of effecting ecclesiastical reform, but Gregory VII used the reforming movement as a means of enhancing papal power, or, to put it another way, he considered reform to include the enhancement of papal power. This led him into conflict with the German rulers, a conflict not settled until the Concordat of Worms (1122), and even then only tenuously. So much for the outline, now the details.

While the papacy was still wallowing in its corrupting dependence on the local house of Tusculum, sounds of Christian renewal could be heard off in the distance and even in the far distance. At different times and in different regions reforms occurred, some were monastic, aimed at restoring fidelity to the spirit of the Rule of St Benedict, while others were directed towards the secular clergy, who had the care of souls at a time when churches – what we might call 'parishes' – were multiplying. The area which was the 'Middle Kingdom' of the grandchildren of Charlemagne – the land between the kingdom of the East Franks and the kingdom of the West Franks – witnessed reforming efforts beginning in the tenth century, which should force us to see that century not merely in grey tones. By the eleventh century these efforts had influenced other regions of Western Europe and finally reached Rome in mid-century. The most famous is the movement associated with the monastery at Cluny in the French duchy of Burgundy. There in 909 William, the duke of Aquitaine, founded a monastery which would spawn hundreds of daughter houses and which would give its name to a monastic movement. It was intended as a reform monastery, returning to the Rule as articulated by Benedict Aniane (see chapter 5). Other monasteries with similar purposes were founded at about this time by wealthy patrons. What set Cluny apart was its independence. The very charter by which Duke William set an abbot and twelve monks down in this valley provided for the free election of the abbot by the community and for the pope, rather than local bishop or duke, to be its protector. In time, Cluny's claim to be exempt from local jurisdiction and answerable only to the bishop of Rome gave Cluny the self-confidence to develop into a major force for ecclesiastical reform. William of Aquitaine's charter declared 'that our foundation shall serve for ever as a refuge for those who renounce the world and, as poor men, bring nothing but their good will'.

Cluny has not lasted 'for ever', as William wished, for it fell victim to the excesses of the French Revolution in 1791, its bells melted down for cannon and a road soon pushed through what had been the centre of the great abbey church. Yet, at its beginning, monks came to this valley to live in wooden huts and to worship in a wooden church. They spent long periods of each day in utter silence, raising their voices seldom save for periods of oral prayer. These two features – silence and oral prayer – became the hallmarks of Cluny. Its abbot Odo (926–44) crystallized its customs and became a missionary for the reform of other monasteries. By the mid-tenth century only five monasteries were subject to Cluny. In time, hundreds of daughter houses (called priories) were established or recreated from existing monasteries. Hundreds of others were to become associated with Cluny, accepting its spirit and customs, although not part of what was in reality a religious order. The abbot of Cluny was *pater et abbas* (father and abbot) not only of the monks at Cluny itself but also of all the monks of its satellite priories. Under Abbot Mayeul, or Maiolus (954–94), these daughter and associate monastic houses were dotted throughout France, extending beyond, even into parts of Christian Spain and northern Italy. In 1077 Cluny established a priory at Lewes in England and, in time, had thirty-five houses in England and four in Scotland. That was in the future. Cluny by the end of the tenth century had become the single most powerful spiritual force in Western Europe. The reformed monasteries of the Romance-language-speaking peoples largely took their lead from the abbey of Cluny, which stood then near the pinnacle of its

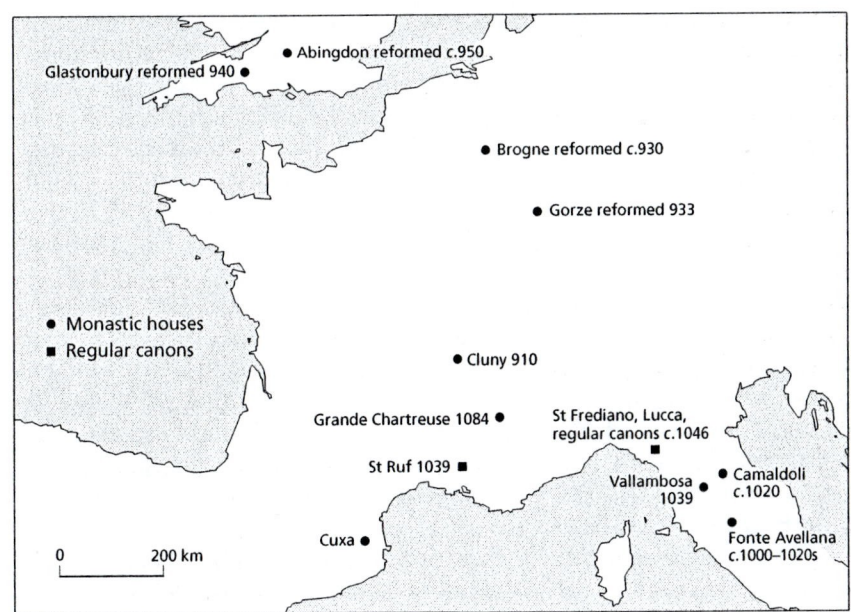

Map 8 Centres of reform in the tenth and eleventh centuries.

power. Before the end of the eleventh century it produced two more long-ruling, sainted abbots, Odilo (994–1049) and Hugh (1049–1109), and placed on the chair of St Peter two popes of exceptional abilities, Urban II (1088–99) and Paschal II (1099–1118).

Yet not by Cluny alone was reform brought to Western monasticism. In the German-speaking lands, notably in the areas of the Mosel River valley and the nearby Rhineland, monastic reform took root. The abbey of Gorze near Metz in 933 provided much of the stimulus for this renewal of Benedictine life. Monks from Gorze revitalized the ancient monastery at Trier, and monks from Trier brought their spirit of reform into the region centring on Cologne, where they founded new monasteries and renewed old ones. And, even somewhat earlier, the bishopric of Liège felt the reforming impulses from the monastery at Brogne. All this took place in Lorraine, which made it one of the principal centres of reforming ideas in the eleventh century. In England, where the dislocations of the Viking invasions and land-taking left most of the surviving monasteries as little more than communities of married clerics, it was St Dunstan who was the driving force for reform, and he had lived at the Brognean monastery at Ghent. These centres of reform were merely that: they did not blanket the map north of the Alps. Yet they did represent a growing sentiment in favour of the revival of the church, in which strong personalities, ecclesiastical and lay, played significant roles. The archbishop of Cologne, himself the brother of Emperor Otto I, encouraged events there. In England in the late tenth century there were three exceptionally able monastic bishops, all intent on reform: Dunstan at Canterbury, Ethelwold at Winchester and Oswald at Worcester. Also in England, King Edmund (939–46), King Edred (946–55) and King Edgar (955–59) gave the reformers the support essential to their task, and the revived monasteries of strict Benedictine observance such as Glastonbury, Abingdon and others were the result. In France, the second king in the long line of the Capetian dynasty, Robert the Pious (996–1031), supported the mission of Cluny. His contemporary in Germany, Henry II (1002–24), succeeded in bringing reform to the hitherto resistant abbeys of Fulda, Reichenau and others. His grandson, Henry III (1039–56), married a French noblewoman with close connections to Cluny. Henry's association with Cluny and with the broader reform movement provides an example of a Christian monarch not interfering in church affairs but fulfilling his obligation as an anointed king. It was Henry III who was to set in motion the reform of the papacy itself, which, in turn, was to change essentially the scope and direction of reform. As the end of the first millennium approached, there was a clearly identifiable impetus towards reform, and Cluny and Lorraine were the principal instruments in fostering a commitment to spiritual renewal.

The conditions in Rome, with the pope little more than a puppet in the hands of local families, scandalized much of Christendom, and, when Henry III marched on Rome in 1046, he did so to set in motion papal reform. The synod he convoked at nearby Sutri marks for many historians the beginnings of the papal stage in the movement of reform. Three contesting 'popes' were dismissed, and Henry imposed the German bishop of Bamberg on Rome as its bishop, yet the new pope died within ten months but not before crowning Henry III emperor. The new emperor imposed another German on the papal throne, but he died, probably of malaria, within twenty-three days. It was with the next pope, another German bishop imposed by Henry III, that the programme of papal reform began in earnest. Leo IX (1049–56), as bishop of Toul in Lorraine, had vigorously sought the reform of religious men and women as well as the secular clergy. Now on a larger scale, strengthened by his ties of kinship to the emperor, he instigated a bold programme to reform the universal church. From the time of Leo IX the pope was taking charge.

Leo IX brought with him from Lorraine men steeped in the culture of reform. Chief among them was the passionate and, as events would prove, extreme and rigid Humbert of Moyenmoutier, who soon became cardinal bishop of Silva Candida. A politically well-connected reformer who came to Rome with Leo was Frederick of Lorraine, brother of Godfrey, duke of Lorraine: both brothers will reappear in this story, Frederick as abbot of Monte Cassino and Pope Stephen IX and Godfrey as husband of the formidable Matilda, countess of Tuscany. Also in Leo's entourage was the Roman monk Hildebrand, who, in the tumult of 1046, fled north with Gregory VI, whose secretary he was and whose name he was later to take as pope. From Italy itself there came to Rome at about this time a monk from an abbey nestled in the Apennines, Peter Damian, himself later (1057) to become cardinal bishop of Ostia.

The newly chosen pope approached the city of Rome not in triumphal splendour but in the garb of a humble pilgrim, and, once there, he refused to be crowned pope until the emperor's selection of him was confirmed by the Roman clergy and people. One might see in this the first step in the papacy's attempt to throw off the power of secular rulers, even the well-intentioned intervention of men like Henry III. Conflict about the intervention of secular rulers lay in the future. The pressing issue in 1049 was reform, and less than two months into his reign as pope Leo IX convened a synod at Rome which deposed several bishops and castigated unworthy clergy. One month later he packed his bags and left Rome to convene synods at Pavia, Rheims and Mainz, at which his personal presence vividly highlighted the exigency of reform. In a papacy of only about five years he also went in person to southern Italy and to Langres, Trier, Pressburg, Ratisbon, Augsburg and Mantua, spending less than six months at Rome. Energetic and vital, Leo was clearly in control in an active way unknown to his predecessors, and his agenda was one of reform.

The reforming agenda needs spelling out. Two major issues preoccupied Leo and his 'cabinet' of advisers: simony and clerical concubinage. Simony took its name from Simon Magus, the man in the Acts of the Apostles (8, 9–24) who tried to buy from St Peter the miraculous power of laying on of hands. Although in a general way simony meant the buying and selling of holy things, its meaning in the eleventh century focused on the paying for an ecclesiastical office (e.g., a bishopric or abbacy) or for ordination, and those buying these holy things were denounced as simoniacs. In time, Cardinal Humbert took the view, in his *Adversus simoniacos* ('Against Simoniacs'), that the sacraments conferred by a simoniac were invalid. Thus, in his view, a priest ordained by a simoniacal bishop was not a priest and could not validly say Mass or perform other priestly functions. More moderately, Cardinal Peter Damian held that it was indeed gravely sinful to buy an office but the sacraments conferred by a simoniac were valid: their validity did not depend on the worthiness of the minister. And Damian's view prevailed. If Humbert had won the day, one can only wonder at the confusion and severe crises for souls, even, and especially, for the devout, that would have ensued. Good sense saved the church from the excesses of radical reformers.

Clerical celibacy was another matter and much less clear-cut. While a few would defend the buying and selling of church offices or ordinations as part of a gift-giving culture, the practice was widely condemned. Clerical marriage, however, was not so obvious a matter of right and wrong. No biblical text could be cited prohibiting it and requiring priestly celibacy. Most of the apostles were known to be married. The practice of the Eastern Church was – and, indeed, is – to allow married men to become priests. Even in the West an unmarried clergy only slowly and not at all uniformly became the rule. Individual councils legislating for their regions and even individual popes, responding to individual cases, called for married men who became priests either to put their wives aside or to live with them as brother and sister. Married clergy not following these injunctions could be found in almost every part of the West, and even a rigorous canonist would have had to admit that their situations were allowed by legitimate custom, at a time when long-standing custom was considered to replace even contrary law. A lively debate on this issued ensued: Peter Damian arguing for celibacy and others, like the bishop of Imola in central Italy, arguing that celibacy was a vocation distinct from the vocation to the priesthood. Those reformers favouring a celibate secular clergy were mostly monks, who were by definition and choice celibate. Damian was a monk of Fonte Avellana, Humbert a monk of Moyenmoutier, Hildebrand a monk of Santa Maria on the Aventine Hill in Rome. From 1073 to 1119 the papacy itself was held by former monks, something unrivalled in its long history. More was at stake here than the matter of clerical celibacy: it was the ideal of Christian perfection. That ideal, it was held by Damian and others, was to be found in the life of a monk, but, if one could not become a monk, one should live as close as possible to the life of a monk in the world. And for the secular clergy, the reformers believed, that required a celibate life. The real struggle was over the soul of Christian spirituality, and the monks won this round, although the matter of clerical celibacy was not settled until the Second Lateran Council (1139) ruled that a priest, a deacon and even a subdeacon could not contract a valid marriage; if any were already married, they were to lose their benefices.

Against these two perceived evils Leo IX and later reformers appealed to ancient practices by extracting texts from early synods, papal directives and the teachings of the Church Fathers. The reform was accomplished by invoking tradition and pristine practice, not by fulminating new decretals, new laws, new texts. Thus, collections of such texts were compiled. One can almost see the reformers at Rome, scouring through existing collections of old texts in search of references to use for their own contemporary needs. The collection made by Burchard of Worms (before 1020) had reached Rome by mid-century. Both Burchard and a collection in seventy-four titles, which was made at Rome, were used by the greatest compiler of canon-law texts of the time, Ivo, bishop of Chartres, in the 1090s. To him should be given much of the credit for establishing canon law as a scholarly discipline. And Anselm, bishop of Lucca, in the mid-1080s produced a collection of canons strongly supportive of the papal power to reform. With such canonical references in hand the reformers could insist on a renewal of traditional church practices. Resistance there surely was, but Leo IX, presiding over provincial synods, simply rolled over opposition by intimidation and sanctions, not hesitating to depose reluctant bishops. Reluctance to accept reforms, particularly clerical celibacy, led to near riotous scenes at Rouen and Paris, at Erfurt and Passau and elsewhere. But reforms were imposed, and canon law played a considerable role in this process.

Leo's reign, however successful its early years, ended in personal failure. Younger sons of noble families in Normandy, serving as mercenaries (or freebooters), had invaded southern Italy by the time of Leo's accession and were threatening church lands there. Leo raised an army under the papal banner and personally led it against these Norman Christians. It was a fatal error. His army was quickly defeated and Pope Leo was captured and kept in benign imprisonment for nine months. Within a few weeks after his release in April 1054, the first of the great reforming popes died, dispirited and disillusioned.

Subsequent popes continued this programme, convening synods, but not travelling so widely themselves, instead sending legates across the Alps to act in their name. There still remained the crucial issue of papal elections. Leo's successor, Victor II (1055–57), was the last imperially selected pope. A change of momentous significance occurred within months of the coronation of his successor, Nicholas II (1058–61). He issued an electoral decree that, with some later changes, has regulated the election of popes ever since. The pope was to be elected by the cardinal bishops. While 'saving the honour and reverence' due to the emperor, the decree did not include him in the election process. A word must be said about cardinals. Seven bishoprics in the suburbs around Rome were served by bishops who came eventually to provide, first, liturgical services and, later, administrative services for the pope. They became the *cardines* (hinges) of the Roman church; they were cardinal bishops. The presiding priests of the great Roman basilicas adopted the term 'cardinal' as, in time, did certain deacons in the papal service. Thus, three orders of cardinals developed: cardinal bishops, cardinal priests and cardinal deacons. By Pope Nicholas's decree it was the cardinal bishops who had the initial voice in the selection of future popes, their choice to be confirmed by the other cardinals and, finally and only formally, by the clergy of Rome. It was the function of cardinals in the election of popes that was to give them in time a corporate sense, the sense of being a 'college'.

The purpose of the election decree was to make the election free, devoid of external influence whether from German emperors or from the Roman aristocracy. The decree was soon tested by the death of Nicholas II in 1061. The German king, Henry IV (1056–1106), was but a boy, and a ten-year regency complicated the situation. Only the firm action of Hildebrand ensured the application of the new decree. The election of Alexander II (1061–73) created a storm in Germany, and the Germans elected their own pope (known to history as an anti-pope). Intense negotiations and a flexible Alexander II resolved the matter in his favour.

A long pontificate, longer than his six predecessors combined, gave Alexander opportunity to carry forward the work of reform, to which he had been long committed. He sent a legate to Aragon, one of the Christian outposts in northern Spain. He even involved himself in the succession of the English crown. When King Edward the Confessor died early in 1066, Duke William of Normandy sent a mission to Rome, seeking papal support for his claim to the English crown: Harold, the claimant, had perjured himself and Stigand, the archbishop of Canterbury, had received the pallium from an anti-pope. One source, whose reliability is not universally accepted, relates that the pope actually sent a blessed papal banner, under which William defeated Harold at Hastings. The dubious banner apart, papal support was given to William, and Alexander II sent two papal legates to preside over a synod at Winchester (1070), which deposed Stigand and other bishops. The bishop of Lichfield, a married man with children, resigned his see and took himself to a monastery. With the learned Lanfranc, abbot of Bec in Normandy, now at Canterbury, the English church had become a part of the papal reform programme and England was drawn towards the Continent from its remote, comfortable insularity.

Central to any historical view of this whole period lies the figure of Hildebrand, who, in 1073, under exceptional circumstances became Pope Gregory VII. His twelve-year pontificate created considerable controversy not only for his contemporaries but also for modern historians. His supporters in the historical profession have given his name to the reform movement, of which he was but a part and arguably not the principal part. The view presented here is that the pontificate of Gregory VII was a failure, perhaps even a monumental failure. He disturbed the forward progress of reform by picking unnecessary fights with secular rulers. What betrayed his papacy was that perennial scourge of the church, 'the priest in politics'.

The unusual nature of his election was an augur of things to come. At the funeral of Alexander II, according to sympathetic accounts, Hildebrand was spontaneously selected by the Roman populace and, despite his unwillingness, he was ordained priest and consecrated bishop of Rome. Most obviously, this procedure, however the truth of his reluctance, stood the Nicholas election decree on its head. In the future his enemies would attack him for the manner of his election.

Not content to push forward the usual programme of reform against simoniacs and married priests, Gregory VII added a new issue: lay investiture. To say succinctly that lay investiture meant the investing of a bishop or abbot with the insignia of his office by a layman (a king or prince) is not to say enough. Lay rulers, as has been seen, viewed their office as a holy one, a view which, for example, led King Henry III of Germany to descend on Rome in 1046 to sort out the problems there. Such a ruler would have a voice, often a definitive voice, in the selection of bishops and abbots. In addition, these ecclesiastical officials generally held considerable lands from the king or prince. Thus, when the person took office, he took an office both ecclesiastical and secular, and the ruler understandably felt that he had rights. When a man became a bishop or abbot, the sacramental rites were performed by the appropriate ecclesiastic, but it was the secular ruler who very frequently invested him with ring and staff. To Gregory this constituted gross interference by the laity in ecclesiastical matters. Papal claims in the growing controversy were to change the Gelasian image of God handing one key each directly to the pope and emperor to the image of God granting both keys to the pope, who, in turn, gave one to the emperor. There logically followed a papal claim to the power to depose secular rulers. Matters moved very far very fast, and the catalysts were Pope Gregory VII and King (later Emperor) Henry IV.

Trouble began early in Gregory's pontificate. In the first week of Lent 1075 a Roman synod strongly attacked so-called lay investiture, an attack aimed with little subtlety at the Germans:

> If anyone receive a bishopric or abbey from the hands of a lay person, he shall not be considered a bishop or abbot . . . Likewise, if an emperor, king, duke, margrave or anyone vested with secular power presumes to invest a person to bishoprics or other ecclesiastical offices, he shall likewise be condemned.

Henry IV, king but not yet crowned emperor, was soon free of troubles in Saxony and turned his attention to the Lombard lands which he held, particularly to the vexed problem about the great see of Milan. Two claimants to that see had been in contention for several years, and King Henry, perhaps imitating his father's action during the papal crisis of 1046, secured the elimination of the two claimants and the consecration of a third. This infuriated the pope, who, on 8 December 1075, threatened Henry with excommunication and deposition for interfering in the appointment of bishops. Within weeks Henry had gathered a synod at Tribur, which deposed the pope, claiming his election invalid.

To about this same time – possibly in the spring of 1076 – can be dated one of the most tantalizing and puzzling documents of this whole period. It is the *Dictatus papae*, which means the dictations of the pope to a secretary. It consists of twenty-seven simple statements. They all concern papal power and seem to be chapter headings for a canonical collection never made or, if made, now lost. Several of these 'dictates' illustrate its general thrust:

> 9. That the pope's feet and no else's are to be kissed by all princes.
> 11. That his title is unique in the world.
> 12. That he may depose emperors.
> 19. That he is to be judged by no one.
> 27. That he may absolve subjects from their fealty to evil persons.

The twelfth 'dictate' would not be long in being tested, for at the Lenten synod at Rome in 1076, the pope not only excommunicated the German king but went much further:

> I deprive King Henry, son of Emperor Henry, who has audaciously rebelled against the church, of the government over the whole kingdom of Germany and Italy, and I release all Christians from allegiance sworn to him.

Henry quickly responded by presiding over a church council in June 1076, which excommunicated Gregory 'not pope but false monk'. But Henry had misjudged his support among the Germans, a people not sympathetically disposed to centralizing kings. Confronted with this opposition, Henry agreed, in October 1076, to appear before an assembly at Augsburg in February of the following year, an assembly over which the pope would preside and whose purpose it would be to consider Henry's position. Few would have bet on Henry's chances for surviving the greatest crisis of his reign. Yet he did.

Pope Gregory, to break the long, hazardous journey from Rome across the mountains in winter on his way to Germany for the assembly, stopped over in late January at the castle at Canossa in northern Italy, nestled in the Apennine Mountains, where he was the guest of the formidable Matilda, countess of Tuscany. There he was to receive a visitor. Henry IV, desperate to keep his crown, donned the guise of a penitent pilgrim, slipped out of Germany with but a few companions, fellow pilgrims, to intercept the pope. This he did at Canossa. Henry arrived there on 25 January and begged the pope's absolution. For three days Gregory kept him waiting, barefoot in mid-winter outside the castle gates. Who knows what went on within the castle? Matilda counselled the pope to absolve the penitent king. So too did Abbot Hugh of Cluny. One suspects that they may have played a behind-the-scenes role in this dramatic meeting and that the whole choreography may have been pre-arranged. On the third day Gregory absolved Henry. Having saved his crown, Henry immediately returned to Germany. A substantial group of German nobles refused to accept him and raised a reluctant Rudolph of Swabia as king, and Germany was engulfed in a bloody civil war. The usually decisive, even impetuous, Pope Gregory delayed taking sides in the civil war, and, when he did in favour of Rudolph in 1080, it was too late. Henry had all but defeated Rudolph, who, in any event, died shortly after the papal decision. The penitent's garb long since put away, an angry Henry marched on Rome, installed a new pope and had himself crowned emperor. Thirteen of the cardinals – a majority – defected, and Gregory was in full retreat. He fled Rome and sought refuge with his Norman supporters, moving south to Monte Cassino and, finally, to Salerno, where, on 25 May 1085, he died. His last words, echoing Psalm 44, are said to have been, 'I have loved justice, hated iniquity and, therefore, die in exile,' to which he might have added, 'And I die a failure.'

There was no winner in the investiture controversy just as there was no right party and no wrong party. It took over thirty years for the controversy to be resolved by compromise. Pope Urban II (1088–99) lowered the temperature of papal rhetoric and pretensions, but most remarkable was the solution proposed by Pope Paschal II (1099–1118). He could see that the core of the problem over investiture was the fact that bishops and abbots held territories from kings and princes, since, besides being spiritual rulers, they were secular rulers. The pope recognized that the king clearly had rights with respect to the temporal possessions of these ecclesiastics. The problem would not exist if these bishops and abbots ceased to be secular rulers. Hence, with unassailable logic, Paschal, in February 1111, ordered the bishops and abbots of Germany to return their temporal possessions to the king. 'The church,' he said, 'will remain free', dependent on the free-will offerings of the faithful for its needs. Many modern historians consider this proposal a naive non-starter, but the danger here (as elsewhere) is to read history backwards and to conclude that, because the proposal failed to be accepted, it was bound to fail. This gesture of Paschal II must be judged among the boldest made by the medieval popes. Our minds boggle at what the subsequent history of the church would have been had the church renounced temporal possessions in the early twelfth century. As it was, the church held on tenaciously to its territorial possessions until 1870, when Piedmontese troops took Rome and the pope became 'the prisoner in the Vatican'. In 1111 vested interests, particularly among the German bishops, helped to defeat the initiative of Paschal II.

The resolution of the investiture struggle, when it came under Calixtus II (1119–24), left the king and pope both able to claim victory. Troubles in England between King Henry I and Anselm, archbishop of Canterbury, had been settled in 1107 in a way which provided a precedent for the eventual compromise: the king gave up his practice of giving the bishop his pastoral staff, and the bishop would give homage to the king for lands which he held from the king. The Concordat of Worms (1122) made a similar distinction: the election would be free, although in the presence of the king, but the latter would not invest the bishop with symbols of his office, receiving instead homage from the new bishop. Somewhat different terms would apply to parts of the empire outside Germany. The fundamental issue between pope and emperor over jurisdictions still remained, and future clashes would occur.

The Eastern church

An event vividly remembered in the Eastern church occurred in the afternoon of Saturday, 16 July 1054, at the great church of Santa Sophia in Constantinople. Unexpectedly, while services were about to begin, three Western ecclesiastics walked briskly down the nave to the high altar. They turned and faced the startled congregation, said something unintelligible (probably in Latin) and then placed a document on the altar. Not waiting for a reaction, they retraced their steps, and, at the door, they turned and shouted, 'Let God see and judge.' They were papal legates sent by Leo IX, and the document was a bull deposing and excommunicating the patriarch of Constantinople. Few events in the history of the medieval church have provoked such wildly different interpretations. Dismissed by some as but a minor bump on the road of East–West relations, it is seen by others as the crucial moment when occurred the schism between the churches of East and West, which, despite flickering moments of reunion in 1274 and in the 1440s, has continued to the present day.

The situation in Italy sparked these events, at least in a proximate way, although long-standing differences between the churches of the East and West were clearly at work here. The political landscape in Italy was seemingly straightforward at this time: the north under the control of the Germans, the middle under the popes, the south under the Byzantine emperors. Yet on the ground the situation was not so clear-cut, and this was particularly true in the south. Theoretically the Byzantines held jurisdiction south of a line drawn across the boot from Terracine to Termoli. In fact, the Lombards controlled two duchies (Spoleto and Benevento) as well as several towns including Naples. Byzantine rule from Constantinople extended to the almost totally Greek province of Calabria and to Apulia, which had mixed Greek and Latin populations with churches serving both peoples. The matter became more complicated in 1020, when Latin Apulians rose against Eastern rule and invited the help of warriors from Normandy. These soon became the dominant force in southern Italy, even threatening Rome itself. Pope Leo IX decided that the crisis required an alliance with the Byzantine emperor against the rampaging Normans. It proved a disaster, when, after the briefest of campaigns, the pope's forces were defeated in June 1053 and Leo IX was held as an honoured prisoner of the Christian Normans. Not only were the Normans Christians, they were Latin Christians and had insisted on Latin liturgical usages in southern Italy and did not allow Greek churches to follow their traditional practices.

There entered the scene at this point the redoubtable patriarch of Constantinople, Michael Cerularius, who, in response to the Normans, caused Latin rituals to cease at the Latin churches in Constantinople. Cerularius also objected, in the most strenuous of language, to the Latin practice of using unleavened bread at Mass. The pope, in January 1054, responded by sending three legates to Constantinople, headed by the tactless reformer, Cardinal Humbert, whose extreme views on simony we have already met. With two leading roles being played by such unpredictable men like Cerularius and Humbert, an explosive condition existed. The first meeting of the papal legates with the patriarch ended with the legates abruptly walking out. Matters deteriorated from there. The legates, the patriarch asserted, were not true legates for their documents had been tampered with and, in any case, the pope who had issued them had already died (15 April 1054). At one point during the subsequent weeks, Humbert in a moment of anger insisted that one of the patriarch's spokesmen was the son of a whore. It was thus in this atmosphere of mutual distrust and of great ill-temper on both sides that the legates excommunicated the patriarch at Santa Sophia. The patriarch responded with his own excommunications.

Was this, then, the crucial moment in the relations between the churches of East and West, the defining moment of the schism? The bump-on-the-road historians hold that contemporaries did not see it as a decisive moment. After all, they argue, the legates had excommunicated only the patriarch, and, in any case, their power had died with Leo IX before the excommunications. Also, Cardinal Humbert, far from being seen as a failure, was treated as a triumphant hero on his return to Rome. Furthermore, subsequent popes were in communication with the East without a word of the events of 1054 being whispered.

There is much truth in all this, yet the belief grew in the West that a schism had occurred at this time. This can be seen in several contemporary chronicles. Also, subsequent popes could have but did not repudiate the legates for acting beyond their authority. The excommunication itself merits a closer look. The crucial part reads,

> We subscribe that our most reverend pope has denounced Michael and all those who follow him in these errors and presumptions, unless they repent. They are excommunicated. Maranatha. Amen. Amen. Amen.

What should be seen here is that the legates did more than excommunicate Cerularius: they excommunicated all who supported his positions, some ritual and some theological. Of course, most of the positions attributed to him were patently untrue (e.g., that communion was forbidden to men with beards), yet the crucial theological issue concerned the *filioque* ('and from the Son') clause in the creed of faith. Essentially, the *filioque* dispute concerned how the three persons of the Trinity (Father, Son and Holy Spirit) were related to one another, especially the Holy Spirit to the other two. The Eastern position held that the Holy Spirit proceeded from the Father through the Son, whereas the Western position held that the Holy Spirit proceeded from the Father 'and from the Son' (*filioque*). The whole matter might seem arcane to the modern mind, yet at this time it was seen as a crucial element in the description of the Christian God. The Eastern church rejected the *filioque*, and, hence, the anathema pronounced by the legates had a wider application than we might at first believe: it could be read to include the whole Eastern church. By the fourteenth century the widespread view in

117

the East was that the schism dated from the excommunication of 1054. It had been a view long held in the West. So persistent has been this belief in both churches that, on 7 December 1965, Pope Paul VI and Patriarch Athenagoras of Constantinople, in a dramatic expression of irenic goodwill, embraced and mutually repudiated the excommunications of 1054 and expressed the wish that the excommunications and accompanying offences and insults be erased from Christian memory, a wish that even a respectful historian cannot honour.

The First Crusade

The first thing that must be said about the First Crusade is that no one at the time knew it was the *first* crusade. When Pope Urban II preached this crusade at Clermont in France in 1095, he had no idea of beginning a movement, whose ambitions would grow beyond the retaking of the Holy Land to encompass and, indeed, justify attacks against the infidels elsewhere and even against fellow Christians. The very word 'crusade' and the neat numbering of the Crusades were the inventions of a later period. For all the romance and adventure popularly associated with them, the crusades were marginal events in the general flow of medieval history. The central lines of the history of this period would remain essentially unchanged if the crusades had never occurred: the crusades were but one element among many in medieval history and clearly not in the first rank. No historian would deny that the life of the church was influenced by soldiers fighting war with papal authorization under the banner of the cross, yet the temptation to overemphasize the place of the crusades in the life of the church in the Middle Ages must be resisted.

All that having been said, it must be added that in one particular aspect the crusades have had an enduring effect on the history of Western civilization, an effect whose influence it would be difficult to measure. In its beginning Christianity was a religion of peace. There resonated in the ears of the early Christians the words of their founder: 'Turn the other cheek' (Matt. 5, 39); 'Those who live by the sword shall die by the sword' (Matt. 26, 52). The pacificism of the early church received reinforcement from the fact that the army in which Christians would have fought was the army of an empire hostile to Christianity. The conversion of the Roman Empire in the fourth century clouded matters, and Christian men, particularly in the West, took up arms in support of Christian rulers. The teaching of St Augustine of Hippo (354–430) allowed warfare by Christian rulers under severely limited restrictions, but such restrictions were often forgotten or overridden in the turmoil of actual war. A culture giving heroic stature to the warrior developed and long remained a fixture of Western life. Yet the pacifist view never died, and exponents of it can be found in virtually every generation, reminding contemporaries of the injunctions of their founder. By restating the ideal, if only in a partial and, at times, half-hearted way, a peace movement emerged. In the closing decade or so of the tenth century church councils in Aquitaine urged that the clergy and poor be spared from

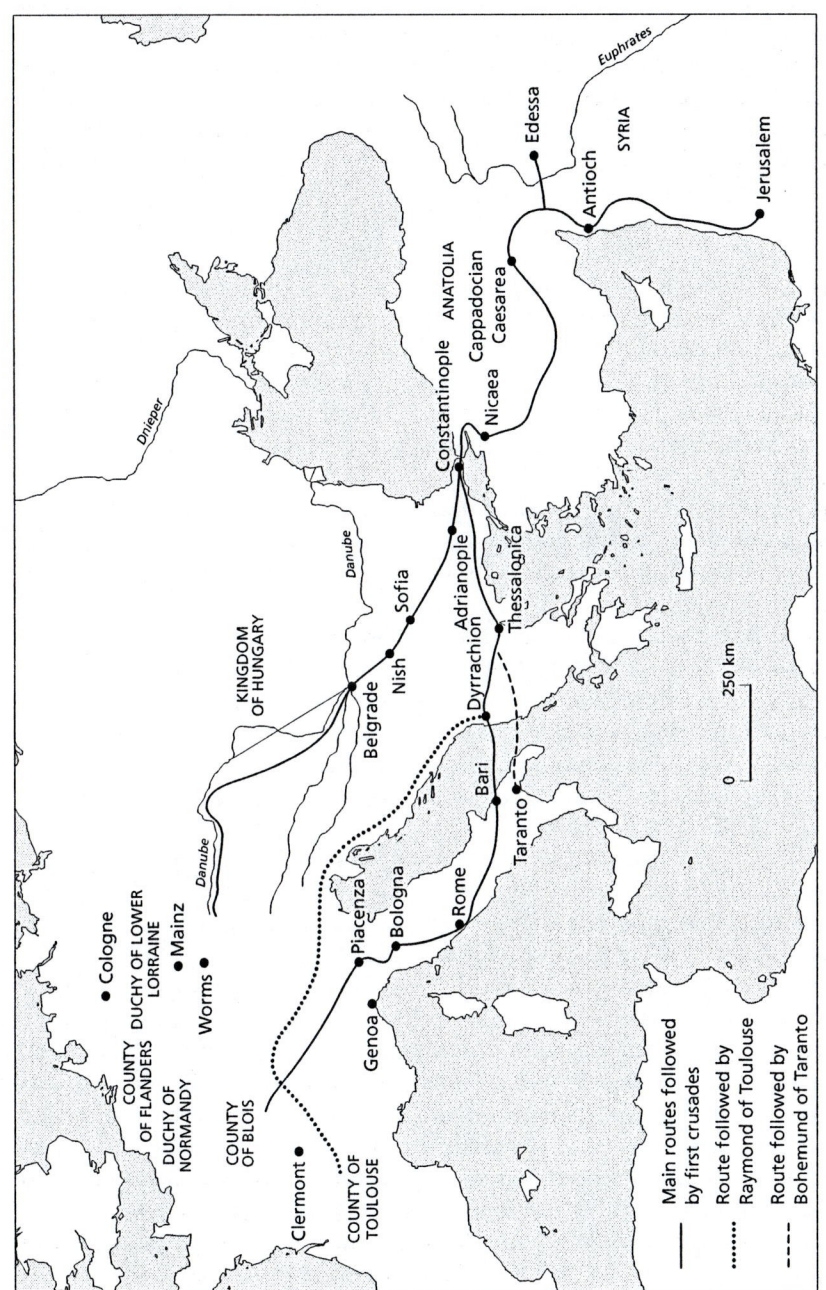

Map 9 Routes of the First Crusade.

violence. At Poitiers, in 1000, a council forbade, under pain of excommunication, the settlement of disputes by arms. The French king supported this for his lands as did other regional councils in France. Oaths were taken to this end, and the Peace of God came into being, the expression of the yearning for a settled life, free from the human consequences of violent warfare, a peace supported by religious principles. More important was the kindred movement, the Truce of God. This called for a total abstinence from war – a truce – during specific times. At first, it was limited to the daylight hours of Sundays and holy days. (Even the troops on the Western Front observed an unofficial Christmas truce in 1914 to the consternation of their officers.) By the middle of the eleventh century, the period of the truce was extended to include the period from Wednesday evening to Monday daybreak, and much of Europe accepted this, at least in theory. Duke William of Normandy, in 1042, not only accepted the truce but extended it, yet this did not stop him from fighting against King Harold at Hastings on 14 October 1066, a Saturday. Not effective always and everywhere, the peace movement at least provided some restraint against unlimited violence in a society containing some but few other restraints.

A war called by a pope, preached by bishops and priests and fought under the banner of the cross against unbelievers seemed to legitimize the use of armed force to resolve human problems. The First Crusade and the others which followed served not only to allow war but to sanctify it: war had become holy. Indeed, 'holy wars' existed in the West before 1095, but these were limited to campaigns in Spain and Sicily. With the First Crusade we have the beginnings of a movement whose ideals were accepted by the vast majority of Christians in every part with only some voices of dissent. In almost every subsequent war between Christian countries each side prayed to God for victory, believing that God was on their side. Some may argue that the brutalities of war needed an approving God to justify them.

On Tuesday, 27 November 1095, Pope Urban II mounted a platform in a field outside the gates of Clermont in central France and before a throng numbering in the thousands announced a holy war. Four different accounts, each written some time after the event, attest to the dramatic sermon. Three of the chroniclers may have been present; one says that he was. The exact words of the pope were not recorded, and what we have are attempts to reconstruct the substance of Pope Urban's address. The Turks were threatening Christian brothers in the East and desecrating their shrines. It was time (in the words of one version) for 'you, who are girt with the belt of knighthood, who arrogantly war against your brother, who cut each other into pieces, who oppress children, plunder widows, commit crimes of murder, sacrilege, robbery' to become soldiers of Christ and now fight against the heathen. Did he ask the warriors of the West to recapture Jerusalem from the Muslims? Probably not. At any rate, soon thereafter he was to include as the goal of the crusade the 'freeing' of the Holy City and, particularly, the Holy Sepulchre, where it was believed Christ had been buried. At Clermont his listeners shouted repeatedly, 'Deus le volt' ('God wills it'), and the crusades had a motto. The bishop of Le Puy cast himself on his knees before the pope, offering to go, and hundreds of others did the same. The crusades had begun.

What lay behind this dramatic pronouncement at Clermont? We should distinguish between remote and proximate factors leading to the pope's call for a crusade. Historians, looking at the remote factors, agree in seeing the meeting of two elements here: pilgrimages, particularly to Jerusalem, and the holy war. They disagree on the weight to be given to each of these. Pilgrims had been going to Jerusalem for centuries. The city had fallen to Muslim Arabs in 636, yet they did not hinder the pilgrims from access to the holy places. From the tenth century pilgrimages from the West became more common and included high-born ladies such as the countess of Swabia and the duchess of Bavaria as well as prominent bishops and abbots. In the eleventh century monks of the Cluniac family helped to organize pilgrimages, and there was a corresponding increase in the number of pilgrims, especially from France and Lorraine. Two great archbishops – of Trier and Mainz – were among them as was Duke Robert of Normandy (1035). The Norseman Harald Hardrada, who in 1066 was to try to conquer England, went on pilgrimage in 1034. In 1051 Earl Swein Godwinson, whose brother Harold was to succeed Edward the Confessor as king of England, for his many sins, including the seduction of an abbess and treacherous action towards the king, went as a penitent pilgrim and died on his way home in 1051, as he was walking barefoot through the mountains of Anatolia. In 1065 a band of German pilgrims, probably numbering about seven thousand, travelled the pilgrim route to the sacred places. And so it went, the annual, untroubled trek of pilgrims to the Holy Sepulchre. And after the conversion of the king of Hungary (975) an overland route was possible. Alternatively, many sailed from ports on the west coast of Italy, especially Bari, across the Adriatic and then overland through the Balkans. The immediate destination in either case was Constantinople on the Bosporus, from which pilgrims, generally in large groups, made their way across Anatolia (the Asiatic part of modern Turkey), then south to Jerusalem. Events were to disturb this peaceful arrangement.

The caliphates that ruled the Islamic world were largely at peace with their Christian neighbours. The Fatimid caliphate, centred at Cairo, controlled Palestine and did not disturb Christian pilgrims. To the east the Abbasid caliphate, centred at Baghdad, provided a buffer against the warlike peoples of central Asia. A crisis occurred at Baghdad in the eleventh century with the result that it could no longer prevent the intrusion of large numbers of Turks in search of new lands, particularly Seljuk Turks. And a Turk soon ruled at Baghdad. During their migration west from central Asia the Turks accepted the religion of Islam. By the 1060s these Muslim Turks were in Armenia and threatening the Byzantine Empire. The defeat of the Byzantine army at Manzikert in Armenia in 1071 left Anatolia open to Turkish penetration. In the same year Turks took Jerusalem from the Fatimids. Christians in Jerusalem did not suffer harsh treatment from their new rulers, although in 1091 some priests who were suspected of intriguing with the Fatimids were expelled. Pilgrims continued to travel to Jerusalem, but their numbers were greatly reduced because of the difficult passage across Anatolia. The pilgrimage to the holy places, which had become a popular expression of religious fervour, was no longer feasible except for the very few. The call of Urban II to recover the Holy Land resonated deeply in the religious sensibilities of Western Christians.

Not so much need be said of the other factor, the holy war. The Christian kingdoms in the north of Spain, never conquered by the Muslims, had begun in earnest a war to reconquer the Muslim lands to the south. In 1063 Pope Alexander II supported their cause by helping to raise an army to fight in Spain; Gregory VII actively supported an expedition in 1073 and again in 1080. (He also toyed with the idea of sending Christian knights to fight for the Eastern emperor, but it all came to nought as Gregory became involved in the great conflict with Henry IV.) Knights from Christian Europe, particularly from France, crossed the Pyrenees to fight the infidel in Spain. Most of the ingredients for the crusades are visible here: papally endorsed or organized military campaigns by Christian knights against unbelievers. Add the ingredient of regaining pilgrim access to Jerusalem, and we have the First Crusade.

It is only when we draw back a distance from the day-to-day events of the time that we can join these two factors of pilgrimage and holy war and see that they created the climate in which the First Crusade took place. Yet it was the day-to-day, year-by-year advance of contingencies that, in the final analysis, produced the crusade: even given the two powerful remote factors, it is to the immediate events that we should turn in locating the reason why this crusade took place. The essential fact is that Pope Urban II was asked by Emperor Alexius I for troops against the Turks. The what-might-have-beens of history are not really history, but one may legitimately wonder if the crusades would have happened if the emperor had not requested military assistance. His position was not perilous in 1095: he had the situation in Anatolia well under control and the Turks posed no immediate threat. What Alexius needed were fresh recruits for his army, since the traditional recruiting grounds were not as accessible as they once were. With one major offensive he felt he could drive the Turks completely out of Anatolia and, thus, effectively destroy their military power once and for all. To this end Alexius sent envoys to a papal council held at Piacenza in March 1095. They asked the fathers of the council to urge knightly warriors to fight for Alexius; it would serve, they argued, to reopen the routes for Christian pilgrims to reach the Holy Land. And it was later, in November, of that year that Urban II gave his rallying cry at Clermont. What Alexius wanted was Western mercenaries; what he got was the First Crusade.

Recruitment for the crusade posed no problem. Leaving Clermont, the pope preached the crusade at Limoges, Toulouse, Angers, Tours and elsewhere in France. Great princes took the crusader's oath, sewed the cross on their shoulders and prepared for the journey east: Raymond, count of Toulouse, Robert, duke of Normandy (eldest son of William the Conqueror), Godfrey, duke of Lower Lorraine, and his younger brother Baldwin as well as others from the noble class, each with his own army. Back in Italy in August 1096, Urban got support from Genoa, Bologna and, especially, after a slight delay, from the Normans in the south, where Bohemond, son of their leader, Guiscard, took the cross. To avoid or, at least ameliorate, discord among these ambitious princes, Urban appointed the bishop of Le Puy as leader of the crusade, directly responsible to the pope.

Now, as happens occasionally in history, a person stepped out of near obscurity to play an unexpected part. Peter the Hermit began preaching the crusade within weeks of Clermont, travelling by donkey through parts of France and Lorraine. His fervour and eloquence so electrified crowds wherever he went that, by the time he reached Cologne in April 1096, he had with him perhaps as many as 10,000 who had responded to his call. At Cologne he attracted Germans to follow him, and when he left there his crusade numbered about 20,000. Often called the People's Crusade, Peter's crusade was more than that. Indeed, his followers were drawn in large numbers from the peasantry, but they also included many warriors from the knightly class, who would provide the military leadership of the expedition. A lack of discipline soon appeared. Peter's crusaders killed 4,000 inhabitants of one town in Hungary. When they reached Belgrade, they savaged the population and fired the town. At Sophia they were given an escort to accompany them to Constantinople, which they reached on 1 August 1096. One can only imagine the interview between the resplendent, sophisticated emperor and the unwashed, coarse, simple hermit from Picardy. Alexius had the sense to move them quickly across the Bosporus, but in Anatolia they suffered a disastrous defeat on 21 October. A remnant dispersed, and Peter, escaping the fate of the army and later surviving the disgrace of desertion, was still later to enter Jerusalem with the conquering Christian army.

Before following the main part of the crusade in its march across Europe and Asia Minor, a difficult question must be asked: what motivated the crusaders to take up the cross and join a military expedition to the Holy Land? The most difficult area of the past which any historian faces is individual human motivation. What was in the minds of countless men, whose names are lost to us, as they left home, family and country to go on the crusade? At the remove of nine hundred years answers do not come easy. These cautions should not stop historians from asking why men volunteered for the crusades, but they should oblige us to think in the subjunctive mood.

An Italian priest's remarks on this subject were reported by an early twelfth-century chronicler:

> Different reasons are given by different people. Some say that all
> pilgrims are moved by God and the Lord Jesus Christ. Others say that
> the Frankish nobles and a majority of the people have set out on
> their journey motivated solely by frivolous reasons.

That remark places the matter at its sharpest dichotomy. The non-religious reasons can be summarized. A burgeoning population, recent flooding in 1094, drought and famine in the next year, vulnerability to attack by outlaws and hostile neighbours – these were all facts of life in the years leading up to the crusade. Younger sons with slim prospects could be found everywhere in a society which set high store on the manly art of warfare. There was the prospect of gaining land in the East and, for princes, perhaps their own kingdoms or principalities. Yet, when a knight bade farewell to his wife and children, he could not know what lay ahead, quite possibly death in battle, or, at least, years of separation. Since much human motivation is very often mixed, it is difficult in all this to exclude entirely a spiritual element. To go to the Holy Land as an armed pilgrim, to enter Jerusalem, to kneel at the Holy Sepulchre and to venerate the cross of Jesus would have moved many a conventionally pious Christian. Added to that must be the 'crusading indulgence', often misunderstood even in the eleventh century. The Council of Clermont granted an 'indulgence' for those going on the crusade. The text merits quoting,

> To whoever solely out of religious devotion and not for acquiring honour or wealth proceeds to liberate the church of God at Jerusalem his journey will count for all penance.

What the council meant was that the church would remit the penance due for their sins if they went on a crusade for pious reasons. It did not mean that their sins would be forgiven – these had to be sincerely repented of and confessed – but that the penance required to be performed would be remitted. In other words, the journey to Jerusalem was considered to take the place of the required penance, and this applied only to those crusaders motivated by religious ideals. All this having been said, the rhetoric of preachers could lead audiences to conclude that the crusader would gain remission of all his sins, although, it should be added, the evidence of exaggerated preaching is scanty at best for this crusade. The promise of heaven or something akin to it would have made taking the cross attractive, perhaps even compelling, for thousands for whom life after death with eternal rewards or eternal punishments formed a fixed part of their view of life.

Three crusading armies raised in Germany to fight the infidel in the East began their crusade by slaughtering Jews in the West. At Worms, in May 1096, they killed all the Jews in the ghetto and even those given sanctuary by the Catholic bishop. These crusaders then went on to Mainz, where there was a massacre of Jews that lasted several days. Next to Ratisbon, and another massacre. They murdered Jewish communities at Neuss, Wevelinghofen and Xanten. In Bohemia they exterminated Jews at Prague. Despite the attempts of local bishops to protect the Jews, barbaric savagery was carried out in the name of the cross. Many contemporary observers saw a divine judgement on these crusaders for they met disastrous defeats in Hungary. What motivated these crusaders in their treatment of the Jews? Probably greed and hatred and the excuse of having 'unbelievers' close at hand.

The main body of crusaders travelled east, using the traditional pilgrim routes: either overland through Hungary and the Balkans or across the Adriatic Sea to Dyrrachion and then over land. Their destination was Constantinople. The crusaders came in four fairly large armies, but there were smaller groups as well. The earliest journeys of these armies began in October 1096, and by the following May (1097) they had all reached Constantinople. Provisioning an army whose total might have exceeded 60,000 created problems en route, and, when local peoples were unwilling or unable to sell the necessary provisions, violence erupted. Yet the movement of such a large number was remarkably free of major incident.

Emperor Alexius had two immediate aims: first, to acquire oaths of allegiance from the crusaders and, second, to move them out of the area of Constantinople as quickly as possible. The oath required the crusaders to return to the emperor any lands they captured which were previously held by the empire before the Turkish invasion and to swear their loyalty to the emperor for any other lands they might conquer. Only Raymond of Toulouse demurred, but even he took a modified oath. By the end of May 1097, the crusading armies had all been transported across the Bosporus to Asia and away from Constantinople. Alexius accomplished both objectives by diplomatic persuasion and by bounteous gifts

6 Crac des chevaliers (Syria), crusader castle. Reproduced by permission of A.F. Kersting.

to the leaders of the crusade. He could feel optimistic that his capital was safe and the prospects of recovering lands good.

The armies were on their way. On 19 June they captured Nicaea, remembered for its council in 325. On 1 July they handed the Turks a staggering defeat, and the way was now open to cross Anatolia. Only the great city of Antioch lay in their way to Jerusalem. They arrived at Antioch on 21 October, and there the crusade became stalled for eight months. Meanwhile, the ambitious Baldwin, brother of Duke Godfrey, led a spur into the lands of the Armenians, where he was welcomed as a liberator from Turkish control. On 6 February 1098, he entered Edessa, east of the Euphrates River, where he was adopted by the local Armenian ruler as son and heir. By the following March, Baldwin had become count of the county of Edessa. Having attained what he had set out for – a principality of his own – he abandoned the crusade, and the first crusader state had been established in the East.

Antioch with its high walls and its citadel invulnerable on one side by a steep precipice proved a formidable obstacle to the crusaders. It could not be bypassed, lest there be an enemy at their back, and had to be taken. A siege was decided upon, perhaps unwisely. It lasted eight months and ended only on 3 June 1098 with a victorious assault by the crusaders. It took another battle, on 28 June, for their possession of Antioch to be secure. The way was now open to Jerusalem, only two hundred miles or so to the south. Yet before they could recover from the long siege and brutal battle and march to Jerusalem, the crusaders suffered a major setback: the bishop of Le Puy, the pope's legate and the acknowledged leader of the crusade, died. Much of what followed might have been avoided if he had survived.

Despite the proximity of Jerusalem it took more than a year for the less than united crusaders to reach the Holy City. A treacherous route lay before them with many fortified places to be pacified by gifts or taken by arms. Not until the seventh day of July 1099 did the pilgrim-warriors catch sight of the walls of the city. A mighty fortress, Jerusalem was almost impregnable to direct attack. If the crusaders could construct wooden towers, built to the height of the walls and placed on wheels, they might gain entry and then open the gates. The unexpected arrival of ships at the port of Jaffa provided the necessary tools and foraging in Samaria provided the necessary wood. About noon on 14 July 1099, Godfrey of Lorraine and his men forced a bridge across from their mobile tower to the top of the wall, and they were soon in the city. What followed is one of the saddest pictures in the history of the Christian church. The crusaders slew a great number of the inhabitants of Jerusalem in a wild butchery. Muslims and Jews, men and women of every age, children and even infants fell to the savagery of the Christian sword. An observer relates that, on the next morning, he went to the area of the Temple, knee-deep in blood. Soon the crusaders were at the Holy Sepulchre, offering thanks to God for their victory.

It was not long before states were established in what Westerners would call 'Outremer' (overseas). In addition to the county of Edessa, a county of Antioch

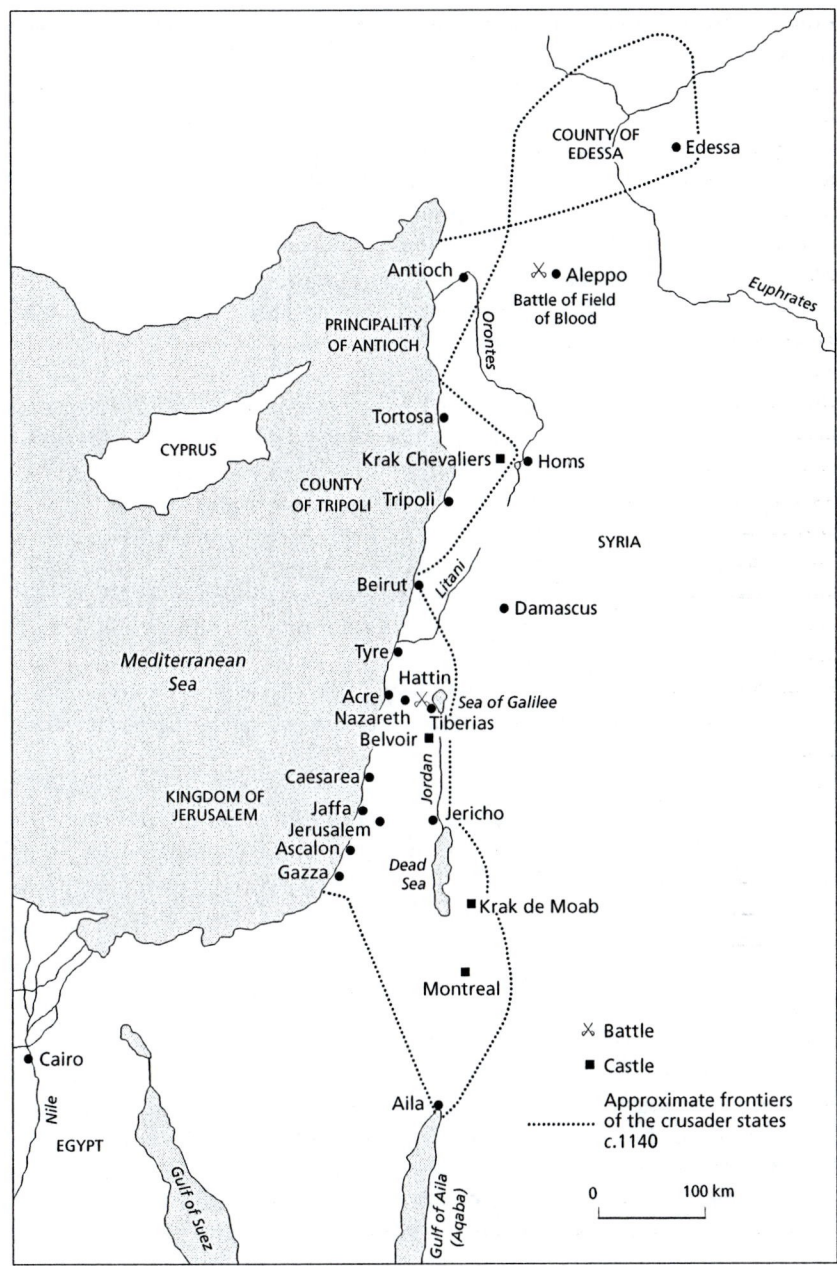

Map 10 Crusader states.

and even a kingdom of Jerusalem were created. Later, in 1109, a county of Tripoli was carved out. These four Crusader States continued as a presence in mid-Eastern affairs into the second half of the thirteenth century. And military orders also appeared.

In 1119, the crusader knight Hugh de Paynes and eight other knights took the religious vows of poverty, chastity and obedience in the church of the Holy Sepulchre. They took up residence on the Temple Mount, and thus their name the Knights Templar. They did not give up their arms but were armed monks, dedicated to the religious life and also to the protection of pilgrims and, more generally, to the protection of Jerusalem from the Muslims. St Bernard of Clairvaux supported them, and they grew in numbers and acquired considerable wealth. Their round churches can be seen in the West, for example, in London and Cambridge. Another order was soon created. In the early 1120s, knights who had given up their swords to care for poor and sick pilgrims took up arms again as Knights Hospitaller. They too prospered. Later, in 1198, from a German hospital established in Jerusalem there developed the Teutonic Knights. Thanks to generous donations from secular rulers, particularly German kings, they ruled over vast territories in Eastern Europe, in the thirteenth century their lands stretching along the Baltic Sea from Gdansk almost to the Russian border. (They feature in the great Eisenstein film *Alexander Nevsky*.) Some, but only a few, found their mission anomalous.

Other crusades will enter into these pages from time to time, but this might be the place to quote the judgement of the doyen of the history of the crusades, Sir Steven Runciman:

> The triumphs of the Crusade were the triumphs of faith. But faith without wisdom is a dangerous thing. By the inexorable laws of history the whole world pays for the crimes and follies of each of its citizens. In the long sequence of interaction and fusion between Orient and Occident out of which our civilization has grown, the Crusades were a tragic and destructive episode. The historian as he gazes back across the centuries at their gallant story must find his admiration overcast by sorrow at the witness that it bears to the limitations of human nature. There was so much courage and so little honour, so much devotion and so little understanding. High ideals were besmirched by cruelty and greed, enterprise and endurance by a blind and narrow self-righteousness; and the Holy War itself was nothing more than a long act of intolerance in the name of God, which is the sin against the Holy Ghost.

Not all will concur with the Runciman judgement, yet it raises issues no serious student of our history can neglect.

Further reading

Many of the themes treated in this chapter and in the next two chapters can be seen in a broader context in Malcom Barber, *The Two Cities: Medieval Europe, 1050–1320* (London and New York, 1992).

On reform as inherent to the Christian church see Gerhart B. Lardner, *The Idea of Reform: Its Impact on Christian Thought and Action in the Age of the Fathers* (Cambridge, MA, 1959). For a measured, well-informed approach to the reform of the eleventh century and for much else see Colin Morris, *The Papal Monarchy: The Western Church from 1050 to 1250* (Oxford, 1989). Gerd Tellenbach has written two stimulating books on this period, the first when he was twenty-nine (*Church, State and Christian Society at the Time of the Investiture Struggle*; tr. R.F. Bennet; Oxford, 1940) and the second which appeared when he was eighty-six (*The Church in Western Europe from the Tenth to the Early Twelfth Century*; tr. Timothy Reuter; Cambridge, 1993). An excellent summary of the monastic reforming movements of this period is Joachim Wollasch, 'Monasticism: The First Wave of Reform', *The New Cambridge Medieval History*, vol. 3, *c.900–c.1024* (ed. Timothy Reuter; Cambridge, 1999), pp. 163–85. Opposing much of the conventional inter-pretation is Geoffrey Barraclough's stimulating *The Medieval Papacy* (London, 1969). Every student of the period should have Brian Tierney, *The Crisis of Church and State, 1050–1300* (Englewood Cliffs, NJ, 1964), whose valuable introduction provides a view of Gregory VII contrary to the view presented here. For a work of mature reflection see H.E.J. Cowdrey, *Gregory VII* (Oxford, 1998). For a broad view of the German king see Ian S. Robinson, *Henry IV of Germany, 1056–1106* (Cambridge, 1999). The classic study of the question of celibacy, now somewhat out of date, is Henry C. Lea, *History of Sacerdotal Celibacy* (3rd edn; New York, 1907). An excellent discussion of the arguments supporting clerical marriage is Anne Llewellyn Barstow, *Married Priests and the Reforming Papacy: The Eleventh-Century Debate* (New York, 1982). See, too, the summary in James A. Brundage, *Law, Sex and Christian Society in the Middle Ages* (Chicago, 1987), especially pp. 214–23.

For matters concerning disputes between the churches of East and West see Steven Runciman, *The Eastern Schism: A Study of the Papacy and the Eastern Churches during the XI and XII Centuries* (Oxford, 1955) and Francis Dvornik, *Byzantium and the Roman Primacy* (New York, 1966). More specific is Richard Mayne's article 'East and West in 1054', *Cambridge Historical Journal* 11 (1954), 133–48.

The literature on the crusades is prodigious and seems to grow exponentially. The starting place will be Sir Steven Runciman, *A History of the Crusades* (3 vols; Cambridge, 1951–54). A multi-authored work is Kenneth M. Setton, gen. ed., *A History of the Crusades* (2nd edn; 6 vols; Madison, WI, 1969–89). The works of Jonathan Riley-Smith have brilliantly opened up a variety of topics. One might begin with his one-volume work, *The Crusades: A Short History* (London, 1987) and his *The First Crusaders, 1095–1131* (Cambridge, 1997). Readers interested in military history should see John France, *Victory in the East: A Military History of the First Crusade* (Cambridge, 1994). An excellent article is E.O. Blake, 'A Hermit Goes to War: Peter and the Origins of the First Crusade', in *Monks, Hermits and the Ascetic Tradition* (ed. W.J. Shiels; *Studies in Church History*, vol. 21, 1984), pp. 79–107. For aspects of the later crusades see N. Housley, *The Italian Crusades: The Papal-Angevin Alliance and the Crusade Against Lay Power, 1254–1343* (Oxford, 1982) and *The Later Crusades: From Lyons to Alcazar* (Oxford, 1992). Stimulating questions are raised in C.J. Tyerman, *The Invention of the Crusades* (Toronto, 1998). For a contemporary

Eastern view see the account by the daughter of Emperor Alexius: Anna Comnena, *The Alexiad of Anna Comnena* (tr. E.R.A. Sewter; Harmondsworth, Mddsx, 1969).

For the peace movement through the ages see Ronald G. Musto, *The Catholic Peace Tradition* (Maryknoll, NY, 1986), *The Peace Tradition in the Catholic Church: An Annotated Bibliography* (New York, 1986) and *Catholic Peacemakers: A Documentary History* (2 vols; New York, 1993–96). For informative essays on the peace movement in France see T. Head and R. Landes (eds), *The Peace of God: Social Violence and Religious Response in France Around the Year 1000* (Ithaca, NY, and London, 1992) and for a detailed explanation of the origins of the peace movement in Aquitaine see Thomas Head, 'The Development of the Peace of God in Aquitaine (970–1005)', *Speculum* 74 (1999), 656–86.

Malcolm Barber, *The New Knighthood: A History of the Order of the Temple* (Cambridge, 1994) is an excellent study of the subject.

8

THE TWELFTH CENTURY

Medieval Europe came of age in the twelfth century as also, it will be argued, did the Christian church. Growth, development, expansion, maturation and even affluence are all relative. Accepting that as a premise, we can still say that the twelfth century experienced all of these in a marked way. More and more land came under cultivation as woods were levelled, marshland filled and marginal lands made arable. No one knows for certain whether the growth in population created the need for more food supply or whether the increased food supply contributed to population growth. When farmers could grow more than sub-sistence required, the possibility of commerce was opened up. Selling the excess to towns, which were growing in number and size, provided the seller with actual money with which he could buy town-made goods, such as finished cloth. Commerce was the essential ingredient in defining a town, and commercial towns soon developed a merchant class and an artisan class, both of which organized themselves into guilds, which had a religious flavour. This rural–urban commercial nexus was the case particularly north of the Alps. Not just London, Paris and Cologne, but places like Worms, Bristol, Tours, Angers and dozens of other towns developed as places of robust commerce. Most importantly, the great towns of Flanders – Bruges, Ghent, Ypres, Lille and Arras – became centres of an international trade in textiles. The fields of England and Wales, many of them until recently woods, were now dotted with sheep, owing in large part to the work of the Cistercian monks (whom we shall soon meet more fully) as England became the largest wool producer in Europe and the principal supplier to the looms of Flanders. South of the Alps the story was somewhat different. There maritime cities developed thanks to an expanded commerce with the East. The crusades had opened up sea lanes, and luxury items (e.g., silks, spices) were imported. Ports such as Genoa, Pisa and, above all, Venice thrived on this trade. A vast market in international trade was held in the French province of Champagne, where fairs attracted merchants from much of Western Europe, who came there to deal in a wide variety of goods. Tin from England, cloth from Flanders, horses from Lombardy, spices from Syria via Italy, furs from Scandinavia and much else were bought and sold at what was Europe's greatest wholesale market.

International commerce demands some form of international banking. Notes guaranteeing actual money were used to facilitate business. Incipient capitalism needed capital, and bankers loaned money at interest, a practice condemned by the church since money could not fructify and, in any case, it was the duty of every Christian to assist others in need without receiving anything – like interest – in return. To provide the need for investment capital it was principally Jewish money-lenders who stepped in and oiled the wheels of commerce. Only later did Christians find arguments to allow their entry into banking free of charges of usury, but Lombard bankers and the great house of Medici were centuries away.

Perhaps as a consequence and clearly as a concommitant of these economic developments were sweeping cultural changes. Educational focus shifted from the monasteries to the towns. Secular schools (i.e., schools run principally by the secular clergy), clustered near cathedrals and other great churches, became centres of a new learning. Paris with its three schools stood above the rest, but notable schools also existed at Laon, Rheims, Tours, Regensburg, Northampton and elsewhere, where the fame of masters attracted students. Universities were to develop later from some of these schools. The curriculum stressed logic and grammar: how to think and how to write. Fuelling this intellectual ferment were texts of the ancients, newly translated into Latin, which began to enter into the West in ever increasing numbers. Translations of ancient Greek texts from Arabic texts were made in Spain; translations were made from Arabic and Greek texts in Sicily. The result was a torrent of scientific, mathematical and philosophical texts. Aristotle was only partially known before, but from the 1130s new translations of logical works began to appear, and by 1240 nearly all his works, including his ethics and metaphysics, were in the hands of Western students. Apart from the schools, a literature in the vernacular blossomed as these languages became the principal vehicles for literary expression. *El Cid* was being recited in Spanish, the *Nibelungenlied* in German and the *Chanson de Roland* in French. And the Arthurian legend entered into world literature. In the south of France troubadours sang songs of courtly love, a love largely unrequited. An increasingly affluent age was enjoying the finer things in life. And before century's end Gothic churches would begin to appear.

In this dynamic environment the church continued to live its life: babies were baptized, couples married, dying men and women received the last rites and the traditional words of Christian burial were spoken over their bodies. Yet in the practical life of Christians new forms developed and old forms changed as religious orders sprang up and devotional practices played a larger role in the daily living of the Christian faith. Popes continued to look more and more like great princes, and the legacy of the First Crusade haunted the West as two further crusades were (unsuccessfully) fought in the 1140s and 1189–91.

Popes and anti-popes and emperors

With the reform papacy in place in the early twelfth century and with fairly amicable relations with the German emperor after the Concordat of Worms (1122) one would expect gentle breezes and full sails for the popes. Such was not to be the case. Internal problems centred about the question of who was pope, and external problems centred about the question of what role the emperor should play in Italy. Uncertainty, turmoil, disruption and even armed violence accompanied the process of resolving these questions, and there was little that was edifying in the process.

The papal election in 1124 was to have repercussions to be felt for decades. The death of Calixtus II only two years after he had brought peace between the papacy and the empire exposed once again the vulnerability of papal elections to the interest of rival Roman families. At that time, the rival families were the Frangipani and the Pierleoni. The majority of the cardinals supported the Pierleoni candidate and elected Celestine II. Meanwhile, a minority supported the Frangipani candidate and elected Honorius II. While Celestine was being installed and the hymn of thanksgiving (*Te Deum*) was being sung, the Frangipani broke into the basilica with swords drawn. They violently tore the papal mantle from Celestine's shoulders and forced him to resign. Honorius also resigned but was soon elected by the cardinals, and the intimidated Celestine agreed to accept this new election. Schism had been avoided, but at the next papal election it became a reality. In 1130 as Honorius lay dying, the Frangipani family, which had supported his election, feared that the Pierleoni would gain control of the next election. Honorius's frail body, still clinging to life, was moved to the monastery of St Gregory the Great on the Caelian Hill. The convention concerning papal elections was that an election should not take place until after the burial of the pope. Sometime during the night of 13–14 February, Honorius died and his body was immediately buried at the monastery. An election by the Frangipani cardinals followed at once. This middle-of-the-night election by a rump of the college of cardinals produced Innocent II, the manner of whose election was to haunt his pontificate. Within hours of this election the majority of the cardinals elected a cardinal member of the Pierleoni family, who took the name Anacletus II.

Western Europe was soon divided in a schism which lasted for eight years. Generally speaking, Innocent II gained support of Christendom north of the Alps, where Christian kings – Louis VI of France, Lothar of Germany and even Henry I of England – acknowledged him as pope. The great transalpine church-men rallied to his cause: Abbot Suger of St Denis (Paris), Peter the Venerable of Cluny, St Norbert, archbishop of Magdeburg, and, especially, St Bernard, abbot of Clairvaux. The latter, the most effective spokesman for Innocent's cause, was moved not by a conviction of the canonical validity of Innocent's election but by the belief that Innocent was better suited to be pope. Anacletus II was acknowledged as pope in Rome and in southern Italy, where he entered into an alliance with Roger of Sicily, the Norman king. It was only with the death of Anacletus in 1138 that the schism ended. The triumphant Pope Innocent summoned the bishops of the Latin West to the Lateran Basilica for a general council. Perhaps as many as six hundred bishops and abbots journeyed to Rome in 1139 for the reforming Second Lateran Council – one even walked all the way from Scotland – but the council produced little new and Innocent used it to act vengefully against the late Pope Anacletus by annulling all his ordinations. Four years of relative calm ensued, but a storm was not far away.

When the storm came, it was a violent storm, which saw armies pitted against armies and which, when stripped of all excesses of rhetoric, was really about who would control Italy. In a general way, it can be said that Italy was divided into three parts. In the south the power of the Norman kings extended from Sicily in a broad swath across the Italian boot. Central Italy, with territories stretching northward along the Adriatic coast, formed what we may now call the Papal States. North of this was a patchwork of city states, each with a hub city and surrounding territories, some having extensive territories (e.g., Milan, Pavia, Cremona); over much of the north the German king-emperor held nominal authority. It was a time-bomb ticking. All it needed was an ambitious emperor, and he came in the person of Frederick, whose red beard gave him the name by which he is known to history, Barbarossa.

Two popes entered into conflicts with Frederick Barbarossa, Hadrian IV and Alexander III, and their conflicts were not about theology or the spiritual meaning of life but were essentially about political matters, particularly about the relationship between pope and emperor with Italy the focus of their conflicts. Nicholas Brakespear, fresh from successes in reorganizing and reforming the church in Scandinavia, was the unanimous choice of the cardinals in 1154 and became the only English pope, Hadrian IV (1154–59). His was not a tranquil pontificate. In the city of Rome itself the 'senate' had proclaimed a republican commune under the sway of the reformer Arnold of Brescia, who preached evangelical poverty and inveighed against the wealth of the church. Arnold was forced by Pope Hadrian to flee the city. He was soon captured by Frederick Barbarossa and handed over to the Roman Prefect, who summarily executed him and then threw his ashes into the Tiber. Soon thereafter the pope crowned Barbarossa as Emperor Frederick I (18 June 1155).

Ten days before the imperial coronation, ominous signs of things to come are visible, at least from our vantage point. Frederick and Hadrian met each other at Sutri, north of Rome: the austere Englishman from Hertfordshire and the handsome, vital German from Swabia. It was an awkward moment. By tradition, protocol required Frederick to lead the pope's mule. This he refused to do. Whatever the reason for this – there could simply have been a misunderstanding by Barbarossa – three days later he performed the ritual act. It was an ill omen. Once crowned, Emperor Frederick faced a hostile Roman commune and returned to Germany not with totally happy memories of his visit to Rome.

Eager to consolidate his power north of the Alps, Barbarossa convened a diet (assembly) at Besançon in October 1157. In the meantime, Hadrian, facing the Normans to his south without imperial support, had little alternative but to enter into alliance with the Norman king of Sicily, William I. To the imperial diet, presided over by an emperor unhappy with this papal-Norman alliance, the pope sent two legates, one, Rolando Bandinelli (the future Alexander III), who read the pope's letter in Latin, which was translated by Frederick's chancellor into German. In that translation it appeared that the pope was claiming the right to confer the empire as a benefice from the pope to the emperor, thus subjecting emperor to pope. So angry was one of the German nobles on hearing this that he drew his sword, but Frederick intervened and ordered the legates to return to Rome. Later, but too late, the pope explained that he meant the Latin word *beneficium* not in the legal sense of a 'benefice' but simply as a 'benefit'. But the damage had been done.

Frederick now turned the attention of his large army to the wealthy Lombard cities, over which he wanted to exercise more than mere nominal power. The pope, now allied not only with Sicily but also with Milan, clearly set himself against the emperor's ambitions by threatening Frederick with excommunication. With tensions at a high point and an imperial army in Italy, Hadrian died unexpectedly on 1 September 1159.

Another disputed election and another schism followed. The election of Rolando Bandinelli as Alexander III (1159–64) could not have been more provocative to Frederick I: this was the very man who had insulted the imperial office at Besançon. Five pro-imperial cardinals elected Victor IV (1159–64). The ensuing schism was to last nearly twenty years. Victor and his two successors received virtually no support outside the empire, whereas Alexander III was widely recognized as pope even by the reconciled kings of France and England, Louis VII and Henry II. (It was the pope's need of Henry II's support that complicated Alexander III's response to the Becket crisis. See chapter 9.) For three years Alexander lived in France, for much of the time at Sens. The resolution of the schism occurred not by quiet negotiations but on the battlefield.

Encouraged by Alexander, the northern cities, led by Milan, formed the Lombard League to oppose the emperor. Two years later the armies of the Lombard League, in one of the major battles of medieval history, thoroughly routed the imperial army at Legnano. So great was the defeat that it was thought that the emperor himself had been slain, until, without banner and shield, he came straggling into Pavia, an emperor almost beyond recognition. Peace with the pope soon followed (July 1177), and the schism was at an end.

To mark its end, Alexander convened a council (Third Lateran Council, 1179). Its chief long-term accomplishment was the reform of papal elections, left virtually unchanged since 1059: it gave each cardinal an equal vote and required a two-thirds vote for election. For the next two hundred years the papacy was not troubled by disputed elections and (except for a brief hiccup in 1328) the challenge of anti-popes, and this procedure, with only the slightest of modifications, still remains in force. The council also forbade tournaments and even denied Christian burial to those dying in tournaments. Alexander III died in 1181 and Frederick I died by drowning in 1190 in Asia Minor as he led a large German army in a futile attempt to recapture Jerusalem from the Turks (Third Crusade). He had arranged, in 1186, a marriage between his son Henry and the Sicilian princess Constance, sister to the king of Sicily. From this marriage, in time, came the involvement of German emperors in southern Italy, a state of affairs at odds with the political interests of the popes.

If these disputes of the twelfth century between pope and emperor appear to the reader to be matters more of politics than of religion, who can gainsay that? We see the pope as one political player among others in the struggle for power in Western Europe, and religion had little to do with it. A papal defence would claim that the pope needed to be independent and free from the coercion of secular rules in order to exercise his sacred mission, and he thus needed strong papal territories in central Italy to guarantee that independence. For the truly religious movements of the time we need look beyond Rome to see the profound changes that affected the living of the Christian life.

New religious orders

The twelfth century witnessed critical developments in the practice of the Christian faith. New religious orders and new forms of religious devotion produced a flowering of practical Christianity, far removed from the seemingly sordid world of papal politics. Historians may debate the reasons for these extraordinary developments – a thriving economy, pressures of demographic growth, maturing of the forms of religion, an individual quest for more than what the material world can give. They may even propose various names to describe this phenomenon – reform, revival, renaissance, even reformation. Yet, whatever the reasons and the names given, the reality is beyond dispute: a religious enthusiasm seldom, perhaps never, witnessed before in the (by then) long history of Christianity. Changes in the life lived by men and women in religious vows (which we, perhaps inexactly, call 'the religious life') were an essential expression of this enthusiasm and near its epicentre.

The traditional religious life was lived for centuries by men and women following the Rule of St Benedict. At the opening of the twelfth century we can see two forms of Benedictine monasticism. In the first place, there were hundreds of monasteries, each independent, united with others only in their use of the same rule and the same garb, the black habit that gave them the name Black Monks. When Benedictine monasticism is referred to for this and later periods, the reference is to this form of monastic life. The other form, which has been met already (chapter 7), was really an order, subject to the authority of the abbot of Cluny. Scores of priories and thousands of monks all over Western Europe owed their obedience to him. Apart from this unusual form of organization, these monks followed the Rule of St Benedict with an emphasis on silence and liturgical prayer. They were simply called Cluniacs. The Columban form of monasticism had receded from its great height of the sixth and seventh centuries and, by the twelfth century, survived virtually only in Ireland. Hermits leading solitary lives remained a constant feature of religious life, but they were always few in numbers. This settled state of affairs was to be transformed in the course of the twelfth century, not beyond recognition – far from it – but, one might think, with a more attractive diversity of shapes and forms and, above all, with newly infused spiritual vitality.

New religious orders came into being in the twelfth century, chief among them the Augustinian canons and the Cistercian monks, but there were also other, smaller yet influential orders. What must be said, above all, about the Augustinian canons is that they were canons and not monks and that they more than any of the other new orders of monks constituted a break with past forms of the religious life. Canons were essentially priests who lived in a community and who normally exercised the care of souls in some way. Those who followed a rule were called Canons Regular (*regula*, rule), while the others were Canons Secular (*saeculum*, world). A word must be said about the so-called Rule of St Augustine. St Augustine of Hippo (354–430) wrote a letter to his widowed sister to encourage her and the other women who lived in a religious community. Within a short time, still in the fifth century, the text of that letter was changed: the gender was changed from female to male and additions were made, aimed at providing an orderly life for a male community. In 1118 some of the more detailed parts of the text were deleted, and what remained was the 'Rule of St Augustine'. It was this rule that was adopted by the Canons Regular, who thus became known as Augustinian Canons. Unlike Benedict's rule, this rule contented itself with general principles, leaving details to be filled in by customary uses. It provided for a life lived in a monastery – large houses generally became known as abbeys, smaller ones priories – by men vowing to live an unmarried life in obedience to their abbot (or prior) and without property of their own. A moderate life resulted. Meat was not absent from their table, and their form of work tended to be more intellectual than manual. The very flexibility of this rule proved to be its greatest asset. Hundreds of Augustinian monasteries were founded within a few decades in Germany, England, France, Spain and Italy, usually modest foundations with modest endowments and modest ambitions. In Spain, they undertook the relief of the poor and the ransom of captives from the Muslims. In England they had large monasteries at places like Colchester and Oxford and literally scores of small priories, numbering in time well over three hundred in all. In addition, there were important hospitals such as St Bartholomew's at Smithfield, London, as well as less well-known hospitals with but a prior and a few canons, following the rule as best they could. Many of the larger houses provided priests for parishes in the neighbourhood. The ability of the Augustinian canons to lead a common life and to adapt that life to other needs made them successful journeymen in the monastic movement. Nothing glamorous or even faintly flashy about them: they

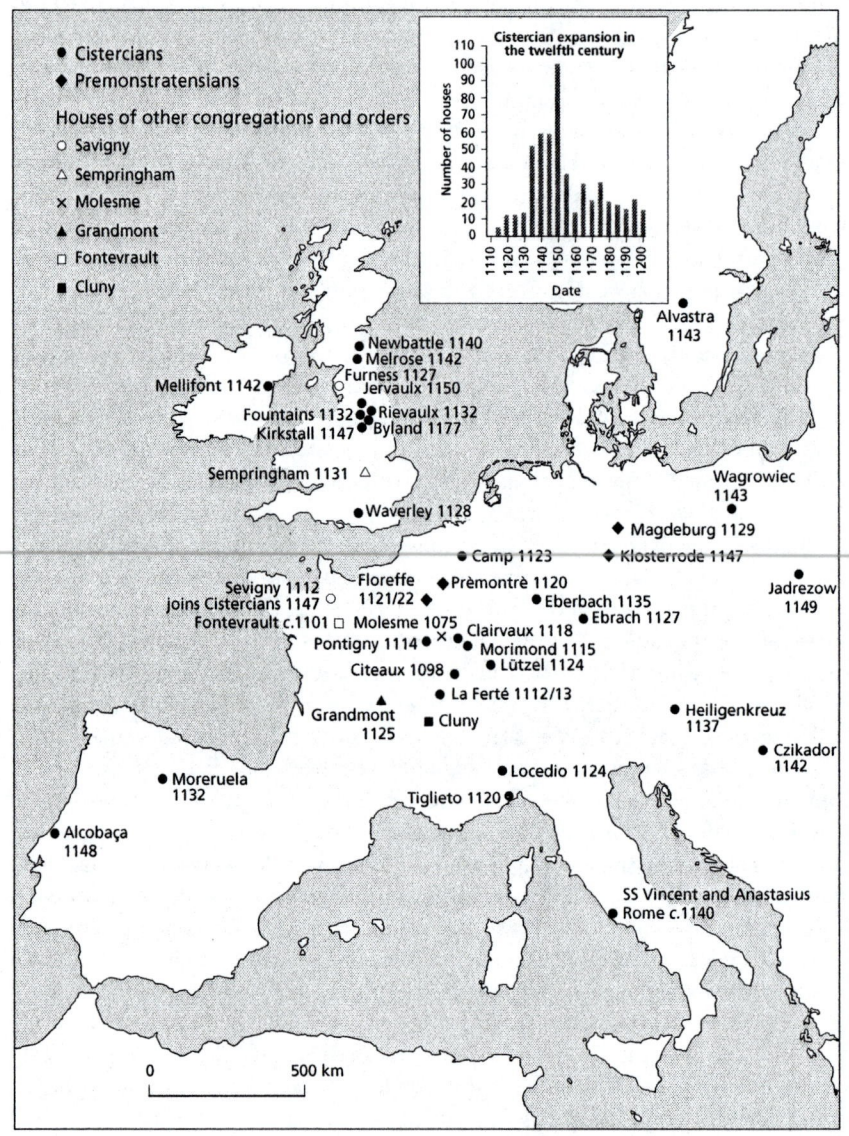

Map 11 Cistercians and other orders: major houses founded by 1150.

said their prayers and led lives of practical Christianity. One medieval commentator summed up their life:

> The habit they wear is neither sumptuous nor ragged, and they thus avoid pride and the affectation of holiness. They do not need many things and content themselves with modest expenditures.

For the sparkling splendour of the religious life we must look elsewhere to the other great order founded at this time.

The achievements of the Cistercian order must stand out as the success story *par excellence* of the medieval church. In 1098 a score or so of somewhat discontented monks left a Benedictine abbey in Burgundy and went deep into a wooded valley in search of a simpler, more primitive monastic life. The valley was Cîteaux and from that valley came the Cistercian order. These discontented monks had no thought of founding a new order, merely the wish to have for themselves a more meaningful monastic life. They found this meaning in the utter simplicity of a poor community situated in a remote place. And so it might have remained, a single house or, at most, a few houses of monks who found their vocation in an austere setting, but events were to lead to greater things. In 1112, the son of a local aristocratic family arrived at Cîteaux, and his biographers would want us to believe that it was this arrival of St Bernard at Cîteaux that was the defining moment in the early history of the order. They probably exaggerate somewhat – for multiple causes are usually at work in human history – yet there can be little doubt of the profound impact of St Bernard on the growth of the order. Even before Bernard, Cîteaux had successes in recruitment, yet his arrival with a retinue of brothers and noble friends breathed fresh life into this young monastery, and he was only twenty-two years old. Three daughter houses were established by Cîteaux in 1113, 1114 and 1115, and in that last year it was the young Bernard, only three years a monk, who was sent to found a new monastery at Clairvaux in Champagne. He was to rule as abbot there for thirty-eight years. During that time Clairvaux established sixty-eight daughter houses, and the charismatic Bernard became the most influential churchman in Europe.

The growth of the Cistercian order, of which the Clairvaux family was but a part, still amazes. Twenty monks or so went to Cîteaux in 1098. By 1152 there were 333 Cistercian abbeys, a growth so rapid that in that year a halt was called to further expansion. Among these foundations were Rievaulx and Fountains in England, Mellifont and Baltinglass in Ireland, Tintern and Neath in Wales, Melrose and Kinloss in Scotland as well as many others in the British Isles. There were Cistercian houses founded in Poland, the Scandinavian countries, Austria, Hungary, Slovenia, Bohemia and Portugal. The impetus was so strong that the establishing of new foundations, halted in 1152, began anew – fourteen new houses in 1162 alone – and by century's end there were 525 Cistercian houses. This remarkable growth in the number of houses was more than matched by the increase in the number of monks at individual houses. Rievaulx in Yorkshire is a good and representative example. Founded in 1132 as a daughter of Clairvaux, at the death of Abbot Ailred in 1167 it numbered 140 choir monks and 500 lay brothers: they must have filled the abbey church for the abbot's funeral.

The mention of choir monks and lay brothers (*conversi*) at Rievaulx reveals something of the social and economic character of these monasteries. Almost without exception wherever Cistercian monasteries were founded in the twelfth century, they were founded in marginal areas. The hills of Wales and vast tracts of Yorkshire, much of them forested were mostly unused or underused. Monks settled in coastal Flanders (modern Belgium) amidst the inhospitable sand-dunes (Abbey of the Dunes). Benefactors did not hesitate to hand over wasteland to these pious monks. What the monks needed was a workforce not of paid labourers but of monks committed to manual labour: what they needed were lay brothers. A two-tier system quickly developed. There were the choir monks, who were educated and devoted themselves to the singing of the offices in the choir of the abbatial church. And there were the lay brothers, who took vows and were monks but of a different sort. They lived and ate together, separate from the choir monks. They spent much of their time working in the fields. When they prayed in the church, they sat not in the choir but in the nave and used a few memorized prayers. They remained *by statute* illiterate: they were not permitted to learn to read and write. What may appear to us as an unattractive life proved to be immensely attractive to contemporary men. These *conversi* came by the thousands from the homes of the peasantry of Europe to live lives of simple piety and hard work. And they came, generation after generation, although in declining numbers from the late thirteenth century until the time of the Black Death (1340s), after which they virtually vanished. This unpaid workforce tamed the wilderness. The fields of Yorkshire soon became vast sheep runs. And sand-dunes became the home of a fleet of Cistercian ships, as western Flanders itself became the centre of northern European commerce, and the monks there farmed 25,000 acres of productive farmland. The white monks were becoming very rich very fast.

Not all the land taken by the monks was uninhabited, and the clearing of land of human beings (not unlike the later clearances of the Scottish Highlands, where landlords preferred sheep – and profit – to people) reveals a darker side of the Cistercian achievement. In Lorraine they did not hesitate to destroy existing settlements. Forced evictions occurred on the lands of Fountains Abbey, where possibly as many as twenty-three settlements were depopulated by the monks, and another forty-six settlements seem to have been cleared by the monks of other Yorkshire monasteries. Some resettlement might have occurred, but the evidence is incomplete. Small wonder that one contemporary critic scathingly complained, 'They raze villages, destroy churches, evict parishioners and even brazenly cast down the very altars; they level everything before the plough.'

The emergence of this new monastic force led, almost predictably, to conflict with the existing monastic establishment, with Benedictine monks and, more especially, with Cluniac monks. What in other circumstance might have been a very minor incident led to a serious conflict between the Cistercians and Cluniacs. A young man related to Bernard, a first cousin, entered Clairvaux, but, finding the life too severe for his liking, he left and entered Cluny. When Bernard heard of this, he went into a barely controlled rage and wrote a letter to the young man, not only seething with anger but also, for most readers, lacking in elemental charity. No one ever accused St Bernard of a surfeit of gentleness and kindness in his letters. The prior of Cluny, said the irate Bernard, was a wolf in sheep's clothing, who commended feasting and condemned fasting, who called voluntary poverty wretched and cast scorn upon fasts, vigils, silence and manual labour. By such sophistries the too credulous boy was led astray and led off by his deceivers. He was brought to Cluny and trimmed, shaved and washed. He was taken out of his rough, threadbare and soiled habit, and he was then clothed with a new neat one.

Although Cluny may have become somewhat lax in the two hundred years from its founding, Bernard was objecting not only to its laxity but to its very being. Even a stricter Cluny was, to Bernard, inferior to Cîteaux. Later, Peter the Venerable, the wise and moderate abbot of Cluny, felt constrained to answer Cistercian attacks. He called the Cistercian critics 'a new race of pharisees', who, in holding themselves superior to all others neglect that chapter of the Rule of St Benedict on humility, where it is written that a monk should consider himself and believe in the depths of his soul that he is inferior to all others. Cluny was far from perfect even by its own standards – in time, Peter the Venerable instituted reforms – yet the seeming lack of charity by the Cistercians in their self-righteous judgement of the lives of other monks must make the detached person wonder what had happened to an order founded on a Charter of Charity (*Carta caritatis*). Initial fervour had apparently given rise to spiritual pride, and, by the end of the century, it was an order little different from the others in evident signs of holiness.

Such decline, although frequent and hardly unexpected in religious institutions, was not universal. Of the Carthusians, founded in 1109, it is famously said, 'never reformed, because never deformed' (*nunquam reformata quia nunquam deformata*). The original community was driven by an avalanche from its place high up in the French Alps. They then settled at lower ground at La Grande Chartreuse, which gave them their name. There and in the monasteries that followed numbers were intentionally limited to a score or so. Theirs was a life of simplicity and austerity lived in solitude, a life for the few. Each monastery was essentially a community of hermits. The hermit-monks lived each in his own little house with a bijou garden, and there in his 'cell' he spent his days and nights, food being brought to him through a hatch each day. The monks went to a monastic church for Sunday Mass, after which they had a communal meal. For evening and night offices they also came together in church. Apart from these occasions each lived his own life, confined to his own space, where he would contemplate the meaning of the Christian life. There too some work would be done, quite commonly the copying and illuminating of manuscript books. The order's growth, unlike the Cistercian order, was in no way dramatic: by the sixteenth century there were just over two hundred Carthusian houses ('charterhouses') in all of Europe, only nine in England. A modern visitor to Mount Grace Priory in Yorkshire – actually, to its ruins – with little imagination can picture the physical arrangement of a typical Carthusian priory. It was, later, at the London Charterhouse (at Smithfield) that Thomas More was to try his vocation, and it was its sainted prior, John Houghton, who was butchered in an act of extreme barbarity at the order of Henry VIII.

Other new religious orders besides the Augustinians, Cistercians and Carthusians fill out the picture. The flexible Augustinian rule was adopted by the followers of St Norbert at Prémontré, who lived a life more severe than the Augustinians. These Premonstratensians (or Norbertines) resembled in many ways the Cistercians in their simplicity and austerity and in their emphasis on withdrawal from the world in silence and prayer. These ascetic followers of the Rule of St Augustine, by the middle of the thirteenth century, had 500 houses in places ranging from Ireland to Palestine. They first came to England in about 1143 and established Newhouse Abbey in Lincolnshire and, by the time of the dissolution, had over thirty houses there.

It was also the flexibility of this same rule that gave rise to another emphasis in the life of Canons Regular: in 1108 the famous scholar William of Champeaux – he was Peter Abelard's teacher – with royal support established the abbey of St Victor in Paris, which attracted men who became scholars (particularly theologians such as Hugh of St Victor), preachers, poets and ascetics, men who followed the Rule of St Augustine. They lived a common life with a strong liturgical element. The Victorines, as they came to be known, grew beyond Paris as other abbeys of Canons Regular adopted their way of life, and by the end of the twelfth century the order had reached its zenith with nearly two score houses in France. The original Parisian house survived to the end of the eighteenth century, when it fell victim to the excesses of the French Revolution.

There had been houses of religious women for centuries. Almost from the beginning of monasticism, holy women formed communities. The sister of St Augustine lived with other women in a community at Hippo. St Benedict's sister, Scholastica, has been called the first Benedictine nun: she lived in a community of women a few miles from Monte Cassino. In the years following the conversion of the Anglo-Saxons and the Germans a number of high-born ladies became abbesses of nunneries, which were peopled with the daughters and widows of the aristocracy. Also, 'double monasteries' had existed in Christian Gaul as early as the seventh century: men and women lived separately and generally worshipped together in the monastic church. In reality, most of these double monasteries were nunneries to which male communities were attached so that the men could serve as priests at the altar or perform manual and business tasks. The head was almost always a woman, frequently of a princely family, who ruled both communities. By the eleventh century such institutions had virtually disappeared or were essentially changed. When St Norbert established at Prémontré the order of canons, he provided a nunnery for women next to the male house, yet the nuns acted not as co-equals to the canons but almost as their servants, sewing and doing laundry for the men. Even such humble roles attracted hundreds of women. Norbert's successor separated the two communities in such a way that the nuns were required to move to a new home some distance away. Even these Norbertine nuns failed to survive much beyond the twelfth century, since it was forbidden to admit new nuns in the late 1190s. Benedictine nunneries continued much as they had done for centuries just as houses of Benedictine monks continued. But the establishment of the Cistercian order presented a problem. Women were drawn to this life of austerity and simplicity and even established themselves in communities, living a Cistercian life, but the order considered itself a male order and was adamant in refusing to accept such communities into their order. In fact, when the order finally admitted convents of women in the early thirteenth century, it was done only reluctantly and, apparently, under pressure from powerful, even royal, patrons. In practice, it is not always clear which nunneries were incorporated into the order and which merely followed the Cistercian customs and traditions. Such developments are but part of a marked growth in the number of nunneries in general. This development, once thought to pertain to the thirteenth century, is now known to have existed in parallel to the growth of male institutions in the twelfth century. In France and England alone about 400 new nunneries were established in the years between 1070 and 1170. The enthusiasm for the religious life in the twelfth century was clearly not an exclusively male phenomenon.

Two new orders of women stand out in the twelfth-century picture, each with its peculiar characteristics, one French and one English: Fontevrault and Sempringham. Robert of Arbrissel (d. 1117), a Breton hermit turned itinerant preacher, attracted to himself the poor and outcast of society, particularly women in search of a new, often reformed, life. Some were prostitutes, others the victims of life's misfortunes, even lepers. About the year 1100 he established for them a house at Fontevrault (near Saumur and the Loire River). A subordinate house for men religious was placed under the authority of the female abbess. The abbey of Fontevrault quickly prospered, and an early tally recorded a population of 150 nuns and 50 brothers. The original emphasis on catering to the spiritual needs of the less fortunate continued for some decades, but, almost inevitably, the monastery's very success undermined this early intention as aristocratic ladies showered gifts upon Fontevrault and soon took over. Principal among these women was Eleanor of Aquitaine, wife of King Henry II of England, who, in the final hours of her life, actually took the veil as a nun of Fontevrault. She was buried there as later were her husband, King Henry II, and her son King Richard I. The original crude buildings by then had been replaced by the fine buildings which visitors can still see. In time, houses were founded in other parts of France, four in England (mostly under royal patronage) and even some few in Spain: a total of nearly fifty before the death of the first abbess in 1149.

In a remote Lincolnshire village the local priest, eager to encourage girls of the parish to devote themselves to the spiritual life, built a structure for them against the north wall of his church. Seven girls (*puellae*) lived as anchoresses there, access to them possible only by a window, through which food was brought to them by laywomen. From these beginnings in 1131 was to grow the only specifically English religious order, sometimes called the Order of Sempringham (after the village) and sometimes called the Gilbertine Order (after the priest).

7 Cloister walk, Fontevrault. Reproduced by permission of the Courtauld Institute of Art.

The small structure at Sempringham by 1139 had become so inadequate to the numbers who wanted admission that a priory was constructed near by for their use. In that same year a daughter house was established. Already the servant-women who brought the food had become lay sisters and male workers had become lay brothers. The attempt of Gilbert of Sempringham to have the Cistercians accept his houses failed. He soon provided his nuns with a rule, and an independent order emerged. Canons, who would live with the lay brothers, were now introduced to serve the liturgical needs of the nuns, and double houses resulted. As many as twelve such communities, all founded in the twelfth century, survived until the dissolution under Henry VIII. At each house two communities were to live quite separately, a priest coming to the nuns' church to say Mass, but neither priest nor nuns could see each other, even at communion. The male community had its own oratory and cloister. Such rigid separation of the sexes probably came as a response to the unspeakably barbarous punishment imposed, about 1150, on a pregnant nun and her lay-brother lover at Watton Priory and to the charges of sexully scandalous behaviour raised by rebellious lay brothers in 1165. But the introduction of canons posed a threat to Gilbert's original design, for after 1150 all new priories were priories of canons and the later history of the double houses shows that real authority lay in the hands of the canon prior.

The new religious orders of the twelfth century undoubtedly tapped a contemporary need. The response was widespread and cut through every social and geographical part of sociey. The desire to go to the wilderness at Cîteaux or to become enclosed at Sempringham or to work in the fields wearing a monk's habit cannot be totally explained in social and economic terms nor in terms of mass psychology, as real as all these undoubtedly were. Although we cannot see into the deep recesses of another's soul, we should give room here, in some measure at least, for a higher vision, an idealism framed by religious belief, a willingness to endure physical and emotional hardships for spiritual reasons. It should be immediately added that all of these new orders – saving always the Carthusians – by the end of the twelfth century had diverted from their early intentions. The Cistercians had become wealthy landowners, who often depeopled their lands. The Augustinian canons had settled into a comfortable routine that would characterize their subsequent history. The Premonstratensian canons, once committed to preaching, had become focused inward almost exclusively on their own spiritual development. Fontevrault had been taken over by aristocrats and Sempringham by males. While institutions were changing, so too were the religious devotions and practices of Western Europe, to which we should now turn.

Popular devotion and practical piety

Virtually every village in Western Europe in the twelfth century had a church building, usually a parish church but sometimes only a chapel. They were mostly simple structures in the Romanesque style, and scores still remain, for example, in parts of rural France where they were not replaced when the Gothic style became the fashion. The village church served as the centre of Christian life for the local community. Its walls were covered with coloured paintings of subjects from the Bible and from the lives of the saints, and in the most prominent place was a large crucifix, not a mere cross, but a cross with the body of the dead Christ, the emphasis on his physical sufferings and humanity. The local church was the usual place where babies were baptized, couples married and the dead dispatched to their eternal reward, and it was more than that. It was the place that the Christian community came to mark the Lord's Day and the great feasts of the Christian calendar.

The central act of Christian worship in all the churches and chapels of Europe was the Mass, often called the eucharistic celebration or simply the Eucharist, and it now had taken on the decided aspect of a drama. Ambiguity had existed for some time about what the Eucharist celebrated. Was it the Last Supper, when the apostles shared bread and wine? Or was it the Crucifixion, when Christ offered his life in propitiation for the sins of the whole human race? The second view was now in the ascendancy. The faithful were attendants rather than participants; they watched rather than shared in the Mass. And what they wanted to see was the bread wafer (called the host) and chalice of wine at the moment of consecration, when these elements, they believed, were transformed into the body and blood of Christ. They wanted to 'see' Jesus, which they did as the priest elevated the consecrated elements. It was why they had come to church. There was a reverential hush within the church as bells pealed above it. And in order that the moment of seeing Jesus could be sustained, in some places the priest was encouraged to prolong the elevation. In time the exposition of the consecrated host was done outside Mass in a monstrance. In the thirteenth century the feast of Corpus Christ (Body of Christ) was instituted by the pope, and it was to become perhaps the most popular religious festival of the later Middle Ages.

The consecrated host was viewed as having miraculous powers. There was the bleeding host and the host bearing the sorrowful face of Jesus and the host providing the sole source of nourishment for a pious communicant. At Arras on Easter Sunday in 1176 a woman was said to have taken a communion host from her local church by wrapping it in a cloth. She secreted it in a well, but the host shone through the cloth, and, when it was removed, it had blood stains. It was quickly placed in the cathedral – the writer Gerald of Wales saw it there on the Sunday after Easter – and the Host of Arras soon became a popular object of pilgrimage. St Bernard of Clairvaux is said to have cured a bewitched man by holding above the man's head a sacred vessel containing consecrated hosts. Stories of miraculous cures multiplied and became the staple of preachers.

By the twelfth century extra-liturgical dramas were added to the Mass. The earliest, the *Quem quaeritis*, although known in a simple form earlier, was now frequently performed at Easter with different persons playing the parts of holy women and an angel at the empty tomb:

> 'Whom seek ye (*Quem quaeritis*) in this tomb?'
> 'We seek Jesus of Nazareth who was crucified.'
> 'He whom ye seek is not here, but go quickly to Peter and his disciples and tell them "Jesus is risen".'

From the core of these three lines or words like them there developed at the Easter liturgy a dramatic presentation with costumes, gestures, lamentations and additional dialogue. Other feasts soon had their dramatic scenes. For Christmas the Easter text was changed to read,

> 'Whom seek ye in the manger?'
> 'We seek our saviour, Christ the Lord, a child wrapped in swaddling clothes.'

And so also there were dramatic presentations for other feasts and other biblical stories: the story of the Magi from the East, the story of Lazarus being raised from the dead, the story of Daniel (scenes of handwriting on the wall, fiery furnace, lion's den) and many others. Removal of such dramas from the church building soon followed, and in these developments we should probably see the birth of the modern drama.

Beyond the Eucharist and its associated devotions and practices were the dramatic growth and vitality of devotion to Mary, the mother of Jesus. She was simply called the Virgin or the Blessed Virgin or the Blessed Virgin Mary, since it was believed that by divine intervention Jesus was conceived not by man but by the power of the Holy Spirit. She was called *mater dei* (mother of God), which is an incorrect translation of the Greek Θεοτόκος (theotokos), bearer of him who is God. She was also called in Latin *Sancta Maria* (St Mary). In France she was usually called *Notre Dame* (Our Lady) and in Italy *Madonna* (My Lady). The multiplication of names, in a way, reveals the ubiquity of Marian devotion, its familiarity, its penetration to a place near and, for some, at the centre of Catholic devotional life. The twelfth-century phenomenon was not limited to one area of Europe: she was venerated in Scotland and Ireland as well as in the Mediterranean lands. Every Cistercian monastery from Cîteaux and Clairvaux in the French heartland to Strata Florida and Cymner in remotest Wales bore the title of St Mary. Every cathedral in France, no matter what title it had previously, became a cathedral dedicated to Notre-Dame. In Sicily the magnificent cathedral at Monreale was dedicated by the Norman king William II (1172–89) to the Virgin, and a contemporary mosaic shows the king offering the new cathedral to her with the approving hand of God above. In England almost half of the twelfth-century monastic dedications were to St Mary, and this figure excludes the Cistercian houses.

St Bernard in hymn and sermon sang and preached her praises as the mediator whom the most wretched of sinners could approach to intercede for them at the throne of her son. Associated with St Bernard is the hymn *Ave maris stella*:

Ave, maris stella,	Hail, star of the sea,
dei mater alma,	Nurturing mother of God,
atque semper virgo,	And ever virgin,
felix coeli porta.	Happy gate of heaven.

Sumens illud 'ave'	You, who took the 'ave'
Gabrielis ore,	From Gabriel's mouth,
funda nos in pace,	Reversing the name 'Eva',
mutans 'Evae' nomen.	Grant us peace.

And the Latin poet Adam, a canon of St Victor's Abbey in Paris, composed a dozen or so hymns to the Virgin. Among them,

Imperatrix supernorum,	O empress of the highest,
superatrix infernorum,	Mistress of the lowest,
eligenda via coeli,	Chosen way to heaven,
retinenda spe fideli,	Fastholding by faithful hope,
separatos a te longe	Those separated far from you,
revocatos ad te junge	Now called back to you, unite
tuorum collegio.	In your band.

When Dante in the *Divine Comedy* approached the divine throne in paradise, he chose St Bernard as his guide to present him at the throne of the Virgin, so that she would introduce him into the presence of the very God. In Bernard's mouth the poet placed the words:

> Vergine madre, figlia del tuo figlio,
> umile ed alta più che creatura,
> termine fisso d'eterno consiglio,
> tu sei colei che l'umana natura
> nobilitasti sì, che il suo fattore
> non disdegnò di farsi sua fattura.
> <div align="right">(<i>Paradiso</i>, canto 33)</div>

Dante's prayer of St Bernard, in turn, was translated in part by Geoffrey Chaucer and placed in the mouth of the second nun in the *Canterbury Tales*:

> Thow Mayde and Mooder, doghter of thy Sone,
> Thow welle of mercy, synful soules cure,
> In whom that God for bountee chees to wone,
> Thow humble, and heigh over every creature,
> Thow nobledest so ferforth oure nature,
> That no desdeyn the Makere hadde of kynde
> His Son in blood and flesh to clothe and wynde.
> ('The Second Nun's Prologue', ll. 36–7)

A figure not just for poets, Mary was a common subject for visual artists, particularly sculptors. The commonest image of the Virgin had her seated on a throne, her lap serving as a throne for her son. Hundreds of statues of this image

8 Virgin and Child, tympanum, west portal, Chartres Cathedral. Reproduced by permission of the Courtauld Institute of Art.

survive from France alone. Later came the image of the son sucking at his mother's breast. From Carolingian times the cathedral of Chartres had a special shrine dedicated to Notre-Dame. It had the most treasured relic of the Virgin, what was believed to be the gown which she wore when the Archangel Gabriel appeared to her. With this background, it is no wonder that she was given a prominent place in the iconographical scheme for the cathedral's grand west entrance, the Royal Portal, when it was built in the middle of the twelfth century. Above each of the three doors there is a story in stone, and together they tell a single story. The tympanum above the central door has Christ in glory, surrounded by the symbols of the four evangelists. The left tympanum has the figure of Christ with angels about him as he ascends into heaven. We are, of course, reading the story backwards, for above the right door is the story of the coming of Jesus (the 'Incarnation', God-taking-flesh). This tympanum has the Virgin crowned and seated on her queenly throne, her seated body serving as the throne for the young Jesus.

At Senlis the sculptors took yet another Marian motif for their west portal, a motif long popular in the East, the dormition (not death) of the Virgin and her assumption into heaven. St Bernard wrote a series of sermons on the assumption of the Virgin. Devotion to Mary's assumption led to the dedication of the new cathedral at Salisbury to her under that title in the next century. Devotion to her under the title of the Immaculate Conception can be found at the same time, but controversy was to attend the theology supporting it for some centuries. The Immaculate Conception is not to be confused (as it often is) with the Virgin Birth. It simply held that alone of the human race Mary was exempted from original sin: she was conceived in her mother's womb without the stain of the sin of Adam, that is, conceived immaculately. Bernard and Thomas Aquinas both opposed it on theological grounds, yet it persisted, was approved in the fifteenth century with its own Mass and was finally defined as a doctrine of faith by Pope Pius IX in 1854.

This outpouring of Marian devotion raises questions not easy to answer. The most obvious question is why? Why did the Christian church and people place Mary on such an exalted level in their devotional lives? And why did they do so with such fervour? Why was this devotion so widespread, apparently universal, gainsaid by none, not even by the apparently impious and wicked? An easy answer is that it was imposed by a celibate clergy, for whom Mary was the woman in their lives. Some would suggest a latent, subconscious sexual component. Yet there is no evidence that Marian devotion was imposed on an unwilling people. On the contrary, it was greedily accepted by married men and by women alike. Some see in Marian devotion an oedipal component for both males and females. Also, a near universal yearning for a female goddess, particularly in a rural society, it is sometimes said, found fulfilment for Christians in Mary: she was goddess and her son god. Besides these is the faith factor: the belief that God was seen to intervene in human affairs and, if one prays to God through his mother, the prayer will be heard, for the son Jesus will not contemn the will of his mother. Such explanations can only point towards an answer.

This chapter has come a long way from popes and emperor in dispute, the political side of the medieval church, to humble Christian men and women in remote churches, kneeling in prayer before the Eucharist and before images of the Virgin. Two sides of the church: the church at its most institutional, involved in affairs of this world, and the church in its devotional, affective role, touching deep the souls of men and women. Both sides formed essential parts of the historical church in the Middle Ages.

Further reading

The classic work on the twelfth century is Charles Homer Haskins, *The Renaissance of the Twelfth Century* (Cambridge, MA, 1927; often reprinted). Still a good read for its enthusiasm and romantic flavour is Henry Adams, *Mont-Saint-Michel and Chartres* (Washington, 1904; also often reprinted), a better book than some modern critics would allow. For a general study of Frederick Barbarossa the reader may find useful Peter Munz, *Frederick Barbarossa: A Study in Medieval Politics* (London, 1969) and, in a more general context, Alfred Haverkamp, *Medieval Germany, 1056–1273* (tr. H. Braun and R. Mortimer; Oxford, 1992). Barbarossa's nephew, Otto of Freising, wrote an official life, *The Deeds of Frederick Barbarossa* (tr. C.C. Mierow; New York, 1953). A fascinating

Latin poem about Frederick Barbarossa's campaigns in Italy has been translated into English with an introduction and bibliography, *Barbarossa in Italy* (New York, 1994).

An important book of historical analysis (with comprehensive bibliography) is Giles Constable, *The Reformation of the Twelfth Century* (Cambridge, 1996), which, despite its title, is about the religious orders. Key chapters on the religious orders of this period, particularly the Cistercians, can be found in C.H. Lawrence, *Medieval Monasticism* (3rd edn; London, 2000). An excellent treatment for one region is Janet Burton, *Monastic and Religious Orders in Britain, 1000–1300* (Cambridge, 1994). The distillation of a lifetime's work can be found in Adriaan H. Bredero, *Bernard of Clairvaux: Between Cult and History* (Eng. tr.; Grand Rapids, MI, 1996), which contains a description of the issues involved in the Cluniac–Cistercian controversy. Constance Hoffman Berman argues that the Cistercian movement developed into an order only in the second half of the twelfth century: *The Cistercian Evolution: The Invention of a Religious Order in Twelfth-Century Europe* (Philadelphia, 2000). An excellent study of the Cistercians in a region outside France is David H. Williams, *The Welsh Cistercians* (Leominster, Herefordshire, 2001). For the social consequences of Cistercian land policy on local people see R.A. Donkin, *The Cistercians: Studies in the Geography of Medieval England and Wales* (Toronto, 1978). The Rule of Saint Augustine in 'an interpretative translation' is conveniently available in paperback (Cistercian Publications, Kalamazoo, MI, 1996). For religious women there are two useful collections of articles: Derek Baker (ed.), *Medieval Women* (*Studies in Church History, Subsidia*, vol. 1, Oxford, 1978) and John A. Nichols and Lillian T. Shand (eds), *Distant Echoes* (*Medieval Religious Women*, vol. 1, Kalamazoo, MI, 1984). See also Bruce Venarde, *Women's Monasticism and Medieval Society: Nunneries in France and England, 890–1215* (Ithaca, NY, 1997), which provides data about the growth of communities of nuns; Sally Thompson, *Women Religious: The Founding of English Nunneries after the Norman Conquest* (Oxford, 1991); and Penelope D. Johnson, *Equal in Monastic Profession: Religious Women in Medieval France* (Chicago, 1991). Definitive on its subject is Brian Golding, *Gilbert of Sempringham and the Gilbertine Order, c.1130–1300* (Oxford, 1995). For a somewhat revisionist account of the founder of Fontevrault see Jacqueline Smith, 'Robert of Arbrissel: *Procurator Mulierum*', in Derek Baker (ed.), *Medieval Women* (Oxford, 1978), pp. 175–84. A detailed monograph is Berenice M. Kerr, *Religious Life for Women, c.1100–c.1350: Fontevraud in England* (Oxford, 1999).

On the Eucharist see Gary Macy, *The Theologies of the Eucharist in the Early Scholastic Period* (Oxford, 1984) and *The Banquet's Wisdom: A Short History of the Theologies of the the Lord's Supper* (New York, 1992); also Miri Rubin, *Corpus Christi: The Eucharist in Late Medieval Culture* (Cambridge, 1991). Two interesting studies on the Virgin are Jaroslav Pelikan, *Mary through the Centuries* (New Haven, 1996), a series of well-informed, discursive essays, and Michael P. Carroll, *The Cult of the Virgin Mary* (Princeton, 1986), which presents a psychoanalytical explanation. More generally, the reader will find that Bernard Hamilton's *Religion in the Medieval West* (London, 1986) provides an excellent explanation of what Christians believed and how they expressed their religious beliefs at this time.

THREE TWELFTH-CENTURY PROFILES

A period in history, such as the twelfth century, can be seen as the rush of events – 'one damn thing after another', in the words of one critic – and as useful and, indeed, necessary as that is, occasionally one should stop the projector and look at a few individual frames to get a more nuanced view. Thus, we shall take another look at the twelfth century, a look focused on three individuals whose life experiences will allow us to see the twelfth-century church in a fuller, more personal dimension. The three persons – two men and one woman – were neither popes nor monarchs, yet they show us different aspects of the church as it lived out its life in the complexities of a Europe coming of age. One was near the centre of power, Thomas Becket as chancellor to King Henry II of England. And through the experience of another, Peter Abelard, we catch sight of the world of the schools and the contentiousness, personal and intellectual, in which he found himself. We come to an entirely different place when we meet Hildegard of Bingen, not merely because she was a woman in a man's world, but also because she was a visionary prophet and perhaps much more. To them, then, let us turn.

Peter Abelard (*c*.1079–1142)

Peter Abelard has fascinated observers uninterruptedly from the twelfth to the twenty-first century. Depending on which glasses one may be wearing, he is seen as a rebellious malcontent, a male chauvinist seducer, a paranoid personality, an original and seminal scholar or an unhappy monk, and there is some evidence to support each of these views. Every generation rediscovers Peter Abelard, and no generation feels satisfied that it fully understands him. Almost inevitably and probably unfairly, he is known in every generation largely because of his love affair with the young Heloise and equally inevitably moral judgements about his actions towards her are made and are almost always negative.

There is no scarcity of sources about his life, but even these, like Abelard himself, are not without controversy. There are his scholarly works on logic, ethics and theology as well as sermons, letters, hymns and perhaps even love songs. It has been estimated that his surviving works run to about one million words, and that obviously does not include the works which he is known to have written but which have not survived. Our principal source for his life is a series of eight letters, the first of which is the autobiographical *Historia calamitatum* ('Story of My Calamities') and the next seven letters are to and from Heloise, his lover and then wife. This correspondence will be relied upon to a large extent in what follows and is quoted, but there is a problem. Scholarly voices, few in number, it is true, have been raised, questioning the authenticity of these letters. Their argument runs along these lines. The correspondence, which was reputedly written during the 1130s, exists today only in nine Latin manuscripts, the earliest of which was written 150 years after the supposed date of the correspondence. In addition, one looks in vain for any reference to this collection of letters in the intervening century and a half. Computer analyses of the texts of the letters have led to ambiguous results. Besides those who think the whole correspondence a later forgery, there are others, still a very few, who suspect that the entire correspondence, including the letters of Heloise to Abelard, were written by Abelard himself. Another collection of love letters has been found, and some scholars attribute it to Abelard and Heloise. The major events of Abelard's life are attested to by other sources and are hardly in dispute, yet, as we use the correspondence, it is always with the faint, nagging fear that some day new evidence may appear, proving it fictitious. Suppressing that fear, let us look at the life of Peter Abelard.

Born in the westernmost region of France, in Brittany, Peter was probably not Breton, but a descendant of a knightly family with roots in neighbouring Poitou. Le Pallet, his birthplace, was at the southern edge of Brittany, south of the Loire River near Nantes. Not much is known about his family. He was the eldest son, destined to be a knight, but he chose instead to become a student. His parents, in later life, by mutual agreement entered the religious life. He was simply Peter, and, perhaps only as a nickname, he later added Abelard.

Sometime about the year 1093 Peter left his native Le Pallet and became a peripatetic student. By then the centres of learning had largely shifted from the monasteries and their monastic schools to the newly emerging and maturing towns, where schools grew up around cathedrals and other great churches. What attracted students to particular schools tended to be the fame of individual masters. And it was not unusual for a student to move from school to school in order to study with different masters. And so it was with Peter Abelard: he went on a circuit of schools, which led him eventually – almost inevitably – to Paris. As he wrote in his autobiography,

> I travelled about in the provinces, disputing, wherever I had heard
> that the study of dialectic flourished.

By dialectic he was referring to the study of logic. Peter's exact itinerary cannot be traced, but there were schools and teachers near by at places like Nantes and Vannes in Brittany. It is known that he studied, perhaps for several years, at Loches and Tours with the master Roscelin, a logician of international fame, a man whose foray into theology had created problems for him in 1092. 'I arrived finally at Paris, which was truly outstanding.' This was in about 1100, and by Paris he meant the cathedral school at Notre-Dame. There he listened to the master, William of Champeaux. They soon clashed. The young Abelard – he was about twenty-one at the time – gained the enmity of William and his fellow students by attempting to refute the most renowned teacher at the most renowned school in Christendom. Two years or so at Paris and anxious to flee the resentments of his enemies, Peter Abelard left not to study elsewhere but to open his own school, and he was still a young man. First he went to Melun, south-west of Paris and then, after a couple of years, nearer to Paris at Corbeil, where he attracted students in direct competition to William of Champeaux. By about 1105 he had worn himself out and experienced what was probably a mental breakdown. He returned to Le Pallet, where his family nursed him back to health.

Abelard returned from Brittany, not to Corbeil, his last school, but to Paris, and not only to Paris but to Notre-Dame as a student once again of William of Champeaux. Amateur psychology has no place in the study of history, yet one may wonder if part of Abelard's health problems had to do with a fixation with his old teacher and if he felt that he needed to return to the scene and to the person of his tribulations. Whatever the reason, he again attacked William of Champeaux. The precise issue was universals.

To the modern mind the problem of universals might seem particularly recondite, but it was hardly so to medieval intellectuals. What is a universal? When schoolmen spoke of universals, they referred to a word like *homo* (human being), which applies to all *homines* (like Plato and Aristotle or, as we would say, Jack and Jane). Does *homo* really exist? Or, take a commonly used example: tree. Does the universal 'tree' exist or only individual trees (this maple or that oak)? The problem of universals concerned the kind of existence which one can attribute to a universal term. Two general positions were taken. Realists would say that *homo* is more than a term and exists apart from individual human beings and that 'tree' exists independently of individual trees: these universals and others like them have a real existence. But the Nominalists held that a universal is merely a name (*nomen*) and nothing more: all that really exist are individual things. William of Champeaux championed the Realist position, whereas Abelard, following his former master, Roscelin, gave no reality to universals, asserting the Nominalist position. Roscelin had said that a universal (e.g., *homo*, tree) was merely *flatus vocis* (i.e., an exhaling of the voice, a sound). Abelard held that they were more than that: the word has meaning and was more than just a sound. The mind recognizes, he said, the elements in common to Jack and Jane and uses a mental construct for which the word *homo* stands. It has meaning as the spoken (or written) sign of that mental construct, yet it has no real external existence. Jack and Jane do not 'share' humanity: each is human independent of the other. We simply, by means of abstraction, focus on one aspect of each individual which they have in common (i.e., humanity), abstracting it from other, differentiating characteristics (age, sex, colour of eyes and dozens of others), and construct a concept of a universal and give to it the word *homo*. For Abelard the ultimate basis for universals was to be found in the ideas which God had when he created individual beings having these characteristics. But, when one turns one's focus on God himself, problems arise. Roscelin was suspected of heresy when he used his Nominalism to explain the doctrine of the Trinity. Since he held that only individuals exist, it could, therefore, be inferred that he held that the universal 'divinity' does not exist, merely three divine persons, Father, Son and Holy Spirit, which sounds like polytheism. Later, Abelard was to encounter his own problems in trying to explain this same doctrine.

In Abelard's telling he was so successful in challenging William of Champeaux on universals that William had to modify his position – it might merely have been a clarification – and, as a consequence, William was abandoned by some of his students. Abelard's ambition to be master at Notre-Dame failed at this time, and he withdrew briefly to Melun. When he returned to Paris, it was to the church of Sainte Geneviève, outside the walls of the town, where he set up a rival school. Dates are not easy to come by in all this, but it was probably from 1109 to 1113 that Abelard taught at Mont-Ste-Geneviève, for it was in 1113 that his life took another turn, which led to yet further controversy.

Up to this time Abelard had studied philosophy (or logic, we might say). Now, for reasons that elude us, he turned to the study of divinity, not at Paris, but at Laon to the school of Anselm of Laon (not to be confused with St Anselm of Bec or Canterbury). Perhaps Abelard envisioned a career as a churchman. Although he was not a priest at the time, he was almost certainly a cleric in minor orders. Whatever his motives, Abelard soon found himself in conflict with his new teacher. Like the student who thinks he knows more than the teacher, Abelard held Anselm in contempt, first, by cutting his classes and then, still but a novice student of divinity, by presuming to give lectures on the Bible. Quite understandably, Anselm was furious and silenced Abelard, who also gained the enmity of two influential fellow students, Alberic of Rheims and Lotulf of Lombardy. Despite this unpleasantness at Laon, Abelard returned to Paris in 1114 to the place which he had long wanted: he became master at Notre-Dame.

The next three or four years must have been the most satisfying of his life. He taught within the cloister of the cathedral; he drew students from far and wide; he had become the successful, popular teacher at a renowned school. But trouble was not far off. As a master, Abelard was a canon of the cathedral. One of his fellow canons, obviously very senior, was Fulbert, who had a house in the cathedral precincts. Canon Fulbert, by renting rooms to Abelard and by arranging for him to tutor his niece, the young girl Heloise, set in motion a string of events which have forever linked the names of Abelard and Heloise. Who was this woman? She was at this time probably a teenage girl, yet she had a wide reputation for learning: 'A gift for letters is so rare among women that it made her even more attractive', Abelard later wrote. He schemed to seduce her and feared no rebuff: 'My reputation was so great and I was so youthfully handsome that I feared rejection from no woman.' So eager was the naive Fulbert that he encouraged Abelard to spend more time with his niece: 'I was astonished at his simplicity.' The hitherto chaste Abelard abandoned himself to his carnal desires:

> With our studies as an excuse, we gave ourselves to love. We withdrew to a private room, ostensibly for study, but our books lay unread before us. We spoke more of love than of books, and there was more kissing than learning. My hands were more often on her breasts than on our books. Love drew our eyes to each other far more than the lesson drew them to the page before us.

So absorbed was Abelard in his love relationship that he spent less and less time preparing his lectures, relying instead on old themes, delivered with no inspiration and with increasingly evident boredom. Such bliss was not destined to be eternal and, in 1118, ended in great tragedy.

Fulbert caught them in the act; like Mars and Venus, Abelard was to say. One can only imagine Fulbert's fury. The drama was accentuated when Heloise joyfully told Abelard that she was pregnant. At once, he secretly sent her to his family to have the child, a son, whom they called Astralabe. Fulbert's fury became uncontrollable when he discovered that his niece had been sent to Brittany, as it were, a hostage to his inflicting harm on Abelard. In the most self-serving terms, Abelard sought an interview with the offended uncle:

> I accused myself of the deceit forced on me by love . . . I reminded him how, since the beginning of the human race, women had brought the noblest of men to ruin. To assuage his feelings I made a magnanimous offer which he could never have expected: I offered to marry the girl I had wronged, provided the marriage be kept secret.

Fulbert agreed to what was patently not a magnanimous gesture. Why, we may ask, the condition of secrecy? Obviously Abelard did not want the world to know, but why? There was no legal reason, since, not in priest's orders, he was not bound by celibacy, but he seems to have been bound by an elephantine self-centredness and did not want his career as a master of Notre-Dame complicated by the fact he had married. And so it was agreed. A private ceremony took place. Heloise is said to have protested, 'We shall both be destroyed.' How prophetic. Returning secretly to Paris, Heloise joined Abelard at daybreak at a church, where, with only Fulbert and a few others present, they were married. What is often lost sight of in this almost stereotypical shotgun wedding is the fact that Abelard and Heloise actually became husband and wife. Yet the secrecy was to be their undoing, for it was not kept. Fulbert and his kinsmen soon divulged the secret, and it was Abelard's response to this disclosure that brought the issue to its ultimate point. Feeling betrayed, he sent his new wife to the nunnery at Argenteuil outside Paris, where she had been as a child. There she was now dressed in the habit of a Benedictine nun save for the veil, the final sign of commitment. Abelard had made a tragic error: it was his dispatching of Heloise to a convent and not his affair with Heloise that raised Fulbert to a monumental rage. Canon Fulbert believed he had been betrayed, that Abelard had rid himself of Heloise by making her a nun. The revenge was swift and cruel. Kinsmen of Fulbert burst into Abelard's bedroom and, while he resisted in vain, they cut off his testicles. It was a barbarous act by any standard, and news of it quickly spread around Paris and soon beyond to the far reaches of Christendom: Abelard, the great Parisian master, had been castrated.

The next morning a crowd of Parisians, crying and grieving, gathered outside his house: 'My students tormented me with their unbearable weeping and wailing.' Yet not all response was sympathetic. Roscelin, his one-time master, cruelly commented that he could no longer call him Peter since that is a masculine name. As soon as he could, Abelard fled Notre-Dame to enter the royal monastery of St Denis as a monk. At his urging Heloise agreed to take the veil and become a nun of Argenteuil. In his autobiography the ever self-serving Abelard had Heloise say, as she took the veil, the words of an ancient poet:

Why did I marry you and cause your downfall?

The story could end there, tragic as it was, with Abelard, an emasculated monk, and Heloise, an unwilling nun, but it did not.

Wherever he went Abelard seems to have created problems for himself, and the pattern continued at St Denis. He denounced the monks as worldly and scandalous and their abbot as notoriously evil-living. His position became untenable, and it was arranged that he go to a dependent priory, not an unheard of way of dealing with difficult monks. This priory, it seems likely, was in Champagne, near one of the great crossroads of France. Students discovered where he was and crowds went there to be taught by the master, now famous not only for his teaching but for his physical mutilation. They would have likened him, as he did himself, to the great Father of the church Origen (d. *c.*254), who had suffered (but at his own hand) a similar mutilation.

Abelard's intellectual interests, save for the brief interlude at Laon, were hitherto devoted to the liberal arts, particularly to logic; they now turned to the serious study of divinity, which befitted his new status as a monk. Although he was virtually untrained in this subject, Abelard did not hesitate to turn to its study. Self-doubt seldom disturbed his mind. This study he called 'theology', a term which he, perhaps more than any other master, caused to become popular. During the years between 1118 and 1121 he wrote *Theologia*, which he was to continue to rework during most of his subsequent life. It got him into trouble in 1121.

Abelard's behaviour at Laon appears to have so incensed Alberic and Lotulf that they conspired to have the charge of heresy brought against him at a council held at Soissons in 1121. The accusation was that in his *Theologia* Abelard had taught that there were three gods. Called before the council, Abelard tried to defend himself, but his explanations went unheard, and he was forced by the council to throw his book into the fire. He thought this an even greater injury than his castration.

> The earlier betrayal was small in comparison to this. I mourned much more for the harm done to my reputation than the harm done to my body, since the latter came upon me through my own fault, whereas it was only sincere intentions and love of the faith that brought this open violence upon me.

He subsequently acknowledged two faults of character – lechery and pride – and that God had provided him a remedy for both: 'first, for my lechery by depriving me of the means to practice it, and for my pride by the burning of my book.' (It should be noted that, although Abelard reluctantly hurled his book into the flames, he had saved another copy.) He returned, humiliated, if not humbled, to his monastery at St Denis.

Abelard soon offended his fellow monks by questioning the identity of their patron saint. Flight soon followed, and an accommodation was arrived at that allowed him to live as a hermit. This he did at a secluded place near Troyes, accompanied only by a single cleric. A rough oratory was built of reeds and thatch. In time, Abelard named it after the Holy Spirit: 'the Paraclete'. Students eventually came to him there, where, at first, they lived in primitive huts, but, as the self-subsistence hoped for became impractical, economic need required Abelard to establish a school. It was at about this time that he put together a treatise, *Sic et non* ('Yes and No'), in which he acknowledged contradictions in theological sources and, by his use of reason, tried to resolve them. It remains his best-known scholarly work.

The monks of the monastery of St Gildas in far western Brittany, where it overlooked the sea, elected Abelard as their abbot, possibly as early as 1125. If the monks made a bad choice in choosing Abelard, then Abelard made an even worse choice in accepting the election. It was probably at this time that he was ordained a priest. He had little in common with the Celtic-speaking monks. His attempts to reform these 'wild' monks, in his account, led at one point to their attempting to kill him by poisoning the altar wine. Real threats or another instance of Abelard's paranoia? Whether the threats were real or not, Abbot Abelard looked for opportunities to spend more and more time away from his abbey. By now Heloise was prioress of Argenteuil, and the expulsion of the nuns from there in 1129 gave Abelard the opportunity to come to their rescue and, in effect, to be absent for very long periods from St Gildas. He offered the exiled nuns of Argenteuil the Paraclete and then saw to the settlement there of a number of these nuns and to the appointment of Heloise as their abbess. Let tongues wag, he said; he would give comfort to these unfortunate nuns.

About this time (say, 1131) Abelard is said to have written his autobiographical *Historia calamitatum* ('The Story of My Calamities'). A copy by accident fell into the hands of Heloise, and there ensued their celebrated correspondence. Despite Heloise's pleas, Abelard would give her only spiritual advice. She complained that she deserved more:

> You belong to me by the obligations of marriage which unite us, and you are even under greater obligation because, as the whole world knows, I have ever loved you with a boundless love.
>
> *(Letters, 2)*

She reminded him that she had tried to dissuade him from the marriage but that he had persisted and prevailed.

> With God as my witness, if Augustus, the emperor of the world, offered me marriage and the whole world as a wedding gift to have forever, it would be more precious and more honourable to me to be called your whore than the wife of the emperor.
>
> *(Letters, 2)*

How cold his response must have seemed when, in reply, he merely counselled her to pray. She answered that this was not easy, for even at the most sacred moments at Mass 'lewd images of our pleasures seize my hapless soul'. Abelard, in turn, confessed what his motives had been: 'My love, which led us both into sin, should not be called love but lust; I took my pleasures from you and that was all the love I had.' Then he described the manner of life which nuns should live. Some may think this but a pious response; others may find Abelard's replies among the most honest deeds of his life.

His theological troubles were far from over, and opposition to Abelard's theology was led by the formidable and unfathomable Bernard of Clairvaux. He was a Cistercian abbot, but he was more, much more. During the 1130s and even the 1140s Bernard was the most powerful ecclesiastic in Western Europe. In a moment of rare self-mockery, he wrote to his friend Pope Eugenius III, 'People say that it is not you but I who am pope.' Author of some of the most sublime works of Christian spirituality – his sermons on the Song of Songs perhaps his masterpiece – Bernard was also the master of scathing invective. A reading of his numerous letters reveals a man seemingly lacking in subtlety, tolerance and, it must be added sadly, elementary Christian charity. He called the bishop of Winchester, 'the whore of Winchester'. The archbishop of York he said was 'not created but execrated', 'a Simon Magus', 'an idol', 'the devil', 'a thief', 'a wild beast ravaging the Lord's vineyard', 'rotten from the bottom of his feet to the top of his head'. In 1227 the archbishop was recognized as a saint. Abelard had the misfortune to come into Bernard's sights, and his fate was to be worse than that of these two English bishops. The differences between Bernard and Abelard were, indeed, personal, very personal, but they were also more profound than that. What differentiated Bernard and Abelard were essentially different views of the Christian life. Bernard accepted on faith alone the mysteries of the Christian religion. He accepted that the Father is God and the Son is God and the Holy Spirit is God, yet there is but one God. For him no effort of the human intellect was necessary to try to understand this doctrine of the Trinity. So great was God, he felt, so utterly transcendent of anything human, that one should merely prostrate one's self before the unutterable, unknowable deity. It would be, for Bernard, the greatest human arrogance to use human reason to try to understand what is utterly beyond the reach of human reason, since wholly other. On the contrary, Peter Abelard, the greatest logician of his day, saw nothing wrong with using human reason to study God: that is what theology meant for him. How can one believe – say 'Credo' ('I believe') – without trying to understand the object of one's credo? For him, it was not contrary to faith to theologize but the very fullness of faith. These two strong personalities and their two different approaches to Christian belief were almost bound to collide, and collide they did with Abelard being vanquished and Bernard displaying the most unattractive side of his character. Bernard wrote of Abelard,

> He has defiled the church; he has infected with his own blight the minds of simple people. He tries to explore with his reason what the devout mind grasps at once with a vigorous faith. Faith believes; it does not dispute. But this man, apparently holding God suspect, will not believe anything until he has first examined it with reason.
>
> (Bernard, Letter 338)

And Bernard's attack then became acutely personal:

> Outwardly he appears a monk, but within he is a heretic having nothing of the monk about him save the habit and the name . . . He is a monk without a rule, a prelate without responsibility, an abbot without discipline. He argues with boys and consorts with women.
>
> (Bernard, Letters 331, 332)

Bernard's pen seemed to know no restraint.

The climax to their controversy came at the show trial of Abelard at Sens in 1141. In its notoriety it can be compared to any of the celebrated televised trials of modern times. The king of France, Louis VII, as well as a large number of the nobility of France and bishops and abbots and many others went to Sens in June 1141 to see what they thought would be the trial of the century. They had come to see Bernard and Abelard in personal combat. Nineteen propositions had been drawn up, attributed to Abelard and alleged to be heretical. They concerned such doctrines as the Trinity, the nature of faith, the Redemption and the nature of sin, although this last was not particularly emphasized. Bernard himself undertook the prosecution and stood before the assembled churchmen and the audience of the famous and powerful. He dramatically confronted Abelard with these propositions. Abelard must have known that in the previous evening Bernard had dinner with the bishops and convinced them to find the propositions heretical. Under such circumstances what could Abelard do? He could hardly argue that the propositions were not heretical in the face of the pre-trial decision by the bishops. Nor could he admit that they were heretical, for this would be an admission that he was a heretic. It was possible for him to argue that they did not accurately represent his teachings, that, in fact, they were distortions. Instead, he simply said, 'I appeal to the pope' and left immediately, leaving behind a disgruntled Bernard and a disappointed king. The council at Sens in 1141 was hardly a triumph for Bernard and is seen by some as the moment when bishops successfully resisted his de facto power: they may have condemned the propositions, but they did not condemn the person Peter Abelard.

Less than a year was left in Abelard's life. Perhaps he recognized his failing health while at Sens. On his way to Rome, he stopped at the abbey of Cluny, where its abbot, Peter the Venerable, one of the most attractive persons of the era, advised him not to proceed to Rome and took him in as a monk of Cluny. His appeal, in any case, fell upon deaf ears in Rome, and Pope Innocent II, immensely dependent on Bernard for being restored (see chapter 8), not only condemned Abelard but, according to one account, personally presided over the burning of

9 Tomb of Heloise and Abelard, cemetery of Père Lachaise, Paris. Reproduced by permission of the Courtauld Institute of Art.

his books in St Peter's. Abelard moved to a priory of Cluny, Chalon-sur-Saône, where his health continued to fail. A face-to-face reconciliation with Bernard occurred at some point as also his absolution from the papal condemnation. And there at Chalons-sur-Saône, Peter Abelard died on 21 April 1142; he was about sixty-three years old. Peter the Venerable, in response to the request of Heloise, personally conducted Abelard's body to the Paraclete, where it was buried in the sanctuary of the chapel. When Heloise died about twenty-two years later, her body was placed next to her husband's. Their grave was disturbed during the French Revolution, but their bodies now repose in Père Lachaise cemetery in Paris, although there is even some lingering doubt about that.

Romantics might see in this story the tragedy of violence destroying love or, more subtly, the tragedy of a young girl who never recovered from her first love, the rest of her life but a long postscript to a teenage love. Still others might find the tragedy elsewhere, in Abelard being more remembered for his relationship with Heloise than for his being one of the greatest scholars of the twelfth century.

Thomas Becket (c.1120–70)

The death of Thomas Becket in Canterbury Cathedral in 1170 has recommended him to the ages, the man of principle slain by order of a king, Henry II, intent on extending the power of the state. His martyrdom created a saint, to whose tomb came countless pilgrims for centuries until another Henry, removing every symbol of resistance to the growing power of the Tudor state, had that tomb violated, its gold and precious stones carted off to the royal treasury and the bones of St Thomas removed and either burned, his ashes thrown to the winds, or buried in an anonymous grave, where it still remains unhonoured. Dramatic stage productions have attempted to portray him in various lights. T.S. Eliot in his verse play *Murder in the Cathedral* and, later Jean Anouilh in *Becket* (later a 1964 film) found ready audiences for their own views of the martyred archbishop. Neither a dramatist nor a hagiographer nor indeed a propagandist, the historian must attempt to sift the wheat of truth from the chaff of fiction.

First, his name. He was named Thomas for the simple reason that he was born on the feast day of St Thomas the Apostle, 21 December. The year is not certain, but 1120 cannot be far off. His parents were both Norman by birth (*pace* Anouilh), among the many Normans who came to England from Normandy in the wake of the Norman conquerors. Becket was probably his father's nickname. The name probably derived as a diminutive from 'bec' meaning 'beak' or 'nose'. In an age when surnames were not fixed and not limited to a single name, Thomas was known as Becket probably only as long as he lived in London. When he left, he was called Thomas of London and, after he became archbishop, Thomas of Canterbury. If he is referred to here throughout his life by his boyhood name, it is only by modern historiographical convention. As to 'a Becket', that appellation is a later, unfortunate confection.

Thomas's parents lived at Cheapside in the city of London. After his death, Thomas's sister had a hospital built on the site of the family house; it later became the site of the Mercers' Company. His father was a successful merchant, who mixed in the social circles of the Norman elite in London. Thomas grew up speaking French with the great men of rank and wealth who visited the Becket house at Cheapside. Although the son of foreign-born parents, Thomas was a Londoner and spent the first half of his life in and around London.

At the age of ten Thomas was sent by his father to study with the Augustinian canons at Merton Priory, about fifteen miles from London, a monastery recently founded (1114) and enjoying the patronage of prominent Normans. He stayed only a few years and then went to a city school, possibly at St Paul's Cathedral. Two sources say that Thomas then went to Paris to continue his studies. If so, then Thomas Becket would have studied at Paris in the company of John of Salisbury, who, in his many writings, makes no mention of Thomas at Paris. In any account, he soon appeared in London, where his father had suffered financial reverses and his mother, the only woman in his emotional life, had died. Thomas left his father's house, perhaps aged twenty or thereabouts, to learn practical administration with a rich kinsman, who was involved in the London money market. Three years there and Thomas made a move that was to lead to an almost meteoric rise to high offices in church and state. At the age of about twenty-five Thomas of London entered into the household of Theobald, archbishop of Canterbury.

In Theobald's household, he had his real schooling. This household was a cradle for future bishops, including four archbishops and six bishops. It was clearly a place for ecclesiastical high-flyers. When Becket arrived there, John of Salisbury had just returned from a brilliant success at Paris and Vacarius had come from studying law at Bologna. At one point, although the matter is a bit obscure, Thomas seems to have taken a sabbatical leave to study canon law at Bologna. Archbishop Theobald led a peripatetic life, spending time not only at his residences in Canterbury and in London (at Lambeth), but also elsewhere in his province on archiepiscopal business and also abroad at Rheims and, perhaps, even Rome. Contemporary descriptions agree that Thomas was a handsome man of impressive appearance and that he was a personality of great charm. His memory for specific detail impressed all who knew him throughout his life. He quickly became a favourite of Archbishop Theobald. Thomas took at least minor orders and probably proceeded as far as subdeacon. After almost ten years in the archbishop's household, in 1154 Becket was appointed archdeacon of Canterbury, the office in the diocese of Canterbury second only to that of archbishop and an office which was often a springboard to higher preferment: his immediate predecessor had become archbishop of York. Now he took deacon's order, but his direct exercise of his archdeaconry was to be limited since he was appointed within a matter of weeks to high secular office, the chancellorship of the realm.

The newly crowned Henry II (1154–89) chose Becket to be his chancellor no doubt upon Theobald's recommendation. It would be saying too much and too little to say that Becket was now the king's prime minister, too much because the modern term relates to a popularly elected, democratic government and too little because, as the right hand of an autocratic king, he wielded more power than a modern prime minister. Thomas, then about thirty-five, quickly became friend and confidant of the new, twenty-one-year-old king, and it was this friendship that elevated the office of chancellor from keeper of the king's secretariat and the authenticating seal to that of the king's closest adviser; in addition, he became the king's best friend. Henry by an astute marriage to Eleanor of Aquitaine extended his holdings on the Continent to include not only Normandy and Anjou but the great duchy of Aquitaine; he now held close to half of France. He was a very great man in the Europe of his day, and the chancellor of such a great man was himself a great man. And Thomas Becket lived the role: fur-lined capes, silken garments, tables laden with plate and vessels of gold and silver, hospitality unmatched in munificence even by the young king. When, in 1158, Becket went on an embassy to the French king in Paris, according to a description of the mission, he took with him an enormous retinue. French villagers wondered in amazement who this could be. The chancellor of England on his way to see the French king, they were told. 'What a great man the king of England must be.' Becket served his king not merely in household and by elaborate diplomatic matters, but, although still an archdeacon, served King Henry on the field of battle. In 1159, dressed in the armour of a soldier, he led a successful campaign in Aquitaine, commanding an army of seven hundred knights and some thousands of mercenaries against the king's enemies.

An easy relationship developed with the king, who often without notice, dropped in to see his friend, sometimes for a drink or a chat. They hunted together, they hawked together, they played fierce games of chess together. On a winter's day they were riding through London, when the king noticed a poor man huddling from the cold. He and Thomas dismounted, and the king, in a playful mood, told his chancellor to give the poor man his new, miniver-lined cloak. The two friends, laughing all the while, wrestled on a London street, before Becket obeyed Henry's order. One biographer said, 'Never in Christian times have there been two friends more at one than these.' The closeness of their friendship only emphasizes the tragedy of their great falling out.

It was Becket's great success as chancellor that was to be his undoing. He was clearly the king's man, even in matters touching the church. When Archbishop Theobald, to whom Becket owed his career, lay dying in late 1160 and early 1161, he begged Becket to come to his deathbed, but the busy chancellor, in an act seen by many as gross ingratitude, failed to visit his dying benefactor. With Theobald's death (18 April 1161) only two obvious candidates for Canterbury could be seen in the field, the learned monk-bishop of Hereford, Gilbert Foliot, and the king's chancellor, Thomas Becket. Whatever the canonical niceties, the king selected *his* archbishop, and the king now chose his friend and loyal chancellor, a choice which, before long, he was to deeply regret. With his chancellor of six years as the principal bishop of his kingdom, the king, with ample justification, felt he would have no challenge from the church to his exercise of royal power. On consecutive days in June 1162 Thomas Becket was ordained priest and consecrated bishop. The king was startled when, almost at once, Becket resigned the chancellorship. Trouble was not far off.

A profound change was quickly noticed in the lifestyle of the new archbishop. The worldly chancellor became an ascetic priest. Early morning prayer, private washing of the feet of the poor, the constant irritation of a hair shirt, the scourging of his body, private prayer, the study of the scriptures and the company of learned ecclesiastics were all part of his new life. His table was still magnificent, and he entertained generously, but, we are told, he himself ate simply, almost indifferently. Historians will long debate the nature of this transformation. Had Becket experienced a conversion of soul and become a new man? Had he, rather, lived out his roles consistently, as chancellor adopting the worldly display of a great king's great man and as archbishop adopting the way of life of a man of the spirit with his eyes on a heavenly goal? Whatever the explanation, a dramatic change clearly occurred.

The first major confrontation with the king – there were earlier skirmishes – concerned the constitutions issued by Henry II at Clarendon, near Salisbury, in January 1164. The king demanded that the bishops give solemn assent to the customs observed by his grandfather, Henry I (1100–35). The bishops were extremely reluctant to do so, Thomas Becket particularly. Threats and intimidations followed, and, unexpectedly and to the consternation of the other bishops, Becket agreed and so swore, and the others after him. Henry II then ordered the customs to be written down. As events would show, this was a blunder. It would be one thing to agree to vague, unwritten customs of a bygone period and quite another to agree to explicit, written-down customs. What resulted was the Constitutions of Clarendon and, eventually, the murder of the archbishop. Sixteen constitutions, containing 'some of the recognized customs and rights of the realm', were set down. Six of them were immediately cited as unacceptable to the churchmen. These can be summarized.

> *Constitution 1*: disputes concerning advowson (i.e., presentation of clergy to benefices such as parishes) shall be decided in the king's court.
> *Constitution 3*: clergy, accused of any crime, shall first appear in the king's court, which can then send them to the church court for trial, and, if found guilty there, sent back to the king's court for punishment.
> *Constitution 4*: only with the permission of the king can archbishops, bishops and beneficed clergy leave the kingdom.
> *Constitution 7*: none of the king's tenants-in-chief (the principal men of the realm) shall be excommunicated without the king's permission.
> *Constitution 8*: in ecclesiastical court cases the final appeal shall not be to the pope without the king's consent.

> *Constitution 12*: when bishoprics or certain abbeys fall vacant, the king has the right to the incomes.

In the age of reform, now over a century old, it is almost inconceivable that any bishop in the reforming mode of the times would not raise objections to these six constitutions. Pope Alexander III, later, was to condemn them. Becket now rued what he had done in swearing to the customs, and, when required to seal the document containing them, refused, to the bitter consternation of the king and to the bewilderment of his fellow bishops. A crisis was created.

We must return to those men whom English historiography calls 'criminous clerks', i.e., those members of the clergy who committed secular crimes. Let us look first at church courts and their jurisdiction. These courts came into existence in England shortly after the Norman Conquest (1066). In general, it can be said that cases came before these courts in either one of two ways: *ratione materiae* (by reason of the matter), when the matter of the crime had to do with something that was in some sense spiritual (crimes such as stealing a sacred chalice, laying violent hands on the person of a priest, burning down a church), or *ratione personae* (by reason of the person), when the person accused of a crime was a spiritual person (such as a cleric, monk, nun). Little dispute arose over cases brought to church courts *ratione materiae*. The sticking issue concerned cases *ratione personae*. What should happen if a cleric commits the crime of murder, or if he steals a neighbour's livestock, or if he rapes a young girl of his parish? According to the canonists, although there was some dissent, such a cleric should be tried in the church courts. If he confesses or is found guilty in that court, the ecclesiastical judge should inflict punishment, which for capital crimes such as murder could be degradation (i.e., loss of clerical status) and exile. In a society where the secular courts would have inflicted much more severe punishment, even capital punishment, degradation and exile were seen by many as exceedingly lenient. Also, in the church courts an allegedly criminous clerk could purge himself by denying the crime and finding others willing to swear to his truthfulness. Becket's position was that all cases, ecclesiastical as well as secular, which involved clerics should be tried solely in the ecclesiastical courts, that clerics who are convicted or who confess in that court should be punished in that court and not again elsewhere, that the degradation and handing over to the secular jurisdiction for the future constituted punishment and that clerics receiving this punishment should not be punished again for the same offence in the secular courts. Becket did not create this point of view; he was echoing the current teaching of canon law. The clash here was between two jurisdictions, not one right and another wrong, but both supported by arguments of law and custom. In hindsight, we could say that there was room here for compromise. That none was reached or seriously considered laid the ground for dispute and, in the event, the death of the archbishop.

Dissatisfied with Becket's actions at Clarendon, the king summoned the archbishop to appear before the council of the king and the great men of the realm to answer charges about a matter concerning rightful possession of land on the archbishop's estates. The royal council was to meet at the castle at Northampton in early October 1164. Other charges were soon added, including the charge that Becket had embezzled from the king in his days as chancellor, although the king had discharged Thomas from any such debt. It was clear that Becket was the target of the king's wrath and that almost any issue would do. His brother bishops gave him conflicting advice; several even urged him to resign. In the end, he heeded the advice of his confessor: 'You could easily soothe the king's wrath and keep him as your friend, but you have chosen the service of God, Who will not fail you.' On the morning of Tuesday, 13 October, Becket appealed to the pope, in clear violation of Constitution 8, leaving him subject to a charge of perjury. He then said Mass in honour of the proto-martyr St Stephen, which opens with the words, 'Princes also did sit and speak against me.' Becket feared that threats made to his life would that day be acted upon. After Mass he took with him a communion host to be his dying viaticum (*via tecum*, on the way with thee).

The archbishop upon his arrival at Northampton Castle took the processional cross from his cross-bearer and entered as a priest carrying the sacerdotal sword of the cross. He and a few companions waited on the ground floor, while in a hall above the king met with barons and bishops, the king intent on humiliating the wilful archbishop. The issues had now been reduced to two: Thomas's refusal to render account of his chancellorship and Thomas's allegedly perjurious appeal to the pope. The king's justiciar went down to Thomas to pronounce the judgement on him, but Becket refused to accept it, since a layman had no right to judge an archbishop. He then bolted out of the chamber and, using a side gate, escaped the castle. The breach had occurred. Becket, dressed in the habit of a Gilbertine brother, silently left St Andrew's Priory, where he had been staying, and in a heavy rain escaped the town through the north gate at midnight, Lincoln – and not London – his destination. Accompanied only by a single servant and two Gilbertine brothers, the archbishop stayed at Lincoln in the humble home of a fuller. From there his journeys were now almost exclusively by night, finding safe-houses with the Gilbertines. Certain that he had given the slip to any king's men hunting for him, Becket reached the coast at Sandwich and sailed into an exile that was to last six years.

That the exile was to last six years was the expectation of neither king nor archbishop. That it did owes much to the character of both but also to the situation of Pope Alexander III (1159–81) and the ever precarious relations between the Angevin king of England and the king of France. Alexander had been challenged by an anti-pope and had to spend much of his pontificate in France. (See chapter 8.) He also had to woo the support of both kings, a ticklish task at the best of times, but a task now muddied by an English archbishop living in exile in France. In addition, Henry II, although king of England, was a vassal of the king of France for his substantial holdings in France. Louis VII (1137–80), who allowed Becket sanctuary in his realm, remained a player in the events of this saga. It was in these circumstances that Becket found himself once he was on the European mainland.

Henry II made an almost immediate attempt to have Becket deposed. He used bishops as his agents, and they appeared before the pope at Sens. He refused the king's request and then warily received Becket. Alexander III condemned the Constitutions of Clarendon and released Becket from the oath which he had made at Clarendon. With the pope's help Becket was taken into the Cistercian abbey at Pontigny in Burgundy, where he remained for two years. There he lived an austere life, asking for and receiving the rough, coarse habit from the pope himself. For a few months he followed the sparse diet of the monks, but he fell ill and had to moderate the monastic diet. He considered his stay at Pontigny a penance for his weakness at Clarendon. It was from here that Becket, joined by some members of his household, carried on the dispute with Henry II. Yet the king would not permit his exiled archbishop to enjoy the tranquil life of his Cistercian retreat; he wrote to the general chapter of the Cistercians and threatened to confiscate all Cistercian lands in England if they continued to allow Becket to live in one of their monasteries. It was no idle threat, and the abbots knew this. The abbot of Cîteaux, himself an Englishman, went to Pontigny to see the archbishop about the matter. In November 1166 Becket, to the great relief of the Cistercian grandees, volunteered to leave Pontigny to save his host's embarrassment and their order great loss. King Louis offered him residence in whatever monastery he wished, and Becket chose the Benedictine abbey of St Columba just beyond the north wall of Sens, where, with brief absences, he was to remain for four more years.

Throughout his exile Becket did not experience the unanimous support of his brother bishops, far from it. A hostile party among his episcopal colleagues was led by Gilbert Foliot, rival candidate for Canterbury, now, as a consolation prize, bishop of London. Foliot had the continued support of the bishop of Hereford, the archbishop of York and, depending on the issue, the wavering support of others of the bishops. The position of the archbishop of York was critical. Roger of Pont L'Evêque had been a colleague of Becket in the household of Archbishop Theobald and, in fact, was Becket's immediate predecessor as archdeacon of Canterbury. He inherited the traditional claims of York to primacy over Canterbury, and, when Becket became archbishop of Canterbury, the rivalry of earlier days in Theobald's *familia* was renewed. The bulk of the bishops found themselves in an uncomfortable position: they were in England, facing an angry king, while their leader (and king's enemy) was abroad in France. Their position was to support a resolution to the crisis. In 1167 the pope sent emissaries to meet with Henry II and Becket in an attempt to effect a resolution. They met with no success. Both parties gave negative responses, but efforts continued.

In January 1169 the two adversaries had a meeting at Montmirail, where the French and English kings were settling their differences. It made much sense to settle the issue of the archbishop at the same time. At the field below Montmirail, in a moment planned in advance, the archbishop fell on his knees before his king, the first time they had seen each other since the fateful meeting at Northampton over four years before. Henry then raised Becket to his feet, and they discussed their differences. The archbishop was willing to swear to observe the ancient customs of the realm *salvo ordine suo* ('saving his order'). This clause was seen as an escape clause, rendering Becket's agreement meaningless, for it meant, in effect, that he would agree to these customs insofar as they did not contradict the liberties of the church, and this was the crux of the matter. The king ended the interview, and a chance was missed. On 7 February the kings met again, this time at St Leger, and Becket again met the king with no more success than at the previous meeting. An attempted meeting on 22 February never took place. Many now felt that only nature would resolve the controversy by the death of one of the parties, king or archbishop or pope. It was the lowest hour.

Two months later, on Palm Sunday, 1169, Becket formally excommunicated two of his fellow bishops, Gilbert Foliot of London and Jocelin de Bohun of Salisbury and seven other of his enemies. As angry as Foliot clearly was at this action, he observed the terms of his excommunication. The king, also sensitive to ecclesiastical penalties, feared his kingdom would be placed under an interdict, which prohibited most church services and sacraments except the baptism of infants, confession of sins (but outside the church proper) and the last rites for the dying. As negotiations in the summer of 1169 faltered, the king added to the Constitutions of Clarendon a provision that anyone who brought a decree of interdict into England would be treated as a traitor and punished accordingly. Six weeks after the decree came into force, Henry and Becket made another effort to reach a solution, this time at Montmartre, then outside Paris. When an agreement seemed near, the king refused to give the archbishop the kiss of peace as his guarantee of his sincerity and promise of Becket's personal security. Pope Alexander III, by now safely back in Italy, could be more assertive, and in January 1170 explicitly threatened an interdict if the king refused to settle.

If matters were not intense enough as it was, temperatures rose to white heat when Henry insisted on having his son Henry crowned at Westminster Abbey on 14 June 1170 by Archbishop Roger of York. Henry II overstepped long-standing tradition which reserved coronations to the archbishop of Canterbury, a reservation confirmed as recently as 1166 by Alexander III. It was an insult to Becket owing either to calculation or to gross insensitivity on the part of the king. In either case, the insult was taken. Almost at once Henry seemed to realize that he had gone too far and wrote to the papal legate that he was anxious to make peace with Becket. And within six weeks of the coronation peace was made. The terms followed, in general, the terms recently offered by Pope Alexander. Henry would allow Becket and his companions to return in peace and for Becket to gain full possession of all his property. The controversial constitutions were not mentioned; they would be quietly buried by the king. In addition, Henry would allow Becket to punish the bishops who had participated in the coronation. For his part, Becket agreed to act as an archbishop should act towards his king, saving the freedom of the church. The two met near Fréteval not far from the Loire.

Sitting on their horses, they greeted each other, and before the day was out the deed was done: reconciliation had been effected. Ambiguities obviously remained, but with good will they could be lived with amicably. Yet the king, claiming an oath taken previously, refused to give Becket the kiss of peace, the symbol of the special protection to his life by the king. Nonetheless, it was a victory for the archbishop against the most powerful man in Europe after the emperor. When the two met for the very last time, probably in early October 1170, they had this parting dialogue:

Thomas: I have the feeling, my lord, as we leave, that you will never see me again in this life.
Henry II: Do you think me a man who breaks his faith?
Thomas: May God forbid, my lord.

They were not to meet again in this life. When next they met, the penitent king spent a night of vigil with the lifeless body of his old friend.

At the end of November Thomas Becket was at Wissant, his face turned towards the channel and England. He had papal letters re-excommunicating the bishops of London and Salisbury, recently absolved, for their participation in the coronation. The archbishop of York remained an excommunicate, never having been absolved. Becket sent ahead to Dover a messenger bearing the papal excommunications, who served them on the three bishops, who were themselves at the coast ready to depart for Normandy to see the king. The messenger escaped with his life, but the bishops, particularly the archbishop of York, reacted with a rage, which still flamed when the bishops met the king some weeks later. Meanwhile, with a favourable wind and a placid sea Thomas Becket sailed for England and arrived at Sandwich on the morning of 1 December 1170, six years and one month after he had sailed into exile.

Two welcomes met the archbishop. First, there was the hostile welcome. As so often happens in major disputes – it happens in our own times in the Middle East, in the Balkans and elsewhere – one demonized one's enemy, and, consequently there were many supporters of the king, including those who had profited from Becket's absence, who truly hated the archbishop. So it was that, on the very day of his arrival at Sandwich, the three seniormost royal officials in Kent rode with an armed troop to confront the archbishop. He refused to meet with them until they disarmed themselves. They angrily – and wrongly – charged that Becket believed that the young king's coronation was invalid. They demanded that he remove the excommunications of the bishops. The sheriff of Kent told him, 'You have brought fire and the sword with you to England.' Yet the popular welcome was wholly different. Becket was greeted as a returning hero, even as a patriot, for his courage in standing up resolutely to an overbearing, unpopular king. The twelve-mile progress from Sandwich to Canterbury became a victory parade, the medieval equivalent to a New York ticker-tape reception. At each village priest and people cheered him in a festive way. Chanting monks met him at the gate of Canterbury; the bells of all the churches pealed. And Becket removed his shoes and walked barefoot to his cathedral, where, his face flushed with excitement, he prostrated himself on the stone floor.

At Christmas at Canterbury the archbishop preached on the theme of peace on earth to men of good will, reminding his congregation of the only martyr archbishop of Canterbury, St Alphege. Then, after the bidding prayers, Becket reiterated the excommunications of the three bishops.

Two parties, each antagonistic to Becket and, indeed, exceedingly angry with him, arrived in time for Christmas with the king at Bures near Bayeux in Normandy. During the course of Christmas Eve and Christmas Day itself they spoke to the king of little else but the treachery of the archbishop. First, there were royal officials who came, spreading the rumour (for which there was not a shred of evidence) that Becket intended to dethrone the young king. The three excommunicated bishops were also there, filling the king's ears with a torrent of abuse of Archbishop Becket. The archbishop of York is reported to have said, 'You will never have peace as long as Thomas is archbishop.' At some point, probably on Christmas Day itself, the king uttered the words that sent four knights on a tragic mission. They are variously reported but in essence were, 'Will no one of my men rid me of this contemptuous, low-born priest?' Four of his knights, upon hearing this, decided to carry out what they saw as the king's wish: they set out from Normandy for the channel, intent on murdering the archbishop at Canterbury. Later it would be said that their intentions were only to seize the archbishop, but account after account state that they headed for England with assassination their clear purpose. Less clear is the king's knowledge of their purpose. He claimed later that he did not know what they planned to do, and writers, sympathetic to Becket, later exculpated the king from ordering Becket's murder, although, it should be added, they were writing while Henry was still alive and, at the height of his power, still an intimidating presence.

The knights were Reginald FitzUrse, who, ironically enough, had come to the king's court through Becket's influence; Hugh de Moreville, who had been Becket's vassal; William de Tracy, a descendant of Henry I; and Richard le Breton, a younger knight with lands in the west of England. They travelled separately, using different ports and rendezvoused at Saltwood Castle on the evening of 28 December 1170, a Monday, there to plot their tactics for the morrow.

Early on Tuesday morning the four knights rode towards Canterbury, a journey of about fifteen miles over the ancient Roman road. Meanwhile, at Canterbury, Becket was following his usual regimen. He attended Mass, said his devotions to the saints at their altars in the cathedral, confessed himself and took the discipline of scourging. The main meal of the day was taken at about two o'clock, and by three Becket sat in his own large chamber with a number of friends and advisers. It was then that the knights entered the archbishop's rooms. What followed has been reported by five eye-witnesses, who tell a uniformly sad tale, each complementing the other in detail.

The knights had entered the cathedral precincts alone, leaving armed guards near the gate to prevent supporters from the town coming to the archbishop's aid and also to prevent the archbishop's escape. The four knights, no doubt led by FitzUrse, having passed through the gate, had stopped briefly at a mulberry tree to leave their horses and their weapons. At the archbishop's great hall they found the meal concluded and the servants eating. The steward went to the adjoining chamber to announce their arrival to Becket. They entered without greeting him nor, indeed, did he greet them. At length, Becket gave the visitors a long stare and spoke, calling FitzUrse by name. The latter said that they came from the king and demanded that Becket lift the excommunications. He said that Thomas had broken the Fréteval peace agreement, which he denied. The knight continued that Becket was also threatening to undo the recent coronation, which he also denied. They were soon shouting at one another, Becket threatening further excommunications and FitzUrse saying that Becket was speaking at the peril of his head. 'Have you come to kill me? You will find me here, a foot soldier in the Lord's army.' The knights ordered the archbishop's servants to guard Becket, while they went to retrieve their weapons. At the mulberry tree they uncloaked themselves, revealing coats of mail, and then put on their hauberks, ready to return to Becket. A loyal servant of the archbishop had bolted the door of the archbishop's hall against them. The knights found a rear entrance up a flight of stairs, but it was being repaired and only by battering through a window with axes did they gain entry. Meanwhile, Becket was seated on his bed, being advised what to do next. At the sound of the axes, a move had to be made, and Becket reluctantly agreed to enter the great cathedral, where vespers (evensong) was being sung. Since the knights had assigned armed men to surround the buildings, another way had to be found for the archbishop's party. An unused passageway which led to the cloister was opened, and Thomas with conscious dignity followed his cross-bearer through the cloister into his cathedral by the north transept entrance. His monks bolted the door of the cathedral behind them, but at his command – 'the church is not a fortress' – they unbolted the door. The monks tried to hurry him up the steps towards the choir, but by then the knights, with FitzUrse in the lead, with bared swords and axes in their hands, had entered the darkening cathedral. 'Where is the traitor Thomas Becket?' Halfway up the stairs, the archbishop turned and said, 'I am here, not a traitor to the king but a priest of God.' He came down the stairs and was standing now in the transept. One of his attackers hissed, 'Run away; you are as good as dead.' But he refused to run. The knights attempted to put the archbishop on William de Tracy's back in an effort to remove him from the church, but Becket resisted, almost throwing FitzUrse to the ground, calling him scornfully 'a pimp'. Now enraged, FitzUrse was the first to strike the archbishop. He struck a blow with his sword at Becket's head, knocking off his cap and taking a slice of his scalp. 'I embrace death in the name of Jesus and the church,' said the archbishop. Another blow and still another blow, both from William de Tracy, felled the archbishop to the stone floor. There with Becket fully prostrate Richard le Breton with a powerful stroke of his sword cut off the crown of Becket's head and broke the sword in two on the pavement. One of their companions, in an act of cruel barbarity, with the tip of his sword scattered the archbishop's brains on the floor. 'This traitor won't get up again,' he boasted. The murderers then fled the cathedral, shouting in shameful triumph, 'King's men, king's men.' And after ravaging their victim's quarters, they left Canterbury, while the stilled body of the archbishop lay where he had fallen, in his own blood and brains. Gradually his friends, scattered during the turmoil, returned, and, as they prepared the body for burial, thunder burst above Canterbury. The king's men had created a martyr.

The revulsion of Christendom was as immediate as the news was passed. Henry II learned of the deed three days later and appears to have sincerely grieved. The pope went into a week's mourning and soon imposed a personal interdict on Henry. The French, who had given refuge to Becket in exile, harboured deep suspicions of the role of the English king. The archbishop of Sens, supported by the whole French hierarchy, imposed an interdict on all Henry's continental lands. The king quickly made his peace with the church. At Avranches in 1172, he agreed to the demands of the pope. He would allow appeals to Rome in ecclesiastical cases; he would restore to the see of Canterbury all its properties; he would take the cross and go to the Holy Land; he would abrogate the customs which he had introduced against the liberties of the church. Later he agreed to exempt clerics from secular courts. In fact, Henry never went on crusade and stated privately that he did not know of any customs like those referred to. Personally, he allowed that, although he did not send the murdering knights to Canterbury, his intemperate and inflammatory words might have provoked his men to commit the murder of Becket. Despite what might sound like self-serving disclaimers, Henry II had capitulated; Becket had won the day.

On 21 February 1173, just over two years after Becket's death, he was declared a saint, St Thomas of Canterbury, martyr, with his feast day to be observed on 29 December. In July of the following year the king approached Canterbury as a penitent pilgrim. Removing his boots at the city gates, he walked barefoot to the cathedral and to the tomb of his once friend. There he prostrated himself, admitted his unwitting role in the murder, and begged the monks of Canterbury to punish him. Each of the eighty monks administered three strokes to the back of the king. He remained there at the tomb throughout that day and the ensuing night. Who knows how calculated this act of penance was? Henry II was beset at this time by a rebellion of his queen and sons, his crown not securely in place. Yet it was a humiliating act for a very proud man. The tomb was fast becoming a shrine, and the long line of pilgrims was to reach into the 1530s, when Henry VIII destroyed the shrine of a priest who dared to challenge the power of the state.

Hildegard of Bingen (1098–1179)

Only in very recent times has the attention of historians been drawn to the remarkable Hildegard of Bingen. One wonders why the delayed recognition. Has she been the victim of a historical establishment dominated by men and largely blind to the accomplishments of women? Or is she now little more than a poster-girl for modern feminists? In a life that spanned much of the twelfth century, Hildegard witnessed the great movements of the time and was in correspondence with the most powerful men of the century. One neglects an examination of her accomplishments at the risk of gaining only a limited and incomplete view of twelfth-century history. Two matters should be cleared away before looking at her life and its historical meaning. She is often called an abbess and a saint. Strictly speaking, she was neither. Hildegard was the head of a religious community, but she was not called abbess but mistress (*magistra*) of the nuns in her community. And for reasons which are now obscure attempts to have her canonized did not succeed, but it should quickly be added that a local cult to 'St Hildegard' survives in parts of Germany with 17 September as her feast day. Only the pedantic would object to her being called 'abbess' and 'saint', although the terms require some stretching.

Hildegard was born at Bermersheim not far from Mainz in the German Rhineland, a daughter of the minor nobility. When she was about eight, Hildegard joined the anchoress Jutta, daughter of a local count, at the male Benedictine monastery of St Disibod (Disibodenberg). They, and other girls who soon joined them, lived in an enclosure perhaps to the south of the monastic church. There, in about 1112, Hildegard professed as a nun and was taught by Jutta to read the holy books. At the death of Jutta in 1136 Hildegard became head of this community of Benedictine nuns. Events were soon to transform her from an almost anonymous mistress of an almost unknown community to a person of Europe-wide fame.

In the preface to her most famous work, *Scivias*, Hildegard described how these events began.

> When I was 42 years and 7 months old, in the year 1141, the heavens opened to me and my brain was flooded by an exceedingly brilliant light. It warmed my whole heart and being in the same way that sun gives warmth. And I instantly understood the meanings of the holy books – the Psalter, the Gospels and the other catholic books of the Old and New Testaments. It was not that I understood the grammar and syntax.

She wrote that she had been experiencing visions since early childhood but that she had not made them known.

> I heard a voice from heaven saying to me, 'Therefore, tell others of these miracles and write them down.'

And, although the voice said, 'I am the living light, who sheds light on hidden things', Hildegard did not heed the call to write and fell ill. She told her secretary, the monk Volmar, about her visions and the command to write them down. He encouraged her, and in the course of the next ten years Hildegard described, in Latin, twenty-six visions. The work was given the name *Scivias*, a shortening of *Scito vias* ('Know the Ways'). The abbot of St Disibod knew and approved of her writings and informed the archbishop of Mainz, who also approved. Then, in a momentous leap, her work was brought to the attention of Pope Eugenius III (1145–53), who actually read aloud a portion of the yet unfinished *Scivias* to the fathers of the Council of Trier (November 1147 to February 1148). St Bernard wrote to his former disciple and now pope a letter urging Eugenius to encourage Hildegard to continue her writing. This he did, and within three years her account of her visions was completed. Hildegard was fast becoming a celebrity. All was not to be smooth sailing.

Hildegard claimed that God had ordered her to move her nuns to a new place. From a practical point of view this made admirable sense: her growing reputation had led to an increase of young women coming to St Disibod with a consequent overcrowding. The abbot opposed this move since his monastery shared in the fame of their visionary nun and, more practically, since the finances of the two communities, particularly the endowments, had become somewhat commingled. In face of this opposition, Hildegard once again took to her bed. The abbot withdrew his opposition, perhaps being pressured to do so by the archbishop of Mainz. In any case, in 1150, accompanied by twenty or so nuns, Hildegard journeyed the twenty miles to Rupertsberg, where on a hill overlooking the Rhine where it is joined by the River Nahe she established her new house. It was near Bingen, which name has been associated with Hildegard since the twelfth century. The abbot of St Disibod's monastery appointed a provost to care for the spiritual needs of the nuns, and he chose Volmar. Hildegard remained 'mistress'. She subsequently experienced long periods of illness, particularly in the late 1150s and late 1160s. A particularly difficult crisis occurred soon after arriving at Rupertsberg, when her favourite nun, Ricardis of Stade, was appointed abbess of Bassum. She was the daughter of the marchioness of Stade and, with Volmar, had assisted in the writing of the *Scivias*. Hildegard's response reveals a very human side of her character. She wrote to the nun's mother in an attempt to thwart the appointment: 'Do not disturb my soul; do not cause tears of bitterness to fall from my eyes; do not wound my heart so severely.' Since she claimed to know the will of God, Hildegard could say with no obvious self-doubt that God did not will Ricardis to become abbess. She insisted on this point in letter after letter. To the archbishop of Mainz, she wrote, 'the clear fountain, truthful and just [God], says, "These legal pretexts for the appointment of this girl mean nothing in God's eyes, for I did not choose them."' When others in Germany failed to see God's will in Hildegard's will, she wrote to the pope, but Eugenius, understandably not wanting to get involved, referred the matter to local officials. Hildegard's will did not prevail. Hildegard then wrote to the new abbess what, to many, may appear to be a love letter:

> My grief rises up to heaven. My sorrow destroys my confidence in
> mankind. I loved the nobility of your behaviour, your wisdom, your
> purity, your soul and every part of your being. May all who have
> sorrow like mine grieve with me, all who, like me, have ever, in
> God's love, so loved a person in heart and soul only to have that love
> snatched away from them as you were from me.

Within a year Abbess Ricardis died, and with her death closes this chapter in
Hildegard's life, a chapter raising questions of human feelings and emotion that
the historian's limited abilities cannot answer.

On another occasion Hildegard's conduct as head of Rupertsberg came under
criticism. Another abbess complained that Hildegard allowed her nuns on feast
days to appear in church with their hair flowing unbound, wearing long white
silk veils that touched the floor and, on their heads, golden crowns, whereas they
should dress with the modesty enjoined by St Paul. Far from denying this practice,
Hildegard defended it as the appropriate way for virgins to approach the High
Priest. Elsewhere she claimed that it was from a vision that she knew that a
virgin's head should have only a white veil and a crown. In addition, the same
abbess registered surprise that Hildegard admitted only noble women into her
community, whereas the Lord chose lowly fishermen and poor people as his
companions. She replied that God created a layered society with a higher and a
lower order and that the lower order should not rise above the higher order.

> What farmer would indiscriminately put in one enclosure all his
> animals – cattle, asses, sheep, goats? It is necessary to be discriminating
> about people, lest people of different status, herded together, be
> disturbed in the pride of their elevation or in the ignominy of their
> decline.

Yet, in Hildegard's defence, it should be said that religious orders over time, by
self-selection of entrants latterly, have tended to produce communities which are
fairly homogeneous in terms of social class. Such criticisms scarcely distracted
Hildegard; she was busy about other things.

From about 1150 Hildegard had a public life, which began soon after the pope
held aloft her *Scivias* at the Council of Trier. Nearly four hundred letters date
from this period. As collected, they are unfortunately not arranged chrono-
logically but in order of the importance of her correspondents. Although she
probably dictated them to a secretary or left her secretary with the gist of what
she wanted to write, she was as much the author of her letters as St Bernard was
of his. In fact, she wrote to the great abbot of Clairvaux, and this letter takes first
place in the collection. Hildegard told Bernard that she had a vision and needed
his advice. In reply, he encouraged her, but his reply has the ring of a stock letter
of spiritual encouragement. She wrote Pope Eugenius III four letters that survive
and at least one other. Writing in 1151, the pope remarked that 'your reputation

has become widespread'. Likewise, she wrote to Pope Anastasius IV (1153–54) – 'you allow evil to raise its wicked head' – and to his successor the Englishman Hadrian IV (1154–59) – 'you are sometimes at odds with your better self.' She was equally severe with the German emperor, Frederick Barbarossa, at the time (1164) when he, for a second time, supported an anti-pope. She told him that he was acting 'like a little boy, like one that has lost his mind'. Nun and emperor had met under more pleasant circumstances in 1152, when Frederick had invited Hildegard to the royal palace. To King Henry II of England she gave stern warning that he should not listen to the devil. And one may wonder what that other great woman of the age, Eleanor of Aquitaine, wife successively of two kings and mother of two kings, made of Hildegard's remark that she was too busy about too many things: 'You have not found rest.'

Much of Hildegard's correspondence took the form of spiritual direction, replies to religious men and women and to priests and prelates who asked her advice or perhaps only her prayers. A monk wrote asking her to intercede with God for his wicked and perverse sins and 'please send me a response by this messenger'. In truth, most of her letters of spiritual direction were written to heads of houses, who, in the face of the changing modes of religious life, felt uncertainties and some even considered resignation. An unnamed abbess wrote, 'I stand in need of your advice concerning my office; how and when will this burden be lifted from me?' Hildegard replied, 'Do not put aside your office because you feel overburdened and weary.' To one severe abbot she advised, 'Impose lighter burdens on those who are unable to carry heavy ones.' To an abbess, impatient with her nuns, she cautioned, 'When you are stirred to anger, put your eyes on the font of patience, and the anger will pass and the storming waters will abate.' Scores of other such letters survive, testimony to her innate wisdom and to the confidence placed in her by a large circle of clients.

In another significant aspect of her prophetic role Hildegard embarked on as many as four preaching expeditions, which took her mostly to monasteries but also, on occasion, to great German cathedrals. At Cologne cathedral she lamented that the clergy by their negligence were responsible for the successes of the Cathars (see chapter 11). At Trier, at Pentecost, 1160, using her most powerful rhetoric, she upbraided the bishops and priests for their laxity. Wherever she went, Hildegard repeated the same message: repent and reform. Her message was fully consistent with the monastic reforming movement of the times.

Her speaking out in monasteries and cathedrals underlines, as do her letters, her self-described role as a prophet, meaning an inspired and fearless speaker of the word of God, although some people, including Barbarossa, expected her to reveal future events to them, which was not the essence of her prophetic role. Like Ezechiel and John the Baptist, she spoke the truth of the divine message, caring not who might be offended and become wrathful at her uncompromising forthrightness. She said that God spoke through her mouth. At the famous Trier sermon she began by saying, 'I am but a poor little one with no claim to learning or courage, but these are the words I have heard', and the sermon, God's words, then followed. The 'words' must have been accompanied by an unflinching sense of self-confidence.

And so she lived her life, preaching and writing. Yet, when death came in 1179, it was preceded by the most troubling episode in her long life. At Rupertsberg, Hildegard had encouraged local rich families to bury their dead in the monastic grounds, a practice not uncommon for religious houses, a practice with spiritual benefits for the deceased from the prayers of the nuns and material benefits for the nuns from the gifts of the deceased's family. In 1178 she allowed the burial of a local nobleman who had been excommunicated. The canons of Mainz cathedral, within days of the burial, ordered his exhumation under pain of interdict, because an excommunicate was by canon law forbidden burial in consecrated ground. She refused to have his body exhumed, claiming that her vision would not allow it. By so doing she cast her community into the consequences of an interdict, which meant that the nuns could not receive communion nor could any liturgical ceremonies be held except in the simplest of forms and never with music or singing. It would be incorrect to see this as a collective excommunication, since excommunication by definition is a casting out from the Christian community, which clearly is not the effect of interdict. Hildegard, besides citing the irrefutable authority of her own vision, argued that the nobleman had confessed his sins and received the last rites before his death. The cathedral canons were moved neither by her claim of a divine imperative to disobey them nor by her description of the deceased's alleged reconciliation, and they refused to budge. According to one account, Hildegard took measures to conceal the grave. Without any apparent jurisdiction the archbishop of Cologne intervened, producing alleged witnesses to the nobleman's absolution, and ordered the interdict lifted. The archbishop of Mainz, in Italy attending the Third Lateran Council, was no doubt displeased by the intrusion of the archbishop of Cologne in a matter beyond his jurisdiction, and he thus confirmed the interdict and remonstrated with Hildegard:

> The church maintained that the man buried at your monastery had in his lifetime incurred excommunication and, although some question remains about his absolution, you acted dangerously when you refused to obey the canons and you were insensitive to the scandal that would be caused.

Nonetheless, the archbishop ordered his cathedral clergy to withdraw the interdict, if suitable witnesses testified to the man's reconciliation. And the crisis ended. Hildegard was then eighty years old and had only six more months to live. She died on 17 September 1179 at Rupertsberg. Her body now rests at Rüdesheim, across the river from Bingen.

If during her lifetime Hildegard was best known as a visionary prophet, she is best known to the modern world as an author. To mention her writings raises instantly the question of authenticity of the writings attributed to her. Within a decade of her life a dossier of writings, which the compilers attributed to Hildegard, was assembled at Rupertsberg. We cannot be equally certain of the authenticity of all the works in this codex and in other collections. Accepting that she used secretaries and scribes, there can be little if any doubt that she was the author of the *Scivias* and the considerable correspondence. The *Liber divinorum operum* ('Book of Divine Deeds'), a description of later visions, raises some questions. Examination of the earliest extant manuscript (at Ghent) suggests to different scholars distinct alternatives, one being her non-authorship, although the evidence for this position seems not compelling. With scholarship divided about some of the works attributed to her, one might put aside for now books of questionable authenticity. These would include a book on medicine. Also, over seventy compositions of sacred music with words and music which are attributed to her clearly came from her monastery at Rupertsberg but might have come from her supervision rather than directly from her hand – still a notable achievement – although her amenuensis wrote, while away, how he missed 'the voice of her melodies and a tongue not heard before'. When the air is cleared of mist, all doubt may well be dissipated and Hildegard's achievement seen in an even brighter light. Yet were she to have written nothing but her letters and the *Scivias*, her place would be absolutely firm as a luminous figure of the twelfth century.

Two copies of the *Scivias* which were made during her lifetime at her monastery have survived, one, lost in 1945, now only in a photographic copy. They contain her visions in three books of unequal length. Each section describes a vision and then presents Hildegard's interpretation. They cover a wide range of topics concerning the Christian life for religious and laity alike.

The nature of these visions interested her contemporaries as it indeed interests moderns. The insistent Guibert of Gembloux, a Walloon monk who later became her secretary, asked Hildegard about how she experienced her visions:

> Is it true that you do not remember at all what you have spoken in a vision once your secretaries have written it down? Do you dictate them in Latin or in German with someone translating the German into Latin? Have you become learned in the scriptures by study or by divine inspiration?

When she failed to answer, Guibert wrote again,

> Do the visions come in a dream while you are asleep or do they come as a trance while you are awake?

Yielding to Guibert's demands, Hildegard gave him (and us) her own explanation of her visions:

> Since I was an infant, I had this visionary gift in my soul, and I have it to this very day. In these visions my spirit is raised by God up to

the heavens and into the winds, and it meets a wide range of people, even those far distant. Since this is the way that I see, my sight is dependent on moving clouds and other conditions. No, I do not hear what I hear with bodily ears nor with the feelings of my heart nor with my five senses. I see them in my spirit with my eyes wide open. Never do I experience a trancelike state in my visions. I am fully awake and see visions both day and night. Still, my body experiences such pain that I feel I might die. Yet with the help of God I am sustained.

The light that I see is not specific and limited. It comes more brightly than the sun shines through a light cloud. Neither the height, length nor breadth of that light can I determine. I have named this light 'the Shadow of the Living Light'. Sun, moon and stars can be seen reflected in water; similarly, writings and words and deeds are seen by me reflected in this light.

The things that I see or learn in vision I keep stored away in my memory for a long time. My experience of sight and hearing and understanding occur all at once. Since I am unlearned and have no other knowledge than my vision, the things that I write are what I see and hear in my vision with nothing of my own added. They are expressed in inelegant Latin, for I hear my vision in that way, since the vision does not teach me to write in the Latin of the philosophers. I should add that the words which I see and hear in vision do not resemble the words of human speech; they are, rather, like a fiery flame and a cloud moving through empty space. There is no way that I can perceive the shape of this light, just as I cannot stare into the sun.

And occasionally I see a light within that light, which I call 'the Living Light'. I can no more explain that light than the other. When I do see it, my sufferings and pains disappear, and I feel like a young girl rather than the old woman that I am.

To this she added that she had the first light which she described, the Shadow of the Living Light, with her always:

It is like looking into the heavens when there is but a light cloud on a starless night. I see in this light the things that I speak of and I hear the responses that I give to those seeking my advice.

This is as full a description as any medieval visionary has given of the visionary experience.

What is the modern reader to make of this? What must be confronted is the question of the historical nature of Hildegard's visions as found in her *Scivias*. Put squarely, did Hildegard actually experience visions from God? If one believes in a God who at times appears to human beings, then the possibility of visions poses

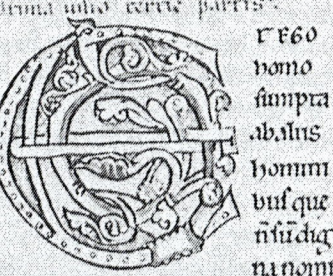

10 Hildegard of Bingen's vision of extinguished stars. Reproduced by permission of Brepols.

no problem. Yet if one cannot intellectually accept the possibility of divine visions or if one feels that it is not proven that Hildegard actually had visions, what then? There seem to be two possibilities. One can say that they were pure fabrications of her imagination, created for personal reasons; this could be true but on the evidence seems unlikely. Or one can say that she experienced something which has a natural explanation but which she felt was divine in origin. The visionary Hildegard could have suffered from migraine episodes, since what she describes fits a classical description of migraine attacks. We often mistakenly think of such

181

attacks solely in terms of headaches, which is not strictly speaking the case. Frequently migraine experiences affect vision. Most commonly, when this happens, one sees a connected series of inverse v's or lightning-like flashes across the field of vision, which do not disappear when one closes the eyes. They are sometimes called 'scintillating scotomata' or 'fortification spectra' (because they can resemble crenellated structures). 'Floaters' often appear in migraine incidents and look like clouds. Hildegard's 'extinguished stars vision', which was illustrated in a contemporary manuscript, closely resembles a form of migraine experience. An aura frequently occurs in the early stage of a migraine attack and can include hallucinations, which the subject can be convinced are entirely objective. The sicknesses which Hildegard experienced frequently in her life are consistent with severe migraine attacks, from which one typically recovers, as did Hildegard, with renewed vigour. Dr Oliver Sacks, long a specialist in the subject, concludes, 'The visions of Hildegard . . . [were] indisputably migrainous'. That her visions may be explained in a neuro-psychological way should not diminish the importance of their content. In such a state with unusual visual experiences occurring, Hildegard might quite understandably have thought them experiences from God and that, consequently, what she was thinking while having such experiences came directly from God. Her *Scivias*, then, could be seen as the outpouring of Hildegard's soul as the result of these experiences. It provides a view, at times brilliant, of the Christian view of life from the fall of Adam and Eve to the Last Judgement and emphasizes the coming of Jesus and his church and its sacraments as well as other themes such as angels, Lucifer and the anti-Christ. Whatever its source, the *Scivias* stands in a commanding place in medieval religious literature and its author in the first rank of remarkable women of any age.

Further reading

The correspondence of Abelard and Heloise, including the *Historia calamitatum*, is available in a Penguin paperback, *The Letters of Abelard and Heloise* (tr. Betty Radice; Harmondsworth, Mddsx, 1974). The best book on Abelard, comprehensive, well-informed, brilliantly incisive, is Michael T. Clanchy, *Abelard: A Medieval Life* (Oxford, 1997). A book that contains more than the title suggests is John Marenbon, *The Philosophy of Peter Abelard* (Cambridge, 1997). For Bernard's letters see *Letters of St Bernard of Clairvaux* (tr. Bruno Scott James; Stroud, Glos., 1998). Constant J. Mews claims that letters found in a collection at the municipal library at Troyes belong to our subject: *The Lost Love Letters of Heloise and Abelard: Perceptions of Dialogue in Twelfth-Century France* (London, 1999), which also provides a translation of these letters.

Two essential books on Becket are David Knowles, *Thomas Becket* (London, 1970) and Frank Barlow, *Thomas Becket* (Berkeley, 1986). For a scholarly treatment of textual evidence see Anne Duggan, *Thomas Becket: A Textual History of his Letters* (Oxford, 1980). In a work of exemplary scholarship the same author has produced an edition (with English translation) of the letters to and from Becket, *The Correspondence of Thomas Becket, Archbishop of Canterbury, 1162–1170* (2 vols; Oxford, 2000). She has also written a fascinating piece of detective work in reconstructing the text of Henry II's reconciliation,

'*Ne in dubium*: The Official Record of Henry II's Reconciliation at Avranches, 21 May 1172', *English Historical Review* 115 (2000), 643–58. An interesting account about the remains of Becket is John Butler, *The Quest for Becket's Bones: The Mystery of the Relics of St Thomas Becket of Canterbury* (New Haven and London, 1995). Written for a general audience by former Canterbury librarian and Oxford don William Urry and published posthumously is *Thomas Becket: His Last Days* (Stroud, Glos. 1999).

An excellent introduction to Hildegard of Bingen is Sabina Flanagan, *Hildegard of Bingen, 1098–1179: A Visionary Life* (2nd edn; London and New York, 1998). Dr Flanagan has also provided a selection of writings in *Secrets of God: Writings of Hildegard of Bingen* (Boston and London, 1996). A *sine qua non* for a study of her life is Anna Silvas, tr. and intro., *Jutta and Hildegard: The Biographical Sources* (University Park, PA, 1998). Other useful titles include Peter Dronke, *Women Writers of the Middle Ages: A Critical Study of Texts from Perpetua (†203) to Marguerite Porete (†1310)* (Cambridge, 1984); Barbara Newman, *Sister of Wisdom: St Hildegard's Theology of the Feminine* (Berkeley and Aldershot, 1987) and, under her editorship, *Voice of the Living Light: Hildegard of Bingen and her World* (Berkeley, Los Angeles and London, 1998). The text of her major visions has been translated into English by Mother Columba Hart and Jane Bishop: *Scivias* (Bethlehem, CT, 1990). Extremely valuable is the English translation of Hildegard's letters, *The Letters of Hildegard of Bingen* (tr. J.L. Baird and R.K. Ehrmann; Oxford, 1994–). Penguin Classics has produced Hildegard of Bingen, *Selected Writings* (tr. Mark Atherton; London, 2001). Dr Oliver Sacks discusses Hildegard's symptoms in *Migraine* (rev. edn; London, 1995).

10

THE AGE OF INNOCENT III

The history of the church is not the history of the papacy. The Christian church was more than its institutional framework, and, even as an institution, the church was more than the papacy. Yet to relegate the papacy to a side-show would be to distort grossly the nature of the church in the high Middle Ages. If any medieval pope dominated the church in the age in which he lived, it was Pope Innocent III (1198–1216). The period at the end of the twelfth century and the beginning of the thirteenth century tested the advances and reforms of the previous century. There were new challenges and new responses, but these were in the context of a reformed papacy, new religious orders, an increasingly urban population and, in the chair of St Peter, the commanding figure of Innocent III.

His immediate predecessors were in continuing conflict with the German emperor. Although peace had been arranged with Frederick Barbarossa in 1177, the next decades saw disputes, particularly about imperial territorial claims in central Italy, settled in 1189 to the benefit of the papacy. The major problem of the possible union of Sicily and Germany arose and would dominate the political issues of the first years of Innocent's pontificate. Also, Jerusalem, held since 1099 by Latin Christians, fell in 1187 to the remarkable Saracen leader, Saladin, and the Christian West called for a third crusade, a second crusade having failed in 1147 to recapture the crusader state of Edessa. The Third Crusade (1189–92), although led by the great kings of Europe (Frederick Barbarossa of Germany, Richard the Lion-Hearted of England and Philip Augustus of France), failed to recapture Jerusalem, although they secured a ninety-mile coastal strip from Tyre to Jaffa for the kingdom of Jerusalem. Innocent's immediate predecessor, Celestine III (1191–98), a defender of Peter Abelard at Sens and, indeed, a friend of Thomas Becket, died at the age of ninety-two, having failed on his deathbed to arrange his abdication and the appointment of his favourite cardinal. Instead on the very day of his death the cardinals elected Cardinal Lothario de Segni, who took the name Innocent.

The political Innocent

Lothario's father was count of Segni, near Rome, and his mother was a member of an even more notable aristocratic family, the Scotti of Rome. Lothario had studied theology at Paris and was to promote his former teacher Peter of Corbeil to the archbishopric of Sens. Later he studied at Bologna, presumably law. A cardinal at twenty-nine, Lothario de Segni became pope at thirty-seven. In his sermon given on the day when he was consecrated bishop of Rome – and, thus, pope – Innocent gave an indication of what might lie in store:

> Only Peter was given fullness of power (*plenitudo potestatis*). You see, then, who is placed in charge of the household: it is Jesus Christ's vicar, Peter's successor, the Lord's anointed, the Pharaoh's god. I am placed between God and man, below God but above man; I am less than God but more than man; I am he who will judge all and be judged by none.

He acted swiftly, according to his biographer. He reduced the size of the papal curia and removed from it greedy young nobles. The Prefect of Rome now took an oath of obedience to the pope and not, as hitherto, to the emperor. Oaths to the new pope were given by the powerful men of Rome. Once in control of the city, Innocent undertook to restore the papal lands, lost over time to imperial jurisdiction. Within a year he succeeded in regaining control over the 'Patrimony of St Peter'. The pope as temporal ruler of significant territory in central Italy faced at once a major political problem.

When the son of Frederick Barbarossa, Emperor Henry VI, died unexpectedly at the age of thirty-two in 1197 as he was preparing to sail from Sicily on crusade, a serious European crisis was created. Henry was married to Constance, heir to the kingdom of Sicily, which included not only that island but also a considerable part of southern Italy (together generally referred to as the *regno*). Henry VI left not only a widow but a young son, Frederick of Hohenstaufen, who would be heir to Sicily and, depending on the German election, possibly successor to the kingdom of Germany. The main premise of papal foreign policy held that the German-controlled lands to the north should not be united with the *regno*. If the Germans had control of both, the popes felt that the Papal States in between would be in real danger of being squeezed, perhaps to the point of extinction, with the loss of papal independence. The papal lands had to be held at all cost, it was argued, for otherwise the popes and the church would not have the freedom to carry out a spiritual mission.

In Sicily Queen Constance became regent for her young son, but she died in November 1198, and Frederick was made a ward of the pope. In Germany the electors were deeply divided as to what they should do. They had, in 1196, taken an oath, at the urging of Henry VI, to recognize the young Frederick as his successor. Few felt constrained to keep that oath. Two factions elected two different men as king, and Western Europe took sides, favouring either Otto of Brunswick or Philip of Swabia. The pope supported Otto, and, when Philip protested, Innocent, in March 1202, issued the letter *Venerabilem* (its first word). Innocent disclaimed any right in the elections in Germany. Yet, since by tradition it was he who would crown a German king as emperor, then he had the right, he argued, to examine that king and judge his fitness. Also,

> If there is a divided election, we can support one of the parties, suitable delays for representations being made, particularly when coronation has been requested of us.

This looks very much like the pope making what is essentially a political decision in the temporal – and not spiritual – order. The death of Philip of Swabia in 1208 resolved the immediate crisis, and Otto IV was crowned in October 1209. Yet, in 1210, Innocent excommunicated Otto for violating his coronation promise not to invade Sicily. The focus shifted now to Frederick of Sicily, whom the pope put forward to succeed Otto, and he was supported in this by Philip Augustus, king of France. In December 1212 the electors elected Frederick as king. Otto, supported by his uncle, King John of England, lost any chance of success when he and John were defeated by Philip Augustus at the crucial Battle of Bouvines (27 July 1214). A year later Frederick II, at age twenty, was crowned king at Aachen, and his claim to the imperial title was confirmed at the Fourth Lateran Council several months later. He surrendered claims to papal lands in Italy and promised Innocent that he would resign Sicily when he was crowned emperor. Innocent III would have been justified in thinking he had won a victory, having gained uncontested control of central Italy and having thwarted the union of empire and *regno*. He died (1216) with this conviction. His successors had to deal with the unravelling of the settlement as the pliant Frederick II turned into an enemy.

Much of this story belongs to the political history of Italy rather than to the history of the church, yet the involvement of the popes in Italian politics by reason of their temporal possessions was bound to have an influence on the church as an institution, since Christian rulers were spiritual sons of the pope yet, in many cases, his political enemies. This situation was bound to complicate and even to compromise the spiritual nature of the church's mission. The events can be quickly summarized.

Frederick II dominated the European stage for thirty-five years after Innocent's death. His enemies portrayed him as amoral, blasphemous, heretical and ruthless. About his personal beliefs there is no convincing reason to think him other than conventionally orthodox. His personal morals were neither better nor worse than many of his contemporary rulers. But ruthless and headstrong he was beyond doubt, and also one of the most intelligent of medieval kings. In 1220 he had his young son, Henry (VII), elected as German king; then he proceeded to Rome, where he was crowned emperor. Frederick had, in fact, established a union in his person of Germany and Sicily, the plan of Innocent now shattered. Frederick's son proved rebellious towards his father and was imprisoned in Sicily. Some of the Lombard cities in northern Italy resented Frederick's exercise of imperial power in these imperially held places. Twice was Frederick excommunicated by Pope Gregory IX, in 1227 for failing to go on crusade – he had embarked but took ill – and again, in 1239, for failing to secure peace with the Lombard cities. Frederick's role in the crusades contains a bitter irony. In 1227, although excommunicated and not under papal banner, he set out for the East with a small army. Having married the heiress to the kingdom of Jerusalem, he held claim to that kingship. Once in the East, he entered into negotiations with the sultan of Egypt and gained control of the kingdom of Jerusalem. On 18 March 1229 he processed into the church of the Holy Sepulchre to be crowned, and, with no priest there, the excommunicated Frederick II crowned himself king of Jerusalem. Not a drop of blood had been spilt; Jerusalem, lost to Saladin in 1187 and its recapture the object of three crusades (III, IV, V), was now in Christian hands. (We shall have to visit the Fourth Crusade shortly.) Instead of congratulations, Frederick was vilified on many sides, some critics openly lamenting that it was not by blood and the sword that Jerusalem was regained. In the following year Frederick made his peace with the pope, and the excommunication was lifted. But Pope Innocent IV (1243–54) actually declared Frederick deposed in 1245, and, whatever the official reasons, the real reason was the emperor's continued efforts to control the Lombard lands. Frederick died five years later, the matter still unresolved. When the pope heard of his death, he said, 'Let the heavens rejoice and the earth exult', sounding more like a political adversary than a shepherd of souls.

To return to Innocent III, it was not only with the emperor that he came into conflict but also with other princes of Europe. He was involved with the emerging kingdoms of the Iberian peninsula (see chapter 13). Also, Hungary, since its conversion in the years just prior to the millennium, was pivotal to the aims of the papacy in evangelizing for the Latin, Western church, yet, in 1203, Innocent III risked this effort by supporting Bulgaria and Bosnia, to the great annoyance of Hungary. Nowhere outside the empire was Innocent's involvement in high politics more evident than in England. There King John (1199–1216) became embroiled in a dispute over the election of the archbishop of Canterbury after the death of Hubert Walter in 1205. The monks of Canterbury Cathedral Priory secretly elected their subprior and sent him to Rome. Innocent halted the process, and, back in England, King John intimidated the monks into electing his candidate, the bishop of Norwich. But this election the pope ruled was uncanonical, and he soon ruled the previous election also invalid. A delegation of fifteen Canterbury monks travelled to Rome and, no doubt following the papal will, elected as archbishop Cardinal Stephen Langton, an Englishman then lecturing in theology at Paris and probably a former fellow student of the pope. Innocent consecrated Langton as archbishop of Canterbury in 1207 in Italy. King John refused to allow the new archbishop into England, and, like Becket before him, Langton spent six years in exile in France, mostly at Pontigny, the place where Becket had stayed for two years. Innocent threatened an interdict on England, and, when the threat failed to move the king, the pope, in 1208, carried through his threat and placed the kingdom of England under interdict. Public religious ceremonies ceased, the bare essentials of infant baptism and the last rites for the dying and little else surviving the papal penalty. The interdict lasted for six years, its precise effects difficult to measure. At a crucial moment in 1209 negotiations broke down and Innocent excommunicated King John. In 1211, faced with the threat of being deposed as king by the pope and with the prospect of an impending invasion by the French king, John capitulated. He did more than allow Stephen Langton to come to England as archbishop of Canterbury; he handed over the kingdoms of England and Ireland to the papacy and took them back as vassal to the pope. King John faced another problem: the opposition of English barons to his exactions. The king was forced to issue Magna Carta on 15 June 1215, but the king's new ally, Pope Innocent III, annulled it on 24 August:

> By violence and fear he [King John] was forced to accept an agreement which is not only shameful and degrading but also illegal and unjust . . . That charter we declare to be null and void for ever.

(Visitors to the British Library in London can see displayed side by side the charter and the papal bull annulling it.) Although the significance of Magna Carta in the development of civil liberties has long since been drastically reduced by modern scholars, the significance of the papal annulment needs underlining, for here a pope not only criticized but declared null what was essentially a secular document. Innocent III was exercising a fullness of power (*plentitudo potestatis*) that would have amazed most of his predecessors and have alarmed some. Yet, when Magna Carta was reissued in 1216, after the deaths of John and Innocent, it bore the seal of the papal legate to England.

The Fourth Crusade (1202–04)

We have already seen the successful regaining of Jerusalem by Frederick II in 1229, in the context of that ruler's ongoing controversies with the papacy. We must now back up twenty years to look at the tragedy of the crusade called by Pope Innocent III in August 1199, referred to by later historians as the Fourth Crusade. It was the failure of the Fourth Crusade that precipitated the expedition of Frederick II twenty-five years later. Innocent's crusade was to be under papal control and its object was to recapture Jerusalem. Neither happened as the pope lost control and as the Christian city of Constantinople, rather than Muslim Jerusalem, was captured by the crusaders. The response to the pope's call was slow in coming, the target date of departure, March 1199, was not met, but the preaching of Fulk of Neuilly kept the idea alive. Actual recruitment began in November 1199, when knights who had gathered for a tournament at the castle of Thibault, count of Champagne, cast down their weapons for the day's sport and took oaths to go on the crusade. Soon joining those knights were others: Baldwin of Flanders, Louis of Blois, Geoffrey of Le Perche, Simon de Montfort and other nobles from Flanders and northern France, followed soon by nobles from the Rhineland and northern Italy. Since only the count of Flanders had a fleet, the three leading crusaders, the counts of Flanders, Blois and Champagne, in 1200 sent emissaries to negotiate with Venice for their transport, and, in doing this, the first of many mistakes was made.

Crossing through Alpine passes and the Lombard plain the envoys of the crusaders arrived at Venice in Lent 1201, where they were greeted cordially by the doge (from *duce*, leader), Dandolo, then ninety-four years old and blind. An agreement, the Treaty of Venice (1201), was made; it proved disastrous. At the request of the crusaders the Republic of Venice agreed to provide ships to transport 4,500 knights and their horses, 9,000 squires and 20,000 foot soldiers – an army of 33,500 men – for the sum of 85,000 marks to be paid in four instalments by April 1202, when the crusaders would be at Venice, ready to ship out in late June. Venice also agreed to provide an additional fifty war galleys, for which they would receive half the spoils of the expedition. The Republic further agreed to provision the crusading army for one year. This agreement meant that Venice would construct about 450 vessels and would provide those vessels with as many as 14,000 crewmen. In early May 1201 Pope Innocent III confirmed this treaty, although he seems to have added as a condition that the crusade not attack Christians. (He was to make such a prohibition in November 1202.) Indeed, it was not in the plans of the crusade leaders to attack Christians, but it was also not in their plans to go directly to the Holy Land. The strategy was to attack Egypt, to take the great Muslim city of Alexandria and hold it hostage until the sultan restored Jerusalem to the Christians. It was a strategy which over the preceding decades had many supporters including King Richard I of England. Within a few weeks of Innocent's approval Thibault of Champagne, the driving force behind the crusade, died aged about twenty-four. In need of a leader, the principal crusaders selected Boniface, marquis of Montferrat in northern Italy, who met them at Soissons, where he took the cross. The pope was not consulted.

By June 1202 the expected 33,500 had not arrived at Venice. The organizers seem to have grossly overestimated the size of their army. Departure dates were repeatedly made and postponed, and, when it became clear that only about 12,000 crusaders had come and no more could be expected, the leaders of the crusade knew that they could not pay the doge the agreed 85,000 marks. The Venetians had built the ships, secured the crews and purchased provisions; they were understandably concerned that only 50,000 marks were being paid them. The crusaders had not fulfilled their part of the treaty. The crusade stood in imminent peril of collapsing. It was a moment of extreme crisis. What happened next sealed the disaster which was the Fourth Crusade.

Two factors now came into play. In the first place, Boniface of Montferrat, the leader of the crusade, was a close friend and ally of Philip of Swabia, who at this time was a contender against Otto of Brunswick for the German throne and, ultimately, for the emperorship (see pp. 185–6 above). Philip was married to Irene, the daughter of the Eastern emperor, Isaac Angelus, who had lost his throne, shortly after his daughter's marriage, at the hand of his brother Alexius, who now as Emperor Alexius III imprisoned Isaac and Isaac's son Alexius and blinded Isaac. The young Alexius escaped and travelled to his sister and brother-in-law in Germany, looking for help.

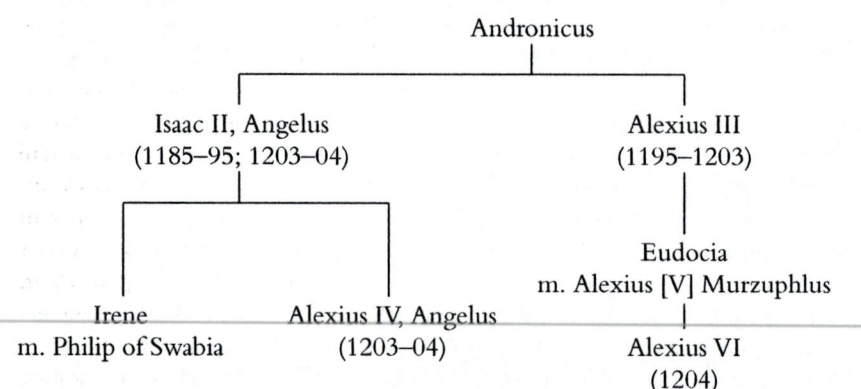

The second ingredient was the Venetian desire to control the Dalmatian coast of the Adriatic Sea. Its chief port of Zara was then in Hungarian hands. Venetian interests would be served if the crusaders could capture Zara. Two deals were struck. First, the crusaders were told that the Venetians would allow them to defer payment yet sail in the ships with crews and provisions, provided that, on the way, they would take Zara. Apart from aborting the crusade, which some contemporaries thought should have happened, there was little else the crusaders could do. An eye-witness to all this, Robert of Clari, commented,

> The barons and the other leaders of the crusade agreed to the doge's plan, but the rank and file of the army knew nothing about it.

They sailed out of Venice on 8 November 1202 and down the Adriatic, where two days later they attacked the city of Zara, which, after sixteen days, they took and thoroughly pillaged. Zara was a Christian city. Pope Innocent III was appalled at this turn of events; excommunication was incurred by all who took part, although it was later removed by Innocent except for the Venetians. What to do now, once in Zara? The agreed strategy was to set sail for Egypt and take Alexandria. Yet the Venetians were negotiating a trading agreement with Egypt and, whatever they might have said to the crusaders, they would probably not have countenanced Venetian ships being used to attack a trading partner. Philip of Swabia and Boniface of Montferrat approached the Venetians with a tempting proposal. Philip, acting on behalf of his exiled brother-in-law, the young Alexius, promised that, if the crusaders would secure the imperial throne for Alexius at Constantinople, Alexius would pay the outstanding debt owed by the crusaders to the Republic of Venice. After much debate and considerable dissent, it was so agreed. An already greatly upset Innocent became enraged and forbade the crusaders to use the sword against fellow Christians, but the crusade leaders conspired to keep this prohibition from their soldiers. The papal legate issued a bull excommunicating the Venetians, yet, despite defections by such as Simon de Montfort, it was agreed at Corfu, where the crusading army had gone from Zara, that the crusaders would sail for the great Christian city of Constantinople, and Innocent III was helpless to stop them. It was a crusade out of control.

On 25 May 1203, on the eve of the Christian feast of Pentecost, the fleet left Corfu and, stopping to replenish supplies en route, sailed through the narrow passage of the Dardanelles and, unimpeded, into the Sea of Marmora, where they came within sight of Constantinople on 23 June. Their plan was to put ashore on the Asian side of the Bosporus and there wait for the surrender of Constantinople, which the young Alexius had led them to believe would occur once they had arrived. They waited and waited, and his uncle, the usurper, Emperor Alexius III, refused to surrender. An attack, which the crusaders had not expected to have to make, was now necessary. Rather than attack Constantinople directly, the strategists in the crusading army decided that they should attack Galata across from the city on the northern shore of the Golden Horn, Constantinople's large and secure harbour, the entrance to which was blocked by a mammoth chain. After fierce fighting, Galata was taken and the chain broken by the iron prow of a Venetian ship at full speed. The fleet sailed into the Golden Horn and took up positions at Galata. The army was ready for its attack on the city itself. After two days of fighting, the walls were breached and the emperor fled. Constantinople had been easily taken. The blinded Isaac agreed to return as emperor and to accept his son, the young Alexius, as co-emperor. On 1 August 1203 the latter was crowned in Santa Sophia after promising to unite the Eastern Church with Rome. With this diversionary action successfully completed, one might think that the crusaders could now go on to the Holy Land. This was not to happen.

Simply put, the young Alexius (IV) and his father were unable to raise the promised money for the crusaders to pay their Venetian creditors. Promises by Alexius that he would pay kept the crusaders at their camps across the Golden Horn into early 1204. Discontent was running high not just among the crusaders but also among the Greeks, who were dissatisfied with Alexius IV for his financial exactions and for his overtures to Rome for union of the churches. A palace coup occurred. Isaac died, and the young Alexius was strangled and replaced by Alexius III's son-in-law (yet another Alexius, the fifth emperor of that name). The crusaders saw their chance of being paid fast slipping away and were convinced that their only option was to take the city by military force and set up their own man as emperor. In their councils the crusaders, no longer really crusaders but adventurers, agreed on the division of the spoils of battle for the

Eastern empire. The new (Latin) emperor would have one-quarter of the city and empire. The remainder would be divided equally between the Venetians and the knight crusaders. A senior crusader, Villehardouin, acknowledged that the crusade was over:

> At the end of March in the following year anyone who wished to leave would be free to go wherever he wished. Those who remained, however, would be subject to the jurisdiction of the emperor.

The first attack on the walled city proved unsuccessful, but then on 12 April 1204, rallied by preachers, the Latin army succeeded in breaching the walls, scattering the ill-trained Greeks, and captured a large section of the city. Fire broke out, wasting a considerable area, and the will of the people of Constantinople to defend themselves vanished. The Latins had taken the most magnificent city in the world, and the leaders allowed their soldiers three days to sack the city.

'The sack of Constantinople is unparalleled in history', Sir Steven Runciman sadly comments. The capture of the city was followed by a ruthless, violent, uncontrolled, barbaric pillaging. Nothing and, indeed, no one was safe from these men as they raped nuns, slew in an awful, random brutality, stole jewels and relics, violated churches and monasteries, destroyed priceless art work: an utterly mindless rampage of collective insanity. They even entered the magnificent Santa Sophia and denuded it of all its decorations, going so far as to smash the altar for

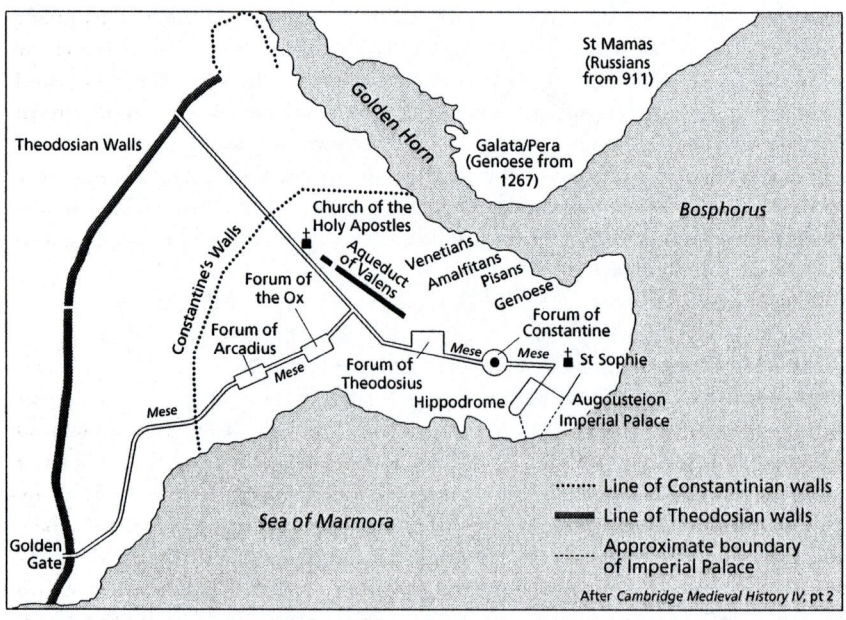

Map 12 Constantinople in the thirteenth century.

its gems and precious metal and were entertained in the greatest church in Christendom by a prostitute seated on the patriarch's throne. They entered houses to wreck them, seizing precious stones for their spoils and women for their pleasure. One Cistercian abbot felt left out and decided to join in but to limit himself to stealing only holy relics, which were later prized by his monks in Alsace. Dandolo, the powerful doge of Venice, whose skilful hand has been seen by many behind the destiny of this crusade, stole four bronze horses from the Hippodrome, and they can be seen today above the entrance to St Mark's Basilica, a symbol now of Venice for the Venetians, but, for many others, a symbol of ineffable hubris and boundless greed. The leaders of the crusade ordered that all booty be brought to a central place – large amounts were concealed by pillagers – for distribution among the conquerors. The debt to Venice, at the centre of this tale, was finally paid.

Innocent III, when he learned of the great outrage, became furious and bitterly denounced the actions of the crusaders:

> Those men were dedicated to seek only the things of Christ and nothing for themselves. Their swords, which were meant to be used against pagans, they have bathed in the blood of Christians. Paying heed neither to religion nor age nor sex, they have publicly committed adultery and fornication and have exposed to the filthy defilement of soldiers the holy women and virgins dedicated to God.

All that remained was for the conquering Latins to select an emperor. Boniface of Montferrat was passed over in favour of Baldwin of Flanders. And, on 16 May 1204, a Flemish knight was crowned emperor, successor to Constantine and Justinian. And soon a Latin patriarch was appointed. But this Latin empire of the East lasted only until 1261, when Constantinople was recaptured by the Byzantine Greeks. The crusading ideal, preached by Urban II in 1095, was now twisted beyond recognition, and the East has never forgotten the Fourth Crusade, which, instead of relieving the Holy Land, succeeded in making permanent the schism between the churches of East and West.

The Fourth Lateran Council (1215)

There can be little doubt that the Fourth Lateran Council was the most important general council of the church in the Middle Ages. It was also the crowning achievement of the pontificate of Innocent III. There came to Rome to meet in council not merely representative bishops from Catholic lands but many more. Every bishop was expected to attend, excepting only a few from each province, who were to send delegates to represent them. Every cathedral chapter was to send a representative as was every collegiate church (i.e., a large church with a number of secular canons such as Beverley Minster in Yorkshire). The heads of the new religious orders (Cistercians, Premonstratensians, military orders)

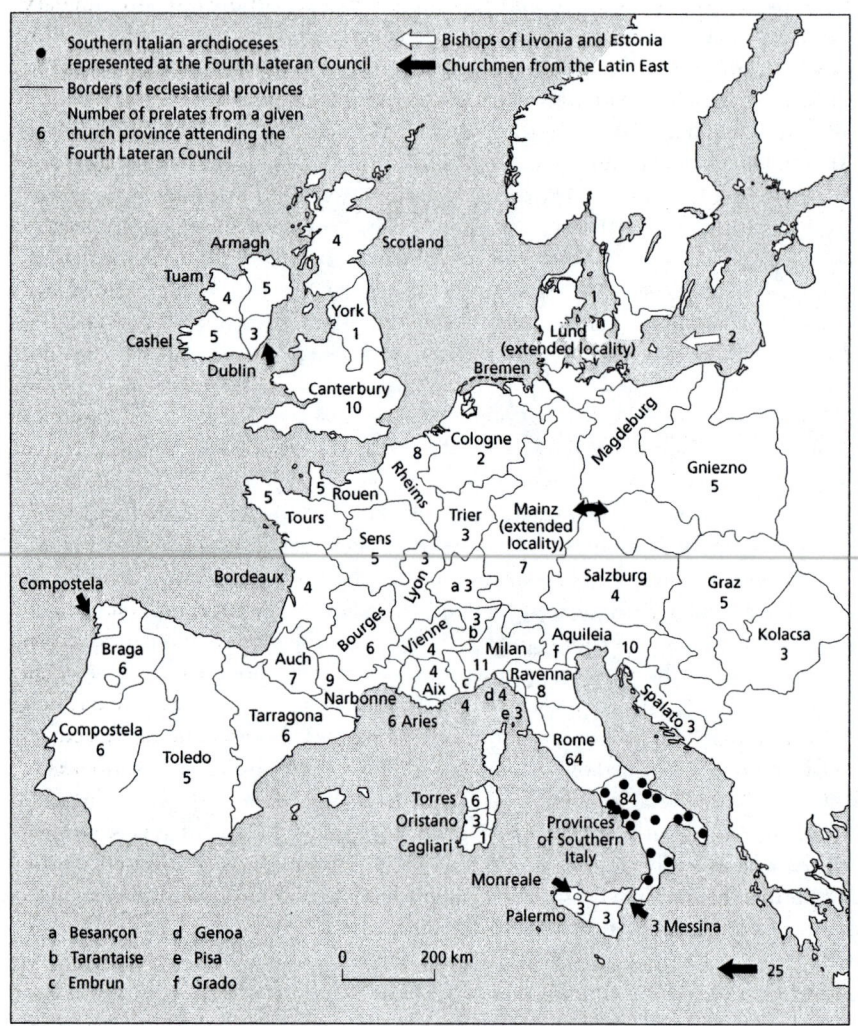

Map 13 Representatives at the Fourth Lateran Council (1215).

were also summoned. Innocent even invited representatives of the Eastern patriarchates to attend. In the event, outraged by the capture of Constantinople in 1204, none came from the East save representatives of the Latin patriarchate of Constantinople and of the patriarch of Alexandria as well as the primate of the Maronite church and proctors from the Latin States. In a move that might have greatly disturbed Gregory VII, Innocent III invited secular rulers to send representatives. Frederick II of Sicily, claimant to the emperorship, sent proctors as did the kings of France and England. Representatives of the kings of Hungary and Aragon attended as did rulers and proctors from the Italian city states. Nothing on this scale had every occurred before: Innocent III, in effect, convoked an assembly of Latin Christendom.

Quietly, at dawn on 11 November 1215, the pope celebrated the opening Mass in the presence only of the cardinals and bishops, about 400 or so. They were then joined by over 800 abbots and religious superiors. When finally the doors of the great basilica of St John, the pope's cathedral, were thrown open, a flood of people pressed their way in, masses of clergy and others. One eye-witness in agitated enthusiasm said there were 'thousands of thousands, even ten times a hundred thousand'. The throng pouring into the basilica is said to have crushed a least one bishop to death. The same eye-witness wrote that so great was the din that he could not hear the pope's address opening the council. He soon secured a copy. Innocent III declared that the aim of the council was twofold: to effect the recapture of Jerusalem and to reform the church. His first aim, as we have seen, proved unsuccessful. What commands our attention is the effort to reinvigorate the spiritual health of the church.

The seventy canons (or decrees), approved by the Fourth Lateran Council, were not debated in council but were presented by the pope. Not a word was changed, not a canon challenged, not an issue debated: the decrees of the council were the work of the pope and his curia. Apart from the first two decrees, which dealt with dogmatic matters, the decrees of the council concerned the practical life of the church. These decrees were to affect the way Christians lived their Christian lives for centuries to come. The most enduring and penetrating actions of the Fourth Lateran Council had nothing to do with crusades or dogmatic niceties but with the pastoral concerns of the church.

A summary of the most significant decrees can only serve to suggest the pastoral dimensions of the council's work. Central to any attempt to elevate the quality of the Christian life as lived by individual Christians in the hamlets, villages and towns of Western Europe was the quality of the clergy charged with the care of souls, which one decree called 'the art of arts'. It is 'better to have a few good priests (*paucos bonos*) than many bad priests (*multos malos*)'. Bishops either personally or through others should instruct candidates for the priesthood as to how they should perform the sacred rites and sacraments. But more, extending an enactment of the Third Lateran Council (1179), it was decreed that each cathedral should have a master of grammar who will instruct the clergy and poor scholars gratis, and in metropolitan churches there should also be a master of theology, who will teach priests and others 'in the sacred page' and who will especially instruct them in those things which pertain to the care of souls. Not quite a modern seminary, itself a creature of the sixteenth century, yet the arrangements provided for the training of the clergy in something more than the mere performance of rituals. More than Mass priests, they were expected to be pastors of souls. The council defined their behaviour in explicit terms:

> Clerics shall not hold secular office nor indulge in commerce, especially unseemly commerce. They shall not attend performances of mimes, jesters or plays and shall avoid taverns except only out of necessity while travelling. Nor shall they play with dice; they should not even be present at such games. They should wear the clerical tonsure and be zealous in the performance of their divine offices and in other responsibilities. Moreover, they shall wear their garments clasped and neither too short nor too long. And they shall eschew bright colours such as red and green as well as ornamentation on their gloves and shoes.
>
> (Canon 16)

The council went on to condemn the conduct of some priests:

> We regret that not only some clerics in minor orders but also some prelates of churches spend half the night eating and talking, not to mention other things they are doing, and get to sleep so late that they are scarcely wakened by the birds singing and they mumble their way hurriedly through morning prayers. There are some clerics who celebrate Mass only four times a year and, what is worse, they disdain even attending Mass. And, if they happen to be present at Mass, they flee the silence of the choir to go outside to talk with laymen, preferring things frivolous to things divine. These and similar practices we totally forbid under penalty of suspension.
>
> (Canon 17)

The clergy are commanded to abstain from drunkenness and the drinking custom in which each drinker matches the other drinkers drink for drink until only one is standing. They are to live chastely, and offenders are threatened with suspension. Bishops should institute only worthy clerics to benefices, and the bishops too are threatened with sanctions.

Decency requires that the clergy have nothing to do with the spilling of blood. They are forbidden to be surgeons and soldiers. Not only may they not condemn anyone to death – 'sentence of blood' – but they may not be present where blood is shed in punishment. And, in a noteworthy provision which was to eliminate a long-standing practice, clerics were forbidden to be involved in ordeals by water and fire. The guilty, many believed, would be rejected by the water (i.e., float to the surface), when they were thrown into blessed cold water, and the innocent would not be infected when they took a blessed hot iron in their hands. Since priests hereafter could bless neither the water nor the iron, these methods of criminal judgement could only fade away, which they did. Similarly, priests were forbidden to engage in hunting and fowling. The priestly life, in short, must be shred of incongruities and irrelevancies and imbued with a commitment to the service of souls.

More than any other provision of the council none touched more people more personally than canon 21, often referred to by its opening words, 'Omnis utriusque sexus'. 'All Catholics of either sex' shall confess their sins to their local parish priest at least once a year and receive holy communion at Easter. Failure to do so would mean exclusion from the Christian community during one's lifetime and from Christian burial at life's end. Annual confession, although urged before this time, now became an absolute requirement, and this decree was to be one of the most influential conciliar decrees of the Middle Ages in its consequences for the devotional lives of ordinary people.

Another matter touching the lives of most Christians concerned marriage. Wedding ceremonies must be performed at church and preceded by the publication of banns; clandestine (i.e., private) marriages were absolutely forbidden. The council, while forbidding clandestine marriages, did not declare them null and void: the parties may commit a sin, even a grave sin, by the clandestine marriage, but they are nonetheless married. It would be many centuries before such marriages would be declared invalid. The complex question of marrying relatives was somewhat simplified. Henceforward, one could marry beyond the fourth degree of kinship, which meant that what was now prohibited was marriage between a man and a woman sharing a common great-great-grandparent or a closer ancestor (i.e., a third cousin or closer). Consanguinity (kinship) was an impediment to marriage based on blood relationship. Affinity was another matter: it was effected by relationship through marriage. When John married Mary, he had a relationship of affinity with Mary's family and she with his. Thus, if Mary were to die, could John marry Mary's sister Catherine or, for that matter, Mary's mother, Maud? These are questions concerning the effect of affinity on the validity of marriage. Hitherto, affinity was an impediment to marriage within the third degree, thus forbidding, in this case, John from marrying his late wife's mother and sister (first degree) and her nieces (second degree) but also her niece's daughter (third degree). Hereafter, only the first degree was forbidden. In a rural society made up of small villages and tiny hamlets with little chance of travel, the choice of a partner was, in the nature of things, limited even with these somewhat relaxed provisions of the council. The new provision regarding affinity would probably have had more practical impact than those relating to consanguinity, given the shortness of life, particularly for women, the small circle of prospective second wives and the involvement of rural properties in these matters. The arrangements were still imperfect but a major improvement on the *status quo ante*.

Pope Innocent, concerned about the multiplication of religious orders and problems of papal oversight, forbade through the council the founding of new rules; new orders would have to adopt existing rules. How this impacted on the newly emerging orders of friars remains to be seen (below, chapter 11). Also, existing religious orders should follow the example of the Cistercians and hold general chapters in each province at three-year intervals in order to ensure the observance of the letter and spirit of their respective rules.

Four decrees dealt with the Jews. They are the last four of the seventy conciliar decrees, and one wonders if they were an afterthought and, if so, why they were added. In the first place, those Jewish money-lenders who charge usurious rates of interest need not be paid until they make reparations for their usury. Secondly, in a justly famous decree, distinctive dress was required of Jews and Muslims and deserves to be quoted:

> In some places, it is not possible to distinguish Jews and Muslims from Christians. It happens now and then that through error Christian men commingle with Jewish and Muslim women and, conversely, Jewish and Muslim men with Christian women. In order to avoid such commingling in the future under the excuse of error as to religious identity, we decree that Jews and Muslims of both sexes, when in public in Christian regions, should always be distinguished from other people by their dress, since even Moses insisted on this [Lev.19, 19; Deut. 22, 5, 115, 11].
>
> (Canon 68)

They were further forbidden to appear in public during certain days in Holy Week, since, the decree stated, it has been reported that some Jews offend mourning Christians by wearing more ornate clothes than they wear at other times. The two remaining decrees about the Jews can be summarized. Since, the council said, it is offensive for Jews to have power over Christians, they should be excluded from public office. And, further, Jews who have voluntarily converted to Christianity should not continue to observe rituals and observances of the Jewish religion.

Some comment is in order. Strictures against usury were not limited to Jews but against usury per se, no matter who the usurer. Ecclesiastical penalties were imposed on Christian usurers and the return of excess interest ordered by church courts. Some may see in this provision of the council an extension of this policy to non-Christian (i.e., Jewish) money-lenders. The exclusion of Jews from public office was first ordered at the Council of Toledo in 589 and was frequently repeated. Jews who were converted to Christianity and who continued to live in Jewish communities where social and religious practices were almost inextricably intertwined must frequently have had to make accommodations, which to the council could appear as compromises and even betrayals. Yet it is the dress provisions which linger in the memory long after the others have been forgotten or have become vague. Jews were required to be recognizable as Jews, as different, ostensibly to avoid sexual mingling with Christians. Whether darker motives lay hidden here it is not possible to say. Muslim rulers frequently required non-Muslims to dress distinctively. This requirement of the council regarding Jewish dress was not immediately adopted, but, in the course of the thirteenth century, a cloth badge of gold or crimson was required in England, France and Germany and in some places a distinctive hat (*Judenhut*) was to be worn. Although laws of dress often required other groups to wear specific dress – priests, prostitutes, physicians, servants – the provision regarding the Jews singled out a group already prone to misunderstanding and raw prejudice. The massacre of over 150 Jews at York in 1190 was but a recent memory. Historians may dispute the severity and impact of the legislation about Jews from the Fourth Lateran Council, yet, to say the least, it further isolated a largely isolated sub-community and further fuelled existing attitudes.

On 30 November 1215 Innocent III blessed the fathers of the council with a relic of the true cross; he was to die within eight months. The bishops and others returned home, copies of the decrees in their baggage. Lest they remain mere mementoes of a Roman holiday, the council itself had provided that in every ecclesiastical province (e.g., Canterbury, Cologne, Rouen, Milan) an annual synod should be held to insure observance of the conciliar decrees and to further the movement for reform. What happened? While annual synods were not necessarily observed in all the Christian lands, synods were convoked almost everywhere to publicize the pastoral aspects of the work of the council. In the provinces of France and Germany – in the latter the situation was complicated by continuing civil unrest – meetings were fairly promptly held. In Ireland the clergy met at Dublin in 1217. The Scots, deprived of their archbishop, did not meet until 1225. In England the bishops of the Canterbury province met at Oxford in 1222, and its decrees were frequently copied: some sixty manuscripts survive. Yet, even before 1222, the bishop of Salisbury, Richard Poore, had issued influential statutes. The Oxford and Salisbury decrees, reflecting the provisions of the Fourth Lateran Council, were incorporated into later provincial and diocesan synodal legislation. Yet equally, if not more importantly, nearly all the Lateran decrees were incorporated into the greatest medieval law book, the collection of decretals issued by Pope Gregory IX in 1234. Called simply the *Decretals* or the *Liber Extra*, this law book was promulgated as the sole, exclusive collection of general church law: any other general ecclesiastical laws previously in force were no longer in force. It was the law book studied at the universities, commented on by generations of legal scholars, used in the administration of the church and applied in the church courts. The inclusion of the Lateran decrees gave the decrees of that council a life beyond their repetition in local synods. With some later modifications, the *Decretals* remained the principal text of church law throughout the rest of the Middle Ages and even, in many places, into the twentieth century.

The emphasis on the care of souls cannot be measured solely by legislation, local or general. Manuals and directives of a practical sort were soon issued in the wake of the council to help the parochial clergy to carry out their duties to the souls entrusted to their care. Some took the form of instructions for hearing confession, now a pressing need in view of the decree mandating annual confession. Others dealt with preaching. Still others dealt with the manner of teaching their flocks the essentials of the Christian religion. The bishop of the diocese of Coventry and Lichfield, about 1230, appended to the usual pastoral canons of a diocesan synod two treatises for his clergy. A treatise on the seven deadly sins, in the form of a sermon to be given to their parishioners, explained the dangers to the soul of the sins of pride, envy, anger, sloth, avarice, lust and gluttony. A treatise on confession insisted, above all, that God forgives no sins unless there is true repentance, and it also was meant as an aid in helping penitents examine their consciences. At about the same time, the bishop of Lincoln, the learned pastor of souls Robert Grosseteste, composed *Templum dei* (*Temple of God*) for his parish priests. He made use of diagrams and tables, providing an easily accessible guide for his priests. For example, with remarkable clarity, Grosseteste shows that all virtue is the mean between two vices: faith between the vices of scepticism and credulity, hope between the vices of presumption and despair, charity between the vices of indiscrimination and hatred. He listed the ten impediments to marriage, the five sins requiring restitution, the three kinds of excommunication and so forth. That the *Templum dei* survives in over ninety manuscripts is testimony to its wide popularity. In the south of France, another learned bishop, Guillaume Durand, in 1291 furnished his clergy with a small book containing instructions for administering the sacraments as well as canons to govern their mission as priests. In this tradition, which grew out of the council's pastoral emphasis, none is more representative than the explicit instructions given in 1282 by John Pecham, archbishop of Canterbury:

> The ignorance of priests casts the people headlong into the pit of error, and the folly and stupidity of the clergy, who are obliged to teach the faithful in Catholic doctrine, occasionally lead them more to error than to sound teaching. To remedy such dangers we hereby order that every priest with the care of souls shall four times each year (once each quarter), on one solemn day or several, either personally or by another, instruct the people using simple English, as follows:
>
> 14 articles of faith
> 10 commandments
> 2 commandments of the gospels about love
> 7 works of mercy
> 7 capital [deadly] sins and their offspring
> 7 principal virtues
> 7 sacraments of grace.
>
> Lest any priest excuse himself, saying that he is ignorant of these, although all ministers of the church are bound to know them, we shall summarize them briefly.

Pecham, the Paris-trained theologian, then did exactly that not in the language of the universities but in simple, easy-to-understand language. This decree became separated from the other decrees issued in 1281 and had a life of its own: it became an important teaching guide for priests well into the sixteenth century. As a schema for popular instruction in the Catholic faith, it had the great merit of clarity, comprehensiveness, practicality and, above all, susceptibility to easy memorizing. Subsequent books of instruction have little improved on Pecham's outline. Through it and similar instructional manuals used elsewhere in Western Europe the effects of the Fourth Lateran Council were felt for centuries.

The provisions of that council were the greatest legacy of Innocent III to the universal church, not to the church as an institution, but to the church of the faithful, of men and women who looked to religion to give ultimate meaning to their lives. The canons of that council, in a practical way, strove to address the needs of these souls, and, in the centuries that followed, the impact was felt in almost every parish in Christendom.

Further reading

A good starting point is Jane Sayers, *Innocent III: Leader of Europe, 1198–1216* (London and New York, 1994). Also useful is James M. Powell, *Innocent III: Vicar of Christ or Lord of the World* (2nd edn; Washington, DC, 1994). The reader should also consult T.C. Van Cleve, *The Emperor Frederic II of Hohenstaufen: Immutator Mundi* (Oxford, 1972).

For the Fourth Crusade, in addition to the general works on the crusades (above, p. 129), see D.E. Queller and T.F. Madden, *The Fourth Crusade: The Conquest of Constantinople* (2nd edn; Philadelphia, 1997), which makes a strong if not entirely persuasive case for the Venetians. Three contemporary accounts are available in English: Robert of Clari, *The Conquest of Constantinople* (tr. E.H. McNeal; Toronto, 1996); Villehardouin, 'The Conquest of Constantinople', in Joinville and Villehardouin, *Chronicles of the Crusades* (tr. M.R.B. Shaw; Harmondsworth, Mddsx, 1963); and Gunther of Pairis, *The Capture of Constantinople: The Hystoria Constantinopolitana* (ed. and tr. Alfred J. Andrea; Philadelphia, 1997). Most comprehensive is the compilation made by Alfred J. Andrea, *Contemporary Sources for the Fourth Crusade* (Leiden, 2000). For the complex situation in the East at this time see Charles M. Brand, *Byzantium Confronts the West, 1180–1204* (Cambridge, MA, 1968).

The decrees of the Fourth Lateran Council can be found conveniently in H.J. Shroeder (ed. and tr.), *Disciplinary Decrees of the General Councils: Text, Translation, and Commentary* (St Louis, MO, and London, 1937), in *English Historical Documents, 1189–1327* (ed. Harry Rothwell; London, 1975) and in Norman P. Tanner (tr.), *Decrees of the Ecumenical Councils* (Washington, 1990). A fascinating account of the council can be found in Stephan Kuttner and Antonio García y García, 'A New Eyewitness Account of the Fourth Lateran Council', *Traditio* 20 (1964), 115–78. For the ordeal see Robert Bartlett, *Trial by Fire and Water: The Medieval Judicial Ordeal* (Oxford, 1986). On reception of the conciliar decrees see Marion Gibbs and Jane Lang, *Bishops and Reform, 1215–1272: With Special Reference to the Lateran Council of 1215* (Oxford, 1934) and Paul B. Pixton, *The German Episcopacy and the Implementation of the Decrees of the Fourth Lateran Council, 1216–1245* (Leiden, 1995). For the practice of the confession of sins see Alexander Murray, 'Confession before 1215', *Transactions of the Royal Historical Society*, 6th series, 3 (1993), 51–81, and Sarah Hamilton, *The Practice of Penance, 900–1050* (Woodbridge, Suffolk, and Rochester, NY, 2001). For pastoral manuals see Leonard E. Boyle, *Pastoral Care, Clerical Education and Canon Law, 1200–1400* (London, 1981) and John Shinners and William J. Dohar (eds), *Pastors and the Care of Souls in Medieval England* (Notre Dame, IN, 1998). A useful example is Robert Grosseteste, *Templum Dei* (ed. J. Goering and F.A.C. Mantello; Toronto, 1984).

11

THE EMERGENCE OF DISSENT AND THE RISE OF THE FRIARS

During the decades surrounding the pivotal pontificate of Innocent III two distinct but clearly related phenomena shook the earth under the church. Neither doctrinal dissent nor the establishments of new religious orders was new, but, when they appeared at this time, they came from quite a different source. Both now emerged from a laity disturbed by the blatant affluence of the church and suspicious of the motives and sincerity of churchmen wearing silken vestments and using golden chalices. It was a laity yearning for a simpler spiritual life. The Christ they knew had been born in a manger and, as an adult, had no place to lay his head. When he sent out his apostles and disciples to preach his message, he told them, 'Take nothing with you, neither staff nor pack, neither bread nor money, not even a second coat' (Luke 9, 3). Essentially there was a quest for a new model for the Christian life. Many felt that it was not necessary to abandon the world for the shelter of a monastery to be a good Christian nor was it necessary to try to live monk-like or nun-like in the world. The Jesus they worshipped lived a holy life in the world, but it was a life of simplicity and poverty: these became the central elements of a new piety. Their attractions touched deep the souls of thousands of Christians, like Waldès and the heretical Waldensians and Francis of Assisi and the orthodox Franciscans. While other elements also helped to shape these and similar movements, at base they all exhibited the desire for a more personal form of religion, one shorn of its accidentals and excesses and centred on the imitation of Christ. Official suspicion greeted almost every expression of this desire, a suspicion leading occasionally to acceptance but frequently to outright condemnation and even to the spilling of blood.

Dissent

Heresy was nothing new to the church. What was new in the late twelfth and thirteenth centuries was the form which it took. Heresy, by its nature, was a departure from accepted orthodoxy, and in the high Middle Ages it was a dissent espoused not by bishops and scholars but largely by lowly priests and unlettered laymen and laywomen, their emphasis, at least at first, not so much on matters of doctrine – that would follow – but on practical piety in everyday life. For this reason it is usually called 'popular' heresy.

When Innocent III ascended the papal throne in 1198, the church was being seriously challenged by strong, independent movements, now generally called 'popular heresies', particularly in France and Italy but not only there. Neither Catharism nor Waldensianism, the two principal dissident movements of the time, was doctrinally uniform, yet the general lines can be discerned. It can be said of both these heresies that each had two elements, an ethic and a doctrine, and we should not think that the latter was equal to the former in attracting recruits. These two movements differed from each other and, indeed, were mutually antagonistic. They need be looked at separately.

The Cathars, it has been persuasively argued, were the most significant medieval heretics, even if judged only by their numbers and their superior organization. The movement began in the 1140s and spread throughout large parts of Western Europe in the subsequent decades, presenting Innocent III with his greatest challenge. Yet it survived his response, only to be dealt its death-blow not by crusade but by inquisition, although there lingered even then a few flickering signs of life in remote areas. Such a striking resemblance appears between the Bogomils, an Eastern sect with its origins in Bulgaria, and the Cathars that it seems that the Cathars to some large extent owe their beginnings to an infiltration of Bogomil teaching into the West, probably in the Rhineland near Cologne, by the 1140s. Both movements shared, among many other things, a basic dualism, a belief in two basic principles, one good and spiritual and the other bad and material, one deriving from God and the other from Satan. The repudiation of material things meant the repudiation of the flesh (and sexual relations) as well as the repudiation of Catholic sacraments.

At Cologne in the 1140s there was ineffective repression of the movement, and, when it reappeared in the West in the 1160s, it was joined by an evangelical element. These were to be the two main ingredients of Catharism, a dualistic theology and an emphasis on a simple, rigoristic way of life. They were not equally emphasized in every place where the movement took hold. The movement's spread was remarkable, even if we cannot plot its course step by step. Nearly contemporary with its first appearance at Cologne, it was also reported at Champagne and Liège. But it was the 1160s which were critical in its spread. By then the Cathars were also in the vicinities of Bonn and Mainz, where they came to the attention of Hildegard of Bingen, who sent an anti-Cathar sermon to Mainz. In 1163, another German preaching against these heretics discussed their name:

> In German they are called 'Cathars', in Flemish 'Piphles', in French 'Texerant'.

It should be added that later, because of their prominence in the vicinity of Albi, they were frequently called 'Albigensians'. The name 'Cathars' derives probably not from the Greek for pure ones but from the spurious allegation of cat-kissing in their ceremonies. Whatever its derivation, it is the term most generally in use by historians.

The Languedoc region of France was to become the ground where Catharism grew more successfully than anywhere else, yet there is no evidence of Cathars there before the 1160s. A region rather than a precise political division, the Languedoc took its name from the form of French spoken there, *langue d'oc* (or Occitan), where 'yes' was rendered 'hoc est' or simply an unaspirated 'hoc' instead of the *oï* of the north (*langue d'oï*). By 1165 the Cathars there were perceived as such a danger that a conference was held at Lombers, near Albi, attended by the archbishop of Narbonne, five other bishops, six abbots and other ecclesiastical officials together with prominent members of the nobility. No effect emerged from what was more a debate than a trial, other than an apparent tolerance of the Cathars by the lay leaders. Also, in the 1160s they can be seen in Lombardy, where a certain Mark the Gravedigger, it was said, was converted by a Frenchman at Concorezzo near Milan; in turn he soon converted others. Before long Cathars were in other parts of Italy: in the north at Desenzano on Lake Garda, Vicenza, Verona and Mantua and in central Italy at Florence and even further south not far from Rome at Orvieto. By the end of the twelfth century there were scores of flourishing Cathar communities in Western Europe, the most successful in southern France and northern Italy.

Attempts were made to repress this heresy. At Cologne in 1144 confessed Cathars were seized from the clergy who tried to protect them and burned by the people. In 1163 further trials were held at Cologne. As early as 1145 St Bernard, abbot of Clairvaux, preached against heretics, quite possibly Cathars, in the south of France at Toulouse, Albi and surrounding villages with apparent success, but a success only of the short term. Generally speaking, the Cathars in northern France and the Rhineland were checked, and their influence faded. To the south the developments were startlingly different. The meeting at Lombers in 1165 had no measurable success, for, among other reasons, the secular author- ities were unwilling to intervene. Other preachers came into the Languedoc, but they had not even the limited success of Bernard. In Toulouse a trial was held in 1177, and a local merchant abjectly recanted, yet four of his sons and their families later appeared as Cathars. Innocent III confronted a serious, seething problem when he became pope in 1198.

What was it that constituted the Catharism to which Innocent III was to respond in a most aggressive manner? In the first place, its organization. Catharism was not a sect within the Catholic church: it was itself a church, one in opposition to the Catholic church. It had bishops and dioceses. In the Languedoc in the early thirteenth century it had dioceses at Agen, Albi, Carcassonne and Toulouse. In Italy the territorial division of the four dioceses there was less clear. A separate church though it was, Catharism had no pope, no overall leader: it was a religion of strong local communities. Three levels of membership were noted as early as 1143 at Cologne, and so that structure continued: the perfect, the believers and the sympathizers. The elite *perfecti* formed the core of the movement: men and women who had passed through a rigorous probationary period, after which they received the *consolamentum* (literally, 'the consoling'), a laying on of hands, which released the person from the power of Satan and now allowed that person to speak to God in the Lord's Prayer. To compare the *perfecti* to Catholic priests or Catholic monks provides some glimpse of their role, but the comparison should not be pressed too far. They bound themselves to an austere life of fasting and abstinence from sex and from all products of coition such as meat, milk, cheese and eggs. It was a code of life more rigid than the most rigid Catholic monastic orders. The *perfecti* tended to live in small communities. Some travelled, preaching and teaching and encouraging others. They formed a class apart, not a priesthood, for there was no Mass, only a blessing of bread while reciting the Lord's Prayer, an elite class deferred to by other adherents, who genuflected to them. Their numbers were never very large, although precise figures elude us. About the lowest order, the supporters, little can be said except that they gave material support to the *perfecti* and listened to sermons. The intermediate order, the believers, was composed of those who had accepted the teaching but were not yet prepared for the consequences of the *consolamentum*. Some believers took that step after several years of intense training. For others the *consolamentum* was a deathbed ritual, since to die unconsoled was to die still in the power of Satan.

To summarize their belief system is hazardous, for it was not exactly the same everywhere. Basic to their world-view was the dualistic dichotomy already mentioned, but, even here, there were differences. Extreme and moderate dualists both saw a world of material, visible, physical reality, the object of our senses, particularly sight and touch, and it was evil. The human body was evil, and to propagate the human body was evil. The moderates believed that Satan, the fallen angel, was created by God, and he in turn created material things. More radically, the extremists believed there are two eternal powers, one of good and one of evil, joined forever in combat. All agreed that the world of the spirit is the world of the good, which derives from God, himself a wholly spiritual, non-material being. The human soul is the spiritual part of every human being, but, while joined with the body, it is under the control of Satan. The ritual of the *consolamentum* released the soul from the control of Satan, liberating it from the power of evil.

Their ethic followed logically from their basic world-view, and its preachers could find passages in the gospels to support their ethic. Renounce the world and all its pomps. Live by the spirit, which can be willing, while the flesh is weak. Abstain from carnality. Fast and abstain from worldly pleasures of all sorts. It was an appeal not that different from that which sent thousands of young men and women into monasteries in the twelfth century. The vital difference was that Catholic teaching, even St Bernard's at his most rhetorical, did not hold that their world-denying life was the only route to personal salvation. For the Cathars it was the only route. Cathar preachers found in the lapses from virtue of Catholic priests and bishops a rich vein to mine. Who could deny such evident evils and who could justify the worldliness and lack of spirituality among the Catholic clergy? The Cathars held that their *perfecti*, having renounced material pleasures, were the only true Christians. Dualism resolved the perennial problem of how a good God can permit earthquakes and illness and disease simply by positing an evil God or, at the least, an evil Satan, to whom material disasters could be attributed. To calculate the numbers attracted to this church is fraught with difficulties. That there existed Cathars among the peasantry in rural areas is abundantly clear, but, only if guesswork were to replace evidence, can actual numbers or even reasonable estimates be given for them. For the towns of Lombardy and the Languedoc some evidence is available. For example 600 *perfecti* gathered together at Mirepoix in 1206; extrapolating from this figure it is possible to say that there may have been as many as 1,500 *perfecti* in the Languedoc. At Béziers, in 1209, about 200 Cathars were identified out of a population of about 10,000. In some villages such as Cambias they formed a majority and, in others, a minority, even a small minority. It was never a mass movement but one that the pope judged he could not ignore.

Innocent III, committed to reform, placed the suppression of heresy as his top priority. Earlier attempts had little success. Almost at once the new pope sent two Cistercians into the Languedoc to preach and to excommunicate heretics. Two others replaced them in 1203, then later another Cistercian was added to the team. Local bishops were not pleased with the intrusion of papal legates into their

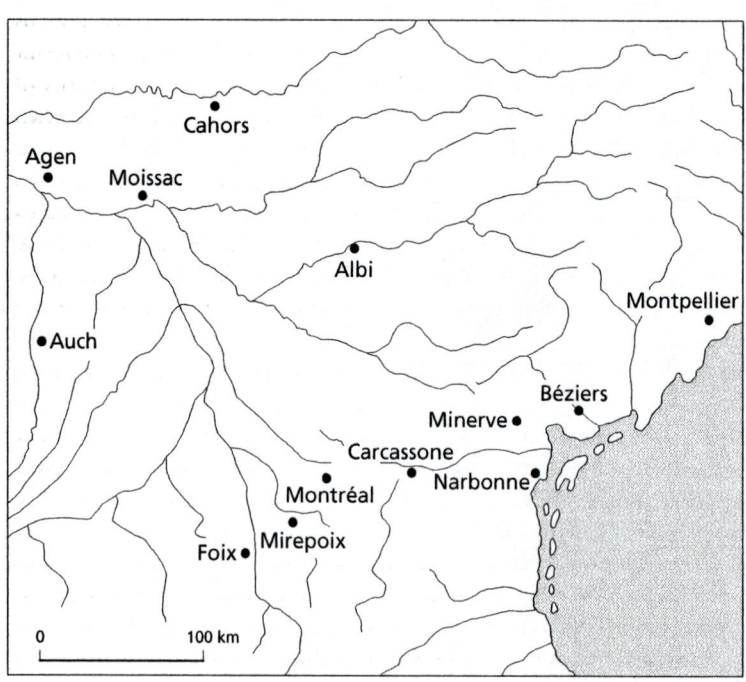

Map 14 Places associated with the Cathars (Albigensians) in the Languedoc.

dioceses. The bishop of Béziers was suspended from office not for heresy but for failing to cooperate with the Cistercian legates. The archbishop of Narbonne was nearly suspended at this time for the same reason, but his suspension did eventually come in 1212. The lay nobles were even less cooperative, and, as a result, in 1207 the count of Toulouse was excommunicated. The preaching mission took on new impetus in 1206 with the arrival of the Spanish bishop Diego of Osma and one of his cathedral clergy, Dominic (later St Dominic). Their plan, approved by Innocent, was that preachers should travel barefoot, eschewing every sign of luxury, in other words, like the Cathar preachers. Also, they should not be reluctant to engage the Cathars in open, public debates. In the following spring, Innocent ordered twelve Cistercian abbots to adopt this preaching method in the Languedoc. Eight days of debate followed at Servian, where Diego and Dominic triumphed. At Montréal the debate lasted two weeks, and 150 Cathars returned to Catholicism. By the end of the summer of 1207 the monks wanted to return to their monasteries, and Diego returned to Osma, where he soon died. Events soon took a dramatic turn. The mission by preaching and example was soon replaced by violence.

On 14 January 1208 the papal legate to the Languedoc, Peter of Castelnau, was assassinated by a knight of Count Raymond VI of Toulouse. The parallel of the Becket murder could not have escaped many. Peter had excommunicated the count and, in the preceding month, had had acrimonious exchanges with him. There is no evidence to suggest the count's complicity in the murder, but his failure to arrest the assassin and to express regret infuriated Innocent. The result was the Albigensian Crusade. Innocent III called on King Philip Augustus of France to lead a crusading army south to suppress the heresy. Preoccupied with difficulties with King John of England and Otto IV of Germany, Philip Augustus refused. The pope appointed a papal legate and promised those taking the cross all the benefits of crusaders going to the Holy Land. Once a movement to recover the holy places in the East from the infidel, the crusade had recently been turned against Christians in Constantinople and now was being used against Christian heretics in the West. A corner had been irrevocably turned in the crusading movement.

The Albigensian Crusade lasted twenty years and was only partially successful in gaining its aims. In late June 1209 a crusading army gathered at Lyons: a large army led mostly by the barons of northern France. On 22 July they arrived at Béziers, which they easily took. The people of Béziers sought safety in their churches. The church of the Magdalene, crowded with frightened inhabitants, was burned as was the cathedral. The abbot of Cîteaux allegedly said, when asked how to distinguish Catholic from heretic, 'Kill them all: God will sort it out.' On to Carcassonne, which surrendered. Other fortified towns in the vicinity, such as Narbonne and Albi, soon followed suit. By then the crusading army was being led by Simon de Montfort, a nobleman from the vicinity of Paris. When, in the spring of 1210, his army took Minerve, they burned alive 140 *perfecti* on a huge pyre. Most of the fortresses in that region of the Languedoc were under the

11 Albi Cathedral. Reproduced by permission of Tim Benton.

control of the crusaders; there remained the region of Toulouse, which was to dominate the hostilities for the rest of the war. Count Raymond VI of Toulouse had thrown his support to the crusaders in 1209, but now the crusade turned on him. When he failed to respond promptly to an order to turn over named heretics, he was excommunicated. In July 1211 de Montfort positioned his army outside Toulouse but was unable to breach the defences. King Peter II of Aragon intervened diplomatically and, in early 1213, convinced Innocent III to halt the crusade. The pope's legates on the ground in southern France subverted the peace, and the crusade started again. Peter II fell in battle near Toulouse in late summer 1213. Desultory fighting continued for the next two years with the crusaders in control of much of the region with the principal exception of

Toulouse. When the Fourth Lateran Council concluded on 30 November 1215, it stripped Raymond VI of his title and made Simon de Montfort count of Toulouse. He took Toulouse in 1216, while Raymond VI was securing fresh recruits from Spain and his son, Raymond VII, was gaining support in eastern Languedoc. In the summer of 1217, while de Montfort was campaigning with little success in Provence, Toulouse rose against his garrison, and Raymond VI returned to a hero's welcome. A siege by the crusaders was set up but failed in June 1218, when de Montfort was struck by a stone projectile that crushed his head. At the pleading of the new pope, Honorius III (1216–27), Philip Augustus sent a royal army south under the command of his son Prince Louis.

The crusade now was but a pretence; the reality was a war being waged by the king of France in the Languedoc for the purpose of extending royal power into the south. What remains of the story pertains more to French political history than to church history. Louis failed in another siege of Toulouse. Truces were made in 1223 and in 1224. By then Louis VIII was king of France and Raymond VII count of Toulouse. Yet Louis's large army had limited success and was weakened by a long siege at Avignon. Tired after twenty years, the count of Toulouse negotiated a peace when he and the fifteen-year-old Louis IX met at the cathedral of Notre-Dame in Paris. He kept much of his ancestral territories, but they would be ceded to the royal family at his death. Then the king of France would have control over most of the south of France. It had been a successful war for the French, but clearly not a crusade. It failed in its stated purpose, to eradicate the Cathar heresy. The counts of Toulouse and most of the other great men of the south were not heretics, despite rumours circulating among the crusaders that Raymond VI was a Cathar supporter and that two *perfecti* were with him constantly ready to give him the *consolamentum*, should he show signs of dying. These southern leaders fought against attacks on their lands. Many heretics were ruthlessly killed, yet Catharism was far from subdued. It would take another campaign, of a different sort, to accomplish that.

The elimination of Catharism was effected by trials and punishment. A new procedure then in use for criminal cases was employed by the popes to eradicate heresy. It was a procedure that vested a papal agent with the power to investigate and to punish the heretics. Its procedure was by way of investigation rather than by accusation. It could be called simply the 'investigation', but it is known to history by a synonym, the 'inquisition', and the papal agents as 'inquisitors'. Canonical legislation against heretics was already in place; it remained to identify them and deal with them. Pope Gregory IX (1227–41) appointed members of the order founded by the preacher Dominic to go into the Languedoc in 1233 with considerable authority. Three Dominican inquisitors arrived at Toulouse. Other inquisitors were soon at Albi, Moissac and Cahors; at these places the dead were exhumed and burned. The presence of the inquisitors led to near rebellion at Narbonne and to their being expelled from Toulouse. The inquisition was particularly active in the early 1240s and by decade's end the back of Catharism was broken.

How did this inquisition proceed? When the inquisitors arrived in a community such as a parish, they summoned the whole parish, and a sermon was preached, exhorting those present to assist in the extermination of heresy. A period of grace was allowed, generally about a week or so, during which individuals could confess, repent, be absolved and punished leniently. Questioning of individual parishioners then began:

> Have you seen a heretic?
> Have you heard sermons preached by heretics?
> Have you witnessed a *consolamentum*?
> Have you supported heretics materially?

And so forth. The questioned would be encouraged to implicate others, who, in turn, would be questioned. When sufficient evidence was acquired about an individual, the inquisitor provided the accused with a statement of the charges but not with the names of the accusers. If convicted, the person would be invited to confess and repent. There is no evidence that confessions were extorted by torture at this time. Punishment depended on whether the person confessed or was contumacious. An analysis of the penalties imposed by the inquisitor Bernard de Caux in 1245–46 is instructive. He questioned 5,605 – every adult in two archdeaconries south-west of Toulouse, all of whom were transported to Toulouse for questioning – and, in the end, pronounced 207 sentences. Only 23 of these were imprisonments; the rest were lighter penances (e.g., pilgrimages). There was some resort at this time to the secular arm for execution: one of every 100 condemned, according to one estimate. The inquisition continued on in the south for some time as did Catharism, but the latter was leading an underground existence, and by the turn into the fourteenth century only remnants could be found in remote places, like Montaillou in the remote hill country of the Pyrenees, kept alive by the example of *perfecti* rather than by their theology. Yet Catharism was not the only heresy confronting the church at this time.

The Waldensians took their name from Waldès, a wealthy merchant of Lyons. According to one version, he was deeply moved by the story of St Alexius, who renounced wealth to live in poverty and, who, when he returned to his father's house, died unrecognized. After taking steps to provide for his wife and daughter, in 1173 Waldès gave up business, wealth and family to become a wandering preacher, giving himself up entirely to a life of poverty. Relying only on alms, he lived sparingly and provided for the needy during the famine of 1176. He soon attracted followers to this simple life, but his new life went beyond poverty and acts of charity. Waldès and his followers preached, and their preaching brought them into conflict with the church. The problem was not what they were preaching – mostly exhortations to live a better Christian life – but that they were preaching at all. These preachers were laymen and, indeed, laywomen, and the church viewed preaching as coming through bishops as successors to the apostles and, thus, restricted preaching to those members of the clergy who were approved by the bishops. Waldès and his followers, however, felt they needed no licence to preach. They heard the words of Christ, sending out his disciples in pairs to prepare for his coming:

> Go barefoot, carrying neither purse nor pack . . . When you enter a town that welcomes you, eat what is put before you. Cure the sick there and say, 'The kingdom of God is near' . . . Whoever hears you hears me and whoever rejects you rejects Him who sent me.
>
> (Luke 10, 4, 8–9, 16)

To Waldès this was a mission for all Christians, and so he and his followers went out barefoot, two by two, to preach repentance and conversion of life, living off what was provided for them. They stood in opposition to the teaching of the church about preaching, and this opposition led in time, almost inexorably, to heresy. A compromise, which proved only temporary, was reached between Waldès and Pope Alexander III at the Third Lateran Council (1179). The pope embraced the poor man of Lyons and approved his life of poverty but allowed him and his followers to preach only if the local priests agreed. To the pope Waldès professed the orthodox Christian faith and renewed his vow of poverty. The compromise was unworkable, principally because very few priests agreed to allow the Waldensians to preach, yet many of them still preached. A new archbishop came to Lyons in 1183 and refused to allow Waldensians to preach there. Still, their preaching continued, and the archbishop expelled and excommunicated them. They were not Cathars or in any way sympathetic to the Cathars, against whom they themselves preached and with whom they debated, yet, in 1184, the Waldensians were condemned with the Cathars at the Council of Verona with little distinction made between them. Their expulsion by bishops merely led to their expansion. In Lombardy, like the Cathars, they found a tolerant atmosphere and fertile soil for their appealing message. Some drifted from a condemnation of bad priests to the position that sacraments, including the Mass, administered by bad priests were no sacraments at all. By the 1190s this was heresy. In parts of Italy Waldensians, who were not priests, celebrated Mass. Some Waldensians denied the existence of purgatory. A line had been passed.

Innocent III, in 1208, reconciled a number of French Waldensians, agreeing that they could continue their lives as poor wandering preachers, now called 'the Catholic Poor'. Two years later a Lombard follower of Waldès was reconciled, and with him others, who formed a Catholic community. Essential to each submission was a profession of orthodox faith, a concern for which had by now replaced the purely disciplinary issue of authority to preach. By this time, the movement had experienced its first of many schisms. In 1205 the Poor of Lyons and the Poor Lombards split over several issues, including personalities, but particularly over the desire of the Italians to form a separate church distinct from the Catholic church, in which they existed as a sect. These two branches of Waldensians remained separate and drifted further apart as each found its separate (if related) place in the ecclesiastical landscape of the times. The Waldensians in France, small in numbers, continued, despite sporadic and largely ineffective persecution, into the sixteenth century. The movement in Italy faded in Lombardy but remained strong in the valleys of Piedmont, where a separate Waldensian church continues to this day. Some evidence suggests that the Waldensians penetrated deep into the German-speaking lands, particularly into Austria south of the Danube and possibly into Bohemia and Moravia, but we should not press similarity of doctrine and practice, known to us principally from their persecutors, so far as to see links back to Waldès, when none is compellingly seen.

Often classified with the Cathars and the Waldensians are the Humiliati (Humble Ones). They also had much in common with the early friars, and a corrected view of their place in history would put them in the company of Francis and his followers rather than with Waldès and his Poor Men or, at least, would see them as a bridge between the two. The Humiliati were mostly artisans from areas in northern Italy, particularly near Milan and Verona. They foreswore luxuries, wearing coarse woollen garments and donating superfluous income to the poor. In addition, they shared with 'heretics' a refusal to take oaths, and it was this that was the sticking point. Humiliati were among those condemned as heretics in 1184, but whether those referred to in the papal condemnation are the same as those who appear in the next decade is not altogether clear. In 1199, they approached the newly elected Innocent III, who, after several inquiries, sanctioned three orders of Humiliati: the First Order for clerics who lived in community, the Second Order for laymen and laywomen who lived separately in community and the Third Order for laymen and laywomen – even married – living in their own homes. They prospered, and, in 1216, an observer wrote,

> This religion has so grown in the diocese of Milan that they now have
> one hundred and fifty houses, men on one side, women on the other,
> not counting those who live in their own homes.

At first, more a loosely linked network of houses than an order like the Franciscans, the Humiliati as a centralized order with a master general, general chapter, annual meetings and annual visitations owes that structure to the canonist-pope Innocent IV, who, in 1246, issued directives to bring about that effect. Two factors have combined to marginalize the Humiliati historically. In the first place, numerous as they may have been, they were a fairly localized order with most of their houses in northern Italy and not international as were the friars or the Cathars and Waldensians. Second, the order fell victim to events in the sixteenth century – including the attempted murder of their cardinal protector by a discontented member of the order – and ceased to exist, unlike the four orders of friars. The order, consequently, has not received the scholarly attention afforded the friars with the unfortunate result that they have tended to be seen more as heretics than as a religious order.

Arising from sources similar to those that gave rise to the Humiliati were the Beguines and Beghards, who formed communities, respectively, of women and men, although some, in the early days, lived singly. Like the Humiliati, they were falsely accused of heresy. Their name, it is sometimes suggested, derives from 'Albigensian'. It was the communities of Beguines that flourished. Their origins lie beyond our sight, but they can be seen in the Low Countries at the turn into the thirteenth century. They did not form an order: they were laywomen who took no vows but promised, while living in community, to remain celibate; many wore simple habits. They were not enclosed, and some of them worked in the towns where their beguinages were located. They could freely leave at any time. While in community, they shared a life of communal prayer. In 1216, Honorius III gave verbal approval to them, and, in 1233, Gregory IX formally took the Beguines under his protection. There were communities at Cologne in 1223, at Leuven in 1232, at Mainz in 1233 and at Namur and Paderborn in 1235. Their reliance on the friars for spiritual direction subjected them to criticisms intended for the friars. Yet they clearly had their admirers. The English scholar and bishop Robert Grosseteste warmly approved of their life, which he found 'perfect and holy'. In the century after the approval by Pope Gregory they flourished, and communities arose in many of the towns of the Rhineland and the Low Countries. At Cologne, by 1309, there were 164 houses with a population estimated at 1,000. At the same time Strasbourg had about 600 Beguines. At the Council of Vienne, in 1312, two hostile decrees were enacted against the movement, and subsequently it began to decline. In many ways, the Beguines presaged the later development of the Devotio Moderna (see chapter 17). Modern visitors to such places as Bruges and Leuven can see excellent examples of beguinages, owing much to their revival in the seventeenth century.

The movements described in this section did not exist in isolation. They formed part of a larger scene in which many Christians found that their increasing wealth did not provide them with what they wanted from life, and, like others before and after them, they renounced the material things of this world, which they had found wanting, and dedicated themselves to a simple way of life, becoming poor not by necessity but by choice. The voluntary poverty of Waldès and others like him was shared, in a strikingly similar way, by Francis of Assisi.

The friars

Any discussion of the friars must begin with St Francis of Assisi. He was the dominant historical figure in the early history of the friars. While there were other notable figures like Dominic and Clare of Assisi, it is Francis of Assisi who, above all others, commands our attention. The unreserved admiration of the ages has been given to the poor friar Francis. He was born in 1181 into a comfortable bourgeois family in the hill town of Assisi, overlooking the Spoleto valley in central Italy. The facts of his early life are a bit sketchy. Yet this much can be said. Francis entered into the family cloth business, perhaps travelling with his father to France. Like other young men of his class, Francis took up arms and fought for Assisi against rival communes. In an engagement against neighbouring Perugia in 1202, he became a prisoner of the enemy. Ransomed, he returned to Assisi, where he suffered from some unnamed illness, perhaps depression. In 1205 Francis undertook to go on a military expedition against the pope's political enemies in southern Italy, but he got only as far as nearby Spoleto. There he experienced a troubling dream, which compelled him to give up his military ambitions. In the next two years Francis left his family and its riches and became a solitary. He lived for a while in the ruins of the church of San Damiano outside Assisi and, at times, in caves that punctuate the hill country of Umbria. He even befriended lepers, in one account embracing and kissing them. Then, in 1208, on the feast of St Matthias (24 February), while at Mass, Francis was deeply moved by the reading of the gospel in which Christ told his apostles:

> Proclaim that the kingdom of God is at hand, cure the sick, raise the dead, cleanse lepers, cast out demons. You have freely received, you must freely give. Do not take gold, silver or copper for your purse. Take no pack for the journey, no second coat, no shoes, no walking stick, for the labourer is worthy of his hire.

Francis, that day, removed his shoes, donned a rough cloak, girded it with a knotted rope and committed himself to the literal fulfilment of the gospel mandate. He had experienced a profound conversion of life and had found his mission. The similarity to Waldès could not be more apparent. Like the poor man of Lyons, Francis became the poor man (*poverello*) of Assisi, reacting to the gospel call to live like Christ, by abandoning worldly goods, caring for the poor and the abandoned and preaching the gospel message of repentance. It was not only Waldès whom Francis resembled but scores of others, including the Humiliati, who renounced the world for a simple Christian life, but, unlike Waldès, Francis escaped the taint of heresy and, unlike the Humiliati, Francis achieved renown and founded an order that is still with us. Francis had no intention of founding an order – he wanted only to live a holy life – but his vision was so attractive that it appealed to young men like himself, comfortable, middle-class, town-dwelling and idealistic laymen. Almost immediately such young men wanted to join him. To them he said that they should sell their worldly goods and give everything to the poor. Some did. Francis and his small band of poor brothers (*fratres minores*, friars minor) walked barefoot, eating what was given them by sympathetic persons and preaching – always preaching – the message of penance. In a word, they were itinerant preachers, like the Humiliati, but with a stricter, more literal commitment to poverty. They owned nothing, and that was the cornerstone of the movement and a source of problems in later decades.

In the summer of 1209 they were eight, and they went out in four pairs, one pair going, it is said, to northern Italy and then to Compostela. Others joined, and soon there were twelve. In 1210 Francis walked barefoot to Rome, probably with the other eleven, to seek papal approval for his band as an order. Several cardinals had misgivings. When the matter was brought before Innocent III, he too felt that the non-possession of property and the austerity of their life could create problems. He was right, as events were to prove. Exactly what Innocent did is shrouded in mist. He gave some sort of approval, which may have amounted to nothing more than oral encouragement. Francis had brought a primitive rule with him, which received some form of papal sanction.

> The most high God directed me to live the life of the gospel. This I had written down in brief and simple words, and his holiness the pope confirmed it.
>
> (St Francis, Testament)

Later, Pope Honorius III (1216–27) was twice to give approval to rules for the order. And, when, in 1227, their longtime supporter, Cardinal Ugolino, himself a nephew of Innocent III, became Pope Gregory IX, their future as an order was assured.

When Francis and his brothers returned to Assisi in 1210, they accepted the offer of local Benedictines to use a dilapidated church. This Portiuncula church on the valley floor below Assisi became their centre. A massive basilica was built around this tiny chapel in the sixteenth century. In the winter of 1210–11 other recruits came to the Portiuncula, so that by the summer of 1211 Francis's band numbered a score or more. During their preaching journeys in that summer others joined them in their life of poverty and preaching. From the sacristy of the Portiuncula, where they were living, they moved to rude huts near the church. It was there, at the Portiuncula, that on Palm Sunday, 1212, a young noblewoman of Assisi, named Clare, presented herself. Other women followed her, and they were given the newly restored church of San Damiano as a place to live. They formed the Second Order, the Minoresses or, more commonly, the Poor Clares. Social and canonical restrictions of the time did not permit them to beg or preach, but they could and did live lives of voluntary poverty. What was once a small band of men had become two orders. It was the order of men (Order of Friars Minor) that was to experience phenomenal growth. They came to Assisi, mostly laymen but some clerics, almost all comfortable and privileged, but no applicants were refused. At Whitsun, 1217, a chapter of the friars was held at the Portiuncula, and a blueprint was devised. Soon there were twelve provinces, half of them outside of Italy. At about this time Francis, in practice, seemed to abandon the actual running of the new, expanding order, although he was still its head. Two vicars were appointed to run the order in 1219, when Francis sailed to the East to join the Fifth Crusade, not to fight but to preach to the Muslims. Under a flag of truce, Francis crossed enemy lines, gained audience of the sultan, preached to him and returned without making any converts. Upon his return to Italy in 1220, Francis gladly gave up any title of authority in the order, his much neglected body now feeling the pains of an illness that would kill him. He wished to retire to the life of a solitary, his first calling. But, first, he and his close associates produced a new rule for the order, the so-called First Rule (1221), which probably elaborated on the skeleton of the rule, now lost, presented to Innocent III in 1210. This new rule was further elaborated two years later in what became known as the Second Rule, when Honorius said that he was ratifying 'the rule of your order approved by our predecessor of happy memory, Pope Innocent'. It codified Franciscan practice and ideals. All friars, it said, are to live 'in obedience, without property and in chastity'. A probationary year for candidates is to be observed. The daily order of prayers is set out. Further, Francis says,

> The friars should appropriate nothing for themselves ... They are strangers and pilgrims in this world, serving God in poverty and humility, and it is this poverty, my dear brothers, that makes you heirs and kings of the kingdom of heaven, poor in material things, but rich in virtues ... To this poverty, beloved brothers, cling with your whole heart, never wishing to have anything else in this life.

While the rule may have resolved some issues, it contained the seeds for disputes about the nature of Franciscan poverty that were to plague the order for some time.

Meanwhile, the order was rapidly expanding. Early missions to France and Germany were ill-planned and failed, and friars who went to Morocco were never heard of again. These were but early setbacks. When Francis went to the East in 1219, there was already a group of friars at Acre in the Holy Land. In the same year there was a community near Paris, and in the next few years communities were founded at Le Mans, Bayeux, Vézelay, Chartres and elsewhere in the north of France. By 1225 there were houses in modern Belgium at Namur, Bruges, Ghent and Ypres. Other missions went to the south of France, at first, in 1217, with no success, and then, in 1219, with long-lasting success. The earliest of these successful southern missions was at Cahors. Dates are elusive, but communities were soon to be found at Arles, Aix-en-Provence, Montpellier, Nîmes and Périgueux. The first mission for Germany and Hungary, which set out in 1219, also proved a failure: none of the friars spoke German or Hungarian, presuming on providence to provide. They were beaten and abused, fortunate to return to Italy with their lives. In 1221, this time led by a recently professed German friar, Caesar of Speyer, a university graduate, a fresh attempt was made. At Augsburg they were warmly received and provided with a house, which became the centre of the German mission. From Augsburg one group with a German friar founded houses at Würzburg, Mainz, Worms, Speyer, Strasbourg and Cologne. Another group of friars went to Salzburg and a third to Regensburg. The German province was quickly divided into four 'custodies': Franconia, Bavaria–Swabia, Alsace and Saxony. No one knows exactly how many houses were founded in Germany in the 1220s, but there must have been dozens.

By 1223 there was a Franciscan presence in Hungary. Into the Iberian peninsula, visited earlier by other friars, came new missions: in 1217, when the friars were mistaken for Cathars and maltreated, and in 1219, when they numbered more than one hundred. Before long the Franciscans had houses at Lisbon, Burgos, Coimbra, Compostela, Barcelona, Toledo and Saragossa, to mention only some.

In England there was a similarly rapid expansion, and here the 1220s was also the crucial decade. We are fortunate to have an almost contemporary account in Thomas of Eccleston's *The Coming of the Friars into England*. Crossing the English Channel, nine friars arrived at Dover on 10 September 1224. Their leader was Agnellus of Pisa, a deacon. Three of the nine were English: Richard of Ingworth, a priest, Richard of Devon, an acolyte, and William of Esseby, a novice. From Dover they travelled to nearby Canterbury, staying there at the cathedral with the monks of Christ Church. After two days the party split. Five remained at Canterbury to establish a house. The other four, including the two English Richards, moved on to London, where they were given hospitality by the Dominicans before receiving use of a dilapidated house on Cornhill. After Agnellus came to London, the two English friars pressed on to Oxford. After a fortnight as guests of the Domincans, who had already been at Oxford for three years, they were given the use of a house from a benefactor. The Franciscans hoped to gain recruits at the university, and they were not to be disappointed. Thus, within six weeks of their arrival they had friaries at Canterbury, London and Oxford, but this was but the beginning. Very soon, probably by 1225, they were at Northampton and Cambridge, later at Norwich, Gloucester, Salisbury and York, all before 1230. By 1240 there were twenty-eight houses in England, scattered throughout the country, but always in towns, from Scarborough in the north-east to Exeter in the south-west. Eccleston said that in 1256 the friars numbered 1,242. And, in 1230, Richard of Ingworth crossed the Irish Sea to found a province in Ireland.

Meanwhile, other friars were founding provinces in Bohemia, Hungary and Poland. It was a growth of almost incomprehensible proportions, greater than the extraordinary growth of the Cistercians a century earlier, like a prairie fire sweeping through Christendom. What did St Francis make of all this, as he lie dying at the Portiuncula in October 1226? We shall never know. The *poverello* of Assisi, his body marked by the stigmata, simply bade those attending him to be faithful to the teachings of Christ. His small band of itinerant preachers was now a vast organization with priests as well as laymen, with university graduates as well as the unlettered and with his Lady Poverty under threat.

Two issues almost immediately surfaced: the owning of property and the education of the friars. Wherever Francis's poor brothers went they received generous gifts from lay benefactors, including the houses where they were to live, yet the rule did not allow individual friars or communities of friars to own anything. Besides houses they would soon want churches. To institutionalize the vision of St Francis, of necessity, required compromises with that vision. How could friars, who could not handle money, contract with workers to build their convents and their churches? And how could friars, who could own nothing, hold their property? In 1230 Pope Gregory IX, long a supporter of the order, arranged a compromise. The friars could appoint agents to handle their financial affairs, and they could remain mendicants, receiving alms from benefactors. His successor, Innocent IV, in 1245, effected a further compromise. He vested owner-ship of their buildings – a great basilica now rising in Assisi and many churches elsewhere – and furnishings and books in the Holy See, which gave the friars permanent use of them. These were compromises which may have resolved strictly canonical issues, but they failed to satisfy those friars who shared the pure vision of St Francis, some of whom, at this time, chose to live in huts and caves. They and those like them would be heard from during the order's ensuing history.

Another issue had risen even before St Francis died: the attitude of the order towards education. He is quoted by an early biographer as saying,

> Some of my friars are being seduced by a curious quest for learning; on the day of retribution they will have an empty hand. It is my wish that they be made strong in virtue so that, at the inevitable time of tribulation, they will have the company of the Lord and their books will be thrown out of windows and packed away in chests.

Although Francis had an elementary knowledge of Latin and, at some point, even took deacon's orders, his sympathies were clearly with the unlettered lay friars. Yet by 1219 his friars were gaining recruits at the University of Paris, where soon masters of theology joined their ranks, including, in 1236, the greatest Parisian theologian of the time, Alexander of Hales. At Oxford they soon established a school of theology and invited the eminent scholar, Robert Grosseteste, a secular cleric, to lecture in theology to them. At Bologna also, before 1236, the friars had a school of theology. At Padua, where a university had recently been founded, their scholar-preacher, St Anthony of Padua, preached to such large crowds that people queued early on the days when he preached and shopkeepers closed their shops. The order was changing, and after 1239 all major offices within the order had to be held by priests. And, in 1257, the friars selected the eminent Parisian theologian, Bonaventure, as their minister general. Under Bonaventure the general chapter, in 1260, restricted admission to educated clerics and laymen of distinction. Although it is true to say that Francis himself could not now have become a Franciscan, it would be a harsh judgement that would condemn the organic growth of any human institution led by honourable men. Both Francis and Bonaventure are venerated as saints, yet each had a different view of the Franciscan vocation. Contemporaries universally praised the personal saintliness of Bonaventure, particularly his attachment to a simple life of poverty, even in the midst of the great university. He recognized that the order had changed, but, he said, so had the church changed in accidental ways while remaining consistently true to its essential self. The basic issue here that will perhaps be debated as long as historians examine

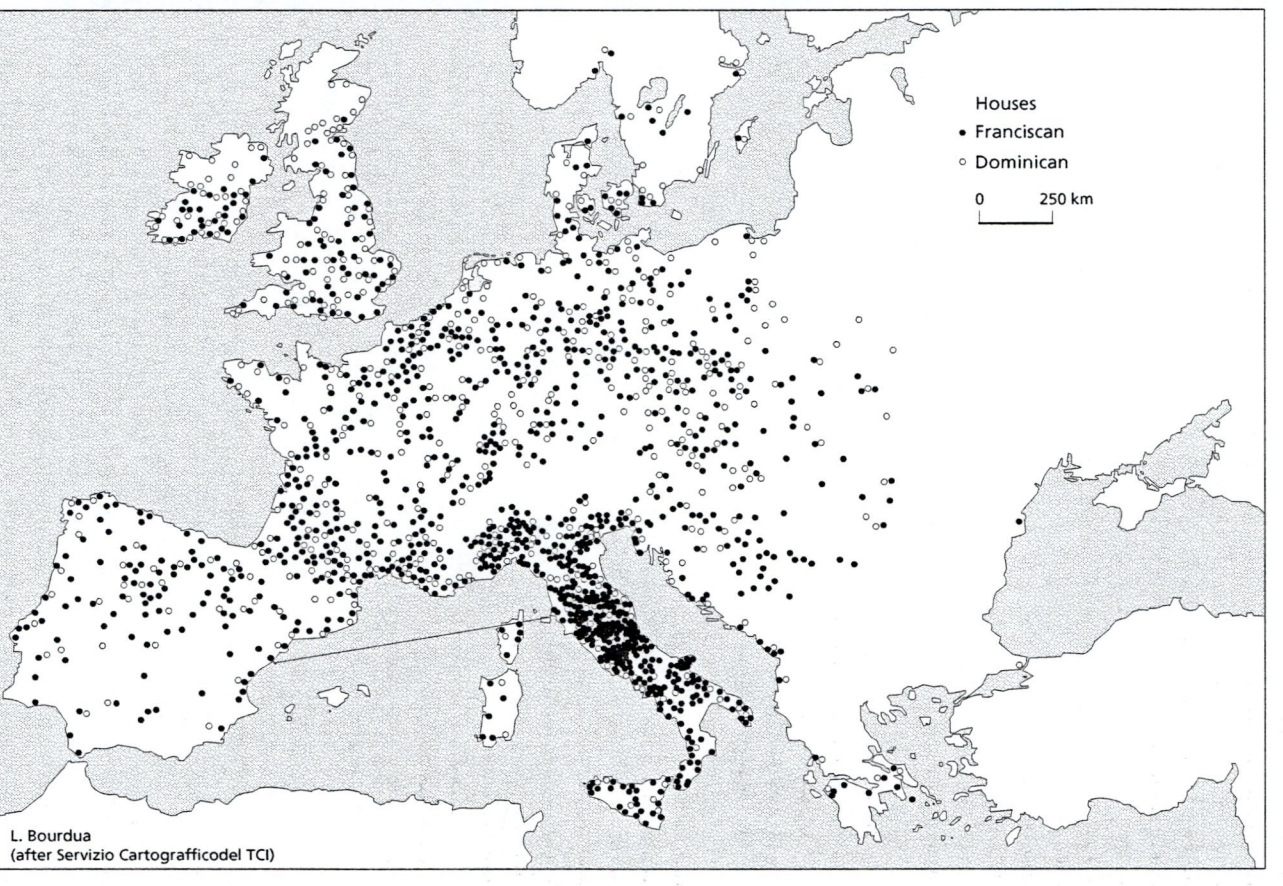

Map 15 Mendicant friars.

it is whether the pristine life envisioned by Francis could survive its organization into an order. Even those, perhaps a minority, who answer in the affirmative must acknowledge the difficulties inherent in such a transition.

The Dominican friars (Order of Preachers), although similar in many ways to the Franciscans, had a distinctly different origin. The founder, the Castilian Dominic of Guzman (c.1171–1221), we have already encountered as a preacher by word and example against the Cathars. Unlike Francis, Dominic was well educated in the liberal arts and theology, and also, unlike Francis, he was a cleric in holy orders when he appeared on the public scene. In 1206 Dominic and his bishop, who was to die in the following year, adopted the simple lifestyle of the Cathars and walked on foot, without a retinue, from place to place in the Languedoc, preaching and even debating with their opponents. Dominic soon established a house for some women converts, who became proto-Dominican nuns. In Dominic eloquence and learning were joined with austerity and unworldliness. Successes were many, but not on a large scale. Innocent III's calling of a crusade against the Cathars undoubtedly affected Dominic's mission. There is no evidence that he was involved in that tragic campaign, although it is true that he was friendly with Simon de Montfort and his family. Dominic continued his preaching amidst the turbulence of the crusade. At Toulouse a group of men, not bound by vows but only by personal loyalty to Dominic, joined his preaching mission. In April 1215 the bishop of Toulouse recognized this nascent community and authorized their preaching. Six months later Dominic was in Rome, where he approached Innocent III for confirmation of the new order. It was just weeks before the opening session of the Fourth Lateran Council. Innocent agreed in principle to Dominic's request but told him to adopt an already-existing rule. He returned to France to confer with his followers. They chose to follow the Rule of St Augustine, to which they added constitutions. Pope Honorius III approved the new order in 1216. Futher provisions were made in 1220. The Dominicans did not become canons, but friars. They were vowed to an evangelical poverty, which did not allow them to live off the rents of lands, as did the monks and canons, but from spontaneous gifts and from what they could beg. The friars were to wear a rough, woollen white habit, covered by a black cloak, which gave them the name Black Friars. The Order of Preachers was now established.

Dominic's vision extended beyond the strife-ridden lands of southern France. On 15 August 1217 Dominic sent forth from Toulouse eleven friars: four to Spain and seven to Paris. And very soon others were sent to Bologna. This was but the beginning. By 1221 the order had expanded to such an extent that what had been two small houses in 1215 was by 1221 an order divided into five provinces: Spain, Provence, France, Lombardy and Tuscany. And the chapter of 1221 projected new provinces in Germany, Hungary, England, Greece, Scandinavia, Poland and the Holy Land. Soon there were these twelve flourishing provinces. To Hungary, in 1221, were sent the Hungarian Friar Paul, a master of canon law at Bologna, and three companions. At the same time the chapter dispatched Friar Christian to Germany, where he established a house at Cologne. Friar Solomon of Aarhus went to his native country, where the archbishop of Copenhagen warmly welcomed him and where, probably in 1223, he founded a priory at Lund. The largest mission went to England. Gilbert de Fresney, an Englishman educated at Bologna, and twelve others landed at Dover in early August 1221, their destination Oxford. Stopping briefly at Canterbury and London, they arrived at Oxford on 15 August 1221. A priory was established, and friars soon became students at the university. Elsewhere, two friars arrived at Cracow in 1222 and soon built the first Polish priory there. Three years later effective plans were made to establish other priories from Cracow: at Wroclaw (Breslau) on the Oder, at Sandomierz on the Vistula, at Gdansk on the Baltic Sea and, further away, at Prague in Bohemia. The growth of the order, if not as spectacular as the Franciscans, was still exceptional, and by 1256 there were about 13,000 Dominican friars.

By then the attachment to universities was an obvious part of the Dominican plan. There were priories already established at Paris in 1217, Bologna in 1218, Palencia in 1220 and Montpellier in 1221, and others were to follow. Richard Fishacre, the first Dominican Oxford graduate, wrote an influential theological commentary. Albertus Magnus at Paris was among those theologians using the philosophical works of Aristotle. His student, Thomas Aquinas, taught at Paris and Naples as well as at Dominican houses of studies and remains the best-known theologian of the Middle Ages. All Dominican priories were to have a resident theologian, and some houses, like Cologne, became centres of advanced study for the Black Friars.

Other orders of mendicant friars also appeared, but the provisions of the Fourth Lateran Council forbidding orders with new rules created a serious obstacle, which the Franciscans avoided by having been approved by Innocent III before the council as did the Dominicans by adopting the Rule of St Augustine. Both the Carmelite friars and the Austin friars emerged as orders from associations of hermits. The Carmelites derive from Western hermits living, in imitation of the prophet Elijah, on Mount Carmel, near Haifa in the Holy Land. They were Westerners, possibly crusaders and pilgrims who stayed on to live solitary lives of contemplation. By the beginning of the thirteenth century they formed a loose association. Sometime between 1206 and 1214 the Latin patriarch of Jerusalem gave them a 'formula of life', which probably described the life which they were then living. These hermits lived in separate cells in the wilderness and came together only for Mass in the morning in their oratory and for a chapter meeting on Sunday. Although Jerusalem fell to the Muslims in 1187, the strip of coastal land in which Mount Carmel lay remained in Christian hands. The continued way of life of the hermits was in peril in the shifting political and military sands of thirteenth-century Palestine. Yet after the fall of Jerusalem the hermits stayed in place and even received their formula of life. There is no suggestion of an exodus of hermits for a half century after the fall. A guide for Western pilgrims, written about 1231, described Mount Carmel:

> On the ridge lies a pleasant place where live the Latin hermits, who are called Brothers of Mount Carmel. They have an oratory dedicated to Our Lady, and many springs flow from the rocks there.

Then they left, not all at once, but in a steady, continuing stream, and returned to the West. The initial reason eludes us, perhaps some specific incident of unpleasantness with the Muslims, but once started it was to continue with groups of hermits from Carmel establishing communities at various places in Western Europe. The contemporary historian Vincent of Beauvais (d. 1264) said that the diaspora began in 1238. Another, not wholly accepted, source relates that hermits from Carmel went to Valenciennes in northern France in 1235. It is safe to say that in the years surrounding the year 1240 they migrated to Cyprus, Sicily, England and Provence, sponsored in all these places, it would seem, by returning crusaders. And for the next decades they continued to come until in 1291 whatever remained of their presence on Mount Carmel was burned down by the sultan's army. One Western visitor in about 1350 claimed to have seen ten Carmelite houses in the Holy Land, but this seems unlikely.

A change took place once they were in the West. They came as hermits who lived solitary lives of contemplative prayer, but they soon became friars with an apostolic mission. This was not their initial intent. For example, when they went to England in 1242, they established themselves in remote places: Hulne in Northumberland and Aylesford in Kent. Their next two foundations were in remote parts of Norfolk and Kent. This was soon to change. Subsequent foundations, almost without exception, were in towns: London and Cambridge in 1247, then York, Norwich, Bristol and Lincoln, all before 1260. And so it went on. By 1300 there were at least a thousand Carmelites in England, and they were definitely friars, like their neighbours in these towns, the Franciscans and Dominicans.

What had happened to the provisions of their formula of life that required them to live as hermits in the wilderness? Almost at once upon their arrival in the West, a party arose among them which wanted to adopt an active ministry like the friars. To settle this matter Pope Innocent IV, in 1247, revised the formula and issued the new document as a rule. They could now live wherever they wanted (i.e., in towns) and were to take their meals in common. They had become mendicant friars with an urban mission. Not only at Cambridge, as seen already, did the Carmelites establish houses but also at other university centres such as Paris, Oxford and Bologna. Yet there were to be continuing tensions, pulling towards contemplation and towards active ministry. About 1270 a former general of the order lamented the abandoning of the life of the desert for the life of the towns. And these tensions were never fully resolved in our period.

The Austin (or Augustinian) Friars, like the Carmelites, were originally hermits. As an order they came into existence by the efforts of mid-thirteenth-century popes to give disparate Italian eremitical groups a common organization. As early as 1223, five hermitages in Tuscany adopted a loose association; they were joined by eight more hermitages in 1228. This collection of thirteen Tuscan groups of hermits formed the core of a new order. In 1244, Pope Innocent IV through Cardinal Annibaldi arranged the formal union of most of the hermitages of Tuscany with the Rule of St Augustine as their rule, to which constitutions were added. Attracting other groups of hermits, the new order had sixty-one houses within ten years. Others were added in 1256, when an order of hermits with three provinces in northern Italy joined this expanding union of hermits as did other groups, especially hermits from the March of Ancona. In that year Pope Alexander IV confirmed the Great Union and gave the order its name, Order of Hermit Friars of St Augustine. Hermit friars they were called, but they were more friars than hermits. They followed the paths of the other orders of friars into the towns and universities of Europe.

Other orders of friars came into existence in the thirteenth century, adopting, as required by the Fourth Lateran Council, one of the older rules, but they never attracted the large numbers of the four major mendicant orders. The Second Council of Lyons (1274) forbade them to accept new members, and they slowly died out.

To an extent that should not be minimized, the friars emerged from forces similar to those that gave rise to heresy, yet the papacy, perhaps having learned from the handling of the Cathars and Waldensians, was able to turn their energies to constructive use within the church. Yet they were more than merely a movement contained within the institution: the orders of friars were the last great innovation of the medieval church. They were not cloistered monks, like the Benedictines, Cistercians and Carthusians, nor semi-cloistered, like the Augustinian canons. They were not bound to live lives enclosed in a monastic setting, intent on perfecting their own souls. They set themselves in the midst of settled populations, their doors open to the spiritual needs of their neighbours. One cannot argue persuasively that this was all planned in advance, that there was an analysis of the needs of the church and that this form of life was thus devised. No study groups; no great plan. In its origins, it was to a significant extent a lay movement characterized by an obvious spontaneity. Within the period of several decades in the thirteenth century the church had taken a leap forward, and the friars became a fixed element in the medieval church.

Further reading

An excellent general survey of medieval heresies is Malcom Lambert, *Medieval Heresy: Popular Movements from the Gregorian Reform to the Reformation* (2nd edn; Oxford, 1992). One may begin a study of the sources of heresy with R.I. Moore, *The Origins of European Dissent* (2nd edn; Oxford, 1985). For the Cathars see particularly Malcom Lambert, *The Cathars* (Oxford, 1998) and Malcom Barber, *The Cathars: Dualistic Heretics in Languedoc in the High Middle Ages* (Harlow, Essex, and New York, 2000). Also useful is Michael Costen, *The Cathars and the Albigensian Crusade* (Manchester and New York, 1997). For one aspect of Cathar history see Carol Lansing, *Power and Purity: Cathar Heresy in Medieval Italy* (Oxford, 1998). For an account of the Waldensians that takes the story into the early modern period see Euan Cameron, *Waldenses: Rejections of Holy Church in Medieval Europe* (Oxford and Malden, MA, 2000). The sections on southern Europe in Gabriel Audisio, *The Waldensian Dissent: Persecution and Survival c.1170–c.1570* (tr. Claire Davison; Cambridge, 1999) may be particularly helpful. Much is to be learned from Bernard Hamilton, *The Medieval Inquisition* (London, 1981). For an English translation of pertinent texts see W.L. Wakefield and A.P. Evans, *Heresies of the High Middle Ages: Selected Sources Translated and Annotated* (New York, 1969). An informed analysis can be found in Heinrich Fichtenau, *Heretics and Scholars in the High Middle Ages, 1000–1200* (tr. D.A. Kaiser; Philadelphia, 1998).

Two important contributions to the study of the Humiliati are the essays by Brenda Bolton in *Innocent III: Studies on Papal Authority and Pastoral Care* (Aldershot, Hants, 1995) and the monograph *The Early Humiliati* (Cambridge, 1999) by Frances Andrews.

The starting place for the friars should be the comprehensive, eminently sound account given by C.H. Lawrence in *The Friars: The Impact of the Early Mendicant Movement on Western Society* (London and New York, 1994). There are many lives of St Francis, not all works of hagiography. The reader will find accessible and readable Adrian House, *Francis of Assisi: A Revolutionary Life* (London, 2000). Also, John Holland Smith, *Francis of Assisi* (London, 1972), provides a fair account, if somewhat flavoured with Jungian psychology. Michael Robson gives an informed analysis in *St Francis: The Legend and the Life* (London, 1997). A valuable collection in English translation is *Francis of Assisi, Early Documents* (3 vols; ed. R.J. Armstrong, J.A.W. Hellermann and W.J. Short; New York, 1999–2001). For a reliable history of the Franciscans see John Moorman, *A History of the Franciscan Order: From its Origins to the Year 1517* (Oxford, 1968). For the early period see Rosalind Brooke, *Early Franciscan Government: Elias to Bonaventure* (Cambridge, 1959) and Cajetan Esser, *Origins of the Franciscan Order* (Eng. tr.; Chicago, 1970). The Dominicans are well served by William A. Hinnebusch in *The History of the Dominican Order: Origin and Growth to 1500* (2 vols; New York, 1965). For Dominic's life see Vladimir Koudelka, *Dominic* (tr. C. Fissler and S. Tugwell; London, 1997). For the Carmelite and Austin Friars there are no readily accessible general histories in English. For the Carmelites one will find useful articles in the journal *Carmelus*; in addition, *Carmel in Britain: Essays on the Medieval English Carmelite Province* (ed. Patrick Fitzgerald-Lombard; 2 vols; Rome, 1992) has relevant information about the largest Carmelite province. For the Austin Friars a good starting place is Francis Roth, *The English Austin Friars, 1249–1538* (2 vols; New York, 1961–66).

12

TWO LEGACIES
Universities and cathedrals

The medieval church, in a sense, is still with us. Much of the ritual – from the rite of baptism to the rite of Christian burial – remains virtually unchanged except for being vernacularized. Theological creeds, although with different emphases and nuances, are still recited. An ethic based on the Decalogue and the Sermon on the Mount continues to elicit broad acceptance, if not universal observance. This chapter focuses on two other legacies, which owe their origins largely to the twelfth and thirteenth centuries. One of these lives on wherever there are institutions of higher learning which have been influenced by the Western European model. Also, in a very physical sense, contemporary places of Christian worship commonly take their form and texture from churches whose architectural styles were formed in those crucial centuries of the high Middle Ages: when one says 'church' today, one usually thinks of a building medieval in origin.

Universities

Modern life owes much to ancient Greece, particularly the use of human reason to ask ultimate philosophical questions, yet it is not to the Greeks but to the Middle Ages that we are indebted for the existence of the university. It was a creation of the Middle Ages and had an almost inherent connection with the church. A line of descent can be drawn from the medieval universities at Bologna and Paris to almost every college and university in the Western world. A line can be seen reaching from Paris to Oxford to Cambridge to Harvard and another line from Paris to Germany to the United States in the nineteenth century. To be sure, as in any vital institution, changes have occurred, yet the essence of the university as an institution has remained unchanged: the meeting of teachers and students around books. The places to look for its origin are medieval Bologna and Paris.

At Bologna, as at other cities, traditional subjects such as grammar and rhetoric, had long been taught, but at Bologna the study of rhetoric led to the study of the drafting of documents, particularly legal documents. The recent recovery of the texts of Justinian's law books (see chapter 3) meant that the study of law could go beyond the mere drafting of documents and concentrate on the study of law itself, jurisprudence. Bologna had the great advantage of being at an important crossroads. It had the even greater advantage of having there the foremost lawyer of the day, Irnerius, who in the years from *c*.1095 to *c*.1125, in addition to practising law, almost certainly taught students the ancient laws of the Romans. There also was at Bologna – perhaps he came to study with Irnerius – a student who was to become the pre-eminent canon lawyer of the twelfth century, Gratian. There is no convincing evidence that he was a monk, and, in fact, very little is known about his life. Gratian's work, commonly called the *Decretum* (Decree), was actually entitled *Concordia discordantium canonum* (The Concord of Discordant Canons). Gratian discussed hypothetical cases and the relevant, often discordant, canons, frequently providing his solution (his concord) to the case. The *Decretum* appeared quite probably in 1140, although it had been in preparation for some time. It was a supremely successful textbook and was used in schools of canon law for almost a century. To these two towering figures at Bologna there should undoubtedly be added others, but the surviving sources fail us as to their identities. Clearly by the middle of the twelfth century Bologna had emerged as the centre for legal studies in Europe. To be sure, liberal arts continued to be studied at Bologna, and, eventually, theology and medicine were added. Contemporaries, in time, would give this type of institution the name *studium*. In the middle of the twelfth century, the fame of Bologna as a centre for the study of law soon attracted students from all over Italy (Cismontane) and also from other countries north of the Alps (Transmontane). It was from the self-organization of students at Bologna that the university was to evolve.

Foreign students at Bologna formed a society principally to protect themselves from local police, who could be harsh, from local landlords, who could be rapacious, and from local booksellers, who could inflate prices. But they also organized themselves, no doubt, for social purposes. These foreign students called their organization by the word *universitas*, which simply meant a guild or association or society. It was a word in common use at the time: for example, *universitas artium* was a guild of artisans. Thus organized in their *universitas*, the foreign students could go beyond self-protection from the townsfolk and companionship. They could and did threaten to boycott their teachers, withhold fees and even to leave Bologna *en masse*, if their demands were not met. Soon, Italian students formed their own *universitas*. Before long the two guilds were acting as one and, in effect, took control of the *studium*. Their threats were far from idle. A number of migrations occurred – to Vicenza (1204), Arezzo (1215), Padua (1222) and, most dramatically, Siena (1321) – and on some migrations the masters joined the students in protest against the commune of Bologna. Yet the students were clearly in control. In the earliest statutes (*c*.1317), almost certainly codifying longtime practices, the student *universitas* insisted on getting value for money:

> No master is allowed to begin his morning lecture before the bell
> at St Peter's finished ringing for the daily Mass.

The master must begin his lecture immediately under penalty of twenty solidi.

He must not continue his lecture after the ringing of the bell for Terce.

The students under penalty of ten solidi must leave at the ringing of the bell.

No master should omit as much as a single paragraph of the law text.

No master should absent himself from Bologna except with the permission of the students, in which case he will deposit the sum of one hundred pounds or an article of equal value to insure that, already having been paid by the students, he would return to complete the course of lectures.

Bologna was a *studium* without an administration. Students paid fees directly to their teachers. The teachers eventually did organize themselves into their own guild, and, although they had control over admitting students as doctors, theirs was always a subsidiary role. The *studium* at Bologna was clearly run by the *universitas* of students.

No roster of early students at Bologna exists, but many, probably the majority, must have been ecclesiastics. Pope Honorius III, in 1219, ruled that no doctors should be made without the consent of the archdeacon of Bologna. Whatever its position before 1219, the *studium* at Bologna was henceforth an ecclesiastical institution. And at some point – no one knows exactly when – the word *universitas* replaced the word *studium* to describe the institution itself. This Bolognese model of the student-controlled university was followed generally in southern European universities such as Montpellier, Naples, Padua, Reggio, Vicenza and Vercelli.

At Paris a *studium* also emerged, but its circumstances were different from Bologna's. Several schools had developed in Paris, most notably one at Notre-Dame Cathedral, where in the cathedral precincts masters taught students, which, indeed, also happened at other French cathedrals. But Paris was blessed by a superb location at the crossroads not of a peninsula, like Bologna, but of Western Europe north of the Alps. From at least the thirteenth century Paris was Europe's leading city. It was also blessed by the quality and popularity of masters, like Abelard, who attracted large numbers of students from France itself and from beyond. At some point in the last half of the twelfth century this centre of study evolved into what we today call a university and what contemporaries, as we have seen at Bologna, called a *studium*. There was no great moment of creation, simply a series of minor changes, which, in sum, changed the school at which Abelard was master in 1118 to a *studium* before the century's end. How did this happen? From what survives it is possible to reconstruct, at least in broad terms, what transpired at Paris. It was the chancellor of the cathedral who permitted masters to teach there. He had authority over granting degrees, as we would say. Actually, he granted successful students a *licentia docendi* (licence of teaching), a teacher's certification to teach a subject as a master or doctor or professor, which were synonymous terms. The admission of a student to this degree (i.e., level) was attended with a certain amount of ceremony and concluded with the welcoming of the new master by those already masters at Notre-Dame with the consumption of food and drink at the new master's expense. A sense of the masters forming a group developed, and soon Paris had its *universitas*, but, unlike Bologna, it was a *universitas* of masters, and it ruled the *studium*. Although in modern times the University of Paris uses the year 1200 as a reference point for anniversary celebrations, the *studium* predates 1200 by at least several decades. Early in the thirteenth century the mutual obligations of members of the guild were written down, and they read like the obligations of other guilds: they were to wear the garments of their profession (academic robes), attend the funerals of other members and observe a common order in their teaching. The students were subsumed into the *universitas* of masters, clearly as junior members, and the *universitas* came to represent both masters and students.

What happened in 1200 was that King Philip Augustus granted the students at Paris exemption from secular jurisdiction because they were clerics or considered clerics. Like so many major moments in the constitutional history of medieval universities, this grant was precipitated by an incident in a tavern. A young German nobleman, then archdeacon of Liège and bishop-elect of that see, was a student at Paris, quite likely of theology. His servant got involved in a tavern brawl. To retaliate students from the German 'nation' attacked the tavern-keeper, leaving him near death. The provost of Paris, in charge of public order, led an armed band of Parisians to the residence of the German students. There they slew several students, including the bishop-elect. The *universitas* was in an uproar, and, fearing they would secede from Paris and take the *studium* elsewhere, the king condemned the actions of the townsmen. The provost was to be imprisoned for life – in the event, he broke his neck in an escape attempt – and the others, if apprehended, were to receive the same punishment. More importantly, the king issued what is sometimes, but misleadingly, called a charter, as if it were a foundation charter, which it clearly was not. In any case, the University of Paris was not founded: it evolved imperceptibly from the cathedral school during the second half of the twelfth century. The king freed the *universitas* from secular jurisdiction and affirmed the place of students as clerics under the jurisdiction of the church:

> Our provost and our judges shall not lay hands on a student for any offense. They shall not imprison him, unless the student has committed a crime that warrants arrest. In this case, our judge shall arrest him without violence, unless he resists, and shall hand him over to the ecclesiastical judge.

Further, the present provost and future provosts were required to take an oath in the presence of the students to observe these provisions. Thus the independence of the *studium* from local secular authorities was assured and its nature as an ecclesiastical institution affirmed. More was to come.

On the eve of Ash Wednesday (*Mardi Gras*) in 1229, a group of students were celebrating in the suburb of St Marcel, where in a tavern they found wine that was 'good and sweet' (*optimum . . . et . . . suave*). When the bill was presented, they felt that the tavern-keeper was trying to take advantage of their condition and had generously padded the bill. Words were spoken, then shouted, and blows were soon struck. Neighbours came to the rescue of the tavern-keeper and inflicted a beating on the students. The latter were not long in seeking revenge. Very early the next morning, the students returned and with them a large number of their fellow students, armed with swords and clubs. Before the neighbourhood was aroused, the students broke into the tavern and committed the outrage of opening the taps on all the wine casks, thus causing a river of the 'good and sweet' wine to course out of the tavern and along the narrow street. The neighbours were now aroused, and they alerted the provost, who with a band of supporters attacked the frolicking students, leaving several of them dead. On hearing of this tragedy, the masters instantly suspended lectures. The Lenten season saw no resolution to the matter, and on Easter Monday the masters announced that they would leave Paris for six years, and the majority of masters did leave, some went to the universities by then existing at Oxford and Cambridge in England, others to places in France like Toulouse, Orléans, Rheims and Angers. In 1231, Pope Gregory IX intervened, and a settlement was reached to the great advantage of the *studium*. The pope gave great praise for Paris, which, even when discounted for rhetorical excess, provides an indication of the high esteem in which Paris was held:

> Paris, parent of studies, city of letters, shines brilliantly and, great in masters and students, she gives great hope.

Gregory enjoined the king of France to see that the privileges of the *universitas* were respected and observed:

> We, in view of the needs of the church, hereby will and order that hereafter our dearest son, the illustrious king of France, shall insure that the privileges of the masters and students be acknowledged.

The right to suspend lectures was explicitly stated:

> If satisfaction for death or for the mutilation of a limb with respect to any member of your university be refused, you may suspend lectures. And, if any of you be unjustly imprisoned, you may immediately cease lectures.

Moreover, the pope addressed the internal tensions within the *studium*. The chancellor of Notre-Dame had to swear that he would not grant the licence to unworthy candidates and, in any case, he would take the advice of existing masters at Paris. Here can be seen a major step in the movement of the *studium* away from the jurisdiction of the cathedral. A physical move away from the cathedral also occurred as the *studium* moved from the streets around Notre-Dame towards the Petit Pont at the Seine, then over the bridge to the left bank, where it created the Latin Quarter, thereafter the site of the University of Paris. It would be a mistake for us to think of the university as a complex of buildings; it was, rather, a community of masters and students scattered in rented houses where lectures were given with faculty meetings being held in local churches and taverns.

Oxford, it was once said, derived from English masters who left Paris in 1167 in the midst of the Henry II–Becket controversy (see chapter 9). It is true – the date is uncertain but probably after 1169 – that Henry II did prohibit English students from going to Paris without royal permission and threatened beneficed English students abroad with loss of their income if they did not return to England, but this did not lead to the founding of Oxford, although the *universitas* that developed at Oxford was of the Parisian model. The number of beneficed English students at Paris probably was not large, and, in any case, there is no evidence that those that returned went to Oxford, although perhaps some did. There were other schools in England, notably Hereford, York, Winchester, Lincoln and Northampton. When the last mentioned had difficulty in the early 1190s in guaranteeing the safety of its students, the *studium* then at Oxford seems to have benefited. Although Oxford did not have a cathedral – it was in Lincoln diocese – nor a major collegiate church, nonetheless it stood advantageously on the River Thames at the border of Wessex and Mercia and at an important cross-roads. England's greatest town, London, would not have its university until the nineteenth century and the great seats of the two archbishops, Canterbury and York, not until the second half of the twentieth century. The origin of a *studium* at Oxford is shrouded in mist. There may have been a school at the church of St George-in-the-Castle, which evolved into a *studium*. Even more persuasively, a nucleus of canon lawyers had gathered at Oxford in the last half of the twelfth century to work in the ecclesiastical courts there, and, as at Bologna, they probably attracted students. Whatever its origins, the *studium* was clearly in place by the mid-1180s, although it was still taking shape. Gerald of Wales (*Giraldus Cambrensis*) described how he read his recently written *Topographia Hibernica* (in about 1187) to the masters and students at Oxford, 'where the clergy in England flourished and excelled'. He reported his visit:

> On the first day he received at his lodgings all the scholars of the whole town. On the second day, all the doctors of different faculties and their more notable students. On the third day, the rest of the scholars as well as many knights, townsfolk and burghers.

This sounds suspiciously like nothing less than a substantial scholastic site, in other words, a *studium*.

The origin of Cambridge can be more clearly defined, although questions still remain. A tragic event or, rather, a series of tragic events at Oxford was the genesis. In 1209 an Oxford student had become involved with a woman of the town, perhaps a prostitute, and, when she died suddenly, the student said it was an accident, but the men of the town did not believe him. Led by the mayor and the burgesses, a crowd of townsmen descended on the student's residence. They seized several of the students and appealed to King John, then near by at Woodstock, who gave permission for the students to be executed. The *suspendium clericorum* (the hanging of the students) proved to be an event of major moment for two universities. The masters at Oxford immediately closed the *studium*, and they and their students – one account says there were 3,000, clearly an exaggeration – migrated to other places like Reading, Paris and some to the sleepy fenland town of Cambridge. There at Cambridge a new *studium* came into being, clearly a daughter of Oxford, and it was soon to have its own statutes and masters teaching the arts, theology, law and medicine. But why Cambridge? The attempts of the ablest modern scholars have not produced evidence of a school already existing there either at a religious house or at a church, a school to which the Oxford men would have attached themselves in 1209. The suggestion is made that some of the migrants were originally from Cambridge. Others suggest that the bishop of Ely, a town only fifteen miles from Cambridge, had Oxford graduates in his household and that they invited fleeing masters to come to Cambridge. As attractive as these suggestions may appear, firm evidence is sadly lacking about the reason for the migration to Cambridge.

While the tragic events of 1209 led to the founding of Cambridge, they had their effect at Oxford itself. Except for a few scabs who carried on teaching there, the boycott persisted until 1214, when the king, then papally excommunicated, made his peace with Innocent III. The resolution of the Oxford dispute quickly followed, brokered by the papal legate, to the humiliation of the townsmen and to the growing independence of the *universitas* from the town. Those men of the town responsible for the outrage on the students were to walk barefoot and cloakless, leading the whole town to where the students were buried, and from there they were to take the bodies to a cemetery for proper Christian burial. For the next ten years the landlords had to reduce by half the rents charged to students. In addition, the town was to provide a sum of money annually for poor students. The masters were free to return, but the scab-masters were not allowed to teach for the next three years. It was agreed that thereafter, whenever a student was arrested by the town, he would be handed over to the *universitas*, which would handle the matter. Both Paris and Oxford, as a consequence of the apparent overreaction of their towns to student misdeeds, gained a significant degree of corporate autonomy.

Other universities were to spring up, generally creatures of the fourteenth and fifteenth centuries. As remarkable as it may seem, Germany had no universities before 1347, when Charles IV, king of Bohemia, established the University of Prague. A francophile, Charles gave the new university a constitution based on

Uppsala 1477

Aberdeen 1495

St. Andrews 1411

Glasgow 1451

Copenhagen 1475

Greifswald 1456

Rostock 1419

Frankfurt-on-Oder 1496

Cambridge 1209–25

Oxford

Louvain 1425

Cologne 1388

Erfurt 1379

Leipzig 1409

Caen 1432

Trier 1454

Mainz 1476

Prague 1347

Paris

Heidelberg 1385

Wurzburg 1402

Cracow 1364

Nantes 1460

Angers

Orléans c.1236

Freiburg i.B 1457

Ingolstadt 1476

Tubingen 1459

c.1250

Bourges 1464

Dole 1422

Basel 1459

Vienna 1366

Pozsony 1465

Poitiers 1431

Grenoble 1339

Pavia 1361

Verona (1339)

Bude 1338

Bordeaux 1441

Vercelli 1228

Piacenza 1248

Vicenza 1204

Treviso 1318

Cahors 1332

Valence 1452

Turin 1401

Venice 1470

Pecs 1367

Orange 1365

Avignon 1303

Padua 1222

Ferrara 1391

Toulouse 1229

Montpellier

Bologna

Palencia (1206)

Aix 1409

Genoa (1471)

Lucca (1369)

Salamanca 1218–19

Valladolid 1300

Husses 1354

Perpignan 1360

Parma 1412

Florence 1349

Coimbra 1308

Siguenza 1489

Saragossa 1474

Lerida 1300

Reggio 1188

Siena 1246

Arezzo 1215

Perugia 1308

Alcale 1499

Gerone (1446)

Pisa 1343

Rome

Lisbon 1290

Barcelona 1450

Studium curiae 1245

Studium urbis 1303

Valencia 1500

Naples 1224

Salerno

Seville (1254–60)

Palma 1483

Catania 1444

(1250) Date uncertain

0   250 km

I. Wei From H. de Ridder-Symoens (ed.)
A History of the University Europe Vol. 1 (CUP, 1992)

Map 16 Medieval universities.

Paris. In 1365, the Habsburg duke of Austria, Rudolph IV, established a university at Vienna 'according to the ordinances and customs observed first in Athens, then at Rome, and later at Paris'. When a university was established at Heidelberg in 1386, both the local ruler and the pope insisted that it be founded on the model of the *studium* of Paris and that it enjoy the same privileges. By then there was a university at Cracow in Poland and two years later one at Cologne and another at Buda in Hungary. The march was on. To mention only a few: Leuven in the Low Countries (1426), Basel in Switzerland (1459), Uppsala in Sweden (1477) and, in Scotland, St Andrews (1413), Glasgow (1451) and Aberdeen (1494). By the end of the fifteenth century Europe was dotted with up to eighty universities. And there were others existing only on paper: Dublin (1312), Verona (1339) and Geneva (1365). What happened at the medieval universities remains to be seen.

Like the modern university, its medieval ancestor had what we would call an undergraduate level and a post-graduate level. The liberal arts were meant to be studied first and only afterwards theology, law or medicine. Some members of religious orders, in the face of stiff opposition, omitted the arts course and went directly to the post-graduate schools. A word first about the arts course. The seven liberal arts, at least notionally, comprised the arts curriculum: the *trivium* of grammar, rhetoric and logic and the *quadrivium* of arithmetic, geometry, astronomy and music. In practice, the *trivium* triumphed over the *quadrivium*, which received less and less attention. And in the *trivium* it was logic that triumphed over grammar and rhetoric or, it can be said, that it was Aristotle who triumphed in the arts curriculum. Logic came to mean philosophy, and Aristotle was known simply as The Philosopher. The availability of the works of Aristotle, mostly through the medium of Arabic translations, had a profound influence on the universities. The length of the arts course varied from time to time, but an early statute required five years in the study of the prescribed texts, leading to the students becoming masters, and then two further years as regent masters, when they taught. Some of these masters of arts went on to study in one of the professional faculties, but the temptation to see masters of arts moving *en masse* into the higher schools must be resisted. At Paris, famous for its school of theology, the number of students in that school was never large, although precise numbers are not easy to come by. The curriculum in theology was a long one, requiring about twelve years of study. By papal decree clerics holding benefices could absent themselves from their benefices for part of their study, hiring a curate with some of their income, the remainder being a type of bursary or scholarship. The theological student first studied the Bible, after which he became a *baccalaureus biblicus* (bachelor of the Bible). Then he studied systematic theology, using as a textbook the *Sentences* of Peter Lombard, which set out theology in four books (about the nature of God, about creation and fall of man, about the Incarnation, Redemption and the virtues, and, finally, about the sacraments and last things), after which he became a *baccalaureus sententiarius* (bachelor of the Sentences). Finally, he performed a series of academic exercises, leading to his becoming a *baccalaureus formatus* (a formed or complete bachelor). His course was then complete. He had only some formalities to observe and was then awarded his licence and became a master of theology. By that time he would have been at least thirty-five years of age. This education provided for a close reading of at least several books of the Old and New Testaments and for a speculative approach to the theological questions raised by the author of the *Sentences*. This textual study was grounded in Aristotelian philosophy. It was an intellectually rigorous and sophisticated approach to the *mater scientiarum* (mother of knowledge).

The word – and variations of it – that is commonly used to describe the medieval university is 'scholasticism'. Those who taught there are called scholastics (or sometimes the variant 'schoolmen'). The danger in using the word 'scholasticism' is that it can be understood to mean what was taught at the medieval universities, as if that teaching formed a monolith. Anyone who reads the works of the scholastics will quickly realize the great variety of opinion. Debates, sometimes heated, were part of and, indeed, essential to the nature of the medieval university. When used to refer to a body of knowledge, even a differentiated body of knowledge, the word 'scholasticism' is being used only in an extended sense. It properly refers not to what was taught but how it was taught, to the form of teaching, to the pedagogy of the medieval university, to which we should now turn.

Two elements comprised the pedagogy of the medieval university, the *expositio textuum* and the *disputatio*. At the core of the first of these was the fact that for each subject there was an authority. For example, in philosophy the authority was Aristotle; in mathematics Euclid; in medicine Galen; in Roman law Justinian; in canon law Gratian and, after 1234, the *Decretals* of Gregory IX; and in theology the Bible. The authority was the source of knowledge, and learning became an exploration of the meaning of the authority. The lecturer read the text and explained it. He did not give an opinion about it, and he did not differ with the authority nor contradict him. He merely exposed the text of the authority as clearly as possible. It was later said that philosophy became not the study of being but the study of Aristotle. That accusation might be credible, were it not for the second element in scholasticism.

The disputation emerged in the twelfth century from problems remaining after the exposition of the text. The master set aside one or two periods each week to discuss unresolved questions, such as the apparent conflict of two texts from the same authority. Soon the master would use these periods to set a question for his students. One student would propose an answer, another would respond and the master would determine (or resolve) the question. These sessions became formalized into the medieval disputation.

The Paris master best known to moderns is Thomas Aquinas. Two series of disputed questions posed by him are known to be extant. His disputations associated with the virtues (book 3 of the *Sentences*) took place in 1269–72. For example, he asked, 'Do we possess virtues naturally?' Arguments pro and con were given by students, each citing authorities and using arguments from reason. Master Thomas responded that 'there is a difference of opinion' and determined that virtue is in us naturally only as an aptitude and not as a perfection. And so it went, a give-and-take which went beyond the formal lecture and which gave a richness to the learning process.

In addition, there was the *quodlibet* (what-you-will) disputation, which was the most popular academic exercise of the medieval university. A master would announce that at a particular time, generally before Easter or Christmas, he would hold a *quodlibet* disputation. He was not required to do so, and many masters never did. The disputation was open to all students and masters and to others as well, and the master was prepared to entertain questions from the floor on any subject (*quodlibet*). Subjects raised often went beyond the terms of academic discussion and could be concerned with current political and ecclesiastical issues such as the suppression of the Knights Templar. To lighten the atmosphere, occasionally frivolous questions might be asked – 'Whether a drunk can be sobered by drinking oil?', 'Whether redheads can be trusted?', 'Whether monks have to be fatter than other people?' In time, the verb *quodlibetare* came into use and is the direct ancestor of our *quibble*. These occasional frivolities of the *quodlibet* aside, the disputation complemented the exposition of the text and produced students who were aware of the accepted opinions and who also had the ability to speculate and to be engaged in intellectual exchange at the highest level. This was medieval scholasticism.

Not many physical remains of medieval universities survive: the churches of St Julien-le-Pauvre and St Séverin at Paris, parts of Merton College at Oxford and Peterhouse at Cambridge but not much else for the period before 1300. What does survive is the institution itself. For medieval physical remains we now turn to actual stone and mortar.

Cathedrals

Scattered across Western Europe today are churches, almost without number, which were built in the Middle Ages. One estimate suggests that in medieval times there was one church for every 200 people. One can visit villages, for example, in remote parts of France or England and find tiny churches that date from the twelfth to the fifteenth centuries, most of them in continuous use since they were built. It was in such simple, often unadorned places that the people of Europe worshipped, where children were baptized, where the feasts of the liturgical year were celebrated, where villagers came on Sundays to Mass and who came on other days perhaps just to sit in the quiet of a holy place and where obsequies were pronounced over the dead. Yet architecturally the crowning glory of the medieval church must be the great cathedrals, the seats of the bishop of a diocese. From Sweden and Poland in the East to Spain and Brittany and Ireland in the West there stood in great towns the cathedral, the centre of religious life for a whole region. There were seventeen cathedrals in England, four in Wales and eleven in Scotland, nearly a hundred in France and even more in Italy. They were large buildings, made to accommodate a town's entire population. The thirteenth-century cathedral at Amiens could accommodate about 2,000 people, which was the population of Amiens. In 1944, when Paris was liberated, General de Gaulle led about 12,000 people into Notre-Dame Cathedral. Frequently sited on prominent hilltops, such as at Laon and Lincoln, the cathedral dominated the landscape. In stone and mortar it was the supreme achievement of the medieval church.

To look for origins one must go back to pre-medieval times, when in the period following the emancipation of the church by Constantine's edict (313) the church was able to construct places of worship. The historian Eusebius wrote

> There was unspeakable joy as we saw that every place, previously reduced to dust by tyrannical wickedness, was now coming back to life and that churches were rising from their foundations.
>
> (Bk 10, ch. 2)

What the church adopted was the style of the Roman basilica (from βασιλική, royal), an administrative building, used as a court and place of public assembly. In the beginning some existing basilicas were actually converted for use as churches. The Christians placed a forecourt (*atrium*) with a central fountain in front of their basilica. The building itself was a rectangle with a semicircular projection (apse) at one end, where the magistrate sat and where now the officiating priest would sit behind an altar; at the other end, through which worshippers would enter, there was usually a vestibule (narthex), but sometimes just a covered portico. Running the length of the basilica were two (sometimes four) rows of columns, which created a wide area in the centre (nave, from *navis*, ship) and an aisle (sometimes two) to the side of the columns. In the course of time, a room was added to one side near the apse for storing materials needed for liturgical ceremonies, and, soon after that, a corresponding room on the opposite side. Thus, unintentionally these projections (transepts) created a cruciform building. Also, in time, the basilica was built on an east–west axis with the apsidal end facing east towards Jerusalem. The superstructure was three storeys high. At the ground level rising from the floor to the tops of arches which bridged the columns was the arcading. The slender columns were joined to one another by typical Roman round arches, and the arcading supported the relatively light weight of the ceiling. Above each row of columns, from west to east, ran an architrave, perhaps four or five inches wide, which, if one stood at the west end of the nave, drew one's eyes eastward towards the apse. The architrave separated the arcading from the second storey, the triforium, an area of wall, perhaps five feet or so wide, which was usually decorated, frequently with mosaics. Above the triforum was a storey with clear windows called the clerestory. A wooden roof enclosed the structure.

A classic example is the church of St Paul-Without-the-Walls at Rome, built in 386, one of the first with an east–west orientation, although what we see today is not the original but an almost exact replica built after the fire of 1823:

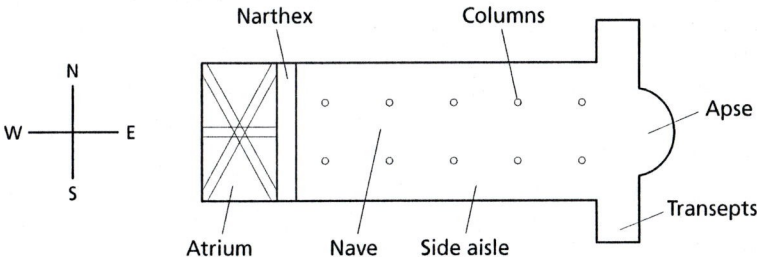

Figure 1 Floor plan of Christian basilica.

a courtyard, narthex, nave, four sets of twenty columns, providing four side aisles, a decorated triforium, fenestrated clerestory and, at the east end, an apse topped by a semi-dome. In Ravenna the church of S. Apollinare Nuovo, completed by Emperor Justinian in the sixth century, with the more usual two sets of columns and two side aisles, has at the triforium level a mosaic of a procession moving towards the apse. Although the Basilican style continued to be used in Italy – San Clemente in Rome was built in the eleventh century – two new forms of church architecture, uniquely medieval, developed. The Basilican style bequeathed to the Romanesque and Gothic two essential elements: the floor plan and the elevations. These continued to be used in church architecture to modern times.

12   St Paul's-Without-the-Walls, Rome, a nineteenth-century print. Reproduced by permission of the Courtauld Institute of Art.

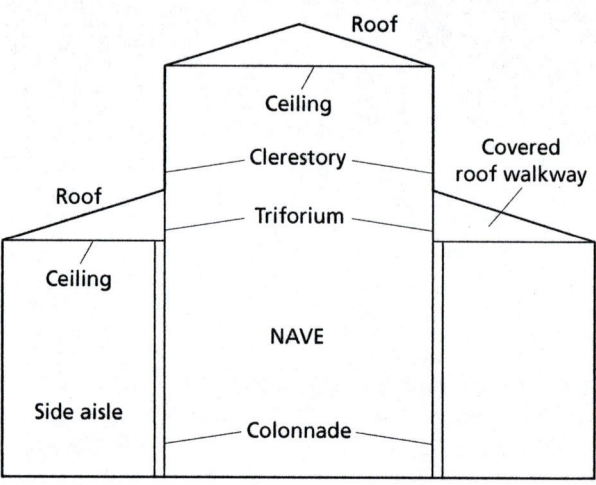

Figure 2 Cross-section of Christian basilica.

The designers of the Romanesque church faced two problems. In the first place, wooden roofs were easily combustible. The solution – not totally successful – was stone ceilings, called vaults. Secondly, since many priests wanted to say Mass daily and since at this time each altar could be used for only one Mass a day – like the priest, it had to be fasting – a church with a simple altar would not meet the devotional needs of the times in monastic and cathedral churches, where there were many priests. The answer clearly was additional altars. The resolution of these problems helped to shape the church of the Romanesque period (*c.*1000–*c.*1150). The floor plan, still basilican, was adapted to create new spaces for altars at the east end. This was fairly easily accomplished by the use of either a staggered or a radiating plan. The staggered plan, used mostly in monastic churches, extended the area of the nave beyond the transept and added side chapels off that extended area (this area east of the crossing now called the choir), where altars were placed. They were also placed in the transepts and at the east end of each aisle. Their orientation was eastward. The radiating plan was to have a more dominant influence. In this plan the side aisles were extended to form a walkway (ambulatory) around the apse, and off the ambulatory radiated chapels that extended as semicircular structures beyond the east wall. The church of St Sernin at Toulouse, begun *c.*1080, has five chapels radiating off the east end and two off each of its transepts. The church of St Martin in Tours, begun in the late 990s, had a similar system of radiating chapels at the east end. The church known as Cluny III (*c.*1120) had fifteen radiating chapels. At the west end of the Romanesque church the atrium of the basilica was now lost, at least in northern Europe. Creating a stone ceiling (vault) over the nave posed serious engineering problems of support. The sheer weight of the vault required the abandoning

13 Nave elevation, ruins of Jumiège Abbey. Reproduced by permission of James Austin.

of the slender columns of the Christian basilica, since they would simply have crumbled under the weight of the stone vault. They were replaced with massive pillars, placed fairly close together and joined by the traditional round arches. Also, the outer walls were vastly thicker. Since the walls supplied most of the

Clerestory

Triforium

Archetrave

Colonnade
(arcading)

Figure 3 Internal elevation of Christian basilica.

support for the vault, little space could be afforded for windows, which now tended to be small in size and few in number.

How was the stone vault shaped? The easiest, least complicated way to cover the space with stone was to use a vault resembling a section of a barrel, a semi-cylinder, which ran from one end to the other. The *barrel vault* at first ran unbroken, but in time arched bands of stone, crossing the nave from pillar to pillar, helped to give more support and, importantly, helped to create the bay, which was to feature in all subsequent church architecture. The bay was formed by four pillars, two on either side of the nave, and the arches connecting them. The space created by the arches AB and CD and the transverse arches AC and BD and their supporting pillars formed the bay ABCD.

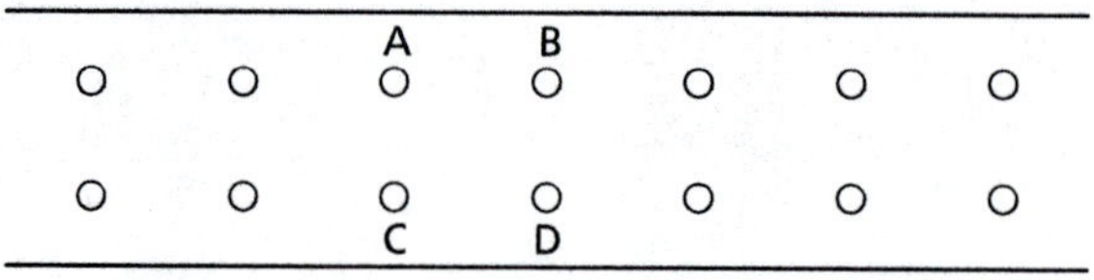

```
              A    B
   O    O     O    O     O    O    O

   O    O     O    O     O    O    O
              C    D
```

Figure 4 Formation of the bay.

The barrel vault was soon modified. The vault over each bay could be formed separately, which resulted in the *groin vault*. It was formed by the intersection of two barrel vaults above the bay. (Another way to look at this development is to consider the bay created where the barrel vault of the nave met the barrel vault of the transepts and to say simply that the vaulting of this bay was replicated in every bay in the nave.) No additional arches were required, just the same arches as for the barrel vault, but now the groin allowed the use of much lighter stone, supported by mortar and the curvature of the stones, since the weight fell not

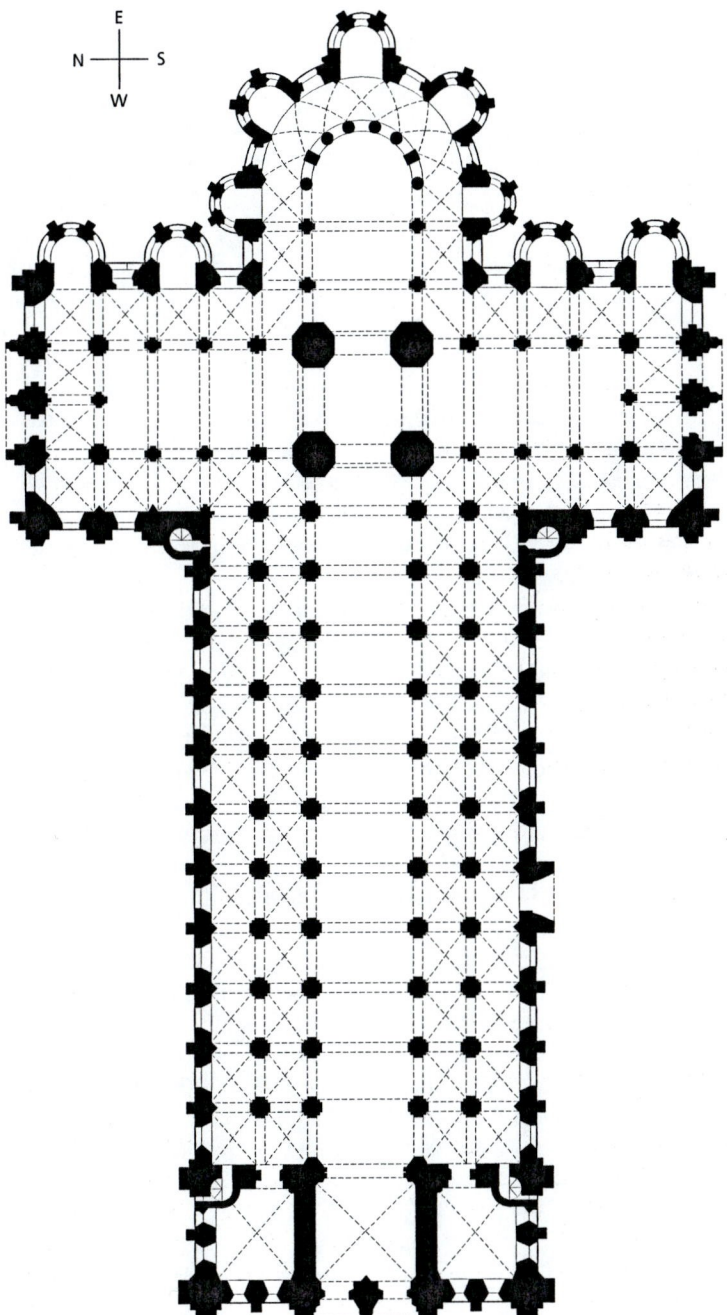

Figure 5 Floor plan of St Sernin, Toulouse.

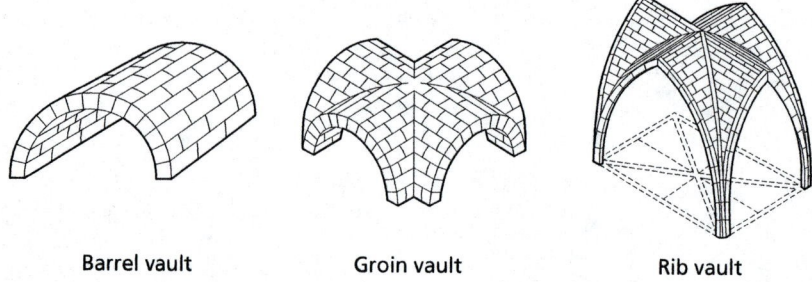

Barrel vault   Groin vault   Rib vault

Figure 6 Vaults: barrel, groin, rib.

evenly along the wall, as in the barrel, but at the four points of the pillars. The shape of the groin vaulting could now allow for more and larger windows. By 1100 the groin vault was covering the naves of many large churches, such as the naves of the church of the Madeleine at Vézelay in Burgundy and the cathedral at Speyer. Within a few decades there emerged from the groin vault a new vaulting that was to give birth to the Gothic.

The *rib vault* made use of the bay division and covered the space of the bay by using three sets of arches: (i) two wall (or lateral) arches, AB and CD, (ii) two transverse arches, AC and BD, in use since the advent of the barrel vault, and, what was new, (iii) two diagonal vaults, AD and BC. By creating a skeleton of these six arches the stone mason could then fill in the spaces (the web) with light stones cut to fit, supported by scaffolding till the mortar dried and then, as in the groin vault, by the weight of the bonded stones in the resulting curvature. Where the rib vault was first used continues to interest architectural historians. Whether in Lombardy, Normandy or Norman England – and there is really no reason to think this development could not have occurred independently in different places about the same time – a look at Durham Cathedral should be instructive. Sited at the top of a promontory at the end of a loop of the River Wear, it dominates the area in such a way that Sir Walter Scott, with typical exaggeration, called it 'half church of God, half castle 'gainst the Scots'. Save for some thirteenth-century improvements at the far east end, it remains to this day little altered from the time when Benedictine monks built their cathedral-monastery as a shrine to St Cuthbert. A very early, perhaps the earliest, example of high rib vaulting can be seen in the

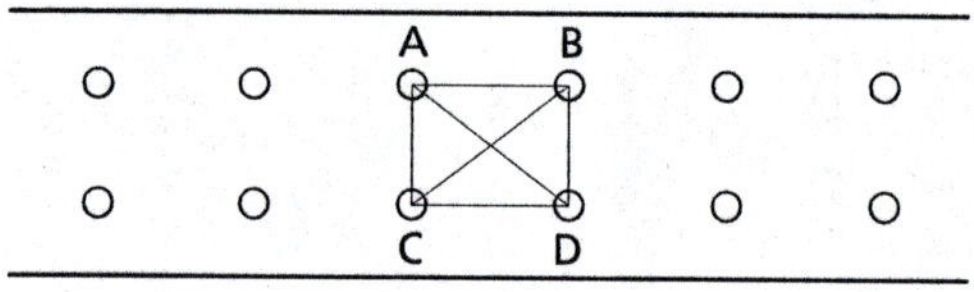

Figure 7 Formation of the rib vault.

14 Durham Cathedral. Reproduced by permission of Durham Cathedral.

choir, which was begun in 1093 and rib-vaulted by 1104, and rib vaulting covered the nave by 1133. Whatever the truth of the claim of Durham that its choir is the earliest use of rib vaulting, it can be said that the cathedral as a whole was probably the earliest structure completely covered by rib vaulting. Gothic was not far away.

Several observations should be made before we look at Gothic. In the first place, it needs to be said that Romanesque church architecture should be seen not merely as a prelude to Gothic: it can stand on its own. The massive size of the pillars and limitations of fenestration produced what is seen today as a fairly dark interior. In the medieval period the interior would have been colourfully decorated or, at the least, whitewashed. Often thought of as French, the Romanesque, in fact, was truly an international style. Parts of Roskilde Cathedral in Denmark (by 1088) and Lund Cathedral in Sweden (by 1146) are in the Romanesque style. On Orkney, the archipelago of islands north of Scotland, at its principal town, Kirkwall ('church bay'), one finds a Romanesque cathedral dedicated to the Norse earl-saint, Magnus, a remarkable structure of red sandstone. At Santiago de Compostela a Romanesque cathedral with a nave more than three hundred feet long was consecrated in 1211; a Baroque façade was added to the west front in the eighteenth century. The cathedral at Pisa has classical Romanesque elevation but is covered by a wooden ceiling. And so it went throughout Western Europe, the widespread use of the Romanesque style but often with local variations.

The Gothic style was many things which the Romanesque was not. It gives the impression of openness and light. It came into use first in the mid-twelfth century and by the second quarter of the thirteenth century had replaced Romanesque for new church construction almost everywhere and remained the style for churches of every size for the rest of the Middle Ages and, in many places, to modern times. To say that Gothic is characterized by the pointed arch and the height of its elevation is merely to describe two of its most obvious elements, but Gothic architecture is a harmonious ensemble of many things. Henry Adams famously compared the rough, heavy masculinity of the Romanesque to the graceful, delicate femininity of the Gothic. Another observer has called it 'perhaps the most creative achievement in the history of Western architecture'. A history professor at Vienna proclaimed that 'the Gothic church is a vision of paradise, the heavenly Jerusalem'. And others similarly. Yet still others have taken a different view. For example, Vasari (d. 1574) said it was 'a malediction of pinnacles'. Here we are on the ground of subjective taste, which the historian should feel quaking under his feet and move on.

The floor plans of most Gothic cathedrals reveal three modifications from earlier styles. The choir, the area east of the crossing of nave and transepts, is greatly extended. At Notre-Dame in Paris the choir is almost half the length of the cathedral. This meant in practice that the laity were further and further removed from the altar; in some churches this separation was further emphasized by the building of a stone screen at the entrance to the choir. Radiating chapels continue to define the east end, as they did in Romanesque churches. Still, the floor plan even with these modifications remains the basilican floor plan, which had been in use since the fourth century. The same three elevations, first used in the Christian basilica, continued to be used in the Gothic.

In examining the Gothic elevations, there can be no question about the significance of the rib vault in its development. Without the rib vault there would not be Gothic as we know it. The ribs provided the framework for the fairly light stone and allowed the bays to be rectangular and the nave to be much taller. The three sets of arches in the early rib vaulting were round arches. If they covered a square, which in the early stages they did, then the wall arches and the transverse arches were of equal size, whereas the diagonal arch, the hypotenuse of a right triangle, was obviously longer. The diagonal arches could reach to a point higher than the crowns of the other arches, thus producing a conical effect. To raise the level of these other arches to the level of the diagonals was accomplished by making these wall and transverse arches pointed in shape. The pointed arch was known before the Gothic but now it was made an integral part of the new style. It was formed not by two straight lines meeting at an angle but by two portions of a circle meeting at an angle. This form of the pointed or broken arch provided a more vertical thrust for the weight of the vault than did the Romanesque. In time, even the diagonal arches might occasionally, although rarely, become pointed. The result consequent upon the use of rib vaulting and pointed arches was greater verticality. Virtually all that was needed to support these increasingly taller structures was buttressing at the outer wall at the exterior points corresponding to the interior pillars. Walls between the buttresses were scarcely needed for support and, hence, could be opened up to allow light to flood the side aisle. The higher the building meant the higher the clerestory and the more window space in the clerestory to bring light to the nave. Of course, higher clerestories required higher buttressing at the point of stress, and this need gave rise to the flying buttress. The external buttress was raised from the level of the side aisle roof to about the level of the nave roof and from it, extended shafts of masonry to the clerestory wall. Neither the rib vault, the pointed arch nor the flying buttress was designed for ornamental or aesthetic purposes. In their beginnings, they were clearly functional or constructional: the rib vault to allow the easy assembly of the stone web, the pointed arch to allow more verticality and the flying buttress to hold the clerestory wall from collapsing outward under the weight of the stone vault. Decoration came later: sculptured programmes in the portals and elsewhere, gargoyles spitting out rainwater from their spouts, stained-glass windows and pinnacles, often by the score, although the latter were also functional. The different periods of Gothic were but variations on the same basic theme.

Gothic emerged in the middle of the twelfth century in the region of France around Paris, the Île-de-France. The earliest known example of Gothic was at the abbey church of St Denis, then just outside Paris. Abbot Suger, a close adviser to the French king, undertook the gradual replacement of the Carolingian church, a shrine to the national saint, a place long associated with the monarchy.

15 Ambulatory, church of St Denis, Paris. Reproduced by permission of the
Courtauld Institute of Art.

Construction of the west façade began in 1137 and what was produced became the standard design for the façades of great Gothic churches: three great portals, which were highly decorated and separated by columns and colonnettes, themselves usually with sculpted figures, and, above the portal, a wheel (rose) window, the whole arrangement framed by towers at each end. Yet it was at the east end, the choir, which was consecrated in 1144, that were first realized those features which are considered the essential characteristics of Gothic. The columns supporting the rib vaults of the ambulatory were slender and the windows in the shallow, radiating chapels produced a richness of light. The impression was one of space and lightness. Time – and the French Revolution – destroyed much of Suger's achievement, particularly in the upper elevations, but the ground floor remains with its forest of thin columns in its double ambulatory. Others followed Suger's example.

Cathedrals in the new style were soon begun at other places in the Île-de-France. At Sens a cathedral was being built at about the same time as St Denis and may have been under construction when Abelard had his famous confrontation with St Bernard in 1141. In its construction additional buttressing was required for the high clerestory walls of the nave, and here, at Sens, was born the flying buttress. Construction began at Noyon (*c.*1150), Senlis (*c.*1153), at Paris (*c.*1163) and at Laon (*c.*1160). Notre-Dame of Paris had a completed choir in 1182 and a completed nave before 1200. The often photographed flying buttresses that support the walls of the choir were added somewhat later. Eugène Viollet-le-Duc, the nineteenth-century architect, saved the cathedral from possible ruin and, in restoring it, effected changes from the original. The cathedrals in the new style were developing a more delicate appearance and were reaching higher and higher. Notre-Dame of Paris reached about 115 feet. At Rheims the cathedral rose to 125 feet, at Amiens to 140 feet and at Beauvais to 158 feet before the roof of the choir collapsed.

In England, fire destroyed much of the east end of Canterbury Cathedral in 1174. An eye-witness, Gervase of Canterbury, described how the fire started in nearby cottages, and, unnoticed, sparks landed on the cathedral roof, fell between the leaden plates and ignited the wooden rafters beneath:

> The three cottages, where the fire had begun, were destroyed and, the general excitement having ended, the townspeople started to go to their homes. Little did they know that the interior of the cathedral was being consumed by fire. But beams and supports were burning, and the flames reached the roof, where the lead began to melt. With the roof now opened, raging winds fanned the flames. The townspeople, turning, saw their cathedral engulfed in flames and shouted, 'Look, look. The cathedral is on fire'.

Reluctantly the monks of Christ Church, advised by the master mason William of Sens, agreed to rebuild the choir. After four years, the same chronicler relates,

16 Nave, Laon Cathedral. Reproduced by permission of the Courtauld Institute of Art.

17 Flying buttresses, Le Mans Cathedral. Reproduced by permission of the Courtauld Institute of Art.

> While William was using machinery to turn the great vault, the beams beneath his feet suddenly broke and he fell fifty feet to the ground, timber and stones falling with him.

In 1184, the east end, which contained the shrine of the recently martyred Thomas Becket was completed by an English master mason, who replaced the injured Frenchman. Both master masons used the Gothic style, and the Canterbury chronicler compared the new (Gothic) with the old (Romanesque):

> The pillars of both the old and the new are similar in style but different in height: the new longer by nearly twelve feet. The old

249

capitals were plain, whereas the new are sculptured exquisitely. The old ambulatory of the choir had 22 pillars; now there are 28. The old arches, as all else, were plain and cut roughly with an axe; the new with a chisel. There were no marble columns in the old, but now they are numerous beyond numbering. The old ambulatory around the choir had plain vaults; the new has ribbed arches and a keystone . . . The new building is higher than the old.

The nave seen by Chaucer's pilgrims and by modern visitors was built in the fourteenth century, and the central tower, Bell Harry, was constructed only in the very late fifteenth century.

Meanwhile, in France nature and man were combining to produce what many art historians consider the crown of medieval artistic genius, Chartres Cathedral. When the earliest church was built at Chartres no one knows, yet the church built there in 743 replaced an earlier church. In 858 fire badly damaged the new church, and it was replaced by a structure that remained till 1020, when it, in turn, fell to fire. In the ninth century, according to a later legend, the Frankish king Charles the Bald gave to Chartres a relic which was to make Chartres the principal pilgrimage place of France: the tunic said to have been worn by the Virgin, when she gave birth to the Christ child. The fire of 1020 enabled a new cathedral to be constructed in the Romanesque style; it was consecrated in 1037. About 1145 two towers, joined by three entrances (the Royal Portal), were built west of the Romanesque church, and the area between this structure and the Romanesque church was covered, thus effecting an extension of the old church. The new portals gave gifted sculptors the opportunity to produce some of the most admired cut stone anywhere. The colonnettes became elongated figures of Old Testament men and women. The tympanums above the doors depict three stages in Christian history. Over the right (south) door is the Virgin enthroned, her lap serving as a throne for her son, the lintels below depicting events in the Nativity cycle. Over the left (north) door is Christ ending his earthly life by ascending into heaven and beneath are lintels with angels giving their message to the apostles. And in the tympanum above the central door is Christ in heavenly majesty, surrounded by the figures of the four evangelists, and in the lintel below are the twelve apostles, flanked at each end by two figures, probably Elijah and Enoch.

Disaster struck at Chartres once again. On the night of 9–10 July 1194 the Romanesque cathedral was destroyed by fire, leaving the new west façade and its windows remarkably undamaged. A new Gothic church was built behind the west façade. Above the level of the lancet windows the wall of the façade was raised considerably higher to provide space for a wheel (rose) window. The work was essentially completed by 1220. The large amount of wall space in the new Gothic church invited large windows and stained glass, for which Chartres has become famous. The red and the blue glass – one writer calls the latter 'supernatural blue' – created a fusion of these colours in the spaces of the nave, choir and aisles. Gifts of windows came from beyond the local community, for the construction of the new pilgrimage church – the tunic, in the crypt, survived the fire – became a national undertaking. Windows were given by the aristocratic houses of the Île-de-France; the much admired windows of the north transept were donated by Queen Blanche, mother of the king-saint Louis IX, and the windows of the south transept by the duke of Brittany. Yet many of the windows were dedicated to local members of the merchant and artisan guilds, who donated them. A vivid account tells how the townsmen, including nobles and burgesses, hauled carts laden with stones up the steep precipice to the site where the towers were being built. The temptation to reduce this symbolic gesture to hysterical pentecostalism would not seem to do justice to the true religious emotion which, at least in part, accounts for the astonishing fact that between 1180 and 1270 eighty cathedrals and five hundred abbey churches were built in France alone.

The Gothic-building movement spread through the Western world from Dublin in the west, where two Gothic cathedrals were built, to Gdansk and Cracow in the east and from Trondheim and Uppsala in Scandinavia to Seville and Milan in the southern peninsulas, everywhere with a local stamp, yet everywhere essentially Gothic. And, when Europeans came to the New World and built churches, they tended to do so in the Gothic mode, adapted to local materials and climate. It had become close to being a universal style.

Appendix
Medieval cathedrals: a select list

This list presents the author's suggestion of some representative cathedrals which were built in the medieval period and which would reward further study.

France
Amiens. Gothic. Built between *c.*1220 and *c.*1280. Considered by many the ultimate Gothic.
Beauvais. Gothic. Choir begun in 1225; its roof collapsed in 1284. Choir rebuilt. Transepts added in the early sixteenth century.
Bourges. Gothic. Built largely in two campaigns (1195–1214; 1225–55). Elegantly tall interior columns and rich stained glass. Façade considered a masterpiece.
Chartres. Gothic. West façade of mid-twelfth century. Most of remainder 1194–1220 (see above pp. 250–1).
Laon. Perhaps best example of early Gothic; begun in the 1160s. Uncluttered, simple, with graceful proportions.
Paris, Notre-Dame. Gothic. Mostly 1163–*c.*1196. West towers by 1250.
Rheims. Gothic. Thirteenth century. Bombarded in two wars, its walls and foundation remained. Successfully restored. 'Like delicate lace'.

England
Canterbury. Gothic. Choir by 1184. Nave fourteenth century (see above pp. 247–50).

Durham. Norman (i.e., Romanesque). Begun in 1093. Vaulted by *c.*1130. Dr Johnson admired its 'rocky solidarity and indeterminate duration'.

Ely. Norman (i.e., Romanesque) nave completed in 1106. Gothic choir by 1251, but rebuilt in the fourteenth century after collapse of central tower, which was replaced by octagonal lantern tower.

Lincoln. Gothic (some Norman features in west façade). Thirteenth century. Two sets of transepts.

Salisbury. Gothic. Built in one campaign, 1220–66. Homogeneity of style: a snapshot of early English Gothic. Several paintings of the exterior by Constable.

Germany

Cologne. Gothic. Built over six centuries (the thirteenth to the nineteenth) and restored after the Second World War. Largest Gothic cathedral in northern Europe.

Magdeburg. Gothic. Thirteenth century. Early example of German use of French Gothic.

Mainz. Romanesque. Consecrated in 1009. Used by the French as an abattoir and stable in 1792 and by the allies as a target in the Second World War. Restored.

Speyer. Romanesque. Mostly eleventh century; nave extended and Baroque decoration added *c.*1700.

Worms. The Kaiserdom. Romanesque. Begun *c.*1000, not completed till the thirteenth century. Dome at the crossing.

Italy

Florence. Italian Gothic. Begun in 1296. Brunelleschi's dome not completed till 1461. Façade nineteenth century.

Lucca. Typical Italian mixture of styles. Fourteenth century. Impressive façade. Marble interior.

Milan. Gothic. Begun in 1386; essentially completed by 1416, yet remained a work in progress for some time. A forest of nineteenth-century pinnacles.

Pisa. Italian Romanesque. Begun in 1063. Wooden ceiling. White marble.

Siena. Italian Gothic. Begun in 1316, but work was halted at the Black Death (1348) and never restarted. A choir and transepts.

Spain

Burgos. Gothic. 1221–30, but dome not completed till 1568. Towers, pinnacles and statues.

Compostela. Romanesque. Begun in 1075 and consecrated in 1211. Eighteenth-century Baroque façade added.

Seville. Gothic. Fifteenth century. Largest Gothic church anywhere.

Toledo. Gothic. Begun in 1227 on the site of Muslim mosque.

Further reading

For the universities an introductory book based on lectures given in 1923 can still be read with profit: Charles Homer Haskins, *The Rise of Universities* (New York, 1923, and frequently reprinted). The classic is the second edition of Hastings Rashdall, *The Universities of Europe in the Middle Ages* (F.M. Powicke and A.B. Emden, eds; 3 vols; Oxford, 1936), which requires close attention by the reader to the editors' notes. More recent works include Helene Wieruszowski, *The Medieval University* (Princeton, 1966); A.B. Cobban, *The Medieval Universities: Their Development and Organization* (London, 1975); R.W. Southern, *Scholastic Humanism and the Unification of Europe* (2 vols; Oxford, 1995–2001), who prefers a later date for the *studium* at Bologna than that given here. For medieval philosophy the standard works are Etienne Gilson, *A History of Christian Philosophy in the Middle Ages* (New York, 1954) and Armand A. Maurer, *Medieval Philosophy* (2nd edn; Toronto, 1982). For canon law an invaluable introduction to the subject is James A. Brundage, *Medieval Canon Law* (London, 1995). An introduction to the study of Roman Law is Peter Stein, *Roman Law in European History* (Cambridge, 1999), and a comprehensive summary is O.F. Robinson *et al.*, *European Legal History* (2nd edn; London, 1994). For theology see Jaroslav Pelikan, *The Growth of Medieval Theology* (vol. 3 of *The Christian Tradition: A History of the Development of Doctrine*, Chicago and London, 1978). Readers will find helpful William J. Courtenay, *Teaching Careers at the University of Paris in the Thirteenth and Fourteenth Centuries* (Notre Dame, IN, 1988). Oxford is well served by vols 1–2 of *The History of the University of Oxford* (gen. ed. T.H. Aston; Oxford, 1984, 1993) as is Cambridge by Damian Leader, *A History of the University of Cambridge*, vol. 1, *The University to 1546* (Cambridge, 1988). The disputation of Thomas Aquinas on virtues can be found in his *Disputed Questions on Virtue* (tr. Ralph McInerny; South Bend, IN, 1998).

A good introduction to Romanesque and Gothic can be found in Spiro Kostof, *A History of Architecture: Settings and Rituals* (2nd edn; New York, 1995). A valuable survey is Roger Stalley, *Early Medieval Architecture* (Oxford, 1999). Paul Crossley's revision of Paul Frankl, *Gothic Architecture* (New Haven, 2000), can be consulted with much profit. For Abbot Suger see Lindy Grant, *Abbot Suger of St-Denis: Church and State in Early Twelfth-Century France* (London, 1998). Gervase of Canterbury's chronicle awaits an English translation. A valuable book is Jean Bony, *French Gothic Architecture of the 12th and 13th Centuries* (Berkeley, 1983). Also useful are Robert Branner, *Gothic Architecture* (New York, 1965) and Otto von Simpson, *The Gothic Cathedral* (New York, 1956). For an explanation of the engineering problems involved in constructing medieval churches see Robert Mark, *Experiments in Gothic Structure* (Cambridge, MA, 1982), which uses computerized models. Readers interested in sculpture will find that Paul Williamson, *Gothic Sculpture, 1140–1300* (New Haven, 1995), provides a helpful summary.

13

DEVELOPMENTS AND FULFILMENTS

The later thirteenth century

By the second half of the thirteenth century there were in full life changes, some long gestating, which affected both the institutional and inner lives of the church. The emergence of strong national monarchies had serious implications for the way in which the church as an institution functioned. If this can be seen most vividly in the high drama of henchmen of a French king physically assaulting the person of a pope, the phenomenon was played out less dramatically elsewhere. Among the Christian kingdoms of Europe must now be factored the monarchies of the Iberian peninsula, for in the second half of the thirteenth century the long process of the Christian recovery of Muslim lands was complete, save for Granada, and the Christians of Castile, Aragon and Portugal had taken their place in the world of medieval Christianity.

Popes and kings

Let this story begin with the death of a French king in 1270 and end with the death of a pope in 1303. The death of Louis IX in 1270 ended the reign of one of Europe's most remarkable kings. Known for his undoubted personal piety, Louis spent considerable time daily in prayer and, in private, he wore the coarse garment of the friars. He constructed the Sainte-Chapelle in Paris to house the crown of thorns, which was believed to be the very crown placed on Christ's head at his trial. Following the conventions of the time, Louis led a Christian army on crusade to the East, but without success. He brought peace between France and her enemies – Flanders in 1256, Aragon in 1258 and England in 1259 – under terms that were equitable and productive of a peaceful realm for his subjects. Taken ill as he was on his way once again to the East, Louis, as he lay dying, advised his son:

> My dear son, the first thing I want to teach you is to move your heart to love God, for without God no one can be saved . . . Love all that is good and salutary; despise evil everywhere . . . Deal with all your subjects in justice and equity, taking particular care for the poor . . .

Be sure to insure that your subjects can live peacefully and honestly
... Love and respect all those who serve the church ... Finally, dear
son, have Masses and prayers said for my soul and for me throughout
your kingdom.

(Joinville)

There died with St Louis the single most effective force for stability in Europe.
In England, Henry III was recovering from a civil war with his barons. Germany
was in a period known as the Great Interregnum, which saw competing rivals
for the kingship and which saw no emperor crowned. And the papacy was
experiencing its longest vacancy in history.

When Pope Clement IV died in 1268, the moment was not conducive to a
quick election, and it was to be a long moment lasting almost three years. Sixteen
cardinals met at Viterbo, where the pope had died, and they were hopelessly
divided, not over spiritual aspects of the leadership of the church but over
the political question of supporting the ambitions of the younger brother of
Louis IX, Charles of Anjou, the papally installed – but papally regretted –
king of Sicily. Exasperated by the incompetence of the cardinals and urged on
by St Bonaventure, head of the Franciscan order, the people of Viterbo on a hot
summer's day stripped the roof from the place where the cardinals were meeting,
locked the doors to bar their escape and threatened to cut off their food supply.
The matter was quickly settled. Yet the man elected, then not even a priest, was
at Acre in the Holy Land, and it was not till six months later that he became
pope, Gregory X (1272–76). His experiences in the East convinced him to seek
a reunion with the Orthodox church. In 1261, Constantinople, in Latin hands
since the Fourth Crusade went awry in 1204, having been retaken by the Greeks.
A reunion with the churches of the East would meet the political needs of the
Greek emperor, now sitting in Constantinople, and such a reunion was patched
together at the Second Council of Lyons (1274). It was not to last. In fact, it
took hold only partially among the clergy and was dead by 1283. The schism of
1054 was not healed, nor would another attempt in the fifteenth century effect
a healing.

The papacy of the last quarter of the thirteenth century suffered from problems
of its own making. In wrenching control of southern Italy and Sicily from
the German kings (Hohenstauffen) and placing their man, Charles of Anjou,
on the throne of Sicily, the popes had created a monster. Charles, young brother
of the sainted French king, quickly became uncontrollable by the popes, and his
ambitions threatened papal independence. Charles controlled a significant
number of cardinals, who could be relied on to support his candidate during
an election. Thrown into this mix was the old story of competing Roman
aristocratic families – the Gaetani, Orsini and Colonna – vying for control over
the papacy. It was an unholy mix, resulting in a number of deadlocked elections
and long vacancies. The provision by Gregory X at the Council of Lyons to lock
the electing cardinals in conclave and starve them into action worked for only a

short time and was abandoned. But, even while it was in force, bad luck produced three short pontificates: Innocent V (21 January to 22 June 1276), Hadrian V (elected 11 July but died 18 August 1276, before even being ordained priest or consecrated bishop of Rome) and John XXI (8 September 1276 to 20 May 1277). There followed a six-month vacancy. Two other long vacancies occurred within the next fifteen years: one of eleven months (1287–88) and another of twenty-seven months (1292–94).

This last vacancy led to one of the most bizarre events in the long history of the papacy. Locked in bitter, seemingly irresolvable disagreement for over two years, the cardinals made a totally unprecedented move. The dean of the college of cardinals read to his fellow cardinals a letter which he had received from a hermit-monk, living in a mountain retreat in southern Italy. This hermit, Peter Murrone, speaking with the unassailable authority of the truly holy, upbraided the cardinals for not providing the church with a pope and said that the wrath of God would fall on them if they failed to elect a pope soon. Not even worldly cardinals could insulate themselves from the prophecy of this otherworldly, non-political, holy man. The dean immediately said that he would vote for Murrone himself, and others of the cardinals quickly followed. The impossible happened: the cardinals elected one whom they called *papa angelicus* (the angel pope), Celestine V. On 29 August 1294 he rode to his consecration seated on a donkey. Not only was he a very old man – about eighty-five – but, more importantly, he was gullible and naive. He became the unknowing puppet of Charles II, king of Naples, whose father, Charles of Anjou, had by now lost Sicily to the Spanish. Almost immediately Celestine named twelve new cardinals, all proposed by Charles. Consecrated bishop in the south, Celestine made no attempt to go to Rome. In fact, he made no serious effort to manage the affairs of the church, and the administration of the church quickly fell into disarray. Keeping with his custom of spending the season of Advent, the four weeks before Christmas, in prayerful solitude, in November 1294 he announced that he would leave the powers of the pope in the hands of three cardinals, while he went on his Advent retreat. When objections were understandably made, Celestine asked for advice. Acting on that advice, on 13 December 1294, the hermit-monk-pope appeared before the cardinals, removed his mitre and ring and resigned the office of pope. One might think that this good man would then have been allowed to go to his mountain hermitage to spend the rest of his days in peaceful contemplation, but such was not the case, as we shall soon see.

On Christmas Eve 1294, on the third ballot the cardinals elected Benedict Gaetani, who took the name Boniface VIII. His was to be a momentous, even tumultuous pontificate (1294–1303). Much could rightly have been expected of him. He was a learned, even scholarly man, proficient, as few other of his generation were, in the law of the church. He was an experienced curialist, who knew where all the bodies were buried. He was a skilled diplomat, who spent nearly three years in England (1265–68) at a most crucial time and who, in 1264 and again in 1290, undertook delicate missions to the French court. Yet his is often judged an unsuccessful pontificate, even a disastrous one. He was burdened by the manner of his becoming pope, since it was he who had advised his predecessor that he could resign and who, further, drew up the actual document of resignation. It should be quickly added that there is no evidence that he used any influence on Celestine V to resign, but his proximity to the process was to make him liable to suspicion and even to unfounded charges. Also, after his election, Boniface, fearing that the ex-pope, Celestine, might become the centre of an opposition party, ordered that the aged hermit be arrested and kept under house arrest at Castel Fumone near Ferentino, where the former pope died in 1296. Further, Boniface's temperament – at this distance we catch only glimpses, making generalizations difficult, if not impossible – may have betrayed him. Others, generally his enemies, describe him as haughty, arrogant and given to moments of irrational rage. In addition, the new pope suffered from what contemporaries called 'the stone', quite probably kidney stones, which meant that he was frequently in considerable pain. In further mitigation of what was to follow it should be said that the dire condition of the papacy owed much to the house of Anjou and its policies in Sicily and southern Italy. Topping his agenda, as he first sat on the chair of Peter, was the task of ensuring that the papacy would be independent of the control of secular princes.

Almost irresistible is the temptation to recount the pontificate of Boniface VIII solely in terms of his encounters with the French king, Philip IV the Fair (*le bel*), but it is a temptation to be strongly resisted. There is no contesting the sheer drama of the dispute of pope and king, but Boniface had much more to deal with than the arrogant, handsome king of France. Boniface gathered together the important papal and conciliar decrees published since 1234, when his predecessor Gregory IX had promulgated his official collection of laws in five books, and added these as a 'sixth book' (*Liber Sextus*). All other laws introduced for the universal church since 1234 were now null. The totality of canon law was to be found in these two great collections. Had Boniface done nothing else, he would have a significant place in the history of law. But he did much else in his nine-year reign.

Two years after issuing the *Liber Sextus*, Boniface called for a Holy Year (or Jubilee Year) to mark the new century. The papal bull decreeing it was issued on 22 February 1300, but the Holy Year was considered to have begun on Christmas Day 1299 and was to run until Christmas Eve 1300. (No concern here about which year marked the beginning of a new century.) Hereafter, in each hundredth year, the pope wrote, there would be a similar jubilee. The form of the jubilee was a pilgrimage to the basilicas of SS. Peter and Paul in Rome. To those who confessed their sins would be given a full remission of the penance due for their sins, the journey to Rome and the visit to the basilicas being considered signs of interior contrition. Pilgrims came to Rome by the thousand, among them representatives from England, including the bishop of Winchester, from Poland, from Hungary and from every Christian country of Central and Western Europe. They came down the Italian peninsula, passing through cities whose residents watched in stunned amazement. At Modena an eye-witness saw people from overseas, some walking and some even carrying aged parents on their backs. At Parma, according to a contemporary, a number, almost beyond counting, passed through: 'barons, knights, noble ladies, men and women of every state, class and condition . . . from Lombardy, France, Burgundy and from every other part of Christendom'. Dante, who may well have been among the pilgrims to Rome, describes a pilgrim,

> Who with joy of spirit travelled from Croatia to see
> Veronica's veil and, who, gazing upon it,
> Lingers there with unsated soul.
>
> (Paradiso, 31, 103–5)

One Italian pilgrim, with understandable exaggeration, said that two million visitors came to Rome during the jubilee. Whatever the exact number, never before in its long history had Rome seen so many visitors. The pope in calling the jubilee apparently had no ulterior motive – not always true of Boniface – other than to satisfy the pious desires of Christian people. In fact, far from dressing like a Roman emperor and parading through Rome during the jubilee, as some of his enemies said, Boniface spent most of that year outside of Rome (from April to October) at his favourite summer place of residence at Anagni. Whatever the actual papal involvement, the Holy Year of 1300 was a moment unlike any other, a clear sign of a church come of age, its people comfortable, perhaps even triumphant, in the security of their beliefs and of the settled order of their society.

At almost the same time, Boniface was sending missionaries to the East: Dominican friars 'to the lands of the Saracens, pagans and Greeks, to the lands of the Bulgars, Cuman, Ethiopians, Tartars' and many others, as the papal letter says, and the Franciscan friars to the Eastern Tartars. Such missions could scarcely succeed without the adequate preparation of the missionaries. The Dominicans had already established schools to train friars for the missions. Ramon Lull, the Majorcan-born intellectual and Christian mystic, who had learned Arabic in order to proclaim Christianity to his Muslim neighbours, travelled to Rome several times, and in the early days of Boniface's pontificate urged the pope to encourage the study of oriental languages. He was not successful at this time, but fifteen years later Clement V, at Lull's urging, created schools in Hebrew, Arabic and Chaldaic at the papal curia (then at Avignon) and at four universities (Paris, Oxford, Bologna and Salamanca):

> We are fully aware that it makes no sense to preach the word of God to ears that do not understand . . . It is our ardent desire that the holy church should abound with Catholic men who have a knowledge of languages used by infidels. These men should be able to instruct them in Christian ways and bring them through baptism into the Christian fold.

Two experts in each of these Eastern languages were to teach at each of these centres, and provisions were made for their salaries. The world of the medieval church was expanding.

The centre piece of Boniface's pontificate, for better or worse, is usually not the missionary activity of the friars nor the pilgrims crowding across the bridges into Rome for the jubilee nor, indeed, the important law collection promulgated in 1298. For modern historiography, the centrepiece remains his disastrous relations with Philip the Fair. Almost inevitably comparisons are made between Boniface and his predecessor one hundred years before, Innocent III. Whereas Innocent successfully dealt with the emperor and kings of England and France, not making a false step, measuring his power and that of his opponents, emerging triumphant, so triumphant that history – and this book – can speak of the 'Age of Innocent III', Boniface, it is said, misjudged both the times and his opponents, using traditional tactics and weapons, only to fail ignominiously, in the end to be stripped even of personal dignity. Another view suggests itself in a historical scene much more complex than can be satisfied by crude comparisons. In Philip the Fair, Boniface encountered an adversary more formidable than any of Innocent's opponents. And Philip was well served by lieutenants moved by overarching ambition. As Thomas Cromwell was to Henry VIII and Cardinal Richelieu was to Louis XIII, so too Flotte and Nogaret were to Philip the Fair: immensely talented, single-minded, ruthless, unbothered by sentiments of justice or morality, moved solely by a lust for power to be gained through their master. Perhaps no pope could win out, arrayed against such foes. A new nationalism, it might be urged, played its role in this conflict. To be sure, the French kings were extending the areas of France over which they held direct authority and wars with the English and Flemish produced some sentiments of 'national' feeling. The king, it may be argued, was expressing these 'national' aspirations and the pope failed to reckon this 'nationalism' into his calculations. Yet it is almost to read history backwards to see in the opening years of the fourteenth century a sense of nationalism not present in reality until the seventeenth century. Philip wanted power, and his advisers wanted access to that power, and nothing and no one would stand in their way, not even the pope. A case can be made that the pope, if anything, was too pliable for too long in his dealing with the French kings.

The story can be briefly told. The immediate issue had to do with the French king taxing the church to help finance his war with England. The clergy of France complained to the pope that the king was taking church money to finance a war not against the infidel but against a fellow Christian prince for purely secular purposes. The powerful Cistercian order pressed their strong disapproval:

> The church is not bound to such extraordinary demands without the authority of the pontiff.

They were soon joined by 'all the clergy of France' in complaining that the king was treating them far worse than the pharaoh had treated the Israelites. The papal response to the complaints from France was the papal bull, known from its opening words, *Clericis laicos* (24 February 1296). It took account of the fact that both the king of France and the king of England were taxing the clergy on income derived from church properties to finance their war. The pope mentioned neither party by name, and his bull was addressed generally, but the meaning was clear. Unnamed laymen (*laicos*) have imposed burdens on the clergy (*clericis*) by exacting parts of their revenues, and some clergy, without receiving permission from the pope (required in such circumstances by provision of the Fourth Lateran Council of 1215), have acquiesced to these exactions,

> fearing whom there is no reason to fear, settling for the peace of the moment, afraid more of offending the temporal than eternal majesty.

Boniface went on to excommunicate rulers who acted in this way as well as clergy who, again, *without papal permission*, made such payments. Experienced diplomat as he was, Boniface gave wiggle room to Philip by using the words italicized here. They could, as indeed they did, provide the space for manoeuvre by both sides. There is every reason to believe that Boniface was caught surprised by the reaction of Philip to this bull. It had not been sent to Philip nor to any other king; Philip learned about it when, almost two months after it was issued, the archbishop of Narbonne asked the king to be excused from paying taxes and cited the papal bull. In an attempt to show even-handedness Boniface then, on the same day, ordered his legates to England and France to publish *Clericis laicos*, thus not putting either party at a disadvantage by losing ecclesiastical revenues. A compromise was in the works. The pope, while retaining the principle of clerical immunity, now allowed that in extreme national emergencies a king could proceed to tax the clergy without the delay involved in obtaining papal permission. Also, the pope chose this time (11 August 1297) to canonize Louis IX, grandfather of Philip the Fair. The matter could have ended there, but Philip sensed a wounded Boniface and pressed for the kill.

The French now conspired with the Colonna family, arch-enemies of the pope and his Gaetani family, to bring down the pope. In May 1297 the Colonna had waylaid a convoy bringing the pope's personal money from Anagni to Rome and made off with a fortune. Infuriated, Boniface threatened the two Colonna cardinals to effect its return or face the consequences. They agreed, and so it happened, but, still furious, Boniface demanded even more. The Colonna cardinals, who in fact had voted for Boniface and who had acknowledged him as pope, now claimed that Celestine could not resign and that Boniface's election was invalid. The cardinals were summarily stripped of their office, and they then added to their accusations against Boniface that he had actually murdered the imprisoned Pope Celestine. The French had found their allies in Italy. Pierre Flotte, chief adviser to Philip the Fair, came to Italy and mischievously told the Colonnas that the French supported their call for a general council to resolve the issue of Boniface's election. Flotte had a broader scheme in mind than merely stirring the Italian pot. He planned to restore a Latin king at Constantinople, who, of course, would be French, and to set up Frenchmen as kings of Lombardy and Arles. Charlemagne revisited and Napoleon anticipated: France was to be in effective control of Western Christendom, the German and English monarchs marginalized and the pope a French puppet, awarded with control over Florence. In the midst of the Holy Year, Pierre Flotte went to Italy again, and, in a meeting with Boniface, told him that people were saying that he was not really the pope, that he had murdered the late Celestine, whom he had imprisoned, and that he was a heretic. At about the same time, complaints were coming to Boniface from French bishops, telling stories of the king infringing their authority. By now Boniface recognized that Philip the Fair was wholly unresponsive to his efforts to alleviate tensions between them. On 18 July 1300 he wrote to the king:

> At length, God's vicar cannot remain silent for fear that he might be accused of being a dumb dog, incapable of speech. For a long time he has waited in patience, hoping that a merciful resolution might be reached, but now he must speak out.

All it would take now was an incident to trigger the almost inevitable explosion, and it happened a year later.

In the summer of 1301 the bishop of Pamiers was arrested by an armed guard and was to be tried on charges before a secular tribunal. Becket had died in defence of the principle of clerical immunity from lay courts. Philip and his advisers, particularly, it would seem, Guillaume de Nogaret, aimed to confront the pope by their clear violation of canon law. Some of the French bishops, hitherto rather silent, protested at the king's treatment of their fellow bishop. Still hoping to resolve the issue but not willing to compromise further, Boniface, perhaps unwisely, wrote a fatherly letter to Philip, *Ausculta fili* ('Listen, son') very late in 1301. The letter was burned when received, and a forgery was quickly produced, which attributed to the pope claims concerning his authority in temporal matters, which had not in fact been made in the letter. When a delegation of French bishops appeared before the pope in June 1302, he denounced by name three French royal advisers as responsible for the forgery and for publicizing it: Pierre Flotte, Robert of Artois and the count of St Pol. Evil things will befall them, the pope prophesied. And just over a fortnight later all three were killed in a battle in Flanders. If the pope needed any reassurance for his position, this was surely it. When less than half of the French bishops attended a council in Rome in the autumn of 1302 and no results were achieved, Boniface issued his most famous decree.

The bull *Unam sanctam* Boniface issued on 18 November 1302, and it remains the best-known pronouncement of a medieval pope. Its principal emphasis is on the unity of the church, its opening words being, 'There is one, holy, catholic and apostolic church'. The pope is head on earth of this one church, and anyone who denies the pope's authority is not part of that one church. For that reason

Boniface asserted that the two swords of power, the spiritual and the temporal, were both given by God for the service of the one church. The spiritual with the goal of human salvation transcends in importance all things material. From this it follows that the spiritual power can and should judge the temporal when it departs from the ways of goodness. The bull's concluding sentence reads,

> We declare, state, define and pronounce that it is necessary for salvation for all human beings to be subject to the Roman Pontiff.

This might sound as if the pope were declaring universal power, but it is a statement concerning his spiritual authority and not about the relations of church and state. Although no mention was made of the king of France or, indeed, any other temporal ruler, the meaning had to be patently clear to Philip: the pope was claiming that Philip had morally erred by his treatment of the church and that the pope had the right and duty to correct him. In response to a papal legate sent to France to threaten Philip with dire consequences should he not reverse his treatment of the church, the king claimed that the pope misunderstood him and his intentions. A clash of wills with dramatic consequences was about to occur.

It was now open season on the pope and his character. The first shot was fired at a meeting of king and council at the Louvre Palace on 12 May 1303, when Nogaret accused the pope of not being pope but of being heretical, simoniacal and guilty of unspeakable sins: he should be tried by a general council. In June the king called an assembly of the great men of the realm, including five archbishops, twenty-one bishops and eleven abbots. An indictment of Boniface was read to the assembly:

> he consults sorcerers
> he does not believe in transubstantiation
> he forces priests to violate the secrets of confession
> he fails to fast
> he commits sexual sins
> he murdered Pope Celestine V
> he hates Frenchmen and says he would rather be a dog than be a Frenchman
> and other charges, twenty-nine in all

The assembly appealed for a general council that would resolve the Boniface problem. French bishop after French bishop subscribed to the appeal for a council; the notable hold-outs were the Cistercians. When the pope learned of these events, probably not till August, he prepared a formal, explicit excommunication of Philip the Fair to be nailed to the cathedral door at Anagni, where the pope was spending the summer. The date set for this was 8 September.

Meanwhile, Nogaret was at Siena, preparing for a personal attack on the pope, whom he planned to abduct physically and bring to France for trial. On

7 September, with a large band of Italian mercenaries, possibly one thousand in number, Nogaret with Sciarra Colonna at his side entered Anagni. In the early evening they forced their way into the papal palace and into the pope's room. They found Boniface sitting on the papal throne, clothed in papal robes and clutching a cross to his breast. Sciarra Colonna was probably intent on murder, and some accounts say that he actually struck the pope. 'Take my head and pierce my breast,' Boniface said calmly. Nogaret intervened, for a martyred Boniface was not in his plans. The tenor of feeling among the townspeople of Anagni quickly turned against the attackers, for, whatever minor grievances they may have held against the pope, he was one of them, a son of Anagni. Nogaret now had to flee for his life. Boniface had a harsh critic in Dante, but even the poet was deeply disturbed by this attack on the pope:

> The fleur-de-lys I see Anagni invade,
> And, in his vicar, Christ is made captive.
> I see Him mocked a second time;
> The vinegar and the gall again renewed,
> And Him slain again between living thieves.
> The new Pilate [Philip] I also see,
> So cruel that he is not even sated by this.
>
> (*Purgatorio*, 20, 86–92)

Broken and weary of life, Boniface returned to Rome to die, and on 12 October 1303 ended the troubled pontificate of this pope of contradictions.

History should perhaps be less severe than was Dante, who at least ten times inveighed against Boniface in *Divine Comedy*. Not by name but by clear reference Dante called him, 'the prince of a new breed of Pharisees' (*Inferno*, 27, 85). The poet reserved a place for him among the simoniacs in the eighth circle of hell (*Inferno*, 19, 53). To be sure, he and Boniface were political adversaries in the impassioned world of contemporary Italian politics, and Dante, the greatest of medieval poets, cannot be seen as a sober detached observer of popes, who by now had become active players in contentious politics, which inevitably distracted them from their spiritual mission. Let the final word be from Dante, who meets St Peter in paradise and puts in the mouth of the first pope the words,

> Wonder not if I change colour
> For, as I speak, you shall see
> All change with me.
> He who on earth usurps my place,
> Yes, my place, my very place,
> Which lies vacant in the eyes of the Son of God,
> Has made my tomb a common sewer of blood and pollution
> Into which the malignant fall.
>
> (*Paradiso*, 27, 139–41)

A harsh judgement, but one aimed at unworthy popes who have polluted Peter's grave. Should history include Boniface among them? Almost certainly not.

Reconquista

By the time of the death of Ferdinand III, king of Castile, in 1252 Christian kings ruled almost all of Iberia. Seville, the great Muslim city and, for the Christians, a great prize, had fallen in 1248, and, in the immediate aftermath, resistance crumbled. Ferdinand's son, Alfonso X (d. 1284), consolidated the victories by annexing two small Muslim states and by beginning a Christian settlement of some of these regions. From the late thirteenth century all that remained of Muslim rule in the Iberian peninsula was the emirate of Granada, which would remain Muslim until 1492. The reconquest of Spain was all but complete.

The use of the phrase 'Reconquest of Spain' to describe the successful taking of Muslim lands by Christian kings has long been in dispute. It has been a dispute not wholly divorced from modern events in Spain, particularly the central event in modern Spanish history, the Civil War (1936–39). Those political considerations put aside, the objection to the use of *Reconquista* is that it distorts the history of the period 711 to 1492. To make the Christian reconquest the central and defining issue, many believe, neglects other, more or, at least, equally significant issues of a social, economic, political and even ecclesiastical nature. It cannot be argued here that the reconquest was the goal of all Christian rulers at all times, for it was not, or that alliances were not struck between Christian and Muslim rulers, for they were, very often against other Christians, or that Christian rulers were always motivated by high principle, for very frequently crass self-advantage lay behind their land-taking. Motivation was seldom pure and probably never wholly altruistic.

The sense of 'reconquest' depends both on contemporary articulations of this ideal and *post factum*, modern historical constructs, although the latter perhaps have had greater influence on historical writing. What can be said is that the expansion of Christian holdings over this long period led in time to the control of the entire Iberian peninsula by Christian rulers. The goal of reconquering was enunciated shortly after the Arab conquest, when, according to a later chronicle, in 722 a Christian prince, in a cave in the Cantabrian Mountains, told his warriors,

> We trust that by the mercy of the Lord from this hill will come the
> recovery of Spain and the restoration of the [Visi-]Gothic army . . .
> We trust in God to restore church, people and kingdom.

Writing about 883, another chronicler said, 'Our glorious lord, prince Alfonso, will rule over all Spain'. There can be little doubt that the reconquest existed as a goal from fairly soon after the Muslim conquest up until the time that the reconquest was completely accomplished, yet it was often little more than a vague and unarticulated *desideratum* and for long periods not a matter of very high priority.

When last seen (chapter 3), Spain was being conquered by a Muslim army that left but a small remnant of the peninsula unconquered. That remnant had no exact borders but extended across the top of Spain from the eastern slopes of the Pyrenees to the Atlantic Ocean on the west. It is mountainous country, dominated by the Pyrenees and the Cantabrian Mountains. It was scarcely worth the effort for the Muslims to try to ferret out the resistance in these areas. Thus, from 719, when the Muslim conquest can be said to have been completed, there were two sets of Christians in the peninsula, those living in the mountainous north and those living under Muslim rule in the rest of the peninsula, the area called al-Andalus. The condition of the latter Christians should be looked at first.

As elsewhere, the Muslims treated their non-Muslim subjects (Christians and Jews) with a tolerance greater than the tolerance shown at that time in most Christian countries to religious minorities. Christians could continue to practise their religion, and no attempt at forcible conversion to Islam was made. There were some minor restrictions regarding the public display of Christianity: not allowed were public Masses and public processions as well as the ringing of church bells. In addition, Christians paid significantly higher taxes than the Muslims, as did the Jews. The Christians, however, with their churches still standing and their bishops still in place, continued much as before the conquest. Yet the powerful Arabic culture had a penetrating influence. Large numbers, while remaining Christians, adopted Arabic ways, including the Arabic language. They were called simply Mozarabs (i.e., like-the-Arabs): cultural Arabs and religious Christians. The so-called Mozarabic rite used by Christians in Spain till the eleventh century is a misnomer, for it was used in Spain before the Arab conquest, and, after that conquest, it was used in Christian Spain in the north as well as in al-Andalus and, in fact, was a Latin-language rite. The Christian scriptures were translated and annotated in Arabic, for, indeed, that language had become the vernacular language of the vast numbers of Christians in al-Andalus. A Christian writer, at Cordova in the middle of the ninth century, lamented this development:

> Many fellow Christians read the poems and stories of the Arabs and study the works of Islamic theologians and philosophers, not to be able to refute them, but to learn correct and elegant Arabic. There is scarcely one Christian in thousands who can compose an acceptable Latin letter to a friend, but the number is countless of those who speak in Arabic and there are even many who can compose in Arabic more artfully than the Arabs themselves.

Yet, even without pressure, many Christians converted to Islam. We may never know how many, but reliable estimates suggest that by the eleventh century a majority or a near majority converted. Their conversions were frequently suspect and, for some time, their descendants (*muwalladun*) were not fully accepted by their Arab masters.

The rule of al-Andalus was originally from the Umayyad caliph in far-away Damascus. When that dynasty fell in 750 and was succeeded by the Abbasids, who moved their capital to Baghdad, a prince of the Umayyad family escaped to Spain and set himself up as emir over Spain, thus creating an independent Umayyad dynasty with its seat at Cordova. There on the site of the Christian cathedral was built the Great Mosque, one of the marvels of world architecture. The emirate and, later, the caliphate of Cordova flourished for centuries. The Muslim settlers were Arabs, the elite leaders of the conquest, who took the prized lands in the south, and the Berbers (i.e., Moors), the bulk of the soldiery of the conquest, who got poorer lands in the northern plateau. Inevitably friction between these two Muslim groups led to at least a partial abandonment of the northern lands by the Berbers, thus leaving something of a vacuum for Christian expansion southward from the mountains. Some evidence suggests that the movement south, now and later, served to relieve serious demographic stresses in the Christian-held regions, where there was a growing imbalance between population and basic resources for subsistence.

The Christian remnant in the far north, within a century or so, appears in several broad groupings. In the north-east, growing up around Barcelona in the

18 Great Mosque, Cordova. Reproduced by permission of the Courtauld Institute of Art.

region soon to be called Catalonia, was the Christian county of Barcelona. To its west in the southern slopes of the Pyrenees was Aragon. Catalonia and Aragon were both to expand to the south, and, in 1137, each having doubled its territory, the two federated, forming what has become known to history as the Crown of Aragon, although Aragon was the junior partner. In the southern regions of the central Pyrenees was Castile. Traversing the Pyrenees at their westernmost part was the Basque principality of Navarre, its principal settlement at Pamplona. Across northern Iberia south of the Bay of Biscay there developed the Christian region of Asturias with Oviedo as its central town and with a shrine to St James (*Santiago*) soon to be built at the field of the stars (*Compostela*). It was from these regions that the 'reconquest' started and grew not steadily but in spurts.

By 911 the king of Asturias had conquered a large part of the lands to his south, much of it underpopulated. Within fifty years the town of Leon had become the centre of Asturian rule and the associated frontier principalities of Portugal and Castile had appeared. Neither exact dates nor exact territorial borders should be expected, but by about 1040 a line drawn across the peninsula roughly from just below Oporto on the west to just below Barcelona on the east, along the Duoro and Ebro Rivers, would give a broad indication of where Christian and Muslim areas met, although Salamanca and Saragossa were still in Muslim hands.

A crucial moment came in 1031, when the caliphate of Cordova fell. For the previous twenty-five years the caliphate was disputed, as various Muslim factions fought one another, some supported by Berbers and others by Christians. When the Arab aristocracy of Cordova finally abolished the caliphate, al-Andalus was already fractured into many conflicting parts. What emerged from these troubles was a collection of a score or so of small Muslim states (*taifas*), ruled by local kings. The Muslim rule in the peninsula was in deep crisis, a crisis of its own making, from which it would never recover. The 'reconquest' was now in the ascendent. At this time, a Christian knight is reported to have said to a Muslim ruler,

> In the beginning the Christians had al-Andalus, until you Arabs drove them into the poor region of Galicia. Circumstances have now changed. Since it is now possible for us to recover these lands by force, we will weaken you, and, when you no longer have money and soldiers, we shall easily conquer the country.

Whether boast or prophecy, the predicted outcome was to occur but not 'easily'.

The Franks had long had an interest in Spanish affairs, particularly in the north-east, where the Carolingians had established counties (e.g., Barcelona), but, in the last half of the eleventh century, the reformed and reforming papacy signalled its interest. Alexander II (1061–73) encouraged Christian warriors to join the fray, and, in 1064, French armies, led by nobles, joined with the forces of Catalonia and Aragon to besiege Barbasto. Although promised safe conduct if they surrendered, the Muslim inhabitants were slaughtered as they made their way out of the city gates, and in the slaughter it was the French 'crusaders' who distinguished themselves by unspeakable barbarities, at least according to Spanish sources. In that same year, 1064, Christian armies took Coimbra, and King Ferdinand I of Leon–Castile appointed a count for Portugal. Further advances were soon to take place in the western part of the peninsulas as Portugal was taking shape. Alexander's successor, Gregory VII (1073–85), encouraged military support for the campaigns in Spain, although, when that support came, it was exercised almost exclusively in eastern Spain between the Pyrenees and the Ebro River. No one knew it in the 1080s, but the future lay with Leon–Castile, the central kingdom, definitively united in 1230 as the kingdom of Castile, which would push further and further south, expanding on broad flanks. In a moment of some drama, the talented king of Leon–Castile, Alfonso VI (1065–1109), won the surrender of Toledo and entered the city on 25 May 1085. For the first time since 712, a Christian king entered what had been the seat of Christian kings before the Muslim conquest, although, for strategic reasons, Alfonso did not move his capital there. Alfonso promised tolerance to the Muslim inhabitants of Toledo and had to be restrained from executing those of his followers who, acting against his wishes, seized the Great Mosque and converted it into a cathedral. Alfonso's victory gave him control over the heartland of the peninsula. The taking of Toledo put the Christian king within striking distance of Valencia and Cordova and must rank high among the principal events of medieval Spanish history.

What Alfonso VI may have forgotten – and what students of medieval Spain should never forget – is the African connection. The Berbers, who had helped to conquer and settle Spain, were North Africans. Across narrow straits from Muslim Spain lay a kindred people, sharing a common culture and religion. After the fall of Toledo the petty kings of the *taifas* panicked. A contemporary Muslim writer commented,

> It is from the edges that a robe unravels, but I see the robe of the peninsula unravelling from the centre.

In this unravelling the Muslim leaders looked to North Africa, to cousin Berbers, to save them from the Christian threat. Enter the Almoravids. Half a century or so earlier, in North Africa, a zealous Muslim preached a fundamentalist interpretation of the Koran. He drew followers from among the Berber tribes of the Sahara. They believed in a strict, even fanatical, interpretation of Muslim laws, fighting against fellow Muslims who disagreed with them. At the time of the fall of Toledo they controlled Morocco and western Algeria. In 1085 they stood poised to cross the straits. It was to these Almoravids that the Muslim rulers turned. They soon regretted their decision. By 1094 the Almoravids controlled al-Andalus and had restored unified Muslim rule at the expense of the local Muslim rulers. At this moment, the man known to history as El Cid (*The Lord*), Rodrigo Diaz de Vivar, captured Valencia from the Muslims and held off an Almoravid attempt to take the city. The El Cid, hero of the *Poem of El Cid*, the

Castilian epic, came to symbolize the *Reconquista*, although the real El Cid was a mercenary, fighting at times for Christian and at other times for Muslim rulers. It is this historical El Cid who comes nearer the representative norm. Valencia, however, was to fall to the Almoravids in 1102 and remained in Muslim hands for over a hundred years. Within twenty-five years of these events at Valencia associated with El Cid, the Almoravid power began to wane as peoples in al-Andalus became restive and new *taifas* began to appear. Christian kings took advantage of this situation. The Aragonese were able, in 1118, to take Saragossa, situated at a strategic point on the Ebro. This positioned them for the eventual taking of the region of Valencia.

From across the same straits another group of Berbers, the Almohads, having already destroyed the Almoravid empire in North Africa, stood ready to do the same in Spain. They arrived in the spring of 1146 and soon controlled parts of southern Spain and the Algarve to the west. Within a year they had seized Seville, Cordova and much of al-Andalus. In this unsettled atmosphere Christian kings once again took advantage of the situation. In 1147 Afonso Henriques, count of Portugal but now styling himself 'king of Portugal', seized Lisbon, aided by over ten thousand crusaders, who had landed at Oporto on their way to the Holy Land. In the same year, Castilians gained Almeria, their window to the Mediterranean, yet it was a short-term gain, for it was to fall to the Almohads. These new Berbers were exerting themselves forcefully and by 1172 controlled most of al-Andalus. Yet, like the Almoravids before them, they soon settled in as but another aspect of the peninsular landscape.

The recently established military orders of knight-monks (see above p. 128) were not happy with this fairly peaceful status quo. The archbishop of Toledo and other bishops also found the situation unsatisfactory. In 1209 Pope Innocent III urged the archbishop to convince the king of Castile to reopen the campaign. The result was a crusade. Innocent granted crusading indulgences, urged Christians, particularly the French, to assist and, further, admonished the Christian kings of the peninsula not to attack one another. At Pentecost, 1212, a crusading army gathered at Toledo. They marched south, French, Aragonese and Castilians. After an early victory the French withdrew, allegedly because of the heat, and their place was taken by Navarrese. At the plain called Las Navas de Tolosa a bloody battle ensued, at which the crusading army triumphed. The Almohad threat had effectively been ended. The three Christian kings of Castile, Leon and Portugal met at Coimbra in November and agreed to put aside their differences and to join together in a push against the Muslims.

Between 1212 and 1252 the momentum from Las Navas de Tolosa led to the capture of town after town, region after region, until all that was left of Islamic Spain was the emirate of Granada. For all intents and purposes, the 'reconquest' was complete: the peninsula, Granada excepted, was ruled by the Christian kings of Castile (lastingly united with Leon in 1230), Aragon (and Catalonia) and Portugal. Population displacement occurred as Christians began to settle in the cities of the south. Conversions of Muslims to Christianity followed, but they

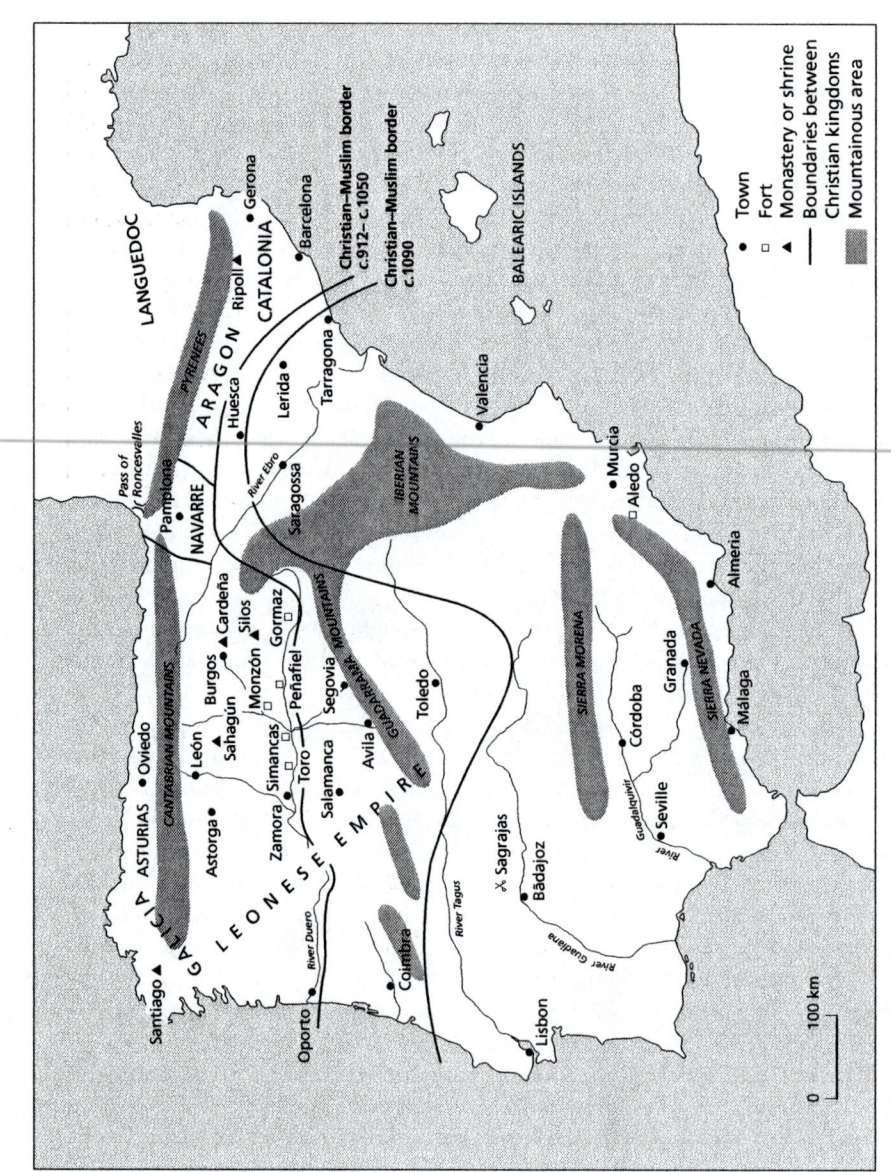

Map 17 Reconquista to *c*.1140.

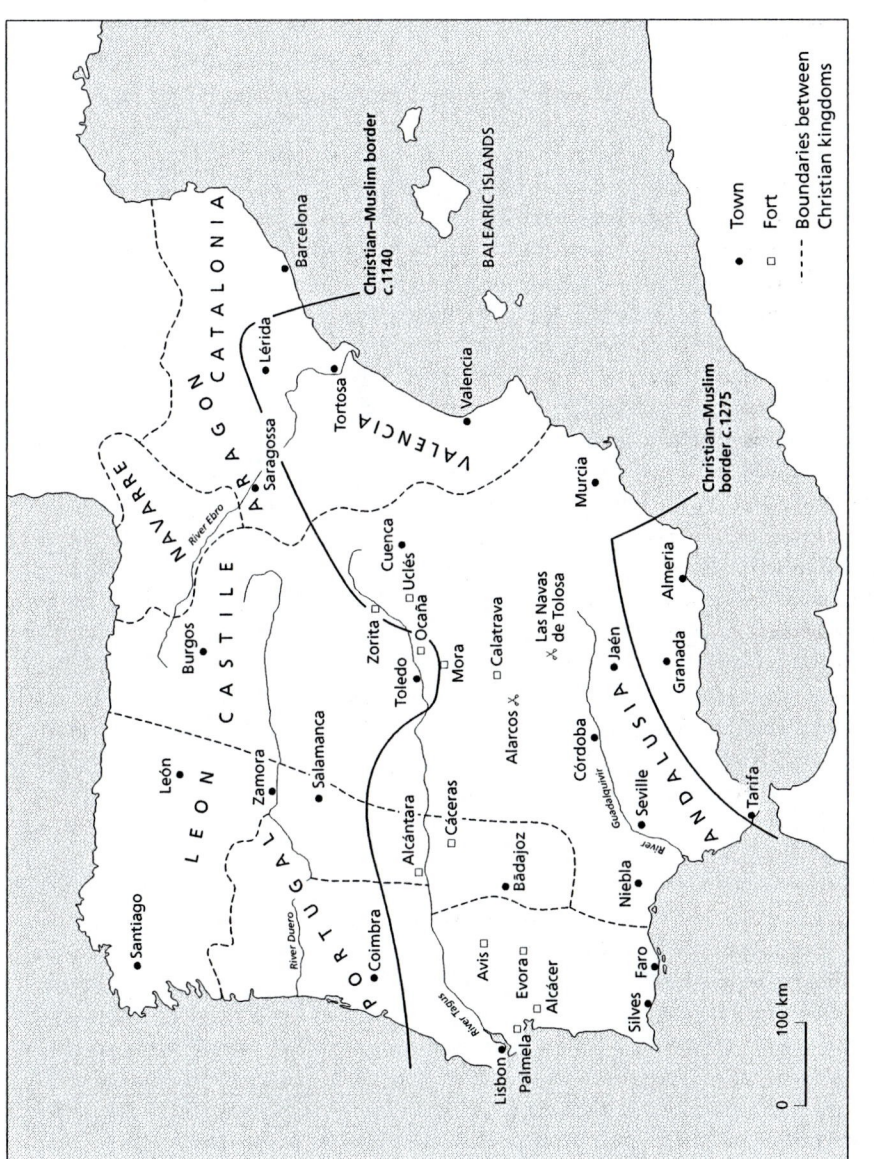

Map 18 Reconquista during the twelfth and thirteenth centuries.

were apparently no more forced than the previous conversions of Christians to Islam in the wake of the eighth-century conquest. The story of the gradual conversion of the bulk of the Muslims has left little by way of record.

An exclusive emphasis on *Reconquista* does not give nearly a full picture of ecclesiastical history in the peninsula. The Christian territories experienced the changes effecting the Western church generally. The impact of Cluny (see pp. 106–8) was early felt, although this is sometimes exaggerated. Bernard of Sediros, a French Cluniac and friend of the reforming Pope Urban II (1088–99), was imposed on the abbey of Sahagún in 1080 and became archbishop of Toledo shortly after its capture. During his long tenure (1086–1124) he helped to insert reforming French bishops into sees such as Valencia, Salamanca, Segovia and Zamora. The winds of reform brought the first papal legate in 1067, and many others were to follow. The new orders of the twelfth century came to Christian Spain, among them the Cistercians, Augustinians and Premonstratensians. In 1140 Alfonso VII of Castile granted lands for the first Cistercian monastery, at Fitero. Fairly quickly thereafter the White Monks were opening houses in recently conquered lands: in 1150 at Poblet and Santa Creus in Catalonia and in 1153 at Alcobaça in Portugal. In the following centuries the friars came very early and prospered. The Dominicans were founded by the Castilian Dominic. A Spanish province was established by 1221, and by century's end there were more than forty priories in Spain. In 1214 St Francis was in Spain, and in 1217 the Franciscan general chapter created a Spanish province and sent friars there to open a mission. They flourished, and centuries later, it was Franciscan friars who went to New Spain to open missions, many surviving to this day. Spanish bishops attended all the general councils of the period: twenty-six at the Fourth Lateran Council (1215). The popular devotions were the same as elsewhere in Western Europe, but with a Spanish flavour. During the reign of Alfonso X of Castile (1252–84) the immensely popular *Cantigás de Santa María* (Canticles of Holy Mary) were composed, over four hundred popular songs in the vernacular, extoling the role of Mary in saving souls 'at the hour of our death'.

Spanish universities were among the earliest, following Bologna, Paris and Oxford. In 1209, the cathedral school of Palencia in Castile developed into a university, and, when it became moribund, its privileges went to Valladolid. Others followed: Salamanca in Leon (*c.*1227), Lisbon in Portugal (1290), which moved to Coimbra in 1355, Lorida in the County of Barcelona (1300) and Huesca in Aragon (1354). The fifteenth century saw the founding of six other universities. The questions asked by theologians at Paris and elsewhere were also raised and disputed at these centres of learning in the peninsula. Iberia had become part of the intellectual world of the Europe of the time.

As important as the contributions of the universities were, it may be argued, of far greater importance to the world of learning was what was transpiring at Toledo. It became the first and pre-eminent centre for the translation of learned works from Arabic into Latin. After the Christian capture of Toledo (1085) many Muslims stayed on and Jewish scholars fled there from the intolerance of the Almohads in the south. These translators were the principal agents for introducing Greek learning into the West. The knowledge of Greek in Western Europe was nearly non-existent in the twelfth century, but the Arabs had long since translated the scientific and philosophical works of Greek antiquity into Arabic. Toledo became a centre where learned men translated the works of the Greek scholars from Arabic into Latin. There became known among Western scholars for the first time almost all the works of Aristotle and Plato (except some dialogues) as well as the works of many other Greeks, including Galen and Hippocrates on medicine and Ptolemy and Euclid on mathematics. The intellectual achievements of Western philosophers and theologians in the twelfth century and, particularly, in the thirteenth century would have been unimaginable without such translations. It might not be too great an exaggeration to say that without a Toledo there would not have been a Paris.

The 'reconquest' must take its place as one among several strands that made up the pattern of medieval Spain. Above all else, what was accomplished during this long period was the shift of the peninsula's axis from Islamic Africa and the Middle East to the Christian world of Western Europe. The 'reconquest' brought Spain back into Europe.

Further reading

Joinville's life of St Louis can be found conveniently in Joinville and Villehardouin, *Chronicles of the Crusades* (tr. M.R.B. Shaw; Harmondsworth, Middlesex, 1963). For the popes of this period one can use with profit the essay by J. Watt in *The New Cambridge Medieval History*, vol. 5, *c.1198–c.1300* (ed. David Abulafia; Cambridge, 1999). For Boniface VIII, still of value is T.S.R. Boase, *Boniface VIII* (London, 1933). For a detailed narrative of the pontificates of this period see Horace K. Mann, *The Lives of the Popes in the Middle Ages*, vol. 18, *1294–1304* (London, 1932). Debra J. Birch's *Pilgrimage to Rome in the Middle Ages: Continuity and Change* (Woodbridge, Suffolk, 1998), although principally concerned with a somewhat earlier period, has a useful section on the Holy Year pilgrimages of 1300. H.L. Kessler and J. Zacharias, *Rome 1300: On the Path of the Pilgrims* (New Haven, 2000) presents an art-history view of Rome in the year 1300.

Medieval Spanish history has benefited from a number of valuable modern works. For a general overview one may start with Joseph F. O'Callaghan, *A History of Medieval Spain* (Ithaca, NY, 1975). For the coming of the Muslims see Roger Collins, *The Arab Conquest of Spain, 710–797* (Oxford, 1989). For the period it covers nothing surpasses Jocelyn N. Hillgarth, *The Spanish Kingdoms, 1250–1410* (2 vols; Oxford, 1976–78). Despite the unpopularity of the title among some historians, Derek W. Lomax's *The Reconquest of Spain* (London, 1978) remains the best account in English. Of considerable value are the works by Peter A. Linehan. His *The Spanish Church and the Papacy in the Thirteenth Century* (Cambridge, 1971) develops the theme of papal influence in Spain, and his *History and the Historians of Medieval Spain* (Oxford, 1993) should be consulted by every serious student of the subject. Bernard F. Reilly has written a series of learned books on medieval Spain; among them is *The Contest of Christian and Muslim Spain, 1031–1157* (Oxford, 1992). Among regional studies, of particular value is Thomas N. Bisson, *The Medieval*

Crown of Aragon (Oxford, 1986). On the Mozarabs see the essay by M. de Epalza, 'Mozarabs: An Emblematic Christian Minority', in S. Jayyusi (ed.), *The Legacy of Muslim Spain* (Leiden, 1992) and Rose Walker, *Views of Transition: Liturgy and Illumination in Medieval Spain* (London, 1998).

14

DEATH AND PURGATORY

The fourteenth century might rightly be thought of as the century during which the popes lived at Avignon. That story awaits the next chapter. Another, more profound reason commends the fourteenth century to our attention: no century in the Middle Ages was more calamitous in terms of the destruction of human life than the fourteenth century. Twice the scourge of massive mortality struck Western Europe, first with a devastating famine and then with the catastrophe of the Black Death. In these tragic circumstances what comfort religion could bring to the dying and to those who mourned them came largely from a belief in an afterlife in which there were not only a heaven and a hell but also a purgatory, heaven's antechamber, a place of cleansing for good but not perfect souls, a place to which all might hope for admission. Death hovered over this century like no other in the Middle Ages.

The Black Death

The church was not immune to the disasters that beset the society in which it lived. The deaths of millions of Christians in the fourteenth century had to affect the Christian church, and indeed it did. The church, it cannot be too frequently repeated, was not merely a structure; it was that, but it was primarily a community of believers. When that community suffered from catastrophic events, as it did in the fourteenth century, then the church also suffered from those catastrophic events. The actual extent of their effect on the church may be long debated, but that the church was deeply shaken can hardly be denied. It also cannot be denied that there was a fairly fast recovery, yet one that left scars.

Often forgotten in the understandable emphasis put on the plague of 1347–50 was the great famine that began in 1315 and, in its severest impact, continued until 1317 and, in some regions, until 1322. Severe, cold winters and very wet summers combined to reduce the food crop drastically, and the consequence was widespread famine. It affected northern Europe: a line from the Alps westward through Lyons to the sea near La Rochelle roughly marks the southern extent of the famine. It reached as far as the British Isles (only northern Scotland escaping) and eastward through the Baltic regions to southern Scandinavia and even as far as Poland. Germany, northern France and Flanders suffered the most. The wheat yields in France are estimated to have decreased by 50 per cent. Prices soared. In London the cost of wheat at market was nearly 500 per cent higher than in pre-famine years. In Holland the price of fish rose to a similar level. The scarcity of feed for livestock was compounded by diseases that ravaged cattle, sheep and oxen. On three estates of an English monastery (Ramsey) in 1319–20 the number of cattle declined from fifty-four to six, from forty-seven to two and from sixty-five to nine. The human mortality is extremely difficult to estimate, since there were variations from place to place and from year to year. Some estimates run as high as 15 per cent and even 20 per cent in the affected places in the countryside and in the towns alike, perhaps with a somewhat greater impact in the towns. In Flanders, according to reliable figures, the town of Ypres lost 10 per cent of its population from May through October 1316 alone. In Bruges an average of ninety-two persons died each week during the same period. At Tournai compelling evidence suggests a mortality rate in 1316 which was 250 per cent above the usual, which led one contemporary to observe, 'There perished every day so many – men and women, rich and poor, young and old, from every rank of society – that the very air stank.' New cemeteries were opened at Leuven in Flanders, at Brussels in Brabant, at Hamburg in northern Germany, at Erfurt in eastern Germany, at Bratislav in Slovakia and at many other places.

The famine was no respecter of persons. In 1316 alone three abbesses of Reinsburg in Friesland died. In the same year, in what is now Belgium at least six heads of religious houses died and by 1319 eighteen others had died. If hunger and famine-related pestilence struck the leaders of monasteries, what should one infer about the lowly monks and nuns and the peasantry working the fields? Stretched by economic necessities, religious house after religious house sold off lands or went into debt. The records describing this process are abundantly rich for Germany, where they show great houses taking drastic measures to survive. There was, in Professor Jordan's words, 'an almost universal crisis for the northern European church'. As drastic as that crisis was, worse – much worse – was to come.

In human terms no other catastrophe in the Middle Ages can come close to matching the plague of 1347–50, known to history as the Black Death. Nature, not always benign, visited Western Europe with a tragedy of monumental proportions, leaving in its wake millions upon millions of humans dead. Economic historians debate the impact of the Black Death, at times in a clinical, almost detached way, but there can be no debating that the middle of the fourteenth century witnessed a phenomenon that caused pain, suffering and death to human beings, their numbers so large as to render numbering them almost impossible and their anguish so profound as to defy description. It was nothing less than a human disaster on a horrific scale. Professionally, historians should be neither reverent nor irreverent, but, when it comes to writing about the Black Death, their pens should be shrouded in awe at the human toll taken by that historical phenomenon.

Some news of disease and famine in central Asia filtered into Europe in the 1330s, but it came from a place where, in the European mind, myth and reality intermingled, and, in any case, it was a far-away place. The stories were of drought and famine, earthquake and flood, and then of plague. It is now known that the plague is endemic to the steppeland of central Asia, where it broke out about 1331. From there it became pandemic, spreading east into China, south into India and west towards Europe. This westward arm of the plague reached southern Russia about 1345. It came to Astrakhan at the Volga delta by 1346. Before long the plague spread to the Crimean peninsula. Although it may have been brought west from other sources in and near the eastern Mediterranean, the Crimean source is best described in contemporary and near-contemporary accounts: it may have been the principal source for the entrance of the plague into Europe. At the port of Caffa (now Feodosiya) in the Crimea, Genoese merchants had sought refuge from the khan's army. A siege lasted for almost three years, since the Western merchants with their back to the sea had access to needed supplies. A contemporary described what happened then:

> Disease afflicted the army of the Tartars and everyday thousands and thousands died. It was as if arrows from heaven were raining on them. Medicine had no affect. The Tartars died as quickly as the disease appeared on their bodies: swellings in the armpit or groin and then a dreadful fever. The Tartar army, overwhelmed by this disaster, turned away from their siege and had the putrefying corpses catapulted into the city, hoping to kill those inside. The Christians could not escape the torrent of bodies thrown into the city. They tried to dump the bodies into the sea, but there were too many. The stench of the corpses poisoned the air and the water, leaving scarcely one in a thousand able to flee.

But some did flee, as the account tells us. A boat, perhaps several boats, sailed from Caffa to Italy in the autumn of 1347. They brought the plague with them. Disease-ridden Genoese galleys arrived at Messina in Sicily in early October, but it is not clear that these were the ships that had left Caffa. At least some of those fleeing Caffa landed at Genoa and, in time, moved on to other ports. We are told,

> When the sailors mingled with the people in these places, it seemed that they had a cargo of evil spirits. Every town, every settlement, every hamlet was struck by the contagion, and the men and women who lived there died. Those afflicted in turn afflicted their families so that even those who were burying the dead themselves died. Death came through the windows.

From Italy the plague moved north until nearly all of Europe had been visited, and it was not till very late in 1350 that it passed from Scandinavia. A giant scythe had cut across Europe.

What caused this devastation? The simple answer is *yersinia pestis*, which is an organism that is resident in the bloodstream of certain rodents and in the stomach of fleas that feed on the rodents. The movement of host rodents and their resident fleas from remote parts of central Asia, probably because of changing ecological conditions such as drought and rodent overpopulation, brought the disease into populated areas. Fleas brought it to humans, and the epidemic had started. It was the black rat, in particular, which carried the organism into Europe. The disease-bearing fleas could live outside their rodent hosts perhaps for weeks at a time and could travel considerable distances. It was black rats and their fleas that arrived in Sicily and Italy in 1347. Contemporaries noticed two sets of symptoms, which describe the two forms that the plague took. The most common symptom was the appearance of large swellings, boil-like, the size of almonds, in the area of the groin or armpit or, less commonly, of the neck. These swellings were called buboes, hence bubonic plague. Fever and severe headaches quickly followed, and, in some cases, interior bleeding led to discolouration of the skin. If the bubo ruptured, there was some chance of recovery. But the bubonic form of the Black Death was fatal in most cases and followed within five days or so after the appearance of the buboes. In this form of the plague *yersinia pestis* attacked the lymphatic system with its principal nodes at the groin, armpit and neck. The poet Boccaccio described what he had seen with his own eyes at Florence:

> The first signs both in men and women were swellings that appeared either in the groin or in the armpits. Some became as large as an apple and others more or less the size of an egg. The people called them *gavoccioli* [i.e., buboes]. They spread quickly from those parts to other parts of the body. Black or livid spots began to appear on the arms and thighs and elsewhere on the body, some large and others small but numerous. Just as the *gavoccioli* are signs that death was approaching, so also are these spots.

Yet the plague, arising from the same organism, also took another form: it affected the lungs, hence, pneumonic plague. While the bubonic form can be traced quite simply to flea bites, the pneumonic plague arose in a more complex way. The initial infection occurred when, in a person suffering from bubonic plague, the organism attacked the lung and that person coughed or sneezed or expectorated, causing the disease-bearing organism to become airborne. When others breathed it in, it attacked their lungs. Alternatively, and probably less commonly, a person might inhale the faeces left by a flea on bedding. In either case, pneumonic plague was the result. The symptoms were shortness of breath, consequent rapid breathing and the coughing of blood. Death was the only release and came within three days. The obvious virulence of pneumonic plague – it was transmitted not by fleas but from person to person – led contemporaries to describe people who went to bed well at night and were dead in the morning. Fear of contagion, in Boccaccio's telling, had dire consequences:

> Brothers abandoned brothers, uncles abandoned nephews, sisters abandoned brothers, at times wives abandoned husbands, and, as difficult as it is to believe, parents abandoned their own children, leaving them uncared for, unvisited, left to their fate like strangers.

Not merely at Florence but in other towns and even in rural areas, the fear of contagion, fed by no exact knowledge of what was happening, added to the disastrous conditions.

The path of the pandemic can be easily seen. When it struck a place, it remained generally for several months before it subsided. Along the west coast of Italy, Pisa and Genoa were struck late in 1347 and in the east Bari and Venice. From these and other ports it went inland, striking almost everywhere so that by the spring of 1348 all of Italy had been visited by the plague. The majority of the population of Piacenza were wiped out, as happened also at Orvieto, Siena, San Gimignano and scores of other places. Boccaccio's estimate of 100,000 dead at Florence, while clearly an exaggeration, may not be too wide of the mark. His description of bodies being piled up outside houses, to be picked up like garbage, remains one of the most vivid images of the plague known to us. At Naples, a contemporary put the deaths at 63,000; at Bologna, a chronicler put the figure at 60 per cent. Milan escaped the same fury, although, even there, up to 15 per cent may have perished. At Pistoia, so severe was the threat of the plague that the city in May 1348 issued ordinances, 'to prevent the sickness now threatening our region from attacking citizens of Pistoia', yet, despite these precautions, the city was not spared. Exact figures are impossible to get, yet Italy experienced a devastation never seen before or since.

The Alps proved no barrier to the movement of the disease. Through Alpine passes the plague reached Bavaria in June 1348 and Austria in November. Vienna experienced it from the next spring, where, one estimate concludes, over 500 people died each day. The exact routes are not known, but the plague was at Frankfurt and Mainz in the summer of 1349 and soon thereafter at Cologne. Then before year's end it was further north at Münster, Bremen and Hamburg; at the latter half the population are said to have perished.

Through southern ports, particularly Marseilles, as well as through mountain passes, in 1348 the plague reached France. At these ports as well as at ports on the west coast of Iberia, the plague struck savagely. Soon it was at Narbonne, Carcassone, Toulouse and, at length, reached the sea at Bordeaux. Situated, as it is, on the Rhone, Avignon, residence of the popes now for nearly forty years, was severely affected in the spring of 1348. A letter sent from Avignon at the height of the plague recounted,

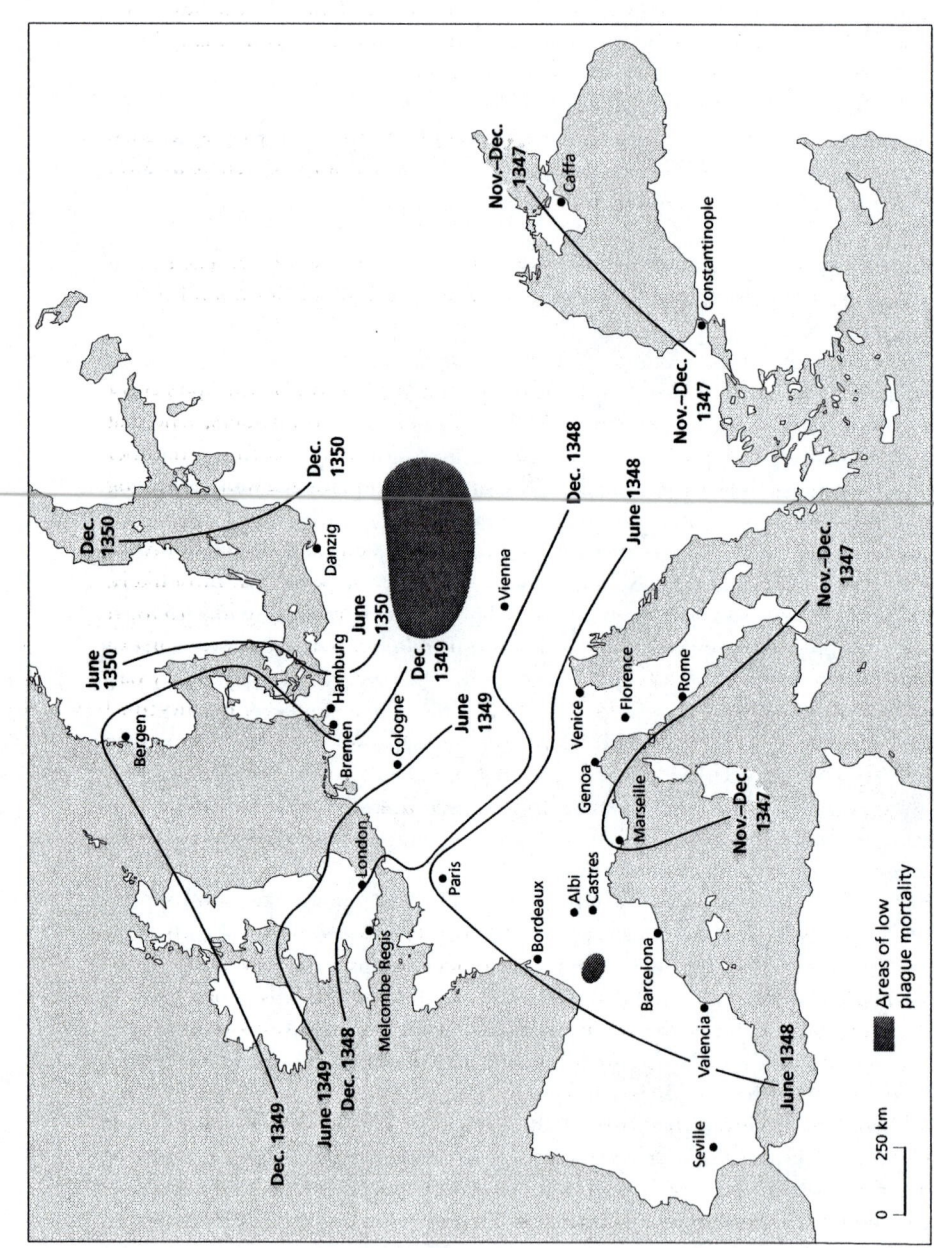

Map 19 Spread of the Black Death, 1347–50.

At least half the population has died. Within the city walls over 7,000 houses are vacant, emptied of their residents by death . . . The pope bought land for a cemetery near the church of Our Lady of Miracles. By 14 March, 11,000 victims have been buried there, while many others have been buried elsewhere in Avignon.

North from Avignon to Lyons and eventually, by June 1348, the plague reached Paris, its gates and walls no defence against the disease. Writing ten years after the events, a Carmelite friar, observed,

So many died that for some time over 500 bodies were taken each day from the Hotel-Dieu to be buried at the cemetery of the Holy Innocents.

Estimates suggest that well in excess of half the population of Europe's most populous city fell victim to the plague. Quickly it spread to Flanders, where at Tournai, a local abbot wrote that at Christmas time in 1348 an enormous number of inhabitants died. Holland was similarly struck, and soon the sea walls encircling the British Isles were breached.

No one knows exactly where the plague first touched England, certainly on the south coast, perhaps in Dorset or at Southampton or Bristol or, most likely, at several places at about the same time, namely, late June or early July 1348. It may have reached London in November, but the city experienced the worst of the pestilence in the next year. Again, no one knows the death toll. The city had a population perhaps between 40,000 and 50,000, and an estimate of one-third mortality is as close to the true figure as we may get. East Anglia, with its close commercial ties with the Low Countries, was devastated. From chronicle after chronicle one can see the progress of the plague through the land. A cleric of Oxfordshire described its further progress:

The joy of the Scots [at the death of so many English] turned to grief. God's wrath, having punished the English, now turned to the Scots and punished them with lunacy and leprosy . . . In the following year it devastated the Welsh as it had the English. Then it travelled to Ireland, cutting down great numbers of the English settlers, but the native Irish were hardly touched.

We know that the pestilence crossed into Ireland in 1349 and that it struck native peoples and settlers alike. A description written by a Franciscan friar, twenty-five of whose fellow friars had died, bears clear testimony to the devastation, his concluding words being his own epitaph:

I, Friar John Clyn of the Franciscans of Kilkenny, related in this book the things of note that have happened in my lifetime, those which I

> myself witnessed or those which I have heard about from trustworthy people . . . Lest this work die with the author, I am leaving space on this parchment for the work to be continued, if anyone should survive and any child of Adam escape this pestilence and continue the work which I have begun.

Another, later hand added, 'At this point the author apparently died'.

The story is told that a merchant ship sailed out of London in May 1349, and, while the ship was at sea, members of the crew experienced the plague symptoms. By the time the ship approached her destination, Bergen in Norway, the entire crew was dead. Those who went out into the fjord to inspect this ghost ship became infected, and so the plague spread to Norway. Whatever truth there may be to the specifics of this story, the Black Death reached Norway at about this time. In the following year the king of Sweden warned his people, 'Norway and Holland are being ravaged, and this death is fast approaching our land'. Ingmar Bergman set his classic film *The Seventh Seal* (1958) in Scandinavia at the time of the plague. The Black Death had reached Constantinople, Greece, Cyprus and probably even the Dalmatian coast before it arrived in Sicily and Italy. Catalonia was an early casualty. From Austria the plague moved to Hungary and, through routes not altogether clear to us, to Lithuania and Poland. Scarcely no part of Europe escaped entirely, although some regions such as Bohemia and parts of Hungary and Poland remained largely untouched.

The recurrence of the plague in 1361, although less severe and less widespread, by ordinary criteria was catastrophic. Another visitation of the plague came in 1369, others in the 1370s and in 1390. Chaucer, writing his famous tales told by pilgrims to Canterbury about 1390, put in the mouth of the Pardoner a tale that took place during a plague:

> There came a privy thief men call Death,
> Who in this country all the people slayeth . . .
> He has a thousand slain this pestilence.
> And, master, 'ere you come in his presence
> Me thinketh that it be necessary
> For to be wary of such an adversary.
> Be ready to meet him wherever you go.
> 'Tis what my mother taught me; I say no more.

Another episode broke out in 1405. And the plague that struck London in 1665 was the final gasp of this pandemic.

The death toll from the Black Death is impossible to measure with anything approaching exactitude. Contemporary estimates are notoriously exaggerated, yet controls on population statistics are possible, and estimates can and, indeed, are made. At one time the estimate ran to 'somewhere between a quarter and a third' of the population of Europe. More recent estimates, based on more local and regional studies, place the death toll between 40 per cent and 50 per cent of the population of Europe. If one accepts a general population of 100,000,000 in Europe, then the Black Death in little over two years took between 30,000,000 and 40,000,000 human lives. Although Europe has seen the loss of human life on large, tragic scales, neither before nor since the Black Death has it suffered such a catastrophic loss of human life from natural causes. One economic historian has said that Europe at the time had an excess population and that the plague had a 'purgative' effect, a proposition, it is safe to say, that would not find much favour with the tens of millions who perished. It has also been said that in addition to the loss of these lives the most significant historical aspect of the plague was a massive psychological reaction, bordering on societal hysteria and that this was compounded by the fear of the plague returning, as, indeed, it did. Contemporary analysis, at one level, traced the plague to the wrath of God. Some saw in the heavens the conjunction of Saturn, Jupiter and Mars in the house of Aquarius, the omen of disastrous catastrophe. At another level, the learned doctors at the University of Paris and elsewhere attributed the plague to bad humours in the air, and, with respect to pneumonic plague, they were not far off the mark. The only remedies were flight and isolation. Massive psychological trauma makes considerable sense, but it is an *a priori* conclusion – what should have happened did happen – and, although anecdotes about traumatic reactions can be cited, the evidence tends to show that the survivors made fairly rapid adjustments to the consequences of this devastation.

The effect of the plague on the church cannot be totally separated from the general effect on society, so interconnected were they. If one looks merely at demographics, the picture is clear: a large number of clergy and religious died from the plague, probably in a proportion to the general population. Accounts show parish priests acting heroically in the face of almost certain death, as they cared for the dying and buried the dead. At Piacenza a priest and the man to whom he gave the last rites were buried together on the next day. In France, it was said that 'in many towns and villages priests, acting like cowards, fled and left the spiritual care of the sick to the regular clergy, who showed themselves, on the whole, more courageous'. At Paris, the same commentator writes, that 'the holy sisters of the Hotel-Dieu, not fearing death, nursed the sick humbly and sweetly, without considering the consequences'. So scarce through death and fear had priests become that the bishop of Bath and Wells told his people,

> If the dying cannot find an ordained priest, they should confess
> their sins, according to apostolic teaching, to any lay person, even to
> a woman if no man is available.

Although the bishop told them that, should they recover, they should confess these sins to their parish priest, it was an extraordinary step. The archbishop of York appointed an Augustinian canon to a parish usually served by secular priests, stating that 'we make an exception now because of the lack of secular priests, who have died from the deadly plague hanging over us'. German sources show that one-third of the higher clergy, the ones most able to flee, perished; among the lower clergy the mortality must have been significantly higher. In Sicily, the archbishop of Catania died in heroic circumstances. The bishop of Paris died as did three archbishops of Canterbury. And the list could go on. Religious, living in enclosed communities, were particularly susceptible to contagious disease and suffered perhaps disproportionately. A hundred and fifty Franciscans at Marseilles died, leaving their priory empty of life. One entire priory of Austin friars perished at Avignon as did sixty-six Carmelite friars. In the far west of Europe, at Coimbra in Portugal, the great monastery of St Peter was devastated. The abbot of Westminster Abbey died as did twenty-seven of his monks. At St Albans the abbot, prior and forty-six monks perished. And there was the nun, the only survivor of a small nunnery, who was found ten years later disorientated, wandering through the lanes of remote Lincolnshire. Reliable estimates suggest that half the religious of England died, monks, canons, friars and nuns, with the friars suffering a somewhat greater loss.

Three further aspects of the plague warrant our attention. In the first place, as in so many massive catastrophes, scapegoats were sought and found. In parts of Spain the Christians blamed the Muslims. Strangers and foreigners were often treated with suspicion, not unlike modern immigrants, with the foreign English suspected at Narbonne and, in Aragon, foreigners and Portuguese pilgrims suspected. More widely, helpless lepers, much reviled as they were, had heaped on them the added opprobrium of spreading the plague. Yet these accusations pale in comparison to those made against the Jews.

Uncoordinated, violent attacks against Jews erupted in many places during the plague. Everywhere the charges were the same. The Jews had poisoned the wells of Christians. It was said that they themselves were taking water from distant streams, which was taken as a clear sign of their guilt. The earliest reported attacks on Jews occurred in the south of France, where, in the spring of 1348, wholesale exterminations took place at Narbonne and Carcassone. At a celebrated trial in September a local Jewish doctor confessed to having imported poison into southern France from Spain, which he then had thrown into the principal wells. At about the same time as this trial, the Jews at Basel were rounded up and put in wooden buildings, which were then incinerated. Burning seemed the usual punishment. In Germany, by early 1349 Jews were burned at Stuttgart, Memmingen, Lindau, Freiburg, Dresden, Worms and Erfurt, to mention only some of the places. The Jews of Speyer were murdered and their corpses placed in wine barrels and dispatched down the Rhine River. In the summer of 1349 the fury had erupted at Mainz and at Cologne.

Some responsible leaders acted with decency and humanity. The pope, Clement VI, threw open the gates of Avignon to Jews fleeing these outrages. He called on Christians everywhere to act with tolerance and threatened with excommunication those who persecuted the Jews. The king of Aragon, Pedro IV, disturbed by persecutions at Barcelona, ordered swift prosecution of the perpetrators there and protection of Jews everywhere in his kingdom. The king of the Germans and the duke of Austria made efforts, which proved largely ineffectual, to stem the attacks. At Cologne, the city fathers also took action to protect the Jews. Neither popes nor kings nor civic leaders were able to stop the fury: it ended only with the passing of the plague.

In another aspect of the plague we must notice the religious hysteria, even if it formed but a small part of the picture of the plague years. The hysteria took its starkest form in the activity of the flagellants. As their name implies, they were men who undertook penance by flagellation. Flagellant penance was not new. Individuals had long seen the scourging of the flesh as a means of bringing its lusts under control and of atoning for sins. Yet, as a group activity, it seems to have first appeared in thirteenth-century Italy. As related to the Black Death, this communal penitential scourging was first seen in Germany. Flagellants were soon found in most regions stricken by the plague. They processed from village to village, from town to town, sometimes by the hundreds in a long procession, two by two, clad in hooded garments, led by a cross-bearer and often by banners of penitential purple. They walked silently except when chanting the haunting words of the *Stabat Mater*, Mary's lamentation at the foot of the cross:

Stabat Mater dolorosa	Stood the mother sorrowful
Juxta crucem lacrimosa,	Beneath the cross weeping,
Dum pendebat filius . . .	Whilst her son was dying . . .
Fac me plagis vulnerari.	Make me wounded by his blows.
Fac me cruce inebriari	Make me by his cross inebriated
Et cruore filii.	And by your son's blood.

Their coming to a village was greeted by the pealing of bells from the tower of the parish church. The parish would come out *en masse* to see these penitential people. The procession wended its way through the crowds of the pious and the curious to the parish church. There they stripped themselves of their cloaks and stood clothed only with cloths that hung from waist to feet. Taking their whips into their hands, they left the church one by one, the eldest leading the way. The first prostrated himself on the ground, his arms outstretched in the form of a cross. The second beat the prostrated one, then prostrated himself and was beaten by the next. And so it went on. They then formed a circle in the marketplace and chanted and scourged, chanted and scourged, chanted and scourged, the tempo increasing like the beat of a drum and with it the emotion of the onlookers. Some of the onlookers were so overwhelmed that they joined the band of flagellants on their pilgrimage of penance.

By mid-1349 flagellants could be seen on the roads and lanes of Poland and Hungary in the east and of Flanders and the Low Countries in the west. From Flanders about 120 flagellants arrived in England, where a chronicler described them:

They went in procession twice each day, barefoot, showing themselves to the people of London, at times at St Paul's and at times at other places. Their bodies were bare save for a linen cloth that covered them from the waist down. Each flagellant wore a hood, on which was painted a red cross on the front and on the back, and each one in his right hand had a whip with three thongs. In each thong there was a knot with a sharp piece of metal, like a needle, which was wedged in the knot in such a way that it protruded at each end. As they processed single file, they scourged themselves on their naked bodies, which were soon red with blood . . . Thrice they prostrated themselves and proceeded to take turns beating each other.

Their stay in England was apparently short, and, few recruits having been made, they returned whence they had come.

At about the same time as the flagellants were scourging themselves in London, the pope at Avignon condemned the movement. In May 1348, Clement VI had actually participated in what were clearly flagellant-like ceremonies at Avignon, but he turned against the movement – was it the religious excess? the lay control? – and, in October 1349, issued a bull of condemnation. By then the worst of the plague had passed except in far northern Europe, and the movement was losing much of its *raison d'être*.

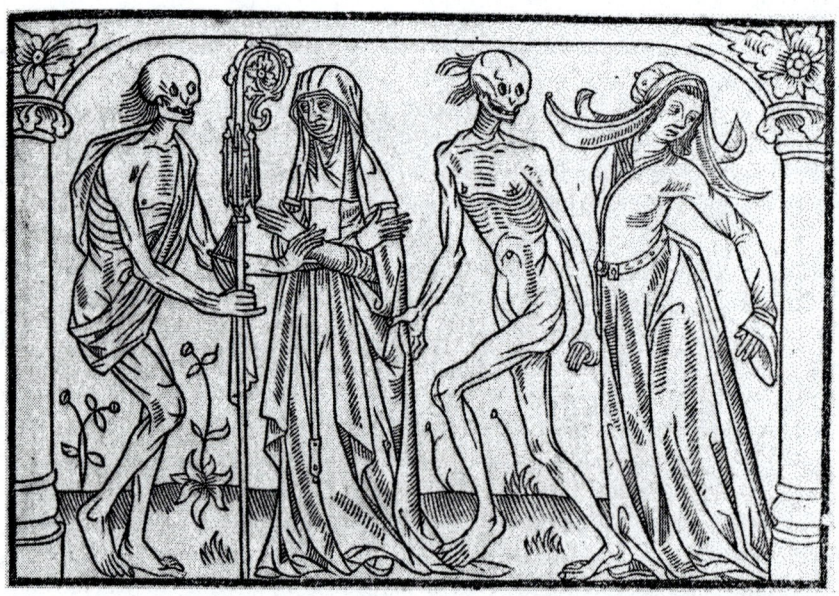

19 Women being led in dance to their death, from *Icy est la danse macabre des femmes* (Paris, 1491); British Library shelf no. IB 39618. Reproduced by permission of the British Library.

Often associated with the Black Death is the *danse macabre* (dance of death). It first appeared in verse of the thirteenth century and, later, in both verse and in artistic representations. Its actual performance in the fifteenth century seems little less than a conceit of lordly courts. In its simplest visual form it shows the dead and the living doing a line dance, led by Death. Among the living were bishop and fool, merchant and thief, old man and child and others, signalling the indiscriminate call of Death. An early printed book, *Danse Macabre* (1485), and woodcuts popularized the image in the late fifteenth and early sixteenth centuries. It is only by inference that we can – and perhaps should – associate the dance of death with the devastating toll of human life taken by the Black Death.

The religious hysteria soon passed. Religious houses by century's end recovered to about 75 per cent of pre-plague numbers. The persecution of the Jews abated but did not disappear. By most standards recovery was fairly rapid. The extent and speed of the recovery should not blind us to the shock that Europe and the church experienced in the mid-fourteenth century.

The emergence of purgatory

The stench of death and the sight of the reaper's scythe cutting down millions indiscriminately focused attention, as nothing else could, on the afterlife. When death comes, is that the end? Do the lights simply go out? The answer was that at this time there was an almost universal belief in an afterlife. In which case, what happens at death? With countless numbers of every age and condition dying from famine and plague, the question had a harsh relevance. Prayers and Masses were said for the dead and alms given in their name, but why? By this time the geography of the afterlife was well established in the belief system of Christians, and it included purgatory. There was heaven for the perfect, hell for the wicked and, in between, purgatory, where the not-so-perfect and the not-so-wicked could be purged of their guilt before entering heaven. It was the waiting room for paradise, and the wait there could be shortened by the prayers and good works of the living.

It would be nearly impossible to exaggerate the significance of purgatory in the life of the medieval church, especially in the way that life was lived by individual Christians. The antechamber of heaven where the good but not perfect souls suffer their temporary punishment had a fixed place in the beliefs of virtually all Christians in the Western church and deeply affected their religious practices. Apart from heretics like the Waldensians and the Cathars and, later, John Wyclif, purgatory was believed in as firmly as the Eucharist, the divinity of Christ, the Trinity and other central beliefs of the church and played a role almost as large as the Eucharist and the Virgin in the daily devotional lives of people. That one could assist one's deceased father and mother and other loved ones and shorten their stay in purgatory led to the development of a rich variety of religious devotions and practices, from which, it is safe to say, no parish in Christendom was exempt. Pope Innocent IV, in a letter of 1254, described this belief:

> The souls who died having repented but not having fulfilled their penance or who die with only venial but not mortal sins on their souls are purged and can be helped by the suffrages of the church.

Two decades later Pope Clement V, in a document associated with the Second Council of Lyons (1274), said virtually the same thing. And Boniface VIII, in calling the Holy Year of 1300, allowed a plenary indulgence of the penance due for sins not only to those who confessed contritely and visited the Roman basilicas but also to those who duly confessed their sins and who died on their way to Rome, an indulgence remitting punishment due in purgatory for penance incomplete at death. During the next two decades Dante was composing his incomparable description in *Il purgatorio*. The doctrine and belief were firmly established by the late thirteenth century. Yet it had been long believed before either pope or poet discussed it.

The belief in an afterlife is essential to Christian belief. The New Testament recounts Christ's many promises of a life beyond the grave in which the good are rewarded and the bad punished. (See, for example, Matthew 25, 31ff.) But belief in an afterlife long preceded the coming of Christ. Readers of ancient texts are familiar with incidents of visits to the underworld. In the *Epic of Gilgamesh*, much of it dating to sometime in the early second millennium BC, we find two such visits. Ulysses in the *Odyssey* (bk 2) descends into a similar underworld as does Aeneas (*Aeneid*, bk 6), who meets Dido, whom he had terribly wronged. Although rabbinical teaching fluctuated, the Hebrews had a *sheol* (hell) and a heaven. Psalm 116 sings,

> I was encompassed in sorrowful death, and I was seized by the pains of hell.

Christ brought a clarity about the afterlife. His teaching had an obvious appeal: the injustices of this life in which the good often suffer and the wicked often prosper will be put aright by an all-just God in the next life. But even this stark clarity of good and evil, heaven and hell, was not without ambiguity. 'I will raise you up on the last day,' Christ taught. Then there would be a judgement, a Last Judgement, and the separation of the good and the wicked. What was unclear was what happened between the time of death and the time of the Last Judgement. It was from this ambiguity that the idea of purgatory arose.

Even from early Christian times prayers were said for the dead, which would be unnecessary if the souls were already saved and fruitless if the souls were already lost. A contemporary account describes the vision had by Perpetua as she was awaiting martyrdom in Carthage in 202. In a dream she saw her dead brother in a place of darkness with others; he was 'all burning and tormented with thirst, filthy of body, clad in rags and his face with the sore he had at death'. He was seven when he died, and in her dream she saw him, still a boy, unable to reach, even on his tiptoes, a basin of water. She prayed night and day for him, and then she had another vision. She saw him, his body and clothes clean, the sore on his face healed and the basin lowered so that he could drink from it. Her prayers had relieved his sufferings in the afterlife. This story of Perpetua's vision became a familiar story in the Middle Ages, as it was told and retold by preachers and others. It served to confirm the idea that the living could help the dead by their prayers.

The works of St Augustine (d. 430) were second only to the Bible in popularity, particularly among the learned, in the medieval centuries. In his immensely influential *City of God* (bk 21) he develops his eschatology (i.e., the study of the 'last things', death and what follows) and affirms a purgatorial fire which punishes some souls in the interval between death and the Last Judgement. Theirs were minor sins or major sins not fully expiated during their lifetime. He left questions unasked, but a purgatorial fire between death and the Last Judgement had by Augustine's time become a firm part of the geography of the afterlife. St Gregory the Great (d. 604) went further and said that there are two parts to the underworld: upper hell, from which souls would emerge and enter heaven, and lower hell, from which no one would ever emerge. In Gregory's upper hell we can see an early description of what would later be called 'purgatory'.

Stories have a way of shaping belief about the afterlife more forcefully than the reflections of theologians. Added to the ever-popular vision of Perpetua was the vision of Dryhthelm, recounted by Bede in his *Ecclesiastical History of the English People* (bk 5, ch. 12), completed in 731:

> A certain man, already dead, came back to life and told of the many memorable things which he had seen.

Bede goes on to recount the vision of this holy layman. He had died one night and returned to life in the morning. During the night he was taken on a journey to the next world.

> My guide was a man of shining countenance, who wore bright robes. We went silently in what seemed to me the direction of the rising sun at the solstice. As we walked, we came to a very broad and deep valley of infinite length. It was to our left. One side of that valley was raging with an exceedingly terrible fire, and the other side was equally intolerable, for it had hail falling furiously and icy snow swirling about and covering everything. Both sides were filled with the souls of human beings, which were thrown from one side to the other as if by the violence of the storm. When they could no longer bear the ferocious heat, the poor wretches hurled themselves headlong into the frigid cold opposite, and, finding no relief there, they hurled themselves back into the ever-burning flames.

Dryhthelm thought he had seen hell, but his guide told him it was not hell and led him on further.

I gradually saw that the place before us, which we were entering, grew darker and darker till there was only darkness. All I could see was the bright garment of my guide. Suddenly before us there appeared balls of fire, first rising and then falling, and then rising and falling again and again. My guide disappeared, and I was left alone and desolate, seeing the balls of fire, spitting up souls like sparks tossed above the flames, only to fall again into the depths.

Dryhthelm then smelled odours of an incomparable stench and heard hideous laughter from evil spirits and horrible lamentations from human souls. He could see the evil spirits dragging souls down into a burning pit. The guide reappeared and led him away from the dreadful scene and placed him on top of a wall.

> From there I could see broad and pleasant fields full of fragrant flowers, so sweet that the awful stench disappeared. And there was a brilliant light, brighter even than the sun at mid-day. In the fields were groups of young people in white robes, sitting around in joyful groups.

Dryhthelm thought that he must be in heaven, but the guide told him that this was not the kingdom of heaven.

> Now I saw in front of me a light more luminous than what I had seen, and I heard the sweet sounds of singing, and I smelled a transcendently beautiful scent.

His guide would not let him enter these fields and explained to him what he had seen.

> The valley that you saw with its bursting flames and frightful cold is the place in which there are tried and punished the souls of those who delayed the confession of their sins until the moment of death. They died before making restitution for their sins. Despite the lateness of their repentance and confession, they will all enter into the kingdom of heaven at the Last Judgement. The prayers, almsgiving, fasting and the celebration of Masses of those who are still alive can help to free many of these souls even before the day of judgement.
>
> Also, that flaming and putrid pit which you saw is nothing else than the very mouth of hell, and those who enter will never leave.
>
> That flowery place where you saw the beautiful and happy people is the place for the souls who practised good works but who are not so perfect as to enter heaven immediately. On the day of judgement all of these will see Christ and enter into the joys of the heavenly kingdom.

Those who are perfect in their every word, deed and thought, once they die, shall enter heaven immediately. This is the kingdom where you heard the sweet sounds of music and smelled the glorious fragrances and saw the splendour of light.

This story, often repeated, provides an afterlife of four places: a heaven for the perfect, a hell for the wicked and two intermediary places, one for the good but not perfect and one for the bad but not wicked. In the course of time, these two intermediary places will be conflated to produce purgatory. What needs under-lining is that Bede, as many before him and very many after him, believed that the living can help those souls by prayers, alms and Masses.

Even more enduring and persuasive was the tale told in the late twelfth century and repeated in countless manuscripts, not only in the original Latin but in almost every vernacular language of the West. It was the story of *St Patrick's Purgatory*. It is based on a legend that held that the entrance to purgatory was through a hole (sometimes called a well or a cave) on an island, now Station Island, in Lough Derg in Co. Donegal. It was popularly believed that, if a truly contrite person entered that hole and spent a night and a day there, that person would be purged of sins and, barring any future sins, at death would enter directly into heaven. In the twelfth century, a story relating to this popular belief circulated. It tells of a knight who went to Donegal to do the penance. After preparing himself he entered the pit and there had a vision reminiscent of Bede's Dryhthelm with some added touches. Throughout his journey into the other world the knight was ten times tormented by evil spirits, whom he dispelled by saying the word 'Jesus'. He saw an earthly paradise, but it was not heaven nor was it hell (the place of the torments) which he had seen. Two archbishops in the earthly paradise explained to him:

> After receiving the faith we have often sinned because of human frailty, and we needed to perform penance for our sins. Yet, since we did not complete all our penance during our lifetime, we did so after our death in the place of torment which you have seen; some stay there longer than others. We came through those torments to this peaceful place. Those whom you saw, excepting those in the pit of hell, will also be saved and come here. Even today some have arrived here. Those suffering such torments know not how long they will so suffer, but Masses, psalms, prayers and alms which are done for them can moderate their torments . . . Even when they come here, they do not know how long they will be here . . . After the time set for us has been fulfilled, we will ascend to heavenly paradise. Our numbers here in this earthly paradise are at once increasing by those rising from the torments and decreasing by those going to heaven.

Other legends placed the entrance to purgatory elsewhere. For example, one such legend placed it in a cave on the volcanic Mount Etna in Sicily. Such popular stories reaffirmed popular belief in an in-between place in the afterlife, a temporary place for souls neither perfect nor wicked, who could be assisted by the prayers and good works of the living.

No more graphic and eloquent depiction can be found anywhere to compare with Dante's *Il purgatorio* in the *Divine Comedy*, which was completed in 1319. Famously, over the gate of hell the poet reads, 'Abandon all hope, ye who enter here.' The detailed sufferings described by Dante in each of the circles of hell, as vivid as they are, do not depict the essential suffering of hell: for the Christian poet hell's greatest torment is the absolute sense of hopelessness. As Dante, led by Virgil, goes from hell into purgatory, whose sufferings he will describe, he is moving into a place, whose essential feature, amidst these sufferings, is the knowledge that the sufferings will end, that there is hope. The contrast is stark.

> How different this entrance
> From the infernal one; here through song
> Is one greeted, there with ferocious lament.
>
> (12, 112–14)

One might compare the individual punishments in hell and purgatory, but the absence or the presence of hope makes the sufferings essentially different. To show this, the poet, as he is led out of hell, looks up and sees four stars: he is outside under the sky. Purgatory is not underground but is a seven-storey mountain on an island above ground. It is a steep mountain, which Dante and Virgil at times can climb only on all fours, and the ancient poet tells Dante not to veer to the left or to the right but to climb ever forward. At each storey souls are purged of one of the seven deadly sins. First, they are purged of pride, then, in the second storey, of envy, where 'each soul has its eyelids sewn with iron threads' (13, 70). In the third storey they are 'undoing knots of anger' (16, 24). The slothful purge their sin by rushing about, unwilling to waste even a moment, and the avaricious walk stooped, looking down on the ground, weeping because of their former preoccupation with earthly things. In the sixth storey the gluttons are so emaciated that their faces have skin drawn taut across their bones and their eye sockets look like vacuous jewel settings. And lastly he sees fire purifying souls of their sins of concupiscence. And then he is led to paradise by his beloved Beatrice. Dante affirmed in sublime verse purgatory as a place of suffering and hope, a place which leads to heaven.

It may long be debated whether the scholarly discussions about the question of purgatory at the schools and, later, at the universities were independent of and parallel to the popular belief of the faithful or, indeed, spurred into action by that popular belief. In either case, theologians seriously addressed the question of purgatory. The agenda for them was set, as in so many other matters, by Peter Lombard in his *Sentences* (*c.*1157), which became the textbook *par excellence* for theology in the universities of the thirteenth century and beyond. For him there are sins of a less serious nature – he calls them venial sins – which can be purged

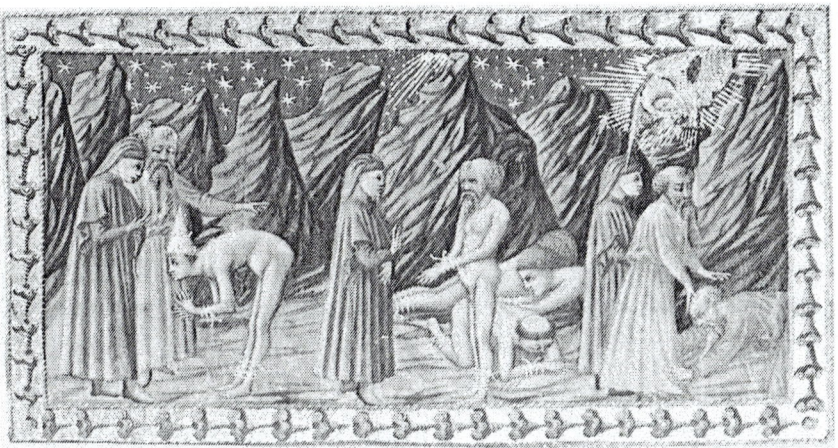

20 Dante and Virgil, wandering in Dante's purgatory, meet Pope Hadrian V, King Hugh Capet and the poet Stasius (from *Il purgatorio*), British Library, MS YT36, fo. 100. Reproduced by permission of the British Library.

after death and before the Last Judgement, the length of this purging varying from soul to soul, and there is, as a consequence, a single receptacle for medium-good and medium-bad souls in the afterlife. William of Auvergne, writing in the 1230s, argued that purgatory was necessary, for souls dying with unexpiated sins cannot enter heaven immediately and that there in purgatory they suffer corporeally from fire. Alexander of Hales, writing at roughly the same time, discussed the question of fire purging venial sins and the penalties due for mortal sins. His fellow Franciscan, Bonaventure, commented at length about the location of purgatory, while the learned Dominican Albertus Magnus answered questions about purgatory in twelve articles. Thomas Aquinas (d. 1274), undoubtedly the greatest theologian of the time, accepted the conventional teaching and went beyond to ask further questions such as: does the actual guilt for venial sin, as distinct from the punishment for venial sin, exist in souls in purgatory? (He answered in the negative.) The theologians were discussing details of what had become by this time an accepted belief, and papal statements of the thirteenth century, referred to at the beginning of this section, were merely statements of what was already a fixed part of Christian belief.

To summarize this belief. At death there is a particular judgement, which decides what should happen to an individual soul. Three options are available: heaven for the perfect, hell for the wicked and purgatory for the not-so-perfect and not-so-wicked. The length of one's stay in purgatory is determined by the number of unrepented venial sins and by the unfulfilled expiation for remitted mortal and venial sins. This time can be shortened by the prayers, Masses and almsgiving of the living. At the end of time, at the final reckoning, in a general Last Judgement, the final Doomsday, God publicly divides the good from the bad, and, as the bad go back to hell, the good, including those souls who were still in purgatory, enter into heaven. The punishment of hell and the joys of heaven are eternal, with absolutely no chance of change. The image of God dividing the good from the bad at the Last Judgement is found illuminated in countless manuscripts and carved in stones over the doors of scores of cathedrals and other churches. The question of one's final fate was difficult to avoid.

The teaching that the living can help the dead had a major impact on the church. This can be seen from at least the seventh century, and in time a day (2 November) for commemorating all the dead and praying for their souls was universally observed. We can see the influence of purgatory on the religious lives of men and women in richer detail from the thirteenth century onward. Scarcely a family in Europe was not affected by this belief. Relatives would pray for their deceased family members. They would see that their bodies were buried with obsequies for their souls and that Masses would be offered on anniversaries of their death. The wealthy often went beyond the usual practices and founded chantries, chapels with a priest to say Masses for their dead. Some chantries were established as separate churches for the sole purpose of having Masses said for a single person or a single family. More commonly, chantries were set up as altars in side chapels in parish churches with funds for Masses to be said for a definite period (e.g., five years) or in perpetuity. During the fourteenth and fifteenth centuries in one small English county (Cambridgeshire) 66 such perpetual chantries were founded. In 1438 an archbishop of Canterbury even founded an Oxford college in commemoration of all the souls in purgatory as well as, specifically, of kings and warriors of the realm. When the English chantries were dissolved in 1547, there were over 250 in London, 44 of them in St Paul's Cathedral alone, and for the country as a whole probably almost 3,000: they fell victim to a new theology that had no room for purgatory.

Moreover, every guild, merchant and craft, prayed for its dead members and arranged annual Masses for their souls. By their earliest statutes the guild of masters at the University of Paris undertook the remembrance of the souls of their deceased members. In addition, confraternities of lay persons, male and female, organized for pious purposes, spread like wildfire all over Europe in the fourteenth and fifteenth centuries. In Italy, Florence had nearly 100, while the village of Linari in Tuscany with a population of only 500 people had 3 confraternities. In France, there were 29 at Rennes, 30 at Nantes and 30 also at Dijon, and at least 25 at Arles. In 1389 King Richard II of England ordered a listing of all such confraternities (often in English called 'guilds'), and, although returns are admittedly incomplete, they reveal 164 such confraternities in Norfolk and 123 in Lincolnshire. This source and others show that there were 162 in Yorkshire with 14 of these in the city of York. Whatever other obligations the members undertook, without exception they undertook to remember in prayers and Masses the deceased members in purgatory. Invariably they would attend the funerals of fellow members. At least one Mass each year would be said for all deceased members. Some confraternities undertook the trentel (a month of

Masses) for each deceased member. Belief in purgatory was an essential feature of these societies.

Thus, woven into the fabric of late medieval religion was the conviction that the living could help the dead. The commemoration of the souls in purgatory took its place with devotion to the Eucharist and devotion to the Virgin as the principal displays of Christian belief from the late thirteenth century through the rest of the Middle Ages.

One cannot leave this subject without discussing indulgences. The teaching on indulgences is based on the twofold consequence of all sins, mortal or venial. In the first place, there is the actual guilt incurred by the sinner in committing the sin. Guilt is removed by sincere contrition and usually by confession to a priest. But something remains after the guilt is removed: the need to make satisfaction for that sin. This was called the temporal punishment due to sin, and it could be satisfied in this life by prayer, pious works and the like. If it was not fully satisfied in this life, then it had to be satisfied in purgatory. Theologians taught that the church as custodian of the infinite merits of Christ could use indulgences to reduce the temporal punishment due to sin. Pope Clement VI, in 1343, expressed what was by that time the accepted teaching. Since the temporal punishment, by definition, was temporal (in time), it could be given time measurements. Hence the pope could declare an indulgence of, say, one hundred days for performing a designated good work, such as donating towards the building of a hospital or visiting a shrine. When the deed was performed, the indulgence was gained and the temporal punishment due to sin was reduced. Exceptionally, those who went on crusade could gain a plenary indulgence, which remitted all this punishment. What is significant about the jubilee indulgence granted by Boniface VIII in 1300 is that it was a *plenary* indulgence. Still, an indulgence could be earned only for one's self by one's self. In time, however, it could be earned vicariously for souls in purgatory. This was a very late medieval development. In 1476, Pope Sixtus IV allowed that the indulgence which was gained by contributing towards the building of a church in Saintes in France could be applied to souls in purgatory. He insisted, as have theologians ever since, that this application was by way of suffrage, which meant that its application depended on God's mercy and was not assured. Two generations later Martin Luther would inveigh against the indulgence preachers who came to Germany to raise money for the new St Peter's Basilica in Rome and who allegedly said that as coins entered the coffers souls would fly out of purgatory. But that takes us beyond the time-limits of this study.

Further reading

Destined to become a classic is William C. Jordan, *The Great Famine: Northern Europe in the Early Fourteenth Century* (Princeton, 1996). A starting point for the plague should be Philip Ziegler, *The Black Death* (London, 1969). In addition to containing translations of many relevant sources, Rosemary Horrox's *The Black Death* (Manchester and New York,

1994) provides balanced, well-informed introductions to the historical questions that concern students of the subject. She also provides an excellent bibliography. Every student of the subject should read the introduction by Boccaccio to his *Decameron* for the best-known contemporary, eye-witness account and, as a bonus, the tales told by those fleeing the plague. Various regional studies provide a wealth of material. For England one should consult Colin Platt, *King Death: The Black Death and its Aftermath in Late Medieval England* (Toronto, 1996). On attitudes towards death in the later Middle Ages nothing surpasses Philippe Ariès, *The Hour of Our Death* (tr. Helen Weaver; Oxford, 1981).

The principal work on purgatory is Jacques Le Goff, *The Birth of Purgatory* (tr. Arthur Goldhammer; Chicago, 1981), which should be read together with the cautionary remarks of Aron J. Gurevich in 'Popular and Scholarly Medieval Traditions: Notes in the Margin of Jacques Le Goff's Book', *Journal of Medieval History* 9 (1983), 71–90. Eileen Gardiner, *Visions of Heaven and Hell before Dante* (New York, 1989), provides the most accessible collection of the texts of visions. Takami Matsuda, *Death and Purgatory in Middle English Didactic Poetry* (Cambridge, 1997) contains a useful summary. For reflections on St Patrick's Purgatory by a modern poet see Seamus Heaney, *Station Island* (London and Boston, 1984). There are numerous translations of Dante's *Divine Comedy*. Many prefer the versions of John Ciardi, the poet, or Dorothy L. Sayers, medieval scholar and mystery writer, although the translation and commentary by Charles S. Singleton, *The Divine Comedy* (3 vols; Princeton, 1970–75) may be preferred by scholars.

The literature on confraternities continues to grow. For Italy one can consult John Henderson, *Piety and Charity in Late Medieval Florence* (Oxford, 1994) and Nicholas Terpstra, *Lay Confraternities and Civic Religion in Renaissance Bologna* (Cambridge, 1995). The classic work for England is H.F. Westlake, *The Parish Gilds of Medieval England* (London, 1919). Among more recent studies one will find useful Barbara Hanawalt, 'Keepers of the Lights: Late Medieval Parish Gilds', *Journal of Medieval and Renaissance Studies* 14 (1984), 21–37; Caroline M. Barron, 'The Parish Fraternities of Medieval London', in C.M. Barron and C. Harper-Bill (eds), *The Church in Pre-Reformation Society: Essays in Honour of F.R.H. DuBoulay* (Woodbridge, Suffolk, 1985), pp. 13–37; and, particularly for the fifteenth century, Eamon Duffy, *The Stripping of the Altars* (New Haven and London, 1992).

15

EXILE IN AVIGNON AND AFTERMATH

For almost seven decades of the fourteenth century the papacy resided not at Rome on the banks of the Tiber but at Avignon on the banks of the Rhone, north of the Alps, in what has been called (wrongly) the Babylonian Captivity. Far from Rome at Avignon, the bishops of Rome became the most flagrant absentee churchmen in medieval history, yet it was an absence which they plausibly – to themselves and to many others – felt they could justify. The question of their subservience to the wishes of the king of France also needs to be explored. The return of the papacy to Rome prompted the worst schism in the history of the Western church, which was to last till 1415.

The Popes and Avignon

From 1309 to 1376 the popes lived at Avignon on the east bank of the Rhone River in what is now France. Seven popes lived there until the last, Gregory XI, at great personal risk, returned the papacy to Rome, fomenting a schism with a pope at Rome and a pope at Avignon. The story of that schism will be told in the next chapter. But now Avignon.

At the outset several points need be made. In the first place, the popes did not leave Rome with the intention of establishing themselves permanently or even quasi-permanently at Avignon or, indeed, anywhere else. After the tragic circumstances of the attack on Boniface VIII by henchmen of the French king, Philip IV (the Fair), in 1303, the papacy was in near disarray. In the turmoil following Boniface's death the cardinals quickly elected Benedict XI, who ruled less than eight months. A long interregnum of nearly a year followed. The pro-French cardinals cleverly secured the election of a non-cardinal, the archbishop of Bordeaux, Bertrand de Got, a Gascon, who took the name Clement V (1305–14). In retrospect, it can be seen as a mistake. He never got to Rome nor did any of his successors for decades. Clement planned to be crowned pope at Vienne, but, bowing to Philip the Fair's wishes, he was crowned at Lyons in the king's presence. For several years he wandered about southern France, a few months here and a few months there. In 1309 he was at Avignon, another stop in his wandering, and resided there at the Dominican friary. Cancer struck the pope, and he remained at Avignon, where the friars nursed him, although he occasionally left the city for months at a time. Clement did not move the papacy to Avignon: he took with him merely those papers needed to carry on the daily affairs of the church as a provisional arrangement at this temporary residence. Why his successors remained there will be visited shortly.

Secondly, the absence of the pope from Rome was nothing new. Many of Clement V's immediate predecessors lived for long periods outside of Rome. For example, Urban IV (1261–64) was never in Rome; neither were John XXI (1276–77), Martin IV (1281–85) nor the hapless Celestine V (1294). And others spent but short periods there. Innocent IV (1243–54) was at Rome a very short time as were Alexander IV (1254–61) and Gregory X (1271–76). It has been calculated that for the period from 1100 to 1304 the popes spent 60 per cent of their time away from Rome. The residence at Avignon should be seen in this context. That having been said, what marks Avignon out is the prolonged residence of the popes in one place and in a place outside Italy.

The third matter that needs stressing is that the seven popes who resided at Avignon were still bishops of Rome. The pope by definition is bishop of Rome: the pope is pope because he is bishop of Rome. When each of these seven popes was installed, he was installed as bishop of Rome. The actual see of Rome was provided with a vicar general, who acted in the pope's name. While at Avignon, the pope was not bishop of Avignon. The popes at Avignon were simply absentee bishops of Rome.

Something must be said about Avignon itself. It was not within the kingdom of France: it was situated on the eastern bank of the Rhone with France on the opposite side, the two banks joined by a bridge known to schoolchildren. The city was situated in the Comtat-Venaisson, which had been in papal control for a hundred years before Clement moved there, although the city itself belonged to the counts of Provence. For most of the papal years there, Avignon was a peaceful place. Excellent water routes made communication with Italy fairly easy, and it was more accessible than Rome to all parts of northern Europe. The convenience is undoubted, but Avignon was not Rome.

Why did the popes remain there for nearly seventy years? Each pope avowed his desire to return to Rome, but, except for the last two, failed to act decisively on that intention. Italy was in near anarchy, they argued persuasively. The political factions that had long plagued the peninsula had erupted into open, almost continuous violence. The Papal States, over which the popes ruled as temporal lords, had as their purpose the insulation of the popes from civil disruption, but they no longer gave that insurance, as these lands were persistently in turmoil. What happened to Boniface VIII at Anagni (see pp. 262–3) cast a long shadow over the fourteenth century, and the not unreasonable fear of the violence of Anagni being repeated on another pope gave reason for pope after pope to hesitate to return to Italy. Clement V lived at the Dominican priory at Avignon. His successor, John XXII, lived there for a while but moved to the bishop's palace, his home when he had been bishop of Avignon. That the popes were to remain at Avignon for some time became clear when John's successor, the reforming Benedict XII (1334–42) constructed a mighty palace. It was this papal palace, soon to be enlarged, that the popes made their residence: a fortress-like structure, its walls thirteen feet thick. Just as importantly, Benedict brought the papal archives from Italy to Avignon. And Clement VI, his successor, bought the town of Avignon from the countess of Provence. The papal court was clearly at Avignon for the indefinite future. In addition, during much of their stay at Avignon England and France were at war, and pope after pope attempted to reconcile the two warring nations so that they could combine their efforts in yet another crusade. This preoccupation, it was said, served as another factor in delaying their return to Rome.

What can be said of the popes, all Frenchmen, who lived there? Often reviled and vilified, the Avignon popes have been condemned by contemporaries and by later historians. The poet Petrarch in his *Book without a Name* refers frequently to Avignon as the modern Babylon, 'the cesspool of crime and scandal, a living hell', which led subsequent writers to call the papal period there the 'Babylonian Captivity', the church, like the ancient Hebrews, taken captive in a sybaritic, immoral place. The same poet describes the labyrinth of Avignon:

> The one hope of salvation is gold. Gold satisfies a wrathful king and defeats the fearful monster. Gold is the thread that guides. Gold reveals forbidden passages, rids the way of barriers and stones. Gold it is that bribes the harsh gatekeeper and opens the gates of heaven. In the end, Christ is sold for gold.

In another place, Petrarch reaches an exceedingly righteous tone and attacks on a broad front:

> Here virtue does not give one protection. Justice has vanished. Freedom has perished. Fairness has been eliminated. What rules is lust. What runs unabated is greed. What boils over is envy ... The wondrous temple built by Jesus Christ, once the invincible fortress against enemies of holy religion, has now in our times become a den of heartless thieves.

There was more than a hint of the Italian patriot speaking in Petrarch, yet his judgement stuck. Ferdinand Gregorovius (1821–91), historian of the city of Rome, declared that the Avignon popes were enslaved to the king of France. The great German historian Ludwig von Pastor (1854–1928) in his memorable history of the popes accused the Avignon popes of being responsible for a decline in religious fervour by their turning the papacy from a universal institution to one that was French. And so it went, the accepted opinion that the period of the popes at Avignon was one of the darkest in the history of the church. Thanks principally to the researches of the French School at Rome another picture, more complex and more reflective of the historical reality, is emerging. We can now get a better view of the popes themselves, and it is to them that we now turn.

Some historians dispute whether Clement V (1305–14) should be called an Avignon pope. Although it is true that he went to Avignon in 1309, took ill there and resided at the Dominican priory, it was not even then his fixed residence. The summer months, for increasingly longer periods, were spent in the cooler hills outside Avignon. In 1313 he spent not only the summer but the winter at a castle near Carpentras, where the curia joined him. With life ebbing from his body in the spring of 1314, Clement decided to return to his native Gascony and left Carpentras but hardly crossed the Rhone before he died. 'Avignon pope' or not, what can be said of him?

Within weeks of his being elected, long before the idea of moving to Avignon, even temporarily, surfaced, Clement named ten new cardinals, one English and the rest French, four nephews among them. More cardinals were created in 1310 and 1312, leaving the college clearly in the hands of the French. Not only did he accede to the wishes of Philip the Fair in moving the place of his installation to Lyons from Vienne, he acceded in much more. Philip, not willing to let his feud with Boniface VIII be buried with that pontiff's bones, demanded that Boniface be tried posthumously for heresy. Clement gave in, and the trial began in February 1309. That it lapsed in 1311 had nothing to do with Clement's intervention, only with the intervention of political exigencies for the French king. Beyond that, in 1311, Clement absolved Guillaume de Nogaret, Philip the Fair's henchman who had led the attack on Boniface at Anagni, and, at the same time, praised Philip for his handling of the problem of Boniface, stating that the king and his men 'were not motivated by any prior malice but only by a praiseworthy and honest devotion for justice . . . and we declare that they were not and are not guilty of the malicious charges made against them'.

Moreover, at the Council of Vienne (1311–12) Pope Clement yielded again to the interests of the French king, who wished to legitimize his seizure of the property of the Knights Templar. This military religious order had come into existence to protect the crusader states in the East. The Templars had grown wealthy, and their properties in France created an irresistible temptation to Philip's voracious appetite. He seized them in 1307, alleging irregularities. Specifically the Templars were charged with spitting and urinating on the crucifix, rejecting Christ, whom they called a false prophet, indulging in homosexual behaviour and worshipping idols. Under torture many members of the order confessed. While the council was sitting, King Philip, accompanied by an armed force, was at Vienne. An English eye-witness noted,

> Virtually all the prelates held in favour of the Order of the Templars, except those prelates from France, who, fearing their king, dared not to act otherwise.

Without discussion, on 3 April 1312, Clement V, with Philip at his right hand and Philip's son at his left, suppressed the Knights Templars. It was a decision forced on the council without debate, or even discussion, about the merits of the charges: a weak pope, suffering from what appears to have been colon cancer, was unable or unwilling to oppose a bullying king. Two years later Clement was dead, and a two-year interregnum followed.

The cardinals were required by canon law to meet at Carpentras, the site of the papal curia at the time of the pope's death. They were divided but not, as might be presumed, into a French and a non-French party. In fact, there were three parties. The largest comprised the ten cardinals from Gascony in the south-western region of France, who were distinctly more Gascon than French and not known for excessive deference to the French king: many were loyal to their duke, who, in fact, was the king of England. Also there was an Italian faction of seven cardinals, who, while united in resenting the presence of the papal court outside of Italy, were themselves split into three subgroups. A third party of six cardinals came principally from parts of France outside Gascony. The need for a two-thirds vote and the unwillingness of the parties to compromise in the early stages led to a hardening of attitudes. Armed mobs attacked the Italians at Carpentras, even burning and looting the houses where the Italian cardinals lived. A mob besieged the conclave, shouting, 'Death to the Italians'. Fearing for their lives, with some justification, the Italian cardinals escaped through a narrow passageway behind the place of the conclave and fled Carpentras. The Gascons also left, returning to Avignon to continue the election without the Italians. Were it not for the flight of the cardinals from Carpentras, there is every reason to think that Carpentras rather than Avignon would have been the place of residence of the popes for decades to come. In response, the Italians threatened to proceed to an election on their own if the Gascons were to proceed without them. The deadlock lasted two years, until June 1316, when the local count locked the cardinals in the Dominican priory at Lyons. The matter was soon resolved, when one group of Italians allied with the Gascons and elected Jacques Duèse, the former bishop of Avignon, who took the name John XXII. He was about seventy years old and, undoubtedly, was seen as a caretaker. In the event, he reigned as pope for eighteen years.

Pope John XXII (1316–34) made Avignon the normal residence of the popes and, for many, remains the creator of the attributes connected with the Avignon papacy. Two characteristics, universally acknowledged, marked his pontificate: centralization of the church apparatus and a fiscal policy that greatly enriched the papal court. The two were interrelated. Pope Clement V had all but emptied the papal treasury by generous, even exorbitant, bequests to members of his family. The new pope recognized the need to restore papal finances to the level adequate for the efficient conduct of papal business. John XXII, as did other popes after him, increased the number of appointments (or 'provisions' as they were called) to benefices reserved to the Holy See, not only to bishoprics but also to lesser ecclesiastical offices. The death of benefice-holders at the papal curia gave the pope the right, so he claimed, to appoint a successor independently of the wishes of local collators. It is now recognized that the papal appointees tended to be better qualified, frequently university graduates with advanced knowledge of theology, than those provided locally. All prelates (bishops and abbots) appointed by the pope were required to pay 'common services', a fee equal to about one-third of the annual income to be derived from the bishopric or abbey. In addition, clerical appointees at lower levels had to pay 'annates', roughly equal to the first-year's income. As the number of papal provisions to benefices grew in the fourteenth century, the income from these taxes came to constitute a substantial part of the papal income. John XXII had a genius for administration. Although papal bureaucracy had long existed, he reorganized with a new efficiency the apostolic camera (or chamber) to deal with finances, the papal chancery to manage the large volume of correspondence, a judicial system to consider petitions, appeals, complaints and the other kinds of litigation coming to Avignon and, also, the apostolic penitentiary, which considered matters of ecclesiastical penalties such as excommunication. And each of these institutions had its subdivisions. Avignon was bursting at the seams, and new suburbs were built outside the old ramparts. Avignon had become second only to Paris in size in 'Greater' France.

Pope John XXII is accused of extravagance with papal revenues. Incidents are not wanting to support this view. For example, on 22 November 1324, he gave a banquet for his great-niece's wedding, quite probably a mass meal for the town, at which were consumed

over 4,000 loaves of bread	9 oxen
over 55 sheep	8 pigs
4 boars	a large volume of fish
200 capons	690 chickens
580 partridges	270 rabbits
40 plover	37 ducks
50 pigeons	4 cranes
2 pheasants	2 peacocks
292 small birds	over 3 hundredweight of cheese
3,000 eggs	11 barrels of wine
2,000 apples, pears and other fruit	

Such excess disturbed the friars, particularly the Spiritual Franciscans, who held to a rigorous, extreme poverty of life.

The dispute about the nature of poverty for the Franciscans escalated under John XXII, when the minister general of the Franciscans espoused the view that neither Christ nor any of his apostles had possessions. In 1328, the same general was summoned to Avignon, where he was detained in house arrest. He fled the city but was deposed by friars loyal to the pope, and the observant friars, probably the vast majority, followed the pope. This long festering controversy over the nature of poverty, dating from the last years of the life of St Francis, would continue to trouble the order and the church for centuries to come.

It should be noted, in fairness, that John ensured that a significant portion of papal revenue be spent in alms to the poor. He established the *Pignotte* to administer almsgiving. Its accounts survive and show that meals were cooked each day for the poor. In the course of an average week the *Pignotte* distributed 67,500 loaves of bread. In addition, clothing and medication were supplied to those in need. It should further be noted that in his personal life John XXII lived in simple frugality, almost to the point of austerity. Also, in his last years he began active moves to return the papal court to Italy, not to Rome, still considered unsafe, but to Bologna, where he felt he might be able to live in security. In December 1334 the caretaker pope, who had been elected as a compromise candidate in 1316, died aged about ninety.

The cardinal electors quickly elected a successor, a Cistercian monk from the south of France, who took the name Benedict XII (1334–42). He was to be a reforming pope. Although he had not lived in a monastery for some time, having served as a bishop and, later, as a curial cardinal, he set about to give new life to the religious orders. One of his first acts was to facilitate the return of apostate religious, those men and women who had fled the religious life, to return to their houses, where, he insisted, they should be received in a spirit of kindness. His own order he endeavoured to reform by insisting on regular visitations. But it was the Benedictines who received his full attention. In 1336 he issued a long, comprehensive bull, which instituted provinces to an order hitherto based on independent houses, reduced the liturgical services and ordered the teaching of grammar, rhetoric and logic – the university subjects – to monks in their monasteries. And in 1339 he issued new constitutions for the Augustinian canons in thirty-nine articles. The Dominican order resented his attempts to restrain their begging and to curb their communal lives of luxury. Also, he found Avignon crowded with secular clergy, who were there seeking personal advantage. Benedict ordered them to return to their benefices.

In the curia itself Benedict reacted so severely to the corrupt conditions that some curialists fled Avignon to avoid punishment. Bribery, threats, intimidations, inflated fees and other behaviour, against rich and poor alike, had been a way of life. He quickly punished those responsible and established firm rules. Unlike his two predecessors, Benedict XII abhorred nepotism. No family members were made cardinals, and, when his niece married at Avignon, the pope forbade any ostentatious display. His nephew was warned not to come to Avignon: 'our master shows no preference to natural feelings'. Benedict XII was the most austere of the Avignon popes.

Yet Benedict did not return the papacy to Rome. Early in his pontificate, he considered the Bologna option, as had his predecessor. Although he expended money to restore St Peter's Basilica and the papal palace at the Lateran, he remained at Avignon, citing the near anarchy in Italy as barring his return. He directed his attention towards a crusade, as had predecessors and successors, and, to that end, towards effecting a peace between England and France. Benedict failed in both. Early in his reign he ordered the construction of the fortress-palace

21 Palais des Papes, Avignon. Reproduced by permission of the Courtauld Institute of Art.

for the popes (Le Palais des Papes) and the transfer of the papal archives from Italy to his new palace. It was this most attractive of the Avignon popes who entrenched the papacy on the banks of the Rhone. His policy of appeasement towards the rebellious factions in Italy proved a failure: he was taken advantage of and laughed at. The pope who followed him, though no more successful in Italy, at least eluded ridicule.

Those observers who view the Avignon popes as worldly, self-indulgent and ostentatious would see in Pope Clement VI (1342–52) the embodiment of those traits. Clement's court, without doubt, was the most sophisticated, resplendent and civilized court in Europe. Like a great secular prince, he delighted in the company of artists and scholars and lavished gifts on all petitioners with an unprecedented benevolence: 'my predecessors did not know how to be pope.' The same generosity, less spectacularly, showed itself when the Black Death struck Avignon in 1348. While, elsewhere, great men fled the towns, Clement remained for much of the plague season at Avignon, where over sixty thousand reportedly died. Moreover, he secured the services of doctors to tend the ill and the dying, purchased a cemetery for the decent burial of plague victims and welcomed into Avignon Jews who were fleeing from the fury of maddened mobs who claimed that they had poisoned the wells.

Early in his reign (January 1343) a deputation came from Rome, conferring on him the rank of Roman senator and entreating him to return to Rome. They were politely received by this aristocratic French pope, but their pleas went unheeded. Clement, in fact, further entrenched the papal court at Avignon by enlarging the papal palace and adorning it with a richness of decoration. His efforts to bring peace to Italy and, particularly, to regain control of the Papal States proved ineffective.

It was his successor, Innocent VI (1352–62), who took the drastic measures needed to pacify the papal lands in Italy. With a stroke of near genius he named the Spanish cardinal, Gil Albornoz, as his legate to Italy with his mission to pave the way for the pope's return. Descended from kings of Leon and Aragon, Albornoz accomplished by war and diplomacy what nearly half a century of vague hopes and half measures had failed to do. The mission of this warrior-cardinal was not fully accomplished during the reign of Innocent VI but, with starts and stops, was well under way. Urban V (1362–70) did, in fact, return the papal curia to Rome, but unsuccessfully. This devout, even ascetic, Benedictine monk within eight months of becoming pope wrote to the Romans that he intended to return the papacy. Against the protests of the French cardinals and the French court, Urban V left Avignon on 30 April 1367. He landed at a port in the Papal States on 3 June, where Cardinal Albornoz greeted him. On 16 October 1367, at last, the pope entered Rome: it was over sixty years since a pope was there. The emperor, Charles IV, came to Rome to be crowned. The Byzantine emperor, John V Paleologus, came to Rome to enlist papal support against the Turks. The humanist Coluccio Salutati told Petrarch:

> If you were now in Rome, you would see temples which lay in ruins now being raised again. I know it would give you joy and your pious soul would praise him who has rebuilt the Lateran, restored St Peter's and given new life to the entire city.

Yet Urban V stayed in Italy for just less than three years. Threats of attacks, the reaction of Romans to his appointing only one Italian cardinal among the eight whom he appointed, the insinuations and rumours of vicious conspiracies against his person – all seem to have contributed to his decision to return to Avignon. And so he sailed for Marseilles on 5 September 1370. When he arrived at Avignon, a triumphant welcome greeted him. Within three months he was dead, but his courage, even if not enduring, meant that the days of the popes on the banks of the Rhone were surely numbered.

Almost immediately the cardinals elected the nephew of Clement VI, the brilliant Gregory XI (1370–78). It was his conviction that, putting aside all opposition, he had to return to Rome. He wrote to the English king:

> From the time that we became pope, it has been our deeply held desire, as indeed it still is, to go to the Holy City, the city that gives us our authority, where, in its environs, we shall establish our residence and the residence of our apostolic court.

Yet he was delayed for various reasons. Peace negotiations between France and England, in which Gregory expected to play a part, were to be conducted at Bruges. Renewed hostilities broke out in Italy, even in the Papal States. He persisted in his plans and eventually announced a date for his departure, but it was postponed, and then he set another date, which was also postponed. The duke of Anjou spoke for many, almost certainly the overwhelming majority of the cardinals, curialists and French nobility, especially the king, when he said,

> You are travelling to a country and to a people, where there is little love for you. You are turning away from the source of faith, that is, that kingdom wherein the holy church has greater authority and perfection than anywhere else in the world. You may indeed cause great harm to the church, for, were you to die there, which your doctors say is quite likely, the Romans – those alien and treacherous people – will control the Sacred College and will elect a pope who suits them.

The duke's words were to prove prophetic. Yet Gregory heard another view delivered with force by St Catherine of Siena:

> Do not delay, for delay has been harmful. The devil is using all his trickery to bar your path . . . Do not resist the will of God any longer: your starving sheep await your return to Peter's see.

Her voice, however powerful, was but one among many and certainly not determinative. Pope Gregory XI knew his own mind and needed neither the encouragement of an Italian partisan nor the counsel of a French nobleman. To the people of Avignon, who urged him to stay, he responded:

> Last year I feared I would die, and it is my belief that the sole reason for my illness was my not living in Italy.

On 13 September 1376 Gregory left Avignon for Rome. Nature seemed to support the naysayers: violent storms at sea forced his ship to return to Marseilles and, later, to seek safety in other ports on the way. It was not till 17 January 1377 that the papal ships landed at Rome. The papacy was back at Rome and, save for forced departures at the hands of Napoleon, it was there to stay. There are reports, however, that, like his predecessor, Gregory XI was dismayed by the state of affairs in Italy and was contemplating a return to Avignon. How much truth these reports contain is difficult to say, but the French cardinals who accompanied him continued in their opposition to the move. What the duke of Anjou feared, in fact, happened: the sickly Gregory XI died on 27 March 1378 and was buried at Rome. Like the duke, Gregory himself had feared what would occur after his death. What occurred was the Great Schism.

The phrase 'Babylonian Captivity' deserves a much too delayed burial. The seven popes who lived at Avignon from Clement V to Gregory XI constituted a remarkably able line of popes, unlike any since the late eleventh–early twelfth century. Three (Benedict XII, Urban V and Gregory XI) were known, even in their own times, for undoubted piety of life, and one of these (Urban V) was subsequently beatified. To none of them can personal scandals be assigned. Even John XXII, the great administrator, lived a simple, sober life, and Clement VI, who lived like a Renaissance prince, showed exceptional compassion and generosity to the victims of the Black Death. But what of their subservience to the French king? While it can be said that the popes while at Avignon were not in French territory and that many of the popes often showed remarkable independence of the French king, it must be added that the desire to please the French king was often present. Consistent papal policy urged the ending of hostilities between France and England in the Hundred Years War, yet the popes were Frenchmen and generally sympathetic to French interests. Clement V, by any reckoning, was subservient to the wishes of Philip the Fair, and Pope John XXII and King Philip VI were friends. The popes, particularly John XXII and Clement VI, allowed the French kings to use ecclesiastical revenues in their wars against the Flemish and the English, an allowance not extended to the adversaries of the French. The popes no doubt thought it a small price to pay for living in a stable place in prolonged peace. For the most part the popes acted independently and often in opposition to the wishes of the French monarchy. Nonetheless, the perception to many contemporaries, particularly to Italians, was that the popes were puppets of the French kings, and, although the reality differed from the perception, that perception itself created the context for what followed after the death of Gregory XI at Rome.

This long line of able popes, acting more or less independently of the French monarchy, had one incontrovertible characteristic: these bishops of Rome lived continuously outside Italy, hundreds of miles from Rome. It was a state of affairs that could not last for ever. The historian must ask the question: how justified were the Avignon popes in claiming that the anarchic conditions in Italy made it impossible for them to live there in peace? Near anarchy accurately describes the situation it Italy at this time, but why would that inhibit the popes from living in the city of Rome? Even if the popes might have been able to control the disputes within the city of Rome itself, the problem of the Papal States might still remain. What good would it be to control Rome but not the Papal States? It was a long-held principle of papal policy that these papal possessions needed to be under papal control in order to give the popes the independence which they felt they needed. (This principle was to continue as the basis for papal policy in Italy until 1870.) The Avignon popes felt that they could not be assured control of the Papal States, a position which can be historically justified, and that, therefore, they could not return to Rome. In a sense, they had become prisoners of their own perceived need to be secular rulers of a large part of Italy.

Two elections and the coming of schism

The return of Pope Gregory XI from Avignon to Rome in January 1377 presaged a return to normalcy after nearly seventy years of the popes living at Avignon. Normalcy was not to be. A long, peaceful reign which overcame early settling-in problems would have acted to solidify the papacy in Rome and to win over those cardinals and curialists longing for the attractions of Avignon. But the pope's health did not cooperate, and fourteen months after his return Gregory XI died. The chronology of events can briefly be summarized and demands more than our usual attention. The pope died on 27 March 1378. On the next day his body was buried in the church of Santa Maria Nuova (now Santa Francesca Romana). By the canon law of the time the conclave to elect a successor could not convene until ten days after the pope's death: it met on 7–8 April and elected the archbishop of Bari, who took the name Urban VI. He was enthroned and crowned on 18 April, Easter Sunday. Five months later, on 20 September, the cardinals, declaring Urban's election invalid, elected another pope, Clement VII. The church was in the throes of a schism. Now the details.

Sixteen cardinals were at Rome when Gregory XI died. Six others had remained at Avignon, and one was away on a papal mission. Of the sixteen who were to elect the new pope, four were Italians, eleven were French and one was Spanish. The political lines were not as clearly drawn as this statement of nationalities might imply. Two French parties, antagonistic to one another, made a clear 'French vote' unlikely. The Limousin region had produced three of the last four popes, and the five Limousin cardinals in Rome wanted still another. A Gallic party of four cardinals wanted a non-Limousin cardinal and were led by the ambitious Cardinal Robert of Geneva, thirty-six years old and cousin of the French king; they were supported by Peter de Luna, a Spaniard. Both of these cardinals were to play major roles in the schism. With such divisions selecting a new pope might not be easy. Added to these difficulties was the temper of the Roman people. They made their desires known by their officials and by mobs in the streets: they wanted a Roman or, at the least, an Italian.

During the days before the cardinals met in conclave, canvassing, not unexpectedly, was quite probably taking place. At its centre may have been Cardinal Robert of Geneva. He was so opposed to the Limousins that he allied with the Italians in order to avoid the election of a Limousin. A close friend of Cardinal Robert later alleged that, in the time before the election, the cardinal, with his hand resting on the scriptures, said to him, 'We shall have no one else as pope but the archbishop of Bari.' The archbishop, Bartomoleo Prignano, was not a Roman, but, at least, he was an Italian, a native of Naples. Moreover, Prignano, as an absentee bishop, had served as a diplomat at the papal curia at Avignon for fourteen years. He had travelled to Rome with Gregory XI, who made him his vice-chancellor for Italy. He was an insider and not an unknown quantity, not a token Italian snatched from a remote, southern diocese. Although not a cardinal himself, he was known to all the cardinal-electors who gathered in conclave on the evening of 7 April 1378.

As they processed into the Vatican palace, the cardinals heard a crowd shouting repeatedly, '*Romano lo volemo*' ('we want a Roman'). Once shut in, they could still hear the clamour from outside. The cardinal-electors proceeded with their business on the following morning. The Limousin cardinals lacked sufficient votes for their candidate; the cardinal of Limoges rose and said to the others,

> I propose the election of a man to whom the people cannot seriously object and who would show himself favourable to us . . . I elect the archbishop of Bari to be pontiff of the holy and catholic church, and this I do willingly and freely.

The others followed suit, first the French and finally the Italians, including Cardinal Orsini, a Roman ambitious for the papal office, who simply said, 'I elect the person elected by the majority', who was Prignano. The cardinals had done what they had come together to do and what had been agreed upon in advance: they elected the archbishop of Bari as pope.

One further matter still had to be dealt with. Since Prignano was not a cardinal, he was not present at the election to give the necessary consent to his election. He had to be sent for and his assent received before the election was complete and before the announcement could be made. Still very mindful of the noisy Roman mob, the cardinals summoned a number of prelates, Prignano among them, to appear. Before they arrived, the rumour spread among the Romans that a non-Roman had been elected. At the palace the summoned prelates were kept waiting, while the cardinals repaired to the chapel and there, again, unanimously elected Prignano as pope. The electors delayed informing Prignano and announcing his election to the Roman people. The crowd grew increasingly agitated and soon burst into the palace. In the conclave chamber cardinals, fearing for their lives, put papal vestments on an aged, feeble Roman cardinal and set him on the papal throne, and then they disappeared. The man on the papal throne protested,

> I am not the pope, and I do not want to be an anti-pope. A better than me has been elected, the archbishop of Bari.

Some of the fleeing cardinals sought safety in the Castel Sant'Angelo, others went to fortified places outside the city and still others simply went to their residences unbothered. The pope-elect, not yet having consented to the election, hid in an innermost room in the papal palace.

The morning of 9 April saw Rome a quiet place, and Roman officials, now informed of the election, were pleased and went to pay honour to the new pope. He said that they should not address him as pope but only as archbishop of Bari. That afternoon the cardinals, realizing there was no threat to them, drifted back to the Vatican palace. They asked Prignano to accept his election. He did and took the name Urban VI. Clad as pope, he was presented to the Roman people:

'*habemus papam*' ('we have a pope'). A strange election it surely was, but it was its validity that would eventually be questioned, even to this day.

The cardinals, far from raising any objection to the election, treated Urban as pope. Within a day of Urban's accepting the election three French cardinals asked for favours in the pope's gift: a cardinal's hat for the nephew of the late pope, his intercession for the release of a prisoner and preferential treatment for friends. In view of later events, what Cardinal Robert of Geneva wrote to the German emperor bears rehearsing here:

> The ten days after the death of the late pope required by canon law having passed, the other cardinals and I were enclosed in conclave. The name of the archbishop of Bari (as he then was) was suggested . . . The other cardinals and I unanimously gave our votes to him.

On Palm Sunday, 11 April, just days after the election, the cardinals took their palms from Urban VI, dressed in papal vestments and seated on the papal throne, and on Holy Thursday, four days later, they gathered with the pope while he issued a papal bull. Enthronement occurred on the following Sunday (Easter), and all cardinals were present and took part in the ceremony. Later that same day one of the French cardinals said to a friend,

> In all my life I have not known such joy as the joy I have today: we have completed this task peacefully. I did have doubts whether the Romans would be satisfied.

The next day all sixteen cardinals sent a letter to their brother cardinals still at Avignon, notifying them of the election. What happened to change their minds?

Almost immediately after his enthronement Urban VI began to alienate the members of his curia. On Easter Monday he condemned churchmen who derived their income from benefices from which they were perpetually absent. A fortnight later he preached on the same subject, berating the cardinals who were present for living luxurious lives: the cardinal of Amiens, he said, should live simply and not beg money from foreign ambassadors, and Cardinal Orsini is a *sotus* (a sot). Urban was soon to strip Amiens of his cardinal's rank. The pope came close to physically assaulting the cardinal of Limoges. The cardinals asked the pope to return the papacy to Avignon, but, not unexpectedly, he refused. Summer was approaching, and, on the pretext of escaping the heat of Rome, the cardinals one by one went to Anagni in the hills south-east of Rome, first the French, then three of the four Italians. (The other lay dying at Rome.) Sixteen cardinals had elected Urban in April, and in August thirteen of them were at Anagni, troubled by Urban's behaviour. Of the other three, one by then had died and the other two had returned to Avignon. The pope refused to join them at Anagni, fearing, with some justification, that he would become their prisoner. There, at Anagni, on 9 August 1378, the cardinals issued their *Declaratio*: the election of Urban was null and void and the papal throne was consequently vacant. Their argument, quite simply, was that they acted out of fear of the Roman mob and that such fear invalidated their action. The thirteen cardinals proceeded to a new conclave, which met at Fondi under the protection of the local count. They entered the conclave on 19 September, observed all the appropriate canonical procedures and, on the following day, announced the unanimous election of Cardinal Robert of Geneva, who took the name Clement VII. There were now two popes or, rather, two claimants to the papacy.

We must pause and ask about the canonical probity of the cardinals' actions. How justified were they in what they did? Conveniently for us they laid out their reasons in the document *Declaratio* of 9 August 1378:

> The ultramontane cardinals agreed to the election of an Italian for no other reason than to escape the danger of death, as they then averred . . . Some of the Italian cardinals stated that, were they to be elected, they would decline because of the evident coercion. All the cardinals, eager to escape the perils facing them, quickly nominated the archbishop of Bari without any further discussion, and they immediately elected him to be pope. He was known to them, and they trusted in his considerable experience in the affairs and customs of the curia. Later experience proved them wrong. In addition, some cardinals said that they elected him as true pope, but this was done solely out of fear for their lives.

Several cardinals, it was argued, had demurred in one way or another and some spoke of retiring to a safe place for a new election. This brief went on to describe an attempt at a second election, which was broken up by armed men who surrounded the cardinals. While acknowledging that all the cardinals took part in Urban's enthronement and subsequently treated him as pope, both in consistory and in liturgical ceremonies, they claimed that they did so only in Rome, where they still felt in danger. The *Declaratio* stated,

> They believed that, if they were to cast doubt on the election, they would have been murdered.

This, then, was their argument: since actions performed out of excessive fear are null and void, the election of Urban VI was not a true election and Urban was not a true pope.

Neither the presence of a huge crowd at the time of the election should be surprising – after all, there had not been a papal election in Rome since the thirteenth century – nor that it had an exuberant, carnival flavour nor that the Romans wanted a Roman pope. That some of the Roman people became boisterous and even unruly and a few, at least, positively threatening seems clear enough. The question must be: how influenced were the cardinals by the Roman mob and was that influence sufficient to invalidate their actions? On the face of it, while admitting the presence of the vociferous Romans, one still wonders why the cardinals proceeded as they did, if they were under such constraint. If they merely wanted to placate the Romans, why not elect a Roman such as the aged Cardinal Tebaldeschi, whom some later clothed as pope in a woeful pantomime? Why did they ratify the election by electing Bari again after an interval of several hours? Why did they ask favours of him, assist at his enthronement and generally treat him as pope for three months, if they felt the election invalid? If there were serious doubts, we would expect that at least one or two of the cardinals would have had the personal integrity and moral courage to disown the election, but none did, not until months later. Although we can never be entirely sure, it is difficult to escape the conclusion that what turned the cardinals against Urban VI was his bizarre, hostile, irrational behaviour after his enthronement on Easter Sunday, 1378. Several cardinals admitted as much. One of the French electors remarked, 'If he had behaved prudently, he could have remained pope.' And the Spanish cardinal, Peter de Luna (later pope in the Avignon line), in a moment of candour, allowed,

> If his behaviour had been different, we would have stayed with him. His violence turned everything upside down.

Either Urban VI after his enthronement revealed a part of his character hitherto unknown to his electors, all of whom knew him, or, quite probably, he experienced a mental breakdown. His rantings against bishops and cardinals exceeded mere intemperance and seemed to know no restraint, leading, in one instance, to his nearly striking one of the French cardinals. Later, in 1384, when Urban learned that six of his new cardinals were so disturbed by his rages that they were seeking a remedy, he imprisoned them, and five were never heard of again, presumably murdered; the sixth, the Englishman Adam of Easton, was saved by the intervention of King Richard II. On another occasion, while the aged cardinal of Naples was being tortured by being repeatedly lifted to a ceiling and dropped to the floor, Urban walked outside in the garden, reciting his office as he listened to the cardinal's screams.

Separated as we are by over seven hundred years from these events, we are in no position to render a clinical judgement about the sanity of the pope, but the evidence that we do have must give us pause to wonder. Whether hidden personal characteristics became apparent or a mental breakdown had occurred, the cardinals by the summer of 1378 recognized that they had made a grievous error in electing Urban. This posed a problem of monumental proportions for them. The easiest solution would be for them to convince Urban to resign. But Urban would never resign, and the cardinals knew this full well. That being the situation, what could the cardinals do? At the heart of the problem thus facing them was a defect in contemporary canon law: there were no provisions for removing a pope, even one who had lost his sanity. Yet the cardinals knew that it was a long-standing principle of that law that actions performed by force and fear (*vi et metu*) had no legal standing and were invalid. Their solution was to claim that the election itself was radically compromised and vitiated by reason of fear; then they could proceed to a fresh election. In doing this the cardinals created an even greater problem by plunging the church into a schism, which was to last almost forty years. The argument can be made that, in a real sense, the Great Schism occurred because of the inadequacy of canon law to provide a remedy for an incapacitated pope. (It may be noted that in the United States it was not until 1967 that constitutional provisions were made for dealing with a president unable to discharge the duties of his office.)

The newly elected Clement VII almost immediately created new cardinals and was anxious to return the papacy to Avignon, yet he did not arrive at the Palais des Papes until 20 June 1379. In the eight months between his election at Fondi and his arrival at Avignon, Clement VII was busy in Italy. He recruited mercenary forces to help establish himself in Italy. He tried to lay siege to Rome, but his men were driven from Castel Sant'Angelo and Clement and his court fled to Naples, where they were welcomed by the queen of Naples but not by Urban's fellow Neapolitans. On 20 June 1379 Clement set sail on the queen's ships for Marseilles, whence he sailed up the Rhone to Avignon.

King Charles V of France, cousin of the new electee, did not rush to his support. Before the election of Clement VII the cardinals had sent two envoys from Anagni to elicit the king's support. Charles summoned a number of the higher clergy to the royal palace in Paris to listen to the envoys: six archbishops, thirty bishops, several abbots as well as doctors of law and theology from the universities of Paris, Orléans and Angers. On 13 September 1378 they reported to the king that the matter needed more clarity before a judgement could be made and that the king would be advised to take a posture of neutrality. At their meeting, opposition to Clement was expressed by some of the clergy from Normandy and from Provence. Charles V then called a smaller assembly of prelates and university doctors, some suggest, hand-chosen to support Clement. On 16 November they listened to Clement's envoys and advised Charles to support Clement. This he did. The king had also approached the University of Paris for its opinion, which was slow in coming. Disagreement was apparent among the masters, some, instead of supporting one or other of the claimants, suggesting a general council be convened, but in May 1379 a majority of the university declared for Clement VII. The call for a general council would be heard again. The support of the king of France was crucial to Clement's claim of legitimacy. It may not be too much to say that without this early support of Charles V the schism might have been but a minor footnote in the history of the church. It became much more.

Support for the rival claimants now took on a geographical and a decidedly political dimension. Looking for wider support, Urban, abandoned by his curia as well as his cardinals, in September 1378 created twenty-four new cardinals, four of whom were non-Italian. He began in earnest to look for political support.

Italy, then and for centuries after, was a patchwork quilt of political entities. The kingdom of Naples went briefly into Urban's camp but then went over to Clement, where it remained till Urban's death (1389), when it reverted to the Roman claimant. Throughout the rest of the schism, while there was some vacillation of loyalties, most of Italy remained obedient to Rome. Also in what became known as the Roman Obedience was England, long a foe of France. The position in Ireland was more ambiguous, but Clement certainly had some support in the province of Tuam in the west and Urban had support elsewhere in what, at best, was a fluid situation. Wenceslaus IV, the German king and emperor-elect, opted for Rome, and most of Germany followed his lead. Scotland, traditional ally of France, chose the Avignon Obedience as also did Savoy, Burgundy and Portugal, although the latter, under pressure from England, switched to the Roman Obedience. The other Iberian kingdoms maintained their neutrality at first, but they eventually went over to Avignon: Castile in 1380, Aragon in 1387 and Navarre in 1390. Scandinavia, Poland and Hungary came into Urban's camp. Some dioceses were represented by two bishops (e.g., Breslau, Constance, Mainz, Basel), but too much should not be made of this: the major divisions were national. Political considerations alone – not canon law, not theology, not piety – dictated these decisions. Europe was now divided between the nations supporting Urban VI and the nations supporting Clement VII. In an expression of the time, the world was at sixes and sevens.

Further reading

The two essential English-language works on Avignon are G. Mollat, *The Popes at Avignon* (tr. Janet Love; New York, 1963) and Yves Renouard, *The Avignon Papacy*, 1305–1403 (tr. Denis Bethell; Hamden, CT, 1970). A judicious summary by Patrick N.R. Zutschi is found in vol. 6 of *The New Cambridge Medieval History* (ed. Michael Jones; Cambridge, 2000). The views of Petrarch can be found conveniently in Norman P. Zacour's translation of Petrarch's *Book without a Name* (Toronto, 1973). The story of the Knights Templar is told admirably by Malcom Barber in *The Trial of the Templars* (Cambridge, 1978) and in *The New Knighthood: A History of the Order of the Temple* (Cambridge, 1994). Geoffrey Barraclough, *Papal Provisions: Aspects of Church History Constitutional, Legal and Administrative in the Later Middle Ages* (Oxford, 1935) is the classic work on that subject.

The narrative of the elections of 1378 is related in John Holland Smith, *The Great Schism, 1378: The Disintegration of the Papacy* (London, 1970). Although sometimes criticized for being pro-Urban, Walter Ullmann, *The Origins of the Great Schism: A Study in Fourteenth-Century Ecclesiastical History* (London, 1948) is a gem of a book.

16

THE GREAT SCHISM

There was one pope; then another claimed to be pope; then, still another. A rupture, a schism, rent Western Europe as never before. Largely along national lines, Europe was divided into two and eventually three allegiances. Confusion, suspicion, distrust, bitterness, even hatred consumed much of Christian Europe. Indeed, there have been other times in the long history of the papacy when there were rival claimants, but none can be compared to the schism (known to history as the Great Schism) that began in 1378 and lasted for almost four decades. And it cast a long, lingering shadow over the subsequent history of the church.

The road to Pisa

Two men, each claiming to be pope and bishop of Rome, each claiming canonical election, established themselves together with full papal apparatus at Rome and Avignon. Both held the same constitutional position: they believed in the primacy of Rome over the church. They differed only about who was the true successor of Peter, the bishop of Rome and, on earth, the head of the church. Each quickly excommunicated the other and began to act as pope. Neither Urban nor Clement, on the human level, had much to commend him as leader of the Christian church. Urban's lapses into apparently demented behaviour led to decisions and actions hardly consistent with the ideals of the religion of which he claimed to be leader. Clement, on the other hand, was the butcher of Cesena. A year and a half before the cardinals elected him pope, the then Robert of Geneva, acting as a military commander, ordered the slaughter of all the inhabitants of Cesena, near Rimini, sparing none, not women, children, the aged, the infirm. As many as three thousand perished, and the streets and lanes of Cesena were said to have been awash with blood. Neither Urban nor Clement was an ideal person to be pope, but one of them was the true pope and the other an anti-pope. The identity of the true pope was the central but not the only question of the schism. How to resolve the schism was the allied question, and it soon became the paramount question. Christians of unquestioned rectitude, belonging to both camps, endeavoured to find answers, and their quest was to last for decades. A Paris theologian lamented, 'Not even a hardened heart can be unmoved at the sight of holy mother the church in such agony.'

In the years immediately following the double election, two German theologians at the University of Paris suggested a radical solution to the problem. They proposed the calling of a general council to resolve the crisis. Henry of Langenstein, who was soon (1383) to become, in a real sense, the new founder of the University of Vienna, wrote that the general good of the church must be the final norm and that the church, as the community of believers, to secure the common good can reverse what cardinals had done. His colleague at Paris, Conrad of Gelnhausen, soon to leave for Heidelberg, where he was to become the first chancellor, also believed that the ultimate authority in the church reposes in the church itself, the community of all Christians, which is superior even to the pope. To those who might argue that only a pope can call a general council he replied that, against the wishes of a heretical or notoriously criminal pope, the Christian people can call a council. Also, if after the death of a pope and before the election of his successor all the cardinals died, only a general council could resolve the situation, even though there was no pope to convene it. Thus, for Conrad, there is not an essential need for a council to be summoned by the pope. True, he continued, there are positive, man-made laws that require that a general council be summoned by the pope, but, like all human laws, there are circumstances which even the wisest of legislators could not have foreseen and in which they would not have wanted the law to apply. He was restating the Aristotelian principle of *epikeia* and applying it to the schism: although canon law requires a pope to call a council, the makers of that law could not have foreseen the current situation and, consequently, that law does not bind. His conclusion quite simply was that a general council can and should resolve the crisis of the schism.

In 1381 these opinions of Henry and Conrad found no ready acceptance; their acceptance would come later. In the meantime, the rival claimants were preoccupied with garnering support for their rival claims and for their rival bureaucracies. The death of Urban VI on 15 October 1389 might have provided the opportunity to reconcile the two obediences. Avignon urged the French king to persuade the cardinals at Rome to elect Clement VII and, thus, end the schism, but it was an opportunity spurned. Eighteen days after Urban's death, without waiting for negotiations, the Roman cardinals elected Boniface IX. Almost immediately he excommunicated Clement VII, who, in turn, excommunicated him. There was to be no quick or easy fix to the schism.

The new French king, Charles VI, was amenable to capturing Rome by military force and imposing Clement VII on the papal throne at Rome. Complications arose, and the campaign failed to materialize, but the use of force was never far from Clement's mind. It led him to support various campaigns in Italy with some but little success and to drain the French church by demanding taxes at an unheard of rate, which led to an increasing alienation of much of the French clergy. Mental illness began to plague Charles VI from 1392, and the real power in France moved to the dukes of Berry and Burgundy. They put a high premium on ending the schism, political calculations playing a large role in their designs.

The University of Paris, in 1384, polled its members and graduates about ways in which to resolve the schism. Three ways emerged: *via concilii generalis* (way of a general council), *via compromissi* (way of compromise) and *via cessionis* (way of resignation). The university recommended the last of these: the mutual resignation of both claimants without judgement about the legitimacy of their claims. The *via cessionis* became the policy adopted by the French authorities. It was to have several manifestations, including forced resignation and even deposition. In its less radical form it was the way of choice.

This way seemed quite within reach when a few months later, in September 1394, Clement VII died. If the Avignon cardinals would not elect a successor and if Boniface IX at Rome could be convinced to resign, a resolution was clearly within sight. To this end the royal council dispatched a letter to the cardinals at Avignon not to proceed to an election. Without acknowledging the letter they went into conclave and elected the Spaniard Peter de Luna, whom we first met at the troubled election at Rome in 1378, and he became Benedict XIII. Luna had taken a pre-election oath, as did the other cardinals, that, if elected, he would strive to resolve the schism, even if it required his resignation. He even repeated the same oath after his election but made it clear that he would in no way consider resignation unless his legitimacy was affirmed. The royal dukes responded by calling an assembly of the higher clergy of France to meet at Paris in February 1395 to give their advice. Over a hundred clergy and scholars attended. The key figure at the assembly was Simon de Cramaud, the titular patriarch of Alexandria, formerly a professor of canon law at Paris and now a royal official. He presided and skilfully presented the *via cessionis*, which carried by a vote of more than four to one. An embassy led by the dukes of Berry and Burgundy, joined by the king's brother the duke of Orléans, proceeded to Avignon. Their pleas fell on the deaf ears of Benedict XIII, but his cardinals were not so deaf. All but one, a fellow Spaniard, agreed to the *via cessionis*, and support began to come from elsewhere. In England, Richard II accepted this solution as part of a larger settlement with France that included a truce and his marriage to the French king's daughter. Castile, England's new ally, followed the English lead and supported the *via cessionis*. Richard II's brother-in-law, King Wenceslaus of Bohemia, soon took the same position. In 1397, representatives of France, England and Castile visited both claimants, urging their mutual resignations.

Another French assembly met at Paris in May and June 1398 and argued for forced cession or subtraction (withdrawal of allegiance). Two months later the French government withdrew its support for Benedict XIII. The cardinals who had been loyal to Benedict crossed the Rhone from Avignon, taking with them the papal seal. All seemed lost for Benedict, but the end of the schism was not to be so easily attained. He had hidden support. The duke of Orléans openly sided with Benedict as did the universities of Toulouse, Angers and Orléans. The king of Castile restored his allegiance in 1402. Aragon remained steadfast behind

Benedict, as it was to continue to be throughout the ups and downs of the schism, almost to his final, almost farcical end. Meanwhile, at Avignon, where he had endured a long siege and humiliating house arrest, Benedict escaped to friendly Provence. Opposition in France began to crumble. The cardinals returned, the royal withdrawal of allegiance was rescinded (1403) and the people of Avignon submitted to Benedict.

Flushed with the sense of victory, Benedict sent an embassy to Rome to make two proposals to Boniface IX: first, that the two claimants meet and, second, that both agree not to create any new cardinals. Prospects for a settlement looked promising, but, by the time the embassy reached Rome, Boniface IX was *in extremis* and died 1 October 1404. The cardinals, before proceeding to an election, tried to convince Benedict's embassy that their pope ought now to resign, but they failed. The new pope, Innocent VII, lived just over a year. At his death another chance was given to resolve the schism, but it too failed. The thirteen cardinals of the Roman Obedience met at Rome, and, before entering the conclave, each swore that, if elected, he would resign if the other claimant would do the same and if the cardinals of both claimants would join to elect a new pope and, further, that he would not name any new cardinals. On 13 November 1406 they elected the eighty-year-old Gregory XII for the sole purpose of having him resign. Almost immediately he wrote to Benedict XIII, saying that he would resign if the Avignon cardinals would join his cardinals to hold an election. Early in the following January, Benedict agreed to a meeting with Gregory to arrange a mutual abdication, providing – with Benedict there was always a proviso – there first be a discussion of rightful legitimacy. They planned to meet on 29 September 1407 at Savona, a coastal town west of Genoa. But the carousel was to continue to go round and round.

Simon of Cramaud served as the go-between and, in shuttle diplomacy, moved between the two papal courts. On the appointed day, the feast of St Michael the Archangel, Benedict was at Savona, but Gregory was almost two hundred miles away at Siena. Benedict suggested another meeting place and sailed to Portovenere, east of Genoa, and Gregory moved to Lucca in this strange chess game. In January 1408 they were but forty miles apart. Other meeting places were discussed and rejected. Gregory was losing interest in an agreement, not under the heady influence of papal incense but under the pressure of his greedy family and others looking for personal advantage. On 4 May he announced that he would never resign and he forbade his cardinals to leave Lucca. He also announced that he would create four new cardinals. On 11 May most of Gregory's cardinals abandoned him, appealing from Gregory to Christ, to a general council and to a future pope. A fortnight later France once again withdrew its support from Benedict XIII and declared its neutrality; England followed suit later in that year. At last, events were moving quickly. Most of the cardinals of both camps met at Leghorn on 29 June 1408 and took an oath to reunite the church by securing the voluntary resignations of both claimants:

> If they will not resign or if they act contumaciously, we will find
> another remedy through a general council. Then we will give the
> church one, true, undoubted shepherd by a canonical election by
> both our colleges meeting as a single body.

They then summoned a general council to meet at Pisa on 25 March 1409. The solution, prematurely proposed by Langenstein and Gelnhausen in the early 1380s, was now chosen as the vehicle for reunion.

It would be easy to dismiss the Council of Pisa, as historians often do, because of subsequent events, yet that would grossly underestimate what the council achieved. Not since the Fourth Lateran Council (1215) had such an impressive assembly been seen in Europe. Twenty-four cardinals from the two obediences attended as did four patriarchs, eighty-four archbishops and bishops and the proxies of a 102 others, 128 abbots and proxies for 200 others, the general superiors of the four orders of friars (Dominican, Franciscan, Carmelite and Austin). Cathedral chapters from most of Europe sent representatives as did thirteen universities. Some 300 theologians and canonists were also present. Ambassadors represented almost all the secular princes of Europe. They came from England, France, Bohemia, Poland, Portugal, Sicily and Cyprus. The great dukes of Burgundy, Brabant, Holland, Lorraine and Austria sent envoys as did the prince bishops of Liège, Cologne and Mainz. Other representatives came from Brandenburg, Thuringia and Savoy. Apart from Scotland and Scandinavia the notable absentees were representatives from Naples and Spain, which was still loyal to its native Benedict XIII. It was an impressive array of prelates, scholars and lay envoys who met at the cathedral at Pisa on the first day of the new year (25 March). In a real sense, Europe came together at Pisa in 1409 in a concerted attempt to bring unity to the church. The events at Pisa in 1409 were not incidental, peripheral to general European affairs. It is not too much to say that in the months from late March till early August the focus of Europe was fixed on Pisa.

One matter and one matter alone concerned the fathers of the Council of Pisa, the reuniting of the church under a single pope. At the opening session Guy de Malesset, who was the only surviving cardinal of Pope Gregory XI (except for Peter de Luna, now Benedict XIII) and who had participated in both elections in 1378. Five times the council summoned the rival popes; they responded by calling their own councils, which, in the event, were piddling, ineffective meetings. The main action was at Pisa.

On 4 May the council answered objections to its legality and declared that by canonical right it represents the community of the faithful with the right to pass judgement on the papal claimants. And judgement soon came. On 5 June 1409 the council declared,

> This sacred synod, acting for the universal church, acts as a court in
> the present case against Peter de Luna and Angelo Corrario, once

known as Benedict XIII and Gregory XII, decrees . . . that they were and are schismatics, nourishers of schism and notorious heretics and that they have deviated from the faith and have committed the notorious crimes of perjury by violating their oaths . . . For these reasons and others they have proved themselves to be unworthy of all honour and dignity, including those due to the papal office . . . This synod deprives, deposes and excommunicates Peter and Angelo and forbids them to act as supreme pontiff. This synod declares the Roman see vacant.

There it was: the deposition of both claimants for reasons of heresy and scandalous crimes. In doing this the council was not instituting a revolutionary constitutional principle; it was adhering to current canonical teaching on the two basic issues: first, that a pope could be deposed for notorious crimes and heresy, a doctrine enunciated in its clearest form by the canonist Huguccio (1188), and, second, that the ultimate authority in the church rests with the whole church as a corporate body, a doctrine classically articulated by Hostiensis (1270). Pisa was adhering to principles with a long tradition.

The Holy See was now considered vacant, and an election was quickly held. The council authorized the cardinals of both obediences to elect the new pope. In order to guarantee acceptance of their choice the council decreed that the new pope had to receive not a two-thirds vote of the combined body but a two-thirds vote of each group of cardinals. After eleven days, they announced the unanimous choice of the Crete-born Franciscan friar, Peter Philargi, the cardinal archbishop of Milan. He took the name Alexander V. It must be underlined that he was not elected by the cardinals as cardinals but by the cardinals as electors delegated by the council; the authority for election derived from the council itself.

The schism was over, or so it could confidently be believed. A new pope of unblemished reputation had been elected. He had the support of most of Western Europe. Two octogenarian rivals could not be expected to long endure, and, in any case, their support was eroding. Gregory, now abandoned by his native Venice, had only Naples, and Benedict had little support beyond Spain. The great princes, churchmen and universities recognized Alexander V as the one pope of the now united church. He retrospectively authenticated the acts of the council that preceded his election. The council in its last session (7 August 1409) called for another council in three years' time to address issues of internal reform. The fathers left Pisa with understandable optimism and with the clear sense that they had ended the schism. Unforeseen events were to prove otherwise.

The road to Constance

Nearly seventy when elected, Alexander V would presumably outlive his two rivals. Such was not to be. A delegation from Rome came to him at Bologna to arrange his triumphal entry into their city, but, before he could do so, Alexander

Papal claimants of the three obediences at the Great Schism

Rome	Avignon	Pisa
Urban VI (1378–89)	Clement VII (1378–94)	
Boniface IX (1389–1404)	Benedict XIII (1394–1423)	
Innocent VII (1404–06)		Alexander V (1409–10)
Gregory XII (1406–15)		John XXIII (1410–15)

V suddenly died. One might speculate what might have happened had Alexander not died in 1410, had he solidified his widespread support, had he been able to take advantage of the shrinking influence of his rivals and had he turned to the internal reform of the church. He would have been hailed as a saviour of the church and not listed by the Vatican as an anti-pope. His death was bad luck, but the choice of a successor would have remedied that bad luck. The choice, in fact, was disastrous, or so says traditional historical wisdom.

Baldassare Cossa, a Neapolitan (as were most of the 'Roman popes' of this time), has had his name blackened by his enemies. Disengaging truth from libel is not easy in these circumstances. As a young man, he had certainly acted in the naval wars of the time, but did he act piratically? He failed to display the customary pieties of a prelate and may even have fathered a child, but did he seduce two hundred women at Bologna, as is frequently said? When Alexander V suddenly died at Bologna, had Cossa poisoned him? And, when the election was held, did he use lavish gifts as bribes to secure his election? There may be some truth to some of these allegations, but to say more than that is to go beyond surviving evidence.

John XXIII entered Rome in April 1411, the beleaguered Gregory XII cowering at Gaeta under the protection of the king of Naples. In the following year Naples abandoned Gregory, who then took refuge at Rimini with the local lord, his last supporter. Gregory was quickly becoming an irrelevance. Meanwhile, John's hand was strengthened even more when, out of the contest for the German kingship, there emerged Sigismund, who abandoned any allegiance he once held for Gregory and pledged his considerable support for the successor of the pope elected at Pisa. John XXIII felt confident enough to appoint eighteen new cardinals, including among them three distinguished scholars: Pierre d'Ailly, Guillaume Filastre and Francisco Zabarella. John's strength had now reached its highest point, and no one would have predicted in 1412 that three years later he would be forced to resign.

The unravelling of John's influence began when the army of the kingdom of Naples, once again changing its political position, marched into Rome in March 1413, thus forcing the pope to flee for his safety to Florence and then to Sutri. Fearing the worst, he appealed to Sigismund for assistance. Cardinal Zabarella, the greatest canonist of the age, led the delegation to Sigismund, who at the time was near Como in northern Italy. What they discussed principally was the calling of another council. The Council of Pisa had required the calling of a reforming

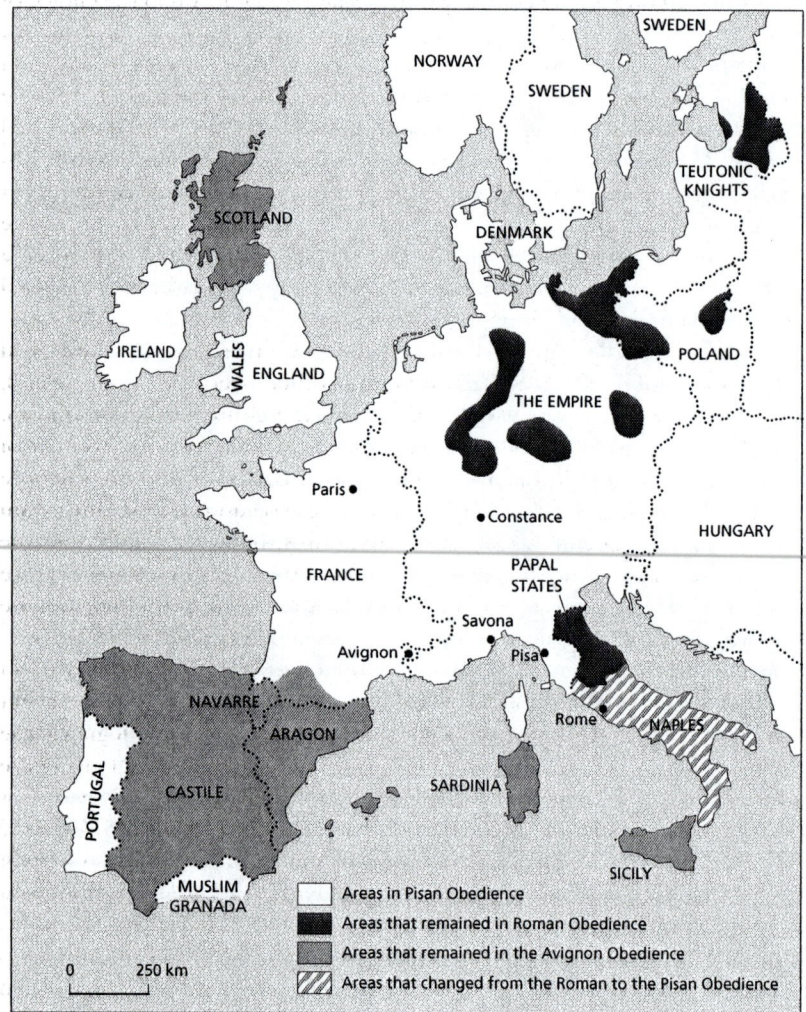

Map 20 The Great Schism: between Pisa and Constance.

council in three years' time. John XXIII had tried to summon such a council at Rome in late 1412, but the unsettled state of affairs in central Italy prevented anything but a small attendance: it was but a brief meeting with only one session. John had promised to call another, fuller council, and, after negotiations of John's legation with Sigismund lasting more than two weeks, the where and when of this council were agreed upon. On 30 October 1413, Sigismund announced that a council would meet on 1 November 1414 at Constance. John then met Sigismund at Lodi for further discussion, and on 9 December he formally called the council. Although it is frequently said that the emperor-elect forced a reluctant pope to call the council, the evidence suggests rather that it was in the choice of place that Sigismund prevailed over the pope. Constance (Konstanz in southern Germany near the Swiss border) was situated in lands that he controlled and, in the turbulent situation then existing in central Italy, was a more appropriate place than Rome, which John favoured. It must further be emphasized that the Council of Constance was not summoned to resolve the schism. It was summoned to complete the work left unfinished at Pisa: the internal reform of the church. That the council took another turn was not foreseen in 1413 when it was called by the one pope with the overwhelming support of Christians. John XXIII made a solemn entrance into Constance on 28 October and formally opened the council on 5 November 1414.

The Council of Constance sat continuously for over three and a half years, had forty-five full sessions, countless committee and other meetings and, in the end, profoundly influenced the very constitution of the church. Its composition, varying from time to time, was even broader in scope than the Council of Pisa: no part of Christendom was unrepresented. Bishops came from remote parts of the British Isles and Scandinavia, from Silesia and Transylvania; even the Iberian peninsula, in time, sent representatives; observers came from the Eastern churches, from Greece and Constantinople. The greatest representative assembly of the Middle Ages it has been called, and that claim might well be justified.

The great array that gathered at Constance, called to complete the work of the Council of Pisa, took a major turn from this original purpose, and the agent of that change was Pierre d'Ailly. He had a brilliant career as a theologian at the University of Paris and became the university chancellor in 1389. During the years of the schism d'Ailly was the towering figure among European intellectuals discussing ways of resolving the crisis. Not particularly involved at Pisa, d'Ailly came to Constance as a cardinal recently created by John XXIII and as bishop of Cambrai; he virtually took control of the council. The Italian bishops in a memorandum of 7 December 1414 wished to limit the council to two actions – to confirm the Council of Pisa and to take a stronger action against the two claimants, Benedict XIII and Gregory XII, particularly the latter – after which the council should dissolve. D'Ailly rose to the challenge and called those wishing to dissolve the council 'promoters of schism and open to serious suspicion of heresy'. Neither he nor his associates questioned that John XXIII was the sole lawful pope and that the others were mere pretenders, but d'Ailly put the unity of the church together with reform as the essential agenda of the council. D'Ailly's party soon urged John XXIII, the good shepherd, to lay down his life for his flock by abdicating: the peace of the church required it. Discussions would follow, but the abdication of John XXIII was firmly on the table. Next d'Ailly turned to the organization of the council. On 7 February 1415 the council agreed to organize itself into four nations: English (including Scots and Irish), French, German (including Poland, Bohemia, Hungary and Denmark) and Italian. In July 1415 the cardinals formed a 'nation' as, later, did the Spanish.

Within each nation voting included not only bishops and abbots but also the proxies of absent bishops and abbots as well as representatives of cathedral chapters and universities and the envoys of secular rulers. In each nation the vote would be by head but in the general sessions it would be by nation. The fear that the Italian bishops by sheer numbers would overwhelm the others if the general session were to have voting by head and the belief that the pope had secretly made fifty additional Italian prelates contributed to the adoption of this method of voting. The attack on John XXIII could now begin in earnest.

During the month of February John XXIII's enemies circulated an anonymous broadside which charged him with great and numerous crimes. It found ready acceptance particularly among the Germans and the English. The unimaginable was becoming inevitable as the anti-John campaign neared its goal, his abdication. In the face of quickly eroding support, not least from Sigismund, John gave the first indication that he might resign on 16 February. Five days later he issued a similar memorandum. In each of these the pope agreed to abdicate on the condition that the other claimants renounce any claim to the papal office. Further discussions took place, and an acceptable formula – not of resignation but of the promise of resignation – was agreed to. On 2 March 1415 after celebrating Mass before the assembled council, John knelt before the high altar of Constance cathedral, while his statement was read:

> I, Pope John XXIII, in order to bring tranquillity to all of Christ's people, do hereby offer, promise, pledge, swear and avow to God, the church and this holy council willingly and freely to give peace to the church by my genuine abdication and to carry out this promise as this council decides, if and when Peter de Luna and Angelo Corrario, known as Benedict XIII and Gregory XII in their obedi- ences, do likewise renounce either in person or by legal proxies their claims to the papal office.

This agreed statement was clear enough: John would resign when the other two resigned. Three of the nations – German, French and English – asked for his immediate resignation. This was predictably unacceptable to John XXIII, who, fearing for his life, fled Constance. In the words of a contemporary chronicler,

> On 20 March 1415 at one o'clock in the afternoon Pope John departed the city of Constance in secret. On a small horse he rode out of the city, wearing a grey cape with a grey hood, wrapped about him to disguise his identity.

The fleeing pope went to a place near by where he was under the protection of the duke of Austria and from where he wrote to Sigismund and the cardinals of his continuing intention of resigning. Although there was a danger that the council would sputter out now that the pope had left, it did not, and John quickly became yesterday's man but not first without some unpleasant formalities. An armed force of three hundred brought him back on what appear to be highly inflated charges. Without his answering them the council on 29 May 1415 proceeded to 'remove, deprive and depose' him. The judgement of one scholar of the period is that

> he was neither better nor worse than his contemporaries . . . He was sacrificed to the desire of the Christian nations for unity, all the sins of the age heaped on him so that he could be deposed with a semblance of legality.

Perhaps this favourable judgement holds much more than a grain of truth. John never appealed his deposition and, in fact, ratified the council's action by resigning. In 1419 he paid homage to the new pope, who made him a cardinal.

The council, after having deposed the pope, the validity of whose election it never questioned, was in an unusual situation. How could there be a council without a pope? A council took its authority from the pope, but now without a pope – negotiations with the other claimants were ongoing – by what right could the council exist? There now came into the open what had been intermittently whispered heretofore, the doctrine of conciliarism: the supreme authority in the church was not the pope but the church itself, represented in a general council.

While John XXIII was on the run, the council asserted its sovereignty. Almost immediately after his flight, even before trying him, the council announced its ultimate authority in the often-cited decree *Haec sancta* (from its opening words):

> This holy synod of Constance legitimately assembled in the Holy Spirit, forms a general council representing the Catholic church militant. It derives its power immediately from Christ, and everyone of whatever position or rank, even the papacy itself, is bound to obey it in all things pertaining to the faith, to the healing of the schism and to the general reform of the church of God in head and members.

It went on to say that any person, even the pope, who refuses to obey a general council will be duly punished. These were unprecedented claims. No council, however turbulent or rebellious, had asserted its supremacy over the pope. This conciliarism had gone beyond the teaching of earlier theologians and canonists that gave a general council extraordinary powers over a heretical or criminous pope: *Haec sancta* attributed to a general council essential power over the pope, even a saintly, fully orthodox pope. In time some conciliarists would moderate this radical view. Zabarella, for example, stressed that the deposing power of a council applied only to popes notoriously guilty of serious offences, but *Haec sancta* made no such distinction. In matters pertaining to faith, ending the schism and reforming the church in head (i.e., the pope) and members the council, representing the church, took its authority from Christ. One might ask, what other matters could there be? Faith has to do with theology, and reform has to do with human behaviour, and schism was a matter of the moment. This was an all-embracing decree. Echoes of it will thunder through the next decades and will be heard centuries later at councils at the Vatican in 1870 and 1963.

The council was without a pope, since, after the deposition and resignation of John XXIII, whose right to be pope was consistently acknowledged by the council, there were still two pretenders, never recognized by the council as popes. Yet, according to *Haec sancta*, a pope was not necessary, and the council continued with its business. Before the council proceeded to disposing of the two pretenders and electing a new pope, a pressing matter had to be dealt with. It concerned heresy.

Wyclif and Hus

This heresy came from Bohemia but had some of its roots in England. John Wyclif, an Oxford don of middling theological abilities, held controversial views, which were condemned at a council at Blackfriars in London in 1382. Two years later he died without having been personally excommunicated, protected by powerful members of the royal family, particularly by the mother of the young King Richard II. Although he was himself an absentee pluralist, holding several benefices simultaneously while residing at Oxford, Wyclif inveighed against the abuses of the church. Churchmen who were not righteous could have no authority in the church of Christ. In addition, he held views on the Eucharist out of step with the received orthodoxy of the times. After the consecration of the bread and wine, he believed, the substance of bread and wine and not merely the accidents (i.e., the appearances) of bread and wine remained. Also, he held that Christ was not physically present in the consecrated species. He further denied the existence of purgatory. All of these ventures into heterodoxy might have remained a purely English affair, of peripheral interest in the wider life of the medieval church, even if ripples continued in England for a few decades. It was the marriage of Richard II to Anne of Bohemia, sister of King Wenceslaus, in 1382, that transported Wyclif's teachings to the tinder-box of Bohemia and gave his name a European-wide recognition. Although the details are not fully known, the works of Wyclif were brought back to Bohemia, perhaps by clerical members of Queen Anne's household after her death in 1394. In Bohemia not England, at Prague not Oxford, Wyclif received a warm welcome. Many of the surviving manuscript copies of his works exist only in Czech libraries.

Even before the reception of Wyclif, Bohemia was experiencing considerable unrest, and the new teachings became part of a larger mix. The indigenous Slavic people, the Czechs, were dominated by the Germans, who formed less than 10 per cent of the population. The centres of resentment were the University of Prague, German-controlled since its founding, and the church, in whose higher ranks the Germans prevailed. One Czech critic described the situation,

> The Germans completely controlled the university. The Czechs were
> helpless . . . And the Germans also controlled the kingdom, having
> the secular offices, while the Czechs had nothing.

This was the world in which the Czech John Hus came of age. He joined the
voices of protest at the Bethlehem Chapel in 1402, while still a theology student.
His eloquence and obvious sincerity won him a large audience, and he soon
became the foremost voice of Czech nationalism and the pre-eminent preacher
of reform in the church, inveighing against the vices of the clergy, his preaching
becoming less and less restrained. At the same time, he discovered the works of
John Wyclif and even translated one of them into Czech.

Of particular appeal to Hus was Wyclif's ecclesiology: since only righteous
churchmen have genuine authority, obedience need not be given to the unright-
eous of any dignity. But it was Hus's violent attacks against simony and clerical
greed that led the archbishop of Prague to restrict his preaching, but to no effect,
since Hus did not feel obliged to obey. When Wyclifite propositions were
condemned at Prague in 1407, Hus refused to join in the condemnation. Two
years later, stirred on by Hus's fiery sermon, a mob sacked the archbishop's palace.
The archbishop burned Hus's works and excommunicated him. Civil unrest
continued, and by 1412 Prague was in near revolt. The touchstone of orthodoxy
was willingness to condemn Wyclifite propositions. After a long silence, Hus, in
July 1412, defended five of these propositions, arguing that an orthodox
interpretation of them was possible. The execution of three followers of Hus for
inciting riots later in 1412 gave the movement its martyrs, and King Wenceslaus
set out to destroy Czech nationalism and the heretical teachings by now
inextricably bound up with it. Hus was solemnly excommunicated. The matter
was moving quickly towards the breaking point. The brief, poorly attended
council held by John XXIII at Rome in February 1413 condemned the writings
of Wyclif, principally because of the growing crisis in Bohemia, but this council
hardly mattered. The showdown was to come at Constance.

Events were to prove it unwise, but John Hus, at the urging of Sigismund and
reassured by the king's promise of a safe-conduct and with the removal of his
excommunication, went to Constance. Perhaps he thought he would be involved
in a university-like disputation with the fathers of the council and that he would
convince them of the rightness of his views. John XXIII before his flight seemed
eager to accommodate Hus, even meeting with him personally, but Hus insisted
that the papacy was a man-made institution and that the church was not built on
Peter but on Christ. Pope John had him placed under house arrest, but, after
John's demise, the council, urged on by Pierre d'Ailly and Jean Gerson, the
chancellor of the University of Paris, turned to the Hus affair. Ironical, as it seems
to us, these two conciliarists and a decidedly conciliarist council found the anti-
papal views of Hus too radical for their taste. A trial was held on 5 July 1415 in
the presence of Sigismund with d'Ailly leading the prosecution. Thirty allegedly
heretical or erroneous propositions supposedly drawn from Hus's work *De ecclesia*

22 Burning of John Hus for heresy, from Ulrich von Reichenthal, [*Chronicle of the Council of Constance*] (Augsburg, 1483); British Library shelf no. IB 5958. Reproduced by permission of the British Library.

(*On the Church*) were presented to him. Hus denied having taught them and, when given the opportunity to abjure them, replied that he could not abjure what he never taught. The following morning after Mass in the cathedral Hus was condemned and handed over to the secular arm, a paper hat bearing the word *heresiarcha* (heretic) placed on his head. The secular authorities acted within hours, and John Hus was devoured by flames.

Rioting followed in Prague, and the Hussites (as they were soon called) became a force in Bohemia, often associated with Czech national aspirations, although many Czech nationalists were not Hussites and the Hussites came to include Germans. Hus having been disposed of, the Council of Constance could return to the business of the other papal claimants and to the election of a new pope.

Back to Constance

Disposing of the two remaining claimants, John XXIII having resigned, proved relatively straightforward. Gregory XII, now nearing ninety and anxious to prepare his soul for death, proved easier to deal with than the increasingly intransigent Benedict XIII. On 4 July 1415, five week's after John XXIII's deposition, Gregory's representatives did two things in his name: they formally convoked the assembly at Constance as a general council, since Gregory did not recognize that assembly as a council, and to that general council submitted Gregory's resignation. Benedict XIII, at Perpignan in the eastern Pyrenees, proved the last obstacle. Sigismund's personal meetings with Benedict and even the pressures brought by Spanish kings had no effect. When these kings and the Scottish legates abandoned Benedict on 13 December 1415, he ceased to be a factor in these matters. All that remained were the formality of his deposition from the office he claimed (16 July 1417), but by that time the council was planning the election of a pope who would be universally recognized.

A significant part of the council wanted to delay the election of a pope until the council took serious measures to reform the church. The stalemate, acrimonious at times, was broken when Henry Beaufort, bishop of Winchester (later cardinal) and nephew of the English king, Henry V, arrived at Constance in early October with a compromise plan: promulgate the reforms already agreed to, elect a pope and defer other reforms to a future council. And so it was agreed. On 9 October 1417, the council by its own authority, promulgated five reforming decrees. They concerned the transfer of bishops by the pope, the papal collection of taxes and, most significantly, the need for future councils. The decree *Frequens*, often paired with *Haec sancta* by historians, provided the vehicle for future reforms:

> A frequent celebration of general councils is a special means for cultivating the field of the Lord and for destroying briers, thorns and thistles, i.e., heresies, errors and schism . . . Thus, by a perpetual edict we sanction, decree, establish and ordain that general councils shall be held in the following manner. The next council shall follow the close of this one at the end of five years. The second shall follow the close of that at the end of seven years. Thereafter councils shall be held every ten years.

There remained only the election of a pope.

Who would elect the new pope? The only uncontested cardinal was the only cardinal still living who had been appointed by Gregory XI (i.e., before 1378), and he was hiding in a Spanish fortress, still protesting that he was pope. (To those who believed the election of Urban VI invalid and that of Clement VII valid Benedict XIII, as successor to Clement VII, was true pope, but that logic won him little support, and he died a sad figure on 23 May 1423.) The electoral body would be made up of the cardinals of the three obediences (twenty-three in number) plus six delegates from each of the nations. The successful candidate would receive a two-thirds majority of the cardinals and a two-thirds majority of each nation. This body met on 8 November 1417 and on 11 November, the feast of St Martin, elected Odo Colonna, who took his name from the day's saint and became Martin V. Some further attempts were made at reform, but the fathers of the council were eager to go home and to postpone all that could conceivably be postponed. Pope Martin entered into some temporary agreements, usually called concordats, about reform with individual countries. Significantly these were with the secular rulers and not the bishops, whose authority was to some extent thus undermined. Although the council did not dissolve until 22 April 1418, the council had essentially ended with the election of Martin V five and a half months earlier. The schism was truly over.

To describe the effect of the schism and the Council of Constance as 'the end of the medieval papacy' exaggerates and even distorts what actually happened. True to say, the papacy in 1418 was markedly different from the papacy in 1378. The institution itself could hardly have been unaffected by competing claimants to the papal office and by Christendom being divided into separate, hostile allegiances. While nations went their own ways, none of them questioned the papacy itself, even the French (the so-called Gallicans). What they questioned was the identity of the pope, although the French and English wanted less papal intervention in the practical affairs of their local churches. The challenge to the papacy itself came from the council and its claim to superiority over the pope. This claim, as we shall soon see, persisted well into the fifteenth century. Yet it was not conciliarism that fomented the great changes of the sixteenth century. After Constance the papacy's principal challenge was the need for reform within the church and for revitalizing the spiritual life of the Christian people.

Further reading

The survey by Howard Kaminsky distils a lifetime of distinguished scholarship on the schism: 'The Great Schism', *The New Cambridge Medieval History*, vol. 6, *c. 1300–c. 1415* (ed. Michael Jones; Cambridge, 2000), pp. 674–96, with a remarkably thorough bibliography (pp. 1031–41), although the article pulls up short, apparently because of constraints of periodization, and consequently has little to say about Pisa and virtually nothing about Constance. Both of these councils are treated summarily by Antony Black in 'Popes and Councils', vol. 7 of the same history, *c. 1415–c. 1500* (ed. Christopher Allmand; Cambridge, 1998), pp. 65–9. A reader looking for a fairly detailed narrative can read John Holland Smith, *The Great Schism 1378: The Disintegration of the Papacy* (London, 1970).

A classic of its kind is Brian Tierney's immensely influential *Foundations of the Conciliar Theory* (Cambridge, 1955). The definitive study of Pierre d'Ailly's thought remains Francis Oakley, *The Political Thought of Pierre d'Ailly: The Voluntarist Tradition* (New Haven and London, 1964). E.F. Jacob, *Essays in the Conciliar Epoch* (2nd edn; Manchester, 1953) contains seminal work on the subject. Among the more recent works in English the reader will find the works of Robert N. Swanson helpful, especially his monograph *Universities, Academics and the Great Schism* (Cambridge, 1978) and his many articles, including 'The Way of Action: Pierre d'Ailly and the Military Solution to the Great Schism', *The Church and War* (*Studies in Church History*, vol. 20, 1983; ed. W.J. Sheils), pp. 191–200.

Several contemporary descriptions of the Council of Constance can be found in *The Council of Constance: The Unification of the Church* (tr. Louise Ropes Loomis; eds J.H. Mundy and K.M. Woody; New York and London, 1961).

17

THE FIFTEENTH CENTURY

Two views can be taken of the fifteenth century, each with merit as historical approaches. In the first place, it can be looked at only with one eye, while the other eye is on the future, to the sixteenth century and to the religious changes that dramatically altered the course of history. The emphasis is on roots, origins, even causes, related to the Protestant Reformation, and no historian of that phenomenon can avoid seeking its historical sources. But, for the medieval historian, this approach poses the real danger of turning the last century of the Middle Ages into a mere prelude to what was to come and of not seeing it in its own right. This second view examines this period not entirely unaware of the great changes around the corner but with the emphasis clearly on the here-and-now of fifteenth-century Europe. It is this second approach which is adopted here: the fifteenth century deserves to be studied for itself, not in an entirely blinkered way, but with emphasis unmistakably on what happened then rather than on what was to happen. What happened then was not decay and decline, as has often been said. It was, rather, a period of unusual richness, a richness in which the church shared and to which it contributed. Recovery from the catastrophic Black Death was fairly rapid. The self-inflicted wounds of the Great Schism and the consequent Conciliar Movement left scars, yet the church as the community of Christian believers emerged as healthy then as the church of the twelfth and thirteenth centuries, perhaps even with a more widely shared sense of the essentially spiritual aspects of religion.

Popes and councils

From the attack on Boniface VIII (1303) through the long, seventy-year exile in Avignon followed by the devastating schism and the humiliation of the councils at Pisa (1409) and Constance (1414–18), the papacy was scarred, deeply troubled, even reeling. Yet fifty years later the papacy had recovered its constitutional position as the supreme authority over the church. Popes would reign who would be among the most splendid in an age of splendour and near splendour.

When Martin V left Constance in 1417, he had much to concern him, particularly the nature of the body that had elected him and its claims and mandates. A pope elected by an assembly claiming to be his superior could scarcely feel comfortable, particularly since that assembly had ordered the frequent meeting of like bodies in the proximate future. Yet Martin V, of that many-pope family the Colonna, had the self-confidence and the subtle diplomatic skill to yield in some things in order not to lose all. And so, in keeping with the requirement of Constance for a council within five years (another within seven from then and others at ten-year intervals), Martin V summoned a council to meet at Pavia in 1423. Few representatives arrived in Pavia for the scheduled opening on 23 April. When plague fell on Pavia in June, the council moved to Siena, where it was officially opened only in November. Little was accomplished because of papal reluctance and also because of poor attendance – only twenty-five 'mitres' (bishops and abbots) at the postponed opening – which was understandable, since the prelates who had attended Constance had been away from their sees for over three years. Practical-minded bishops could see that a system of frequent councils could amount to an almost continuous parliament, requiring bishops to neglect their own pastoral obligations. Some who did attend, like the abbot of Paisley, who had come from Scotland, complained when the council disintegrated in early 1424. Before they went home, the fathers agreed (in accordance with Constance) that another council would be held in seven years time (1431) at Basel, now in modern Switzerland, then an independent city within the empire.

Basel proved the definitive turning point in the Conciliar Movement, being both its pinnacle and its nadir. The conciliarists reigned, perhaps even supreme, for a while, but by council's end they had become what they would remain, academics debating among themselves, far from the real world of power and influence. Many were the agents causing the demise of conciliarism, perhaps chief among them the Greeks.

Before the council met, Martin V had died (20 February 1431) and eleven days later the cardinals elected Eugenius IV, about whose competence as pope historians continue to differ. At his first public consistory, the floor gave way under the weight of the crowd, killing a bishop: an ill omen for a troubled pontificate. On the day of the scheduled opening at Basel only the abbé of Vézelay was present. Others began to straggle in: by April a bishop had come and an abbot as well as representatives of the University of Paris. Small attendance was to trouble the council throughout its sitting. The pope's officials formally opened the council on 23 July 1431, and in late September the papal legate, Cardinal Cesarini, arrived to take personal control. He came straight from a major military defeat in a 'crusade' against the Hussites. He found a mere handful of mitres at Basel. While Cesarini was obsessed with resolving the Hussite problem, Eugenius IV was negotiating with the Greeks in an effort to convince them to attend an ecumenical council with the Latin church to discuss reunion of the churches. More will be said about the Greek factor, but, for now, the Greeks, in preliminary negotiations, preferred to meet in Italy rather than north of the Alps at some place like Basel. In any case, Eugenius held little sympathy for what was happening at Basel and, on 18 December 1431, issued a bull dissolving the council and called for a new council at Bologna. He underestimated the determination of the fathers at Basel as well as the single-mindedness of his legate, who was determined to use the council to resolve the Hussite crisis by peaceful negotiation. The council continued, refusing to obey the papal order, and reaffirmed *Haec sancta* of the Council of Constance, declaring the superiority of council over pope: Eugenius lacked the authority to dissolve a council unless the council approved. It took another year and a half (till 1 August 1433) before the pope withdrew his bull of dissolution. He made further concessions and, on 15 February 1433, abjectly capitulated:

> We decree and declare that the said council from its very beginning was and is a legitimate council and that it should continue . . . as if no dissolution was made. We declare that dissolution invalid and null.

Pope Eugenius IV had surrendered. The victorious council triumphantly repeated the decree *Haec sancta*. The council and, with it, constitutional conciliarism were now in charge, but it was not to last.

Meanwhile, the council fathers – bishops always in a minority – proceeded with the Hussite issue. The fate of John Hus and Jerome of Prague, who, safe-conducts notwithstanding, were burned to death at the Council of Constance, made the Hussites very wary of accepting the invitation to go to Basel. Skilful negotiations by Cardinal Cesarini won their confidence, and, having received iron-clad assurances of their safe-conduct, three hundred Hussites arrived at Basel in January 1433 to put their case to the council. They remained there for three months and returned, unmolested, to Prague with no agreement in hand. But the way was open for further discussions, the council – and not the pope – taking the lead. In November 1433 both sides accepted articles of agreement (the *Compacta* of Prague). The articles addressed the issue of communion under two kinds (i.e., under the species of both bread and wine), which the Hussites had insisted upon: they could administer communion in this way but could not require it, and priests must explain that Jesus is present in the Eucharist – body, blood, soul and divinity – under each species. Free preaching with some controls was allowed, and priests could own property under some circumstances. Further refinements were made to this agreement, and the council ratified it on 15 January 1437. It brought an end to the Hussite Wars and relieved the church of the formidable pressures from the Hussites, although unpacified dissidents remained and would be heard from again. This was the council's greatest achievement.

With the pope effectively sidelined, the council attempted to do two things simultaneously: administer the church and effect reforms. The council sought to replace the papal curia and manage, almost micro-manage, the practical affairs of the church. This consumed more time than was anticipated and siphoned off much of the energy which could have been directed towards meaningful reform. The council did pass reforming decrees, but these had largely to do with the pope and his curia. Theirs was a reform not of 'head and members' but only of 'head': the larger needs of the church were mostly ignored. An opportunity was missed. Although the pope had capitulated and although the council succeeded with the Hussites, the heights had been reached and a steady decline of its fortunes was to end the effective life of the Council of Basel. If the council rose with the Hussites, it fell with the Greeks.

Pope Eugenius may have been seen to capitulate in 1433, but his was a tactical retreat, a holding action, a delay to await a more favourable day. It came. While the fathers at Basel fell into bickering over smaller and smaller matters, the pope continued his pursuit of union with the Greek churches. Understandably, the Greeks wanted any ecumenical council to be held in a convenient place. For a while, Constantinople was seriously considered, then Italy. In the meantime, the council sent emissaries to treat with the Greeks. Many at Basel wanted the assembly north of the Alps at Savoy, Avignon or even Basel itself. The council took a crucial vote on 7 May 1437, and in a babble of voices the majority read its decree, summoning the council to Avignon, while the minority read its decree, summoning the council to an Italian city to be named. Each side then sang the *Te Deum*, as if victorious. It should be said that the system of voting extended voting privileges to academics and members of the lower clergy and that the majority of the mitres were among the minority at Basel Cathedral who favoured a move to Italy. Eugenius summoned a council to meet at Ferrara in January 1438. Many, including the best and the brightest, left Basel. The rump at Basel soon declared Eugenius deposed and elected the lay duke of Savoy, Felix V. His name could scarcely have been less appropriate. With Basel becoming little more than a debating forum for university doctors, led by the Parisians, Felix, a truly devout man, withdrew in 1442. Seven years later he was reconciled with the pope, who treated him generously by making him a cardinal. The Baselites had become irrelevant, and there perished with them any effective conciliarism. It had its greatest support at Constance as the only perceived way of ending the scandalous schism. The radical conciliarists, those firmly committed to government of the church by council, became increasingly fewer in numbers. Practical churchmen with pastoral responsibilities could not justify by ideology the long absences from their dioceses required by frequent councils. Their support for the council and conciliarism faded. Debate continued, but, as a practical matter, the Conciliar Movement was no longer a movement.

The reunion of the Greek and Latin churches, long desired at least in theory, came to fruition at the Council of Florence (transferring from Ferrara early in 1439). That the reunion failed to hold might lead us to underestimate its achievement. What is often said is that the Greeks, with the Turks a force in Anatolia and even in parts of the Balkans and with their posing a threat to Constantinople, turned to the West for assistance and were willing to pay the price of reunion. Such would be an inexact statement of the facts. That there were political considerations and that they played an important part in the quest for reunion cannot be doubted, but the considerations also involved the shared needs of East and West. Not only was Constantinople in peril but so too the Balkans and much of central Europe. Early contacts were made while the popes were at Avignon. The Orthodox monk Barlaam held discussions with Benedict XII in 1339, a century before Florence, and, presciently, the Greek monk argued that only an ecumenical council could achieve reunion. Embassies from the East came to Avignon in the 1350s and 1360s, and at this latter visit preparations were begun for a council. It came to naught, and in the early years of the fifteenth century the initiative came not from the East but from the West. Pope Martin V was on the verge of sending a representative to such an ecumenical council to be held at Constantinople when he realized that he was expected to pay for the council, a burden his empty coffers could not support. Martin and later Eugenius conducted negotiations with the emperor directly or indirectly through the Orthodox church leaders. In the dynamics of the time Eugenius and Basel competed actively to meet with the Greeks to such an extent that it was not known for sure whose invitation the Greeks would accept, even after they landed in Venice in February 1438. That they accepted the papal invitation and went to Ferrara enormously enhanced papal prestige at a great, even lethal, cost to the rump council.

A Greek delegation, seven hundred strong, was led by Emperor John VIII Paleologus. The patriarch of Constantinople attended as did representatives of the other patriarchs (Antioch, Alexandria and Jerusalem), whose cities were under Muslim control. After a fascinating debate over the seating arrangements, Greeks and Latins processed into Ferrara Cathedral and recognized themselves as forming an ecumenical council. The tensions that appeared almost at once concerned not doctrinal differences per se but procedure and order of discussion. The Greeks, prodded by the emperor, who wanted prompt military support from the West, would have preferred a quick bandaging up of old wounds in an ambiguity that would satisfy both sides. Eugenius demanded more. Four issues of difference were finally discussed as representatives of each side presented their views, the Western theologians in an elegant Latinity that captivated their hearers. The centuries-old dispute over the 'procession' of the persons of the Trinity consumed over three weeks in March 1439. In a much earlier time the West had added the word *filioque* to the traditional creed, insisting that the Holy Spirit proceeded from the Father 'and the Son' (*filioque*), whereas in the East the Holy Spirit was said to proceed from the Father through the Son. In the final decree, both sides agreed that their formulas expressed the beliefs of their saints and that their saints, since they are saints, must be teaching the same doctrine. Thus, when the Eastern saints say that the Holy Spirit proceeds from the Father through the Son and when the Western saints say that the Holy Spirit proceeds from the Father and the Son, they must mean the same thing. On the subject of purgatory the Eastern theologians in discussing a place where the souls of the good but not perfect go after death did not speak with one voice, but they seemed to hold that such an intermediate state was not a state of fire and that the final disposition of souls was fixed only at the Last Judgement at the end of the world. They yielded to the Latin view of the geography of the afterlife: after death the good and the wicked are immediately sent to heaven and hell and the good but not perfect remain in another place to purge themselves of the remaining stains of sin, where they can be assisted by the prayers and suffrages of the faithful on earth. The issue of the Eucharist centred on the essential words of consecration, and the dominical words ('This is my body . . . this is my blood') were accepted, leaving room for customary liturgical usages of East and West as well as for the use of leavened or unleavened bread. One matter remained, and that concerned the authority of the bishop of Rome.

While the theological matters just described were dealt with only after much debate, it could be reliably expected that the question of ultimate authority in the reunited church would have provoked the greatest friction. Such was not the case. An agreement happened quite quickly after formulas went from one camp to the other. The agreed statement reads,

> We define that the apostolic see and the Roman Pontiff hold primacy
> in the whole world and that the same Roman Pontiff is the successor
> of blessed Peter, prince of the apostles, and is the true vicar of Christ,
> head of the whole church and father and teacher of all Christians.

The patience of Eugenius, little shown at the beginning of his pontificate but shown at Florence repeatedly as he yielded to the Greeks in minor point after minor point, won the day.

The sixth of July 1439 was proclaimed a civic holiday in Florence. The duomo and the large square in front of it were filled with people as the great men of East and West processed into the cathedral. The Byzantine emperor, resplendent as only an Eastern emperor could be, sat in a prominent place. The pope entered in a magnificent procession, Mass was said, and the bull of union read. It begins with the words from Psalm 95 (96), *Laetentur coeli et exsultet terra* ('Let the heavens rejoice and the earth exult'). The reunion of the churches, long desired and often despaired of, was achieved.

Other churches followed the Greeks. The Armenian patriarch sent two representatives to Florence; they greeted Eugenius as 'the vicar of Christ in the see of the apostles . . . our head . . . our shepherd . . . the foundation of the church'. On 22 November 1439 a document of union with the Armenians was promulgated, at the news of which King Henry VI of England ordered prayers of thanksgiving throughout his kingdom. The Coptic church sent representatives from Egypt, who, on 4 February 1442, agreed to a bull of union. To the Copts of Ethiopia Eugenius sent a letter addressed to Prester John, believed to be the Christian king. (A hundred years later the king of Ethiopia wrote to the then pope, saying that he had a letter and a book from Eugenius, quite likely the letter and copy of the bull of union.) Efforts were made with some success with the Nestorians, the Syrians and the orthodox churches in Cyprus. It all might have worked, but circumstances − not merely the fall of Constantinople in 1453 − conspired against it.

Two deaths provided obstacles. King Albert, successor as German king to Sigismund, died unexpectedly in October 1439, and there followed a dynastic struggle, which precluded a swift response to the pope's plea for military aid for the East. The Greeks, returning from Florence, did not reach Constantinople until 1 February 1440, when Emperor John VIII learned that his wife had died. He entered into profound and prolonged grief. The slow return – six months after *Laetentur coeli* – and the emperor's inactivity gave anti-union forces in Constantinople an unopposed field. If the emperor had immediately and with the full force of his authority promulgated the decree of union, the naysayers might well have had little success in encouraging opposition. The Western forces, when finally gathered, did not reach Constantinople until September 1444 and experienced a devastating defeat at Varna on the Black Sea in modern Bulgaria. Never again would a Christian army of the necessary strength be raised to stem the Turkish forces. Much of the Balkans were already in their hands. Adrianople (Edirne), a hundred kilometres west of Constantinople, had been Turkish since 1362. Under these circumstances one may wonder what the assembled throng in Santa Sophia felt on 12 December 1452 when, at last, the union was solemnly proclaimed. Within four months the walls of the city were ringed with Turkish forces. The two-month siege ended when the defending force of Italians and Greeks, outnumbered twenty to one, finally gave way to the Turks. And the city of Constantine, founded as a second Rome in 330, was no longer a Christian city, its great basilica about to become a mosque, and no longer an outpost protecting Europe from incursions from the east. With the fall of Constantinople in 1453 ended the quest to reunite the two parts of the Christian church. And so it stands.

While the churches sought reunion at Ferrara and Florence, the nation states were confronted with the decision to support Eugenius's council at Florence or to continue supporting Basel. King Charles VII called his clergy together at Bourges in 1438 to determine French policy. What issued was the Pragmatic Sanction, which, while applying some of the reforms of Basel tailored to French needs and being courteous to the pope, maintained neutrality between pope and council. Meanwhile, the German diet that met at Mainz in March of the same year also bided its time by a neutral policy. Poland stopped sending funds to both pope and council. England continued its staunch support of Eugenius. As Basel deteriorated, it became increasingly difficult for supporters to accord it any serious regard. Basel essentially dissolved. Only a shell was left when Felix V became reconciled. Among the able churchmen to abandon Basel was the humanist Aeneas Silvius Piccolomini. In November 1442 he put his talents to the service of Eugenius and Florence. This remarkable man, later himself to become pope (Pius II), went to Germany, where he persuaded Frederick, newly king, to forgo neutrality in favour of Eugenius. By the mid-1440s France, while not formally rescinding the Pragmatic Sanction (not until 1516), had come to terms with Eugenius. The pope died on 23 February 1447, his opponents either reconciled or marginalized and his council successfully completed. Piccolomini concluded his funeral oration by saying of Eugenius,

> There was no greater fault in him than that he was without measure
> and he tried to do not what he could but what he wanted.

The pope's biographer, Joseph Gill, suggests that it would be a more accurate judgement if 'what he willed' were to read 'what he ought to do' or 'what he believed he ought to do'. The new pope, Nicholas V, quickly solidified the papal position, even receiving the homage of the French king. In a moment of comic theatre the remnant of the remnant of Basel (now at Lausanne) 'elected' Nicholas. The crisis was over, but some may see in these circumstances of national churches acting independently for or against a pope or, indeed, a council a precedent for what became a principle in the next century at the Peace of Augsburg (1555): *cuius regio, eius religio* ('in the prince's country, the prince's religion'). Whether the Augsburg formula derived from events of the 1430s and 1440s, no one can say apodictically, for other sources suggest themselves and intervening events created a wider dynamic. Nonetheless, the parallels, at least, show the power of the state in matters of religion. But more was happening to the papacy than its relations with council and princes.

Humanist popes ascended the throne of Peter. Eugenius IV would not fit that profile, yet he was exposed to the new ways while he was at Florence and brought back Fra Angelico to Rome with him. It was his successor, Nicholas V (1447–55), who can be called the first Renaissance pope. A theologian by training at Bologna, he became tutor to an aristocratic family at Florence, and, for him, it was a perfect marriage of time and place. He soon became intoxicated with the world of art and learning, which saw the beauty of nature as not inimical to religion but seamlessly joined with it to fulfil the human spirit. He admired the works of antiquity in letters and stones and, as a young priest, became a bibliophile, according to one story, actually raising money for his obsession by bell-ringing. Once pope, Nicholas set about to begin the restoration of the Eternal City, long neglected by the absence of popes and, later, by their concern with other matters. With peace having been achieved in Italy between the rival states, Rome was ripe for renewal. Nicholas restored and enlarged the Vatican Palace, hereafter the principal residence of the popes, employing the genius of Fra Angelico in the decorations. The pope turned his attention to the repair of churches, bridges, castles and walls. Plans to repair and extend the thousand-year-old St Peter's Basilica were drawn up, although, in time, a new basilica was to be decided upon. Not all was accomplished in his day, but it is not too much to say that Nicholas V presided over the creation of Renaissance Rome. His greatest achievement, however, may be seen in what he did for learning. As a result of the union of the churches, Greek scholars came to the West and found a generous patron in the humanist pope as did Western scholars. Nicholas presided over translations of the canon of ancient Greek writers: the historians Herodotus, Thucydides and Xenophon, the works of Aristotle (known previously chiefly by translations from Arabic), Strabo and many others. The translation of Homer into hexameter Latin verse was incomplete at Nicholas's death. Translators under his patronage rendered into Latin not only Greek secular works but also provided fresh translations of the writings of the great Christian theologians of the East such as Basil, Gregory Nazianzen, Gregory of Nyssa and John Chrysostom. Nicholas's youthful enthusiasm for books became fulfilled: he actively pursued the collection of manuscripts of ancient Latin and Greek works by sending scholars even to remote parts of Europe in search of books. Gutenberg's press was yet to print its first book, and all books were manuscript books. Nicholas acquired over a thousand manuscript books (807 in Latin and 353 in Greek), which were to form the basis for the Vatican Library. His Spanish successor, Calixtus III (1455–58), was said (by his enemies) to have gestured at his predecessor's manuscripts, calling them a waste of the church's treasury.

Pius II (1458–64) we have already met as the brilliant Aeneas Silvius Piccolomini. One of the brightest lights of his age, he not only read the works of ancient authors, but he himself wrote histories, romances, poems, addresses and even an erotic comedy. His *Commentaria* have been translated as *The Memoirs of a Renaissance Pope*. Skilled in diplomacy, he supported Basel and then defected to Eugenius and served effectively on diplomatic missions. He had refused to take priest's orders, for, in his words, 'I fear continence' (*timeo continentiam*). He sired several illegitimate children. Piccolomini travelled widely, reaching even Norway and Scotland, where he suffered frostbite of his feet. In 1445 serious illness led to a personal conversion, and he was ordained the next year. When elected pope, Aeneas Piccolomini took the name 'Pius' because Virgil routinely referred to his hero as 'pius Aeneas'. His years as pope saw him concerned about mounting a campaign in the East, and, unlike his predecessor Nicholas V, Pius did not become the patron of scholars and artists, although, as pope, he produced numerous works, including his already-mentioned autobiography.

A crucial moment may been reached in the attitude of the church towards secular learning. The Middle Ages witnessed an ongoing controversy about the place of secular learning in the life of a Christian. What need do Christians have of such learning, since they have all that is needed in sacred scripture and holy books, it was frequently argued. But humanists at the court of Charlemagne in the ninth century and at Paris in the twelfth century found aesthetic pleasure and intellectual satisfaction in purely secular learning. And in the middle of the fifteenth century two humanists, to be followed by others, became supreme pontiffs of the Christian church. One cannot speak for historical persons, but one can imagine Augustine, Cassiodorus, Alcuin, Abelard, Dante and others like them taking satisfaction and even pleasure at this turn of events. Yet for forces that touched the souls of men and women one must look beyond the courts of Roman pontiffs, who had become successful Italian princes.

Christian piety

The defining form of Christian spirituality from at least the late eleventh century was the monastic life. Christians wishing to strive for spiritual perfection, would be told to leave the world and enter a religious community. The terminology is instructive: they became religious, a term which, without further modification, meant those who took religious vows of poverty, chastity and obedience and who lived in a community with others like them. Theirs was the true life of the spirit. A lay person who desired to live a life of Christian perfection yet was unable or unwilling to take vows and become cloistered could try to live like a religious in the world, in a less than perfect way, distracted by family and other practical concerns of everyday life, at best, a second-rate, inferior spiritual life. The establishing of the life of a religious as the normative form of spirituality defined the medieval ideal of Christian perfection. Attempts at a peculiarly lay spirituality at the end of the twelfth and beginning of the thirteenth century led either to charges of heresy, as with the Cathars and others, or to the absorption of these aspirations into new religious orders, as with the friars. The fifteenth century offered to the laity an alternative model of spirituality, one not second best to monastic piety, but its equal. To seek perfection it was no longer necessary to leave the world and take vows. The new spiritual teaching held that perfection can be sought in the world by laymen and laywomen going about their quotidian pursuits. There were writers and preachers who taught this new way, and individuals committed themselves to following the new way singly or in informal groups. In parish churches they found religious meaning in the rituals of the calendar and in the ceremonies marking the rhythms of life from birth to death and beyond. Lorenzo Valla, writing about 1441, spoke for many when he objected to the use of the word 'religious' to apply only to those who took vows, since it implies that those people have a higher form of the Christian life than other Christians, which, he believed, they clearly did not. This resistance to the traditional religious culture, while not everywhere successful or, indeed, accepted, added a dimension, hitherto mute, to the discourse about religious experience.

Valla was not the first to resent the self-asserted monopoly of religious to that name. In the late fourteenth century Gerard Groote (d. 1384) of Deventer in Holland and his disciples argued not only against the traditional usage but, particularly, against the underlying assumption that religious are more religious. Groote stands as the founder of a new movement, the Devotio Moderna (New Devotion), which swept across much of northern Europe in the fifteenth century. Gerard Groote will never be numbered among the great theologians of his time, yet, far from being a scarcely lettered person, he had spent ten years at the University of Paris. In minor orders, he returned from Paris to Deventer, where, supported by benefices which required no care of soul, he turned his attention to worldly affairs. In 1374 he experienced a conversion of soul and turned over his house and worldly possessions to a group of women, who, in time, became known as the Sisters of the Common Life, i.e., unmarried laywomen living in common. Groote went to a Carthusian monastery near Arnhem, where he remained for three years. When he left, he took deacon's orders so that he could preach. Groote soon became an effective and popular preacher against the evils of the day. His preaching made many of the higher clergy uncomfortable, and, at one point, the bishop of Utrecht forbade preaching by all deacons in order to silence him. Groote became a magnet for laymen and laywomen and members of the secular clergy who desired a more spiritual life. The women living in his house took no vows and carried on their lives as pious women living, without obligation, in a voluntary community. Groote died of the plague in 1384 and soon groups of laymen and secular priests who were committed to his ideals began to appear, first at Deventer, then soon nearby at Zwolle and Kampen. Another branch of followers of Groote established religious communities based on the rule of the Augustinian canons with the Windesheim congregation at its centre. From one of these houses of canons emerged the most influential spiritual writers of the fifteenth century, Thomas à Kempis, about whom more soon.

The Brethren of the Common Life were determinedly not religious, since they took no vows and were free to leave whenever they wished, nor did they form an order, since the Fourth Lateran Council (1215) prohibited the founding of new orders. The Brethren were a mixture of laymen and clerics, and there frequently lived in their houses schoolboys, like Erasmus in 1484–87. Only occasionally did the brothers actually teach the boys – they tended to go to local schools – providing, instead, spiritual direction and some communal spiritual exercises. The brothers themselves spent considerable effort in copying manuscripts of devotional works. An early text describes the Deventer house:

> Our house was established and supported by meagre funds from rents and the sale of goods so that, following the example of the early church, devout priests and clerics and poor laymen can live in this house in common from the manual labour of copying books and from the income from some property. Our purpose is to worship devoutly at church, to obey the bishops, to wear only simple clothing, to keep the canons and decrees of the holy ones, to practice spiritual exercises and to live not only lives beyond reproach but lives of perfection so that we may serve God and perhaps persuade others to do likewise.

Other communities of the Brethren of the Common Life sprang up elsewhere. In the Netherlands there were houses at Delft (1403), Albergen (1406), Hatten (1407), Groningen (c.1433), Gouda (1445) and Utrecht (1474), to mention the more prominent ones. They also spread into Flanders, where communities were established at Ghent, Antwerp, Brussels and Leuven. In Germany the Brethren had houses at Münster (1400), Cologne (1417) and at many other places.

Although they showed some common aims with the Hussites and their less important English cousins, the Lollards, the followers of the 'new devotion' were decidedly within the church. Three components can be said to form the Devotio Moderna: the Brethren, the Sisters and the Canons Regular. The devotion was clearly urban, bourgeois and literate. The classical exposition of its spirituality is in Thomas à Kempis's *The Imitation of Christ*, four different books brought together in 1418 under the Latin title *De imitatione Christi*. A manuscript of 1441 in the author's hand is now at the Royal Library in Brussels. Although he was a canon of Mount St Agnes (Agnietenberg, near Zwolle), his book was intended not just for canons but also for pious souls living in the world, and it was with them — laity and secular clergy alike — that it found its enormous audience.

It is an accessible book, not based on theological arguments but on almost aphoristic phrases, which, if not disdaining theology, show its limitations:

> What good is it if you argue with profound learning about the Trinity, yet, lacking humility, you displease the Trinity? It is not learned discourse but a life of virtue that brings you close to God. I would rather feel contrition than know how to define it.

One can almost hear such phrases, easily memorized, being repeated by readers hungry for easily understood rules of life. Again,

> How foolish to seek riches that only perish and to trust in them. How foolish to be ambitious for earthly honours and strive for worldly advancement. How foolish to indulge the urgings of the flesh and enjoy that for which you will one day be punished. How foolish to want a long life and not care how it is lived. Foolish, too, to think only of the present instead of preparing for the life to come.

A few more examples from the first book, its most widely admired part, can underline further is attraction to ordinary Christians desiring to live a more perfect life:

> Take no credit for yourself for your accomplishments. Think of others with kindness and admiration . . . Do not think of yourself as better than others, however obviously wicked they may seem, for you know not how long you will persevere.

Lest it be thought that the *Imitation* was totally anti-intellectual, Thomas à Kempis reassures the scholar:

> There is no reason to argue with learning, for it is all good in itself and in God's ordering of things. But what must be put first and foremost is a good conscience and a holy life.

Few scholars would argue with that priority of goodness over learning, but, when Thomas tells his readers why they should read the Bible, he tilts away from the scholarly approach:

> We read Holy Scripture not for its literary qualities but for its truth and its relevance to our lives . . . You will read it with the greatest profit, if you approach it in humility, simplicity and faith.

For him the highest motive for all human actions is love for God:

> Frequently when we think we are motivated by love, we are mistaken, for we act for some other reason such as natural inclination, self-will, desire for regard or, even, our own gain. True love is not about self-seeking but is directed solely to the glory of God.

And he reminds his readers to remember that death excludes no one – *memento mori* – and one should keep in mind one's death:

> When you wake in the morning, think that this may be your last day, and, when you retire at night, do not promise yourself another morning.

For à Kempis the Christian is but a pilgrim on earth, life being lived here as a prelude to a fuller life hereafter. This perspective imbues all his writings.

Its simplicity and directness led to the great popularity of the *Imitation* among laity and clergy alike. Translations were quickly made into Dutch (1420) and German (1434) and, in the course of time, into more than fifty languages, including Hawaiian, Eskimo and Swahili. We shall never know how many manuscript copies were made, but more than seven hundred survive in whole or in part. Thousands of copies were printed in the first few decades of printing. Without doubt, no other book of the fifteenth century has had such a profound influence on the spirituality of ordinary people.

In Italian cities of this period religious confraternities, each of them with scores and even hundreds of members, had it as their principal purpose to relieve human suffering. At Florence in 1419, when the confraternities there were reordered, the *della Misericordia* committed its members to visiting the sick and burying the dead, while the *Bigallo* looked after foundlings and orphans. The confraternity of *Santa Maria della Pietà* had a membership which strove to avoid frivolous pursuits, which met for prayer fortnightly, which confessed once a month and which received communion twice a year, yet, for all these pious practices, their principal works was the distribution of food to the indigent. The *Ospedale degli Innocenti* was founded in 1419, its building started then by Filippo Brunelleschi, later the architect of the great dome crowning Florence's duomo; this foundling hospital established a model of its kind. Virtually all Florentines above the poverty level belonged to one or more of the city's charitable bodies. In 1427, it has been estimated, contributions for alms and other charitable purposes in Florence alone was about 108,000 florins, which was about one-sixth of the total income of all citizens.

23 Foundlings, façade of *Ospedale degli Innocenti*, Florence. Glazed terracotta figures by Andrea della Robbia (1463–66). Reproduced by permission of the Courtauld Institute of Art.

Similar works of charity were being done elsewhere. In Pistoia, a town of less than five thousand, there was a hospital with seventy beds (with twenty-five permanent patients) and a staff of two physicians, eight nurses as well as other personnel. There were also other, smaller hospitals, but, in all, there was a capacity of over two hundred beds at Pistoia, a bed-to-population ratio which modern cities can only wish for. In addition to the sick, these hospitals cared for foundlings, orphans, the insane, the homeless, the poor and life's unfortunates, all for free.

These works of charity and others like them were possible because of the increased donation to these confraternities. In Florence such civic charity increased almost twofold between 1427 and 1498. A merchant of Prado, who was encouraged to donate his wealth to a monastery, chose instead to present it to a hospital. Although Tuscany might have led the way, similar pious foundations appeared elsewhere in Italy (e.g., at Venice, Milan, Bergamo, Brescia). Some had a decidedly penitential flavour, but always the purpose was charity to life's less fortunate. Civic charity was clearly emerging, too soon to call it a 'social gospel', but it was a distinct form of Christian piety, seeking religious expression by relieving human suffering.

Central Italy witnessed the spread of the *Laudesi*, groups of laypeople who gathered each evening to pray at their own chapel or oratory. It was a brief meeting of prayers, always including the Ave Maria and ending with a confession of faults. On the first Sunday of every month the members would gather for a solemn Mass and then process through the church, leaving their candles at the high altar. Such monthly gatherings took place at Florence, Pisa, Perugia, Bologna and elsewhere. Their activities began to include public pageants as well as services for the dead. Other, similar lay associations also appeared and helped to shape the increasingly lay devotional piety of the time.

Evidence of devotional piety can be found not only in Netherlandish towns and Italian cities but also in the parishes of urban and rural England, and not merely in the graceful new churches rising amidst the sheep-runs of East Anglia. It can be seen in the cycle of yearly celebrations which touched every parish, even the most remote, and these were celebrations not of a pious few but celebrations of whole communities. On 2 February, when winter was at its greyest and gloomiest and Christmas a fading memory, a feast of the Virgin became a feast of candles: the Purification of the Virgin became Candlemas. It was a day on which the whole parish came to church. The priest blessed the candles and then each parishioner, carrying a lighted candle, joined in a procession which went around the church. At the offertory of the Mass, when the bread and wine were brought to the altar, each person brought a candle to the altar. Margery Kemp, the pious woman of Bishop's (now King's) Lynn, wrote what this ritual meant to her:

> On the feast of the Purification – also called Candlemas – when this creature [Margery] saw parishioners in church with candles in their hands, she could think only of Our Lady offering her holy son, saviour to us all, to Simeon, the priest, in the temple, as if she [Margery] were actually present, making the offering with Our Lady . . . So moved, she could scarcely carry up her own candle to the priest.
>
> (*Book of Margery Kemp*, ch. 82)

Not all enjoyed Margery Kemp's raptures, but all carried candles home with them to light in times of danger. In some bigger towns, such as Beverley, a local guild organized a re-enactment in costume of the presentation of Jesus in the temple with members playing the parts of Mary (carrying a doll), Joseph, Simeon and two angels with large candles.

Similar rituals accompanied the ceremonies of Holy Week, which began with the procession of palms on Palm Sunday and ended with the empty tomb and Alleluias on Easter Sunday. It was the week when parishioners made their annual confession in preparation for Easter communion, which, for most, was the only reception of communion each year. Before Mass on Palm Sunday palms – or the English equivalent – were distributed to the parishioners, who then gathered by a bare cross outside the church as the gospel story of Christ's entry into Jerusalem was read. The priest, carrying the sacrament, approached and sang, 'Behold, Sion, your king cometh'. The procession of palms, with the priest and sacrament at its end, circled the church as flower petals were scattered before the sacrament. They entered the church through its main, western door. When all had entered, three clerics sang Matthew's Passion, each taking a part. After Mass, the palms were taken home, as had the candles weeks before, as a protection for places where they were displayed. On Holy (or Maundy) Thursday, when the priest had completed Mass, the altars were stripped of their linen and left bare, as if to prepare Jesus's body for death the following day. Good Friday was the day of the cross. Three times the priest, before a veiled cross, sang 'Ecce lignum crucis' ('Behold the wood of the cross'), and, after each time, part of the veil was removed from the cross. Then, barefoot, each person approached the bare cross, and kneeling, kissed it. (Henry VIII scandalized many when he did the same thing in a chapel in Westminster Abbey in 1539.) A host, previously consecrated, was solemnly 'buried' in a temporary sepulchre, where it remained, with parishioners keeping watch, till Easter morning. Then the sacrament was removed from the sepulchre, and at Easter Mass the congregation, before the empty tomb, sang 'Resurrexit sicut dixit' ('He has risen as he said'). These were the ceremonies held in every parish church, large or small, across the land, and in some places there were local embellishments. The more recent feast of Corpus Christi (Body of Christ), observed in late May or June, enjoyed a more public expression than those just described, as Corpus Christi guilds in the major towns organized public processions of the sacrament attended with banners, bell-ringing, costumes and even some clearly secular features.

At York a remarkable play was performed on the feast of Corpus Christi. Often called 'mystery plays', it was, however, a single play with fifty 'pageants' – we might say 'scenes' – which recounted the Fall and Redemption of the human race. Each 'pageant' was mounted on a cart by a local guild. A procession of these carts went through the streets of York, stopping at twelve 'stations' to enact their parts of the story. The play began with the fall of Lucifer and the bad angels, followed by creation, the fall of Adam and Eve, the murder of Abel, the flood, the near sacrifice of Isaac by Abraham and Moses before the Pharaoh, to mention only some of the scenes from the Old Testament part of the cycle. Then came carts which performed scenes from the life of Christ, including his birth, the flight into Egypt and the slaughter of the Innocents, Christ's baptism by John the Baptist, his trial before Pilate, his betrayal by Judas and his denial by Peter, followed by his crucifixion and resurrection. The final scene showed the Last

Judgement with the welcoming of the good by God and the casting of screaming souls into the eternal fires of hell. The didactic import of this cycle should not be minimized. York's Corpus Christi cycle was an event of major importance in the civic and devotional life of the city. And there were similar plays elsewhere.

Emphasis on these great procession days could make us overlook simpler observances which engaged the participation of a whole parish. On the Rogation (or Ember) Days, observed on three consecutive days – Monday, Tuesday and Wednesday – four times a year, the parishioners behind the cross processed through their fields which the priest blessed, in the hope of driving away the devil and all wicked things, like blight and famine. After the singing of the litanies of the saints, food and drink were provided by the wealthier members of the parish. And, on the Wednesday, a ritual devil-dragon lost his tail.

It was not merely – or, indeed, mostly – on such days of communal celebration that one looks for external sign of inner piety. It is in the day-to-day, week-to-week living of life. On Sundays virtually whole villages attended Mass. Although the priest said Mass in Latin, often quietly, the laity had their own devotions of prayers – Paters and Aves – or meditative reflections for different parts of the Mass. Yet at the consecration – the sacring – when they believed that the priest's words transformed the bread and wine into the body and blood of Christ, and at the elevation, when, as a bell rang, the consecrated elements were raised for all to see and worship, they raised their arms and silently said a prayer. The fifteenth-century pastoral writer, John Mirk, suggested a prayer such as,

> Jesus Lord, welcome thou be,
> In form of bread as I thee see.
> Jesus, for thy holy name
> Shield me today from sin and shame.
> Shriving and housel, Lord, thou grant me both,
> 'Ere I shall hence go,
> And very contrition of my sin,
> That I, Lord, never die therein.
> And as thou were of a maiden born,
> Suffer me never to be forlorn,
> But when I shall hence wend,
> Grant me the bliss without end.
> Amen.

Other elevation prayers were simpler – 'My Lord and my God' – but, whatever the words, to 'see Jesus' at the elevation was considered by the laity the sublime moment, the essence of the Mass.

No one knows what motivated individual people in the fifteenth century – or, for that matter, in any century. Whether those attending Mass were moved by lofty spiritual reasons or mere social pressure or by a combination of motives or whether motivations varied from time to time we shall never know. That pious woman Margery Kemp recounts that, as she was entering church, a handsome man of her acquaintance made a sexual proposition to her, which she said she seriously considered. Whatever the motivating reason, it seems safe to say that, for all or virtually all, the sacring and showing of the host were considered the moments when they were closest to God.

But how did they learn their Paters and Aves and elevation prayers? The simple answer is by instruction. Before the godparents took the newly baptized infant from the font, the priest told them 'to see it be learned the Pater Noster, Ave Maria and Credo'. These three prayers – Our Father, Hail Mary and I Believe (Apostles' Creed) – formed the basis for instruction. The first is the prayer Jesus gave to his listeners at the Sermon on the Mount, when he was asked, 'How should we pray, Lord?'; the second is the essential prayer to the Virgin and the third a summary of Christian beliefs.

The syllabus of Christian instruction had been set out in the late thirteenth century by John Pecham, archbishop of Canterbury. (See above, pp. 200–1.) Priests were directed to use the vernacular and teach their people the elements of Christian faith: the fourteen articles of the creed, the ten commandments, the two commandments of love of God and neighbour and the groups of seven: the seven works of mercy, the seven deadly sins, the seven virtues and the seven sacraments. It is safe to presume that these were widely known and, easily memorizable as they were, they could be recited with ease by most people. The *Lay Folk's Catechism*, summarizing these teachings in rhyming English verse, was widely circulated, and one bishop gave copies of it to all his clergy at a nominal price. Similar books circulated among the parish clergy, among them John Mirk's *Instructions for Parish Priests*, also in verse to assist them in carrying out their pastoral mission. Parish priests, Mirk wrote, should urge their people to say their private prayers in English, 'for, when you speak in English, you then know and understand what you are saying'. And there was an emphasis on prayer that went beyond the recitation of the Pater and Ave.

Hundreds of manuscripts of primers (often called books of hours) which circulated in the first three-quarters of the fifteenth century still survive. In the decades that followed the establishing of printing presses, tens of thousands of primers were produced for an eager market. They usually contained the little office of the Virgin, the litany of the saints, prayers for the dead, psalms of the Passion, a calendar of the liturgical year and private prayers, such as morning prayers. The primers were prayer books for the laity, and their popularity throughout society – and not just among the upper classes – cannot be in doubt.

The distinct impression that one gets from the extant evidence is that the fifteenth century was a period of vibrant devotional life, which included the laity to an extent hitherto unknown. To be sure, there were saints and sinners, and the vast majority somewhere in between, penitents and recidivists, moving with the tides of everyday life. It is only by externals that one can judge the religious feeling of any age – mercifully, it is not given to historians to peer into souls – and by all these signs the fifteenth century was not a century of decay and decline. Far from it.

Further reading

On the general history of councils of this period an excellent starting point is Hubert Jedin, *A History of the Council of Trent*, vol. 1 (tr. E. Graf; Edinburgh, 1949). More specifically, on Basel, one may consult Antony Black, *Council and Commune: The Conciliar Movement and the Council of Basle* (London, 1979) and, on Florence, Joseph Gill, *The Council of Florence* (originally published, Cambridge, 1959, but with corrigenda, New York, 1982). In addition, the same author has written an accessible biography of *Eugenius IV: Pope of Union* (London, 1961) and has analysed attendance at the councils in 'The Representation of the *Universitas Fidelium* in the Councils of the Conciliar Period', *Councils and Assemblies* (*Studies in Church History*, ed. G.J. Cumming, vol. 7, 1971), pp. 177–95. The source of much that is written on popes of the period is the learned and indispensable work by Ludwig von Pastor, *The History of the Popes from the Close of the Middle Ages* (Eng. tr.; 40 vols; London, 1891–1953). As a papal autobiography, none surpasses *Memoirs of a Renaissance Pope: The Commentaries of Pius II: An Abridgment* (tr. F.A. Gragg; ed. L.C. Gabel; New York, 1959).

The classic treatment of the Devotio Moderna is R.R. Post, *The Modern Devotion: Confrontations with Reformation and Humanism* (*Studies in Medieval and Reformation Thought*, vol. 3; Leiden, 1968). John Van Engen provides us with a book of readings with an excellent introduction, *Devotio Moderna: Basic Writings* (New York, 1988). There are many translations of *The Imitation of Christ*; some may prefer that by Ronald Knox and Michael Oakley (London, 1959).

There is an abundance of excellent studies on civic charity in Italian cities. Among those for Florence the reader will learn much from the seminal essay by Marvin B. Becker, 'Aspects of Lay Piety in Early Renaissance Florence', in C. Trinkaus and H. Oberman (eds), *The Pursuit of Holiness in Late Medieval and Renaissance Religion* (Leiden, 1974), pp. 177–99, John Henderson, *Piety and Charity in Late Medieval Florence* (Oxford, 1994) and Nicholas Terpstra, *Lay Confraternities and Civic Religion in Renaissance Florence* (Cambridge, 1995). For other parts of Italy one can consult the classic work of Brian Pullen, *Rich and Poor in Renaissance Venice: The Social Institutions of a Catholic State, to 1620* (Oxford, 1971), as well as David Herlihy's informative study, *Medieval and Renaissance Pistoia: The Social History of an Italian Town, 1200–1430* (New Haven and London, 1967).

For England one cannot exaggerate the importance of Eamon Duffy's study of religious practice in this period, *The Stripping of the Altars: Traditional Religion in England, 1400–1580* (New Haven and London, 1992), which has made necessary a reappraisal of long-held views. Also, one will find stimulating Christopher Harper-Bill, *The Pre-Reformation Church in England, 1400–1530* (rev. edn; London, 1996). A valuable summary is Robert N. Swanson, *Religion and Devotion in Europe, c. 1215–c. 1515* (Cambridge, 1995). Two specific works can be consulted: Terence Bailey, *The Processions of Sarum and the Western Church* (Toronto, 1971) and Miri Rubin, *Corpus Christi* (Cambridge, 1991). There is a Penguin Classic version in modern English of *The Book of Margery Kemp* (tr. Barry Windeatt; London, 1983; with revised bibliography, 1994). For the religious dramas see Richard Beale and Pamela M. King (eds), *York Mystery Plays: A Selection in Modern Spelling* (Oxford, 1995).

For Germany, in many ways parallelling Duffy's work, is the important book by R.W. Scribner: *Popular Culture and Popular Movements in Germany* (London, 1987).

EPILOGUE

1492: the anatomy of a year

When the Middle Ages end is just as vexing a question as when they begin, and when a book on the church in the Middle Ages should end is equally vexing. Arguments can be made to continue the story to the time of the Fifth Lateran Council (1512–17) and its inadequate response to issues of the day. Other arguments would suggest that Erasmus and Thomas More complete the medieval story. Still others would conclude with Luther and his gesture of defiance at the Castle at Wittenberg in 1517. Such dates can be persuasively argued, yet, in the final analysis, any date or event is bound to be arbitrary, chosen as much for pedagogical as for other reasons. In any case, historical orthodoxy rightly sees a transitional period, when the old (medieval) was fading and the new (modern) was emerging. By the end of the fifteenth century the transition was well under way.

The year 1492 is taken here – other years could have been used – as a convenient place to conclude this account of the medieval church. This is not to suggest that the Middle Ages ended in 1492 or that the church lost its medieval character in that year. Such would constitute historical heresy. The choice of that year affords us the opportunity to consider some events that occurred in 1492 and how they reflect things past and portend things to come.

On 2 January 1492, after a sporadic campaign lasting ten years, King Ferdinand and Queen Isabella received the surrender of the Muslim city of Granada. They led a thousand horsemen and five thousand foot soldiers to the Alhambra, where the banners of the king and queen, each bearing the cross, were hoisted from the tower. The solemn entry into the city took place four days later, on the day of the Epiphany (Feast of the Kings). Although the terms of the capitulation allowed Muslims to continue the practice of their religion, the reconquest was complete, Islam was no longer a presence in Western Europe, and there was widespread rejoicing. Henry VII ordered a thanksgiving service at St Paul's Cathedral in London. The University of Paris sent a message of praise, fulsome in the Latin rhetoric of the time. And the pope was soon to declare Ferdinand and Isabella the 'Catholic Monarchs'. The victory at Granada ushered in or, at least, buttressed a sense of triumphalism, long associated with Spanish Catholicism.

Three months later (31 March 1492) the triumphant monarchs ordered the expulsion of all Jews from their kingdoms. The decree, issued at Granada, gave Jews who did not convert to Catholicism three months to leave, taking with them neither gold, silver, horses nor arms. Many converted, including the chief rabbi; others left in a new exodus, their numbers impossible to know but no doubt in the tens of thousands. The sincerity of these conversions would incur the suspicion of the inquisition in Spain for some time to come. The Jews had been expelled before from other places, for example from Gascony in 1289 and from England in 1290, and soon (1497) from Portugal and, in recent times, from other places, in circumstances of utter barbarity.

At Florence, during the night of 5 April 1492, the great cupola of the duomo was struck by lightning. Lorenzo de'Medici, as he lay mortally ill, took it as an omen that he would soon die. Three days later he sent for the Dominican preacher Savonarola, who gave Lorenzo his blessing; then *Il Magnifico* died. With Lorenzo's restraining hand gone, Savonarola's fiery rhetoric seemed to know no bounds. While delivering a sermon later in the same year, he claimed that he saw a hand holding a flaming sword, on which appeared the words, 'Terrible and swift upon the earth is the sword of the Lord.' And he claimed to hear a voice, which said, 'The time is at hand when I shall unsheathe my sword.' From then his preaching, with increasing fervour, denounced the vices of the church, the corruption of society and the preoccupation with luxuries. His was to become the dominant voice in Florence for six years and he the city's de facto ruler, providing an austerity to Europe's most luxurious city. On carnival day 1497 he encouraged Florentines to feed the bonfire in a main square with their vanities, such as obscene books and pictures, playing-cards, dice, gaming pieces, cosmetics, perfumes, mirrors, dolls, etc. Whether any valuable books or pictures were devoured in the *rogo della vanità* ('bonfire of the vanities'), we shall never know, but the spectacle clearly shows a city high on enthusiasm, almost to the point of uncontrolled hysteria. The religious fervour ended, with no obvious lasting effects. It is reminiscent of the excesses of the flagellants in the darkest days of the Black Death as they entered a community and by chanting, incense and preaching heated the religious emotions to a fever pitch. The Salem witch-trials of 1692 may have fed from a similar source. And some may see parallels between Savonarola's Florence and Calvin's Geneva.

Meanwhile, at Rome on 11 August 1492 a new pope was elected, for many the most infamous in papal history. The Spaniard Rodrigo Borgia took the name Alexander VI. It was an election arrived at by blatant bribery and extravagant promises. As a cardinal, Borgia had sired many children by several mistresses, and, as pope, he continued to indulge his sexual appetites. Through his ruthless son Cesare and his daughter Lucretia he would pursue political ambitions in Italy, even to the extent of trying to appropriate the papal states for the Borgia family. Two of Lucretia's marriages he annulled, and a third husband Cesare murderously dispatched. At one point, when Alexander VI was absent from Rome (1501), he remarkably left Lucretia in charge of the Holy See. It may not have been the worst of times for the papacy, but it surely must have come close. An institution with its share of saints, it also has had its share of men who were apparently wholly secular. The papacy would recover from the excesses of the pope elected in 1492, but the spiritual mission of the papacy continued to be in danger of being compromised because of the pope being a secular ruler, until the Piedmontese army settled the issue in 1870, just two months after Pius IX declared papal infallibility.

There entered Granada with Ferdinand and Isabella on 2 January 1492 a forty-year-old Genoese sailor. Later that year, on 12 October, that sailor, Christopher Columbus, landed in the Indies and immediately fell to the ground on his knees, thanking God for reaching land, which he called San Salvador (Holy Saviour). His men were carrying the banners of the king and queen, on each of which was the Christian cross. Columbus wrote of the people he found there:

> To win their friendship, since I knew they could be converted to our holy faith by love rather than by force, I distributed among them red caps and glass beads, which they hung around their necks, and many other things of similar value, which pleased them much . . . I noticed that they can repeat what is said to them quite quickly. I believe that they would easily become Christians.

And, so, a tectonic shift in world history and, perforce, in the history of the Christian church began on that beach in the Caribbean islands. Tens and tens of millions of white Europeans and countless numbers of black Africans would come to the Americas in the greatest migration in human history. In several senses, it was a new world.

LIST OF POPES, 500–1500

A pope by definition is bishop of Rome. The date of the beginning of his pontificate is the date on which he became bishop of Rome. If the electee was already a bishop, he became bishop of Rome (and, thus, pope) at the time that he accepted election and not at the time of his subsequent coronation. If the electee was not a bishop, he became bishop of Rome (and, thus, pope) at the time of his consecration as bishop. It is this date that is preferred here. The pontificate ended with the death or, occasionally, with the resignation of the pope.

By convention some claimants are called anti-popes, where their claims have not been generally recognized by historians. Yet there will always be room for doubt. These anti-popes are listed in italics.

Symmachus, 498–514
Lawrence, 498–99; 501–06
Hormisdas, 514–23
John I, 523–26
Felix IV (sometimes III), 526–30
Dioscorus, 530
Boniface II, 530–32
John II, 533–35
Agapitus I, 535–36
Silverius, 536–37
Vigilius, 537–55
Pelagius I, 556–61
John III, 561–74
Benedict I, 575–79
Pelagius II, 579–90
Gregory I, 590–604
Sabinian, 604–06
Boniface III, 607
Boniface IV, 608–15
Deusdedit (also, Adeodatus I), 615–18

Boniface V, 619–25
Honorius I, 625–38
Severinus, 640
John IV, 640–42
Theodore I, 642–49
Martin I, 649–54
Eugenius I, 654–57
Vitalian, 657–72
Adeodatus II, 672–76
Donus, 676–78
Agatho, 678–81
Leo II, 682–83
Benedict II, 684–85
John V, 685–86
Conon, 686–87
Theodore, 687
Paschal, 687
Sergius I, 687–701
John VI, 701–05
John VII, 705–07
Sisinnius, 708

Constantine, 708–15
Gregory II, 715–31
Gregory III, 731–41
Zacharias, 741–52
Stephen II (sometimes III), 752–57
Paul I, 757–767
    Constantine, 767–68
    Philip, 768
Stephen III (sometimes IV), 768–72
Hadrian I, 772–95
Leo III, 795–816
Stephen IV (sometimes V), 816–17
Paschal I, 817–24
Eugenius II, 824–27
Valentine, 827
Gregory IV, 828–44
    John, 844
Sergius II, 844–47
Leo IV, 847–55
Benedict III, 855–58
    Anastasius, 855
Nicholas I, 858–67
Hadrian II, 867–72
John VIII, 872–82
Marinus I, 882–84
Hadrian III, 884–85
Stephen V (sometimes VI), 855–91
Formosus, 891–96
Boniface VI, 896
Stephen VI (sometimes VII), 896–97
Romanus, 897
Theodore II, 897
John IX, 898–900
Benedict IV, 900–03
Leo V, 903
    Christopher, 903–04
Sergius III, 904–11
Anastasius III, 911–13
Lando, 913–14
John X, 914–28
Leo VI, 928
Stephen VII (sometimes VIII),
    928–31
John XI, 931–35

Leo VII, 936–39
Stephen VIII (sometimes IX),
    939–42
Marinus II, 942–46
Agapitus II, 946–55
John XII, 955–64
Leo VIII, 963–65
Benedict V, 964
John XIII, 965–72
Benedict VI, 973–74
Benedict VII, 974–83
John XIV, 983–84
    Boniface VII, 974, 984–85
John XV, 985–86
Gregory V, 996–99
    John XVI, 997–98
Sylvester II, 999–1003
John XVII, 1003
John XVIII, 1003–09
Sergius IV, 1009–12
Benedict VIII, 1012–24
    Gregory VI, 1012
John XIX, 1024–32
Benedict IX, 1032–44; 1045,
    ?1047–48
    Sylvester III, 1045
Gregory VI, 1045–46
Clement II, 1046–47
Damasus II, 1048
Leo IX, 1049–54
Victor II, 1055–57
Stephen IX (sometimes X), 1057–58
    Benedict X, 1058–59
Nicholas II, 1058–61
Alexander II, 1061–73
    Honorius II, 1061–64
Gregory VII, 1073–85
    Clement III, 1080, 1084–1100
Victor III, 1087
Urban II, 1088–99
Paschal II, 1099–1118
    Theodoric, 1100–01
    Albert, 1102
    Sylvester IV, 1105–11

Gelasius II, 1118–19
   Gregory VIII, 1118–21
Calixtus II, 1119–24
Honorius II, 1124–30
   Celestine II, 1124
Innocent II, 1130–43
   Anacletus II, 1130–38
   Victor IV, 1138
Celestine II, 1143–44
Lucius II, 1144–45
Eugenius III, 1145–53
Anastasius IV, 1153–54
Hadrian IV, 1154–59
Alexander III, 1159–81
   Victor IV, 1159–64
   Paschal III, 1164–68
   Calixtus III, 1168–78
   Innocent III, 1179–80
Lucius III, 1181–85
Urban III, 1185–87
Gregory VIII, 1187
Clement III, 1187–91
Celestine III, 1191–98
Innocent III, 1198–1216
Honorius III, 1216–27

Gregory IX, 1227–41
Celestine IV, 1241
Innocent IV, 1243–54
Alexander IV, 1254–61
Urban VI, 1261–64
Clement IV, 1265–68
Gregory X, 1272–76
Innocent V, 1276
Hadrian V, 1276 (never consecrated)
John XXI, 1276–77
Nicholas III, 1277–80
Martin IV, 1281–85
Honorius IV, 1285–87
Nicholas IV, 1288–92
Celestine V, 1294
Boniface VIII, 1295–1303
Benedict XI, 1303–04
Clement V, 1305–14
John XXII, 1316–34
   Nicholas V, 1328–30
Benedict XII, 1335–42
Clement VI, 1342–52
Innocent VI, 1352–62
Urban V, 1362–70
Gregory XI, 1371–78

Papal claimants of the three obediences at the Great Schism

Roman	*Avignon*	*Pisan*
Urban VI (1378–89)	Clement VII (1378–94)	
Boniface IX (1389–1404)	Benedict XIII (1394–1423)	
Innocent VII (1404–06)		Alexander V (1409–10)
Gregory XII (1406–15)		John XXIII (1410–15)

Martin V, 1417–31
   Clement VIII, 1423–29
Eugenius IV, 1431–47
   Felix V, 1439–49
Nicholas V, 1447–55
Calixtus III, 1455–58
Pius II, 1458–64
Paul II, 1464–71
Sixtus IV, 1471–84
Innocent VIII, 1484–92
Alexander VI, 1492–1503

INDEX

Abelard, Peter 152–62; abbot of St Gildas 158; autobiography of 153; and Bernard of Clairvaux 159–62; at councils held at Soissons 157–8 and Sens 16–1; education of 153–4; family background of 153; and Heloise (affair with 155–6; correspondence with 153,158–9; marriage to 156); at Laon 155; monk of St Denis 157–8; physical mutilation of 157; and problem of universals 154–5; and Roscelin, the logician 153–5; and scholarly works (*Theologia* 157–8; *Sic et non* 158)

Abrissel, Robert of 143

Adam of Bremen 87–8

Adam, canon of St Victor's 148

Admonitio generalis 76–7

Aethelbert, archbishop of York 62

Aethelbert, king of Kent, his conversion 52

Agiltrude, regent of Duchy of Spoleto 98

Agiluf, Lombard king 36

Aidan, St 26, 56, 62

Ailred, abbot of Rievaulx

al-Andalus 265–9

Alberic of Rheims 155, 157

Albertus Magnus 221, 293

Albi 204, 206, 208–9

Albigensians, crusade against 207–9; *see also* Cathars

Albornoz, Gil, cardinal 305

Alcuin of York 62, 79–80, 82

Aldhelm 59, 62–3

Alexander II, pope 112, 122, 267

Alexander III, pope 135, 166–9, 211

Alexander V, pope 320–1

Alexander VI, pope 86, 352–3

Alexander of Hales 218, 293

Alexius I, Eastern emperor 122, 125–6

Alexius III, Eastern emperor 190–1

Alexius IV, Eastern co-emperor 190–1

Alexius V, Eastern emperor 190–1

Alfonso Henriques, king of Portugal 269

Alfonso VI, king of Leon-Castile 268

Alfonso VII, king of Castile 272

Alfonso X, king of Castile 264

Alfred, king of Wessex 19, 83

Almohads 269

Almoravids 268–9

Ambrose, St 11

Amiens Cathedral 236, 247, 251

Anacletus II, anti-pope 133–4

Anagni: disputed papal election at (1378) 31–11; attack on Boniface VIII at 263

Angers: bishopric 21; University of 317

Anglo-Saxons: conversion of 51–8 (in the south of England 51–55; in the north 55–8); invasion of Britain by 51–2; transmission of learning to 59–63

Anne of Bohemia, queen of England 326

Anselm of Laon 155

Anselm of Lucca 111

Anselm, St, archbishop of Canterbury 115

Ansgar, and conversion of the Danes 86

Antioch: county of 126; patriarchate of 32; siege of city of, by crusaders 126

Aquinas, Thomas 221, 234–5, 293

Aragon 267, 269–71, 314, 317–18

architecture, ecclesiastical 235–52; basilican form of 236–7; Gothic 244–51; Romanesque 238–44; of Santa Sophia 33–5

Arianism 10; conversion of Germans, to 18

Aristotle: place of, in university curriculum 233; works of 19,132

Arnold of Brescia 134

Arnulf, king of East Franks 98

357